LOITER

STAGES, volume 14

Series Editors: Michael Holquist, *Yale University*

Warren Motte, *University of Colorado at Boulder*

Gerald Prince, *University of Pennsylvania*

Patricia Meyer Spacks, *University of Virginia*

ATURE

Ross Chambers

University of Nebraska Press : Lincoln & London

#39477949

Acknowledgments for previously published
materials appear on page xii. Copyright © 1999 by
the University of Nebraska Press. All rights reserved
Manufactured in the United States of America ⊗
Library of Congress Cataloging-in-Publication Data
Chambers, Ross.   Loiterature / Ross Chambers.
p. cm. – (Stages: v.14) Includes bibliographical references and index. ISBN 0-8032-1467-7 (cloth: alk.
paper). – ISBN 0-8032-6392-9 (paperback: alk. paper)
1. Digression (Rhetoric) in Literature. 2. Literature –
Philosophy. I. Title. II. Series: Stages (Series): v.14.
PN56.D54C48 1999 809-dc21 98-33633 CIP

In loving memory of Marie Maclean

Die Parekbasis hat gleichsam die Form einer Wollust. Das Wiederholen des Themas ist das entgegengesetzte dazu.

Digression has something like the form of bliss. Repetition of the theme is the very opposite of that.

Friedrich Schlegel, *Literary Notebooks, 1797–1801*, ed. Hans Eichner (London: Athlone, 1957)

Contents

Foreword

This book is liberally supplied with prefaces. Indeed, it could be charitably described as nothing but a series of prefaces, each of which scarcely gets started on an approach to the topic of loiterature before another starts again from a different but related angle. As a book, it stops, without conclusion, while still in the process of getting going. That is certainly in accordance with loiterature's own affinity for potentially endless digressivity, but it means that the book doesn't really need yet another preface. It is I who need space in which to acknowledge a debt—my personal, long-term debt to Marie Maclean—and also to mention what this book in particular has owed to her, beginning with the fact that even before writing prefaces to loiterature I talked the idea over with her and immediately benefited from her wisdom.

The circumstances were appropriately relaxed: summer twilight crept through the valley of the Rhône, swallows swooped over ancient red tiles. Hector Maclean was in the conversation, too, as always a benign and indispensable mediatory presence. When I said I was thinking of "writing something about episodicity" and mentioned the privilege of not working, it was Marie who reminded me that to work is itself a privilege and spoke of those who are excluded from it. Something began to crystallize for me about loiterature's peculiar relation to both exclusion and privilege. We talked about Colette and *La Vagabonde*, but I knew her remark was in part autobiographical; and as, in the following years, I loitered over loiterature, I have thought of it very often as I watched Marie cling, under very dire circumstances, to the privilege of working. She completed one of her finest articles in the final weeks of her life, and she worked with her students to the end.

A year after the Rhône valley, we met again, the three of us, and sat in Rushcutters Bay Park in wintry Australian sunlight, watching boats bobbing and hearing the roar of Sydney at a tranquil distance. Marie excitedly told me of her "double whammy" theory of what turns women of illegitimate birth (Olympe de Gouges, Flora Tristan, Louise Michel) into social revolutionaries. Out of that insight came *The Name of the Mother* (London: Routledge, 1994), which, by dint of exemplary determination, she was able to research, write, and see through press before her death. Different as the two books are, *The Name of the Mother* and *Loiterature* were largely written in tandem (each of us reading the other's chapters as they were drafted), and there is a kind of digressive relation between the two: each is about the conditions under which it is possible to step out of line. I hope it will not be considered inappropriate, therefore, for me to dedicate *Loiterature* to the memory of a friend whose gentle but pointed criticisms have influenced my work for the better, not only in this instance, but over a quarter century. I do so in deep gratitude for her intense intellectual probity, her unfailing companionship, and her affectionate support.

I hope, too, that the many other friends, colleagues, and students who have similarly helped me with this book will understand why, this time, I don't want the name of Marie Maclean to disappear into what would inevitably become a very long list. For all the insightful questions, comments, and suggestions I've received in public (at seminars and talks), I'm immensely grateful; the friends who gave more private help (reading drafts, putting up with my obsessions, contributing puns) know how appreciative I am. A special word of thanks is due to the students at the University of Michigan (Ann Arbor), the University of Queensland (Brisbane), and the University of Minnesota at Minneapolis (Twin Cities) who tolerated my ramblings and even encouraged them with analysis of their own. Three chapters were given as Messenger Lectures at Cornell University in March 1995 and another was developed as a contribution to the annual French Literature Conference at the University of South Carolina in 1993. For permission to republish, I am grateful to the following: *Michigan Romance Studies* for chapter 4, originally published in vol. 13 (1993), 103–38; *Modern Fiction Studies* for chapter 5, originally published in vol. 40, 4 (Winter 1994), 765–806; *L'Esprit Créateur* for chapter 9, originally published in vol. 34, 2 (Summer 1994), 12–30; *the minnesota review* for chapter 10, originally published in numbers 43–44, 1995, 113–30. All previously published work has been revised.

NOTE TO THE READER: The ordering of chapters in this book is not random, and the volume is intended to have a greater degree of coherence than would be suggested, for instance, by the idea of a "collection of essays." At the same time, the argument I pursue is not obsessively linear. Relations between different chapters tend to be oblique, glancing, and digressive; and the relatively loose organization of the whole leaves plenty of room for the reader to inhabit the volume a bit like a hermit crab in the shell I provide, filling in gaps and making connections wherever that seems desirable.

Each chapter—with the possible exception of the paired chapters 6 and 7—can be read independently of the others, although none is really complete in itself. No single chapter is indispensable, offering a uniquely crucial statement concerning loiterature or a privileged overview of the topic. It follows that the book can be read selectively and that readers are free to invent and follow sequential orderings of chapters quite different from the one foreshadowed in the table of contents.

Prefaces to Loiterature

Divided Attentions (On Being Dilatory)

I've been giving up caffeine for years now, but a caffé latte steams at my elbow. Midsummer:

> Wet heat drifts through the afternoon
> like a campus dog, a fraternity ghost
> waiting to stay home from football games
> The arches are empty clear to the sky.[1]

These verses might have been written (or composed, or generated) only a few yards from where I sit, at the intersection of N. University and S. State in Ann Arbor, the suture point (in my personal myth of the city) where the campus meets the town. No campus dogs in evidence (expensive animals on leashes don't qualify). Times change. When Frank O'Hara came to Ann Arbor in 1950 he was amused by the Midwestern candor of the cafeteria signs that read, bluntly, FOOD;[2] today they're more likely to read *cappuccino*, and it's hard to find a cafeteria:

> (la forme d'une ville
> Change plus vite, hélas! que le coeur d'un mortel).[3]

Sitting lazily at this much frequented intersection, I think about intersections and I think about belatedness, my regret for an Ann Arbor I never knew (and wouldn't have liked), the stab of Baudelaire's midline exclamation point at "hélas!," the image of abstention—better still, of anticipated abstention—in "waiting to stay home from football games." Being belated, one foot in 1950, the other in the 1990s, is (like abstaining and anticipating) a form of divided attention, the "distracted" attention Benjamin thought characteristic of modernity (*was* it Benjamin? I must remember to look it up[4]). One foot in the campus, one in town; one in 1950, one in 1994.

Like a campus dog unable to tear itself away from a likely scent, my mind reverts to O'Hara, his early death, his Whitmanesque love of cities and of men, his astonishing outness, the probable reception of his

campy style by the good citizens of Ann Arbor in the Truman era. I like
the colloquial urbanity of his verse, the poetry of I-did-this-I-did-that
that he developed, the connections he makes between poetry and the
art variously called "just hanging out," "mooching around," "puttering
about," loitering. The O'Hara persona isn't even a *flâneur*, really; it's
enough for him just to fill in some time and to be part of a community—
a community of poets and artists that also includes friends with first
names and Miss Stillwaggon at the bank.

> I walk up the muggy street beginning to sun
> and have a hamburger and a malted and buy
> an ugly NEW WORLD WRITING to see what the poets
> in Ghana are doing these days
>   I go on to the bank
> and Miss Stillwaggon (first name Linda I once heard)
> doesn't even look up my balance for once in her life
> and in the GOLDEN GRIFFIN I get a little Verlaine
> for Patsy with drawings by Bonnard though I do
> think of Hesiod, trans. Richmond Lattimore or
> Brendan Behan's new play or *Le Balcon* or *Les Nègres*
> of Genet, but I don't, I stick with Verlaine
> after practically going to sleep with quandariness.[5]

Of course, "Lady" (Billie Holiday) died that day; there's more to
the poem—or, if you like, even less—than just mooching; there's an
emptiness underlying the strings of ands and ors, the proper names,
the insignificant little first-person verbs (I walk, I go, I get, I don't,
I stick). There's even a moment of pathos pending, but meanwhile
"quandariness" is a nice word. Another form of distracted attention;
you can practically go to sleep from it, as I suppose you can from
belatedness (and certainly from abstention).

My own attention is drawn to a young lady violin player behind me,
her instrument case open to receive coins; she's taking advantage of the
entrance to the arcade because the acoustics are slightly better there and
she is playing Bach. Did Benjamin ever realize that his beloved arcades
spread from Paris, London, and Milan to the outposts, midwestern
college towns or antipodean cities like Sydney, where coffee at Repin's
in Her Majesty's Arcade was a must when I was young? Do those
arches in O'Hara's Ann Arbor poem refer somehow to the Nickells
Arcade? And why is it, after all, that modernity is so Paris-centered?

I quote Baudelaire, O'Hara buys Verlaine and hesitates over Genet. I'd like to think it's because the capital of the nineteenth century was the place where the art of hanging out was first grafted onto the good bourgeois public sphere practices that found their natural site (my authority is Stallybrass and White[6]) in the coffeehouses. Even before the nineteenth century the Palais-Royal (like its own ancestors, the piazza San Marco and the Place des Vosges) was a hanging-out place, already a kind of arcade, and the café de la Régence was its annex. At least, so says Diderot:

> Come rain or shine, my custom is to go for a stroll in the Palais-Royal every afternoon at about five. I'm the person you see always sitting alone on the bench in the allée d'Argenson, my mind elsewhere. I hold discussions with myself on politics, love, taste or philosophy, and let my thoughts wander in complete abandon, leaving them free to follow the first idea that comes along, wise or foolish, like our young rakes whom you see in the allée de Foi running after a prostitute with a giddy look, a laughing face, a sparkling eye and a tip-tilted nose, only to leave her for another, accosting them all and staying with none. Thoughts are whores to me.
>
> If it is too cold or wet, I take refuge in the café de la Régence, where I like to sit and watch the chess-playing.[7]

Of course, in Ann Arbor chess players in cafés have pretty much gone the way of campus dogs. More often what you see are students doing homework or on a first-date-that-isn't-a-date because they're "just having a cup of coffee" together. They rarely seem to just hang out. Still, they're fun to watch too, although their description wouldn't slow my prose the way Diderot's suddenly begins to take its time when he comes to the "courtisane à l'air éventé, au visage riant, à l'oeil vif, au nez retroussé." But Diderot was certainly right to link the errancy of thought, mine like his, with peripatetic desire, and to see that divided attention is distracted because, like desire, it's motivated by something like the sexual cruiser's urge to be comprehensive, to follow a sort of *collecting* impulse that entails "accosting them all," but sticking with none of them, thoughts or whores, for long. Another form of quandariness (or the same?). I wonder whether anyone has ever read the opening of *Rameau's Nephew* as a comment on the scope, the structure, the libidinal energy of the *Encyclopédie*? "Mes pensées, ce sont mes catins," to be sure: what divides attention is desire.

The young lady has put away her violin and moved away. Last year, on the opposite corner where there used to be an old stone bench, a rapper with a bongo drum would hang out regularly, not unlike the philosopher in the Palais-Royal. He would extemporize brilliant doggerel about the passersby and the general scene. *His* thoughts were whorish, as his attention wandered and was caught, maybe, by a student walking her dog, a vehicle quandarizing at the intersection, a pregnant woman or a guy in a suit (both unusual sights hereabouts). With every appearance of spontaneity they flowed, these passerby thoughts, into the choppy rhythm of his dactyls, spondees, and anapests, making a poem of now-this-now-that, all middle, no beginning or end, accosting them all but becoming attached to none. Where the rapper sat is the exact spot I imagine Frank O'Hara hanging out in 1950, making his own poetry of "variations" out of intersections—the campus and the town, the shifting sights of the street and the restless movement of his mind.

The reason I imagine so is that the poem seems to describe its own site as a three-way crossing:

> across the avenue a trefoil lamp
> of the streets tosses luckily.[8]

It's a lucky trefoliation, I guess, because it produces a poetry of felicitous encounters and lucky tosses, like the gas lamp flickering in the wind that Mallarmé noticed in Baudelaire.[9] This section of S. State, it's true, is all three-ways, but the only one with an avenue is right here, at "North U." (N. University Avenue) and State. Ann Arbor's streets, as in most Midwestern towns, are laid out pretty much on a rectangular grid, but the large area of the campus sprawls across the grid and produces a series of three-way intersections in this part of town. Where S. University meets S. State is the site of the Union, now a place of some congeniality again after a long period of near-abandonment. (Is "South U." also an avenue? I must check.)[10] Where E. Liberty sets out in the direction of Main is another café, favored by quieter types and graduate students, if not philosophers and chess-players; and across from it a large bookstore that's a favorite browsing place for all and sundry. Then, in the other direction from where I'm sitting, at the point where E. Williams branches off to the west, is the corner by the church that was Shaky Jake's turf for many years (this summer I haven't seen him). Jake earned his crust there before ever there was a rapper at North U. An elderly black man, vividly dressed, who engaged in cheerful repartee with passersby, sang tunelessly to the accompaniment of a scratchy guitar, and sold postcards of himself, he was the whole city's friend.

Where I'm sitting, though—to come back to N. University and S. State—is the city's glitziest and most assiduously frequented café, where O'Hara would have turned in some campy performances had it existed half a century ago. Here too is the arcade where it's better to loiter than on the street when the weather's cold. Here is the rapper's (O'Hara's?) corner, and opposite that a good wide stretch of sidewalk, almost a fragment of Parisian boulevard, that's sunny in winter and where someone is usually selling something or buttonholing you with a hand out. That's a spot where people seem to like just to stand about, as they do also at the entrance to the arcade and along the stretch of State St. between the arcade and E. Williams. The suture point, where the campus meets the town. The best place to hang out of all.

So what is it about three-way crossings? In *Oedipus Rex*,

> If I understand you [Oedipus says] Laïos was killed
> At a place where three roads meet[11]

—scarcely an auspicious circumstance. But O'Hara seems to have thought trifoliated intersections lucky; and that was certainly the case, historically, for what is now the sleepy French subprefecture of Arles, in the Rhône delta, which in Roman days was a large and thriving city thanks to its position at the point where the roads from Italy, Spain, and Gaul came together. It was strong enough and rich enough to outlast Rome itself by a couple of centuries, the three-way crossing having made money for Arles as it made poetry for O'Hara. That said, there *is* something seedy about three-ways, especially if they are urban, and North U. and S. State is no exception. It's not for nothing that our word *trivial* comes to us from the Latin *trivialis*, meaning having the character of a three-way crossing (and of those who frequent three-way crossings). The sense of "insignificant" that "trivial" now conveys seems to derive, in part, from an association with the medieval *trivium*, which must have been opposed to the *quadrivium* somewhat as the three-way crossing is opposed to more "normal," and "straightforward," four-way crossroads. But before it came to mean insignificant, the trivial was associated with people, places, and practices of ill repute, particularly as they involved the body and the satisfaction of its needs, as opposed to the supposedly higher things of the mind and the soul. Three-way crossings weren't places for triumphal arches and noble monuments; what flourished there were taverns and brothels and gambling dens.

For such intersections were, of necessity, places where many people passed by, and the busier the intersection, the more likely it was one would find eating, drinking, and lodging establishments, places of entertainment, relaxation, and pleasure, and thus on the one hand local citizenry enjoying a moment of détente and on the other folks from out of town, whether honest travelers or vagrants, and among them quite a few rubes and hayseeds just arrived from the country—chickens waiting to be plucked. For shady characters of various kinds, but especially prostitutes and con men, the three-way crossing was therefore the ideal spot to hang out: it provided cover for their apparent idleness, and at the same time a plentiful supply of likely customers or prospective victims. Mingling with those who were enjoying an innocent break, more dubious loiterers hung out with an eye to the main chance, or—in the language of legal codes and police reports—"with intent."

Loitering thus seems always to have had a bad name and to have drawn to it what is called preventive policing. But I'm not sure the reason is solely that loitering provides a ready alibi for would-be evildoers. The truly disturbing thing may well be that, in the absence of an actual crime, the unsavory loiterer is hard to distinguish from legitimate idlers or passersby. Loitering tends to blur the distinctions on which social order depends—between innocence and guilt, between the good citizen enjoying a moment's respite and the seedy character who may just be taking the sun on this bench or idling in that shady doorway, or who may be a prostitute angling to catch a john or a two-bit criminal looking for an easy mark. As Diderot pointed out, the philosopher himself goes whoring in a fashion; and the trivial is a category that breaks down social distinctions and hierarchies of all kinds. The rich and the poor have bodies and bodily needs, as do the powerful and the weak, the law-abiding and the pimps, prostitutes, vagabonds, and parasites who disturb the order of the city. They meet, in the ordinariness of the trivial, like town and gown in Ann Arbor, Michigan, at the three-way intersection of N. University and S. State.

A reason I'm interested in loiterly literature, then, is that it has this characteristic of the trivial: It blurs categories, and in particular it blurs those of innocent pleasure taking and harmless relaxation and not-so-innocent "intent"—a certain recalcitrance to the laws that maintain "good order." In so doing, it carries an implied social criticism. It casts serious doubt on the values good citizens hold dear—values like discipline, method, organization, rationality, productivity, and, above all, work—but it does so in the guise of innocent and, more particularly, insignificant or frivolous entertainment: a mere passing of the time in idle observations or witty remarks, now this, now that, like the philosopher pursuing his ideas as he sits daydreaming on his bench. Or like the poet mooching along, his idleness a contrast to the busy street, going to the bank and the bookstore, doing this, then that.

Loiterature distracts attention from what it's up to, and in that it's a bit like the street conjurer whose patter diverts us from what's really going on. But then, maybe nothing much *is* going on after all. Critical as it may well be behind its entertaining façade, loiterly writing disarms criticism of itself by presenting a moving target, shifting as its own divided attention constantly shifts. Thus what looked for a moment like an acerbic observation or an implied objection may be instantly displaced by another thought, or a weak pun, or a curious anecdote. It can't be summarized or reduced to a "gist," whereas criticism depends, like social order itself, on the possibility of discriminating and hierarchizing, determining what's central and what's peripheral (this is more important than that, the point is such-and-such, the theme is so-and-so; the rest is "just plot" or "descriptive detail"). Supposing there *is* no center, though, and so no periphery? To criticism, loiterature is inevitably a critical genre: it's loitering with intent. But it *may* sometimes be just loitering.

These texts, in other words, resist contextualization—being penned into a single category as either this or that—because they are themselves all the time shifting context, now this, then that. They're sites of endless *intersection*, and consequently their narrator's attention is always divided between one thing and some other thing, always ready and willing to be distracted. But that's how they give pleasure: they enact a relaxation of the constraints by which one's attention is held and one's nose kept to some grindstone or other; they figure the mobility and freedom of the libido, attacking all possible objects of attention without attaching itself to any. And that's why such pleasure is subversive: it incorporates and enacts—in a way that *may* be quite unintended—a criticism of the disciplined and the orderly, the hierarchical and the stable, the methodical and the systematic, showing them to be unpleasurable, that is, alienating. To reactivate Marx and Engels's nice pun in *The Communist Manifesto*, the *ständig* (that which stands on ceremony—the hierarchical) and the *stehend* (that which stands still—the stable) is vaporized.[12]

It may seem paradoxical that a literature of hanging out does not, and can't, stand still. But its art lies not in not moving but in moving without going anywhere in particular, and indeed in moving without knowing—or maybe pretending not to know—where it's going. What makes it loiterly is that it moves, but without advancing. It travels, but it travels, so to speak, on the spot, without needing to leave home. It is prolix and it is dilatory because—like Yogi Berra, who said: "If you come to a fork in the road, take it"—it can't encounter an intersection without accepting the invitation to deviate, its only quandariness arising from hesitation, not about whether or not to deviate, but about which deviation to take next. Thus digression—what years ago, in defining Romantic irony, Friedrich Schlegel defined as *permanente Parekbase*[13]—is loiterature's stock-in-trade, the secret both of its art—a realization of the poetics of pleasure—and of its critical impact, as the enactment of an epistemology of the unsystematic. For digression, as a discursive practice, performs the implications of our divided attentions, the distractedness in which Benjamin discerned a sign of modernity.

The three-way crossing isn't only a site of the trivial, then, it's also a figure for distractedness and digression. Most Ann Arbor three-ways are T-shaped, thus betraying their derivation from a quadrangular street plan. The *ideal type* of the three-way, though, is the Y-shaped version, like a three-pointed star, which also has a secondary advantage: it benefits connotatively from its alphabetic contiguity with, and its topographic difference from, the X that designates the four-way crossing. All crossroads are numinous places, certainly, but the X of the four-way marks a spot and designates a center; its intersection, although it does not preclude digression, organizes the encounter of two linearities. A Y-shaped crossing is, by contrast, a decentering figure because it doesn't permit linear progression in any direction; it's all swerves. It offers a choice—an occasion for hesitancy and quandariness—but a choice within an imperative, the imperative to digress, the option being only whether to digress to the right or to the left.

The world of the three-way crossing, and the kind of world of which the three-way is a metaphor, in which digression is the only option, is a world in which dilatoriness is the rule. Not that a lot of dickering necessarily goes on in such a world, although dickering *is* characteristic of the fussy people we actually call dilatory. But, dicker or not, there are no straightforward paths, in space or time, between any point A and any other point B. *Aporia*, in both its derived sense of undecidability and its etymological sense of pathlessness, is thus the permanent potential of the three-way. And the question in a world figured by the three-way becomes only whether to *minimize* the indirection of digressivity—as I suppose people mainly do, declaring departures from straightforwardness and linearity to be so slight as to be negligible, or else to be disturbing but exceptional, that is, accidental—or whether, on the contrary, and as a long tradition of loiterly writing has done, to *foreground* digression and emphasize dilatoriness. Delay and indirection—the phenomena of mediacy—become at once sources of pleasure and devices of provocation in a larger universe that seems committed to directness, speed, and immediacy (doing it fast, getting there right away). The accidental, here, is no longer exceptional; it has become the rule. "If it can go wrong, it will," is an engineer's maxim. "Since digression can happen, it should," is the maxim of loiterature. Whether such complacency about digressing is synonymous with "going wrong," though, is very much the question loiterature asks us to consider.

How is it, then, that digression *can* happen? I learn with interest from the dictionary that the adjective *dilatory*, like the verb *to dilate*, is etymologically related both to differing and to deferring (which are from the Latin *di-ferre*, whereas dilatory is from its past participle, *di-latus*). Derridean *différance* is therefore, not so surprisingly, intimately bound up with digression and dilatoriness, unless of course it's the other way around. But it's tempting (to me, at least) to work also with a false etymology by virtue of which *di-latus* would mean two-sidedness, and to imagine that dilatoriness has to do with a certain two-sidedness of things in a three-way world. To approach a Y-shaped intersection by any route is to discover that the road inevitably splits into two ways, such that to choose either is to digress. To have a sense of such two-sidedness is to be subject to distracted attention indeed (distraction is from *dis-trahere*, to pull every which way, as differ and defer are from *di-ferre*, to carry in various directions); and to be distracted, I submit, is to be conscious of the permeability of contexts. The context in which one happens to be working is not only not the only context; but another context is actually interfering with the first.

Philosophically, though, it's clear that no context can ever be the whole context and that such interference is therefore generally the case, since the existence of "a" context necessarily depends on there being at least one "other" context—the context in light of which the first context becomes "a" (an incomplete) context. Such a context-of-the-context can no more be separated from "the" context in question than that context can itself be divided from the activities it makes meaningful. And passage from "the" context to the "other" context that contextualizes the first is therefore an easy matter, since the two are in a relation of split, that is, neither fully discontinuous nor wholly continuous with each other. You can do it in a moment of distraction. Digression, then, is a discursive "slide" or "slippage" along a line of continuity that links one context and its other, so that the new position one reaches is both linked with the first and discontinuous with it. One thing leads to another, as people say; and digression may transgress rules of cohesion, but not of cogency and coherence.

Given the permeability of contexts, to maintain what is called one's concentration, not permitting other contexts to interfere and digression to occur, requires an effort; it's a matter of training and vigilance. What makes digression a pleasurable experience is the relaxation of the vigilance, the abandonment of discipline that becomes associated—naturally enough, I suppose—with the way the body impinges on (or distracts from) the activities of the mind, the unconscious on those of consciousness, and with the way desire interferes in matters that are supposed to have nothing to do with libido. Digression is thus readily condemned, from the point of view of the maintenance of a certain cultural order, as a *pente facile* or slippery slope—but it is practiced to the precise extent that such cultural order is maintained at the price of human alienation: alienation from what culture defines as natural. Whence, I suppose, the attractiveness of the erotic genre of the three-way—a kind of libidinal version of the tawdriness associated with three-way crossings in urban environments: the three-way implies that desire can't, and so should not, be confined. For each participant, it's a case of deliciously divided attention and of the pleasurable permeability of contexts. In a novel by Michel Tournier, a cynical fellow by the name of Alexandre reports seeing two dogs, a female in heat and a passing male, fornicating in the street.[14] A third dog, also male, supervenes and is at first discouraged to find access to the female barred. The context is closed and he is excluded from it—until he sees that the fornicating male dog's anus is wiggling invitingly in the air and proceeds to mount *him*. Alexandre is delighted: the third dog has demonstrated that no context is the whole context, that homosexuality is the excluded "other" of heterosexuality, that digression is the way of pleasure. That humans can learn from dogs was ever the cynic's profession of faith; that dogs teach the pleasures of digression is mine.

But if there's pleasure in digression, all the warnings about slippery slopes and open floodgates are nevertheless appropriate. Digression happens because it can happen, but it escalates because what can happen, once it escapes control, will go on happening. Once the three-way phenomenon of two-sidedness is recognized and acceded to, it becomes inevitable to discover that the second side itself has another side, which is therefore the third side of the first, a third that can generate a fourth, a fifth, and so on to infinity. Any local context is thus connected by virtue of a multiplicity of mediations with a globality that, in the end, resists inventory. In this way there comes to be a kind of euphoria of digressiveness, an exacerbation of the divided attention, that loiterly writing—I'm coming soon to Sterne's *Tristram Shandy*—loves to exploit. The pleasures of dilatoriness link with the insatiability of desire—with Diderot's "jeunes dissolus" pursuing every prostitute at the price of becoming attached to none—but also with the philosopher on his bench, pursuing ideas like whores. And an orgy of *comprehensiveness*, generated out of the initial moment when one context opens to another, and two dogs to three, is thus pitted against the forms of *comprehension* that are predicated on foreclosure: limited perspectives, disciplined attention, and closed contexts. In this way mere pleasure tends in the direction of what Roland Barthes would call *jouissance*.[15]

But in that direction only, for the totality it aims for, the comprehensiveness it desires are themselves subject to frustrating limits, which are those of what human language can articulate, the human mind encompass and the human body withstand; and it's thus that loiterature demonstrates Maurice Blanchot's contention that writing inevitably falls short of being the unimaginable *œuvre* whose possibility it nevertheless suggests, and becomes a mere *livre* instead. Not coincidentally,

Blanchot's name for this inevitable failure is *désœuvrement*—being at a loose end, hanging out, demonstrating the quality of loiterliness that's usually translated, in the context of Blanchot, as "worklessness."[16] So digression escalates, the dilatory dilates—but never to the point where it loses all contact with order, linearity, cohesion, and system. This is a matter to which it will be necessary to return, because it means that, like two branches of a Y, digression and linearity, comprehensiveness and comprehension, dilatoriness and directedness or speed, are *themselves* in digressive relation one with the other, a relation of two-sidedness in which each is the other's (permeable) context.

Needless to say, it's not easy to find an economical example of the dilation to which dilatory, digressive texts are subject. But here is Jacques Réda's description, which I offer without comment, of the pleasure of riding a moped on the open road. In this passage the rearview mirror functions as a figure for the "other" context and as the vehicle, therefore, of a distracted attention that escalates into a sort of euphoria or *ivresse*. On a moped,

> you need to keep a weather-eye out all the time. You have to watch not only the whole prospect of the road ahead and its immediate environs (dogs, cats, chickens and children popping up from nowhere) but also what's happening behind you per medium of the rearview mirror. And it's no easy task to learn to use this accessory which reflects no more than a limited area and jiggles continuously from the vibration, so that you're not spared the necessity of turning your head, sometimes dangerously. But it does serve another useful purpose in retaining part of the receding landscape, which otherwise we would miss. It furnishes samples of what the region would look like, something that may well be wholly different, if one were riding in the other direction. Our eyes naturally have a very limited span. But by virtue of the rearview mirror, functioning as a third eye, and the versatility of vision it induces, our compass extends to the full 360° of the horizon. More than truly global, this fragmented vision is, broadly speaking, kaleidoscopic. But from perpetually adjusting and readjusting the pieces, one can ultimately achieve a second vision, as it were, that compensates for our inadequacies and makes us almost all-seeing. The regular, if not exactly exhilarating, speed of one's movement, provided nothing impedes it (ruts in the road or an interminable hill), reinforces this impression and induces a kind of intoxication. And like all intoxications, this one makes you want, for a long time, to get more and more intoxicated; so it sustains the astonishing physical and

psychological stamina one displays, riding beflummoxed on a jolting saddle for hours on end. At this point, it's more the road and the landscape that move, deploying themselves around the fixed point of your exultation. True, this isn't necessarily a state you can reach straightaway. You might as well try to get drunk without drinking. But it can arise on relatively short laps, too short for gradual inducement, as for example between the Invalides and the Alma Bridge. Whence, I suppose, my impatience, my unreasonable insistence on being always and immediately enraptured. The secret, perhaps, is in not knowing where you're going. One ought not assign a precise destination to one's outings, but leave it up to chance. And by chance, then, one would come upon the sources of the Seine: they would spew forth at the culmination of a dizzying and beatific ride.[17]

But if there's a *jouissance* of digression, the option in favor of digressiveness is also, as I've said, a critical act—the critical is, so to speak, the second side of digression's pleasurability. Any digression enacts (although it may not intend) a criticism because, once one has digressed, the position from which one departed becomes available to a more dispassionate or ironic analysis: it must have been in some sense inadequate or one would not have moved away from it. This is the principle of deliberately digressive criticism such as is practiced by writers like Gayatri Spivak or Meaghan Morris.[18] But the option in favor of digressiveness also implies a more general critique, which sometimes becomes explicit, of modes of thought and behavior that regard themselves as disciplined, methodical, or systematic and require progress according to rules of logical progression or closely contextualized cohesion. It's critical, too, of modes of authority (let's say kingship, or the power of the law, or academic authority) that depend on cultural conventions, that is (once again), a restriction of context. To demonstrate, by a shift of perspective, that certain things are the case (certain propositions hold true, certain perspectives are valid) only within a limited context, and that they're dependent on a certain "forgetfulness" with respect to the other-sidedness of a given situation, is to show, on the one hand, that the claims of authority are not universally valid and, on the other, that the condition of intellectual comprehension is a certain failure of comprehensiveness. Plato was applauded for the elegance of his solution to the problem of defining humankind: man, he said, is the featherless biped. The applause faltered, though, when Diogenes, without comment, plucked a chicken and held it up, demonstrating both what Plato's definition forgot and the vulnerability of intellectual authority to any evidence of its limited applicability. Cynical (doglike) philosophy was in large part an art of pointed digression.

Digression's critique is not limited to the local, however, against which it asserts the deflating power of contextual difference. It's also, in diachronic terms, a critique of the present—the local in temporal guise—against which it mobilizes the dilatory as a mode of deferral. The present is a context oblivious of the fact that it has a past that can't be quite forgotten and a future that impinges relentlessly on it. There are thus two ways to enact a criticism of the present, each of which entails a double contextual consciousness and a distracted sense of historical time. To be dilatory is to defer the future, or to express a desire to defer the future, by living the actual movement of time from present to future as if it were an infinite expansion of the present, a dilation sideways, as it were, instead of a direct and inexorable march toward a future that the nature of the present leads one to find unattractive. To be belated is to live in the present, but out of phase with it to the extent that one dawdles psychologically in a remembered past that represents a preferred context because it seems more authentic, more simple, less alienating. To be belated is to be dilatory with respect to the historical present in the way that to be dilatory is to seek to defer or delay, in would-be belated fashion, a predicted historical future. One can thus combine the two: dawdling in the past functions as a judgment on the present and in the present as a judgment on the probable future. But either way, a sense of time as a historical awareness of the permeability of diachronic contexts is asserted against the reification of the present, the correlative construction of history as a series of discrete moments (or periods, or eras), and the linear narrative presupposed by ideologies of both progress and decline.

A hilarious 1989 film by Maurizio Nichetti, *Ladri di saponette* (*The Icicle Thief*) can serve here as an example of digressive criticism from a position of belatedness.[19] A "typical" Italian family of the booming, consumerist 1980s settles down to watch the evening's movie on TV. They watch it, though, because that's where the baby—who was amusing herself channel surfing (i.e. context shifting)—left it when she was put to bed; and meanwhile the son of the house is playing with a Lego set, the father is reading the paper, the mother calling *her* mother on the phone and worried about the advanced state of her pregnancy.

She's more entertained by the commercials than by the film in any case. So this is distracted attention indeed, even though its consequence is that the world of the movie—Nichetti's "Ladri di saponette," a film-within-the-film that is an affectionate parody of Italian neorealism—seems remote. *It* belongs to the economically difficult past, *they* live in the complacent and plethoric present. But meanwhile, at the studio, Nichetti (playing himself) demonstrates his own inaptitude for modern life, incarnating the traditional bumbling clown figure amid all the technological know-how, and sitting silent—a figure both of exclusion and abstention—through the interview in which he might have explained his film. Particularly alarming to him are the commercial breaks that interrupt the mood and style of the neorealist pastiche with jingles, beautiful models in swimsuits and attractive commodities, all in vivid color. Miserable as it is, the world of neorealism clearly represents for him a preferred, more authentic, historical moment, one of genuine feeling and real but relatively simple problems by comparison with the commoditized present. But Nichetti, it seems, is the only belated figure to whom this past time still seems relevant.

The two moments, though, past and present, prove before long to be oddly, and mutually, permeable. For one thing, "Ladri di saponette" is not *Ladri di biciclette* (*Bicycle Thieves*) but a contemporary pastiche thereof, a product of modern nostalgia that belongs, therefore, on the TV along with the *pubblicità* that Nichetti so detests. Consequently, characters soon begin to migrate between the two spheres, and in both directions: a 1980s model dives into an azure swimming pool in the interest of advertising some product, but comes up spluttering and drowning, still wearing her revealing swimsuit and in full color, in the black-and-white world of the river that runs through the industrial neighborhood in which the neorealist drama is set. The wildly digressive perturbations this interference between the two contexts sets off in the plot of the film lead Nichetti to follow her in an attempt to get things back on track; but while Heidi the model contentedly learns Italian and gets accustomed to living in black-and-white (although missing her morning cornflakes), Nichetti's arrival on the scene provokes wildly escalating digressiveness, all the more since Maria and Bruno, the wife and the son of the eponymous icicle thief, have meanwhile slipped out of the neorealist environment into the "heaven" of the commercials. There the child contentedly munches Big-Big snack foods that previously he had only been able to devour with his eyes from his position in the televised film, through the magic of cinematic shot/countershot, while his mother—a member of an all-girl trio back in the world of neorealism—prances, strutts her stuff, and sings her heart out in honor of a detergent.

They are finally fetched back by the itinerant Nichetti and restored to their home in the 1940s, but not before raiding a 1980s supermarket and returning with a procession of loaded shopping carts, to the delight of all. The original plot (involving paralysis, prostitution, and an orphanage) has now been thoroughly diverted from its track by the conversion of the neorealist world to the values of consumerism—but one realizes that, with the the period's longing for food and consumer comforts and taste for song-and-dance numbers to silly ditties like those performed by Maria and her friends, the 1940s already contained the germ of its degraded and commercialized future: the present of the 1980s. If the present remembers, and so is inseparable from, its past, the past itself was once a present on which the future already impinged; that's why "lateral" travel between the two is possible, substituting a digressive pattern of movement between the two co-present contexts for history as inexorable linear progress. This relation of equivalence between past and present is figured by the fact that Nichetti, who plays "himself" in the present, also plays the icicle thief, Piermattei, in the past, each figure being presented in symmetrical fashion as out of phase with its own, respectively already consumerist and now fully consumerist, era. But that too is why these figures of belated authenticity also find themselves ironically compromised with the context they are alienated from: Piermattei is willing to steal commodities to please his wife, and Nichetti—whose nostalgic belatedness is a part of the contemporaneity he inhabits—ends up stuck in the TV set where he rightly belongs.

These ironies, in the economy of digressivity, are those of the critical gesture in general, although they are nicely illustrated by the problematics of belatedness as an abstentionism that forms part of the context it rejects. The critical position is inevitably connected with the position that is criticized because it is sutured, as the two branches of a Y are sutured, to the context of which it is the digressive "other." What makes criticism possible—that is, the circumstance of digressive split—is also what makes it impossible for criticism to occupy a position absolutely exempt from, and unsullied by, what it is critical of. In this, criticism is absolutely homologous with digression as a mode of pleasure, which can function as a pleasurable relaxation of constraint only to the extent that it remains connected with, and hence in the end governed by, the constrictions of discipline, system, cohesion, and linearity that it seeks to relax.

With a quick flick of the channel selector, I can now make a lateral move across a couple of centuries of time to reach Laurence Sterne, author of *Tristram Shandy*, and certainly the major progenitor of modern loiterature (although he has plentiful predecessors of his own in figures like Burton, Rabelais, Montaigne, and Cervantes). Actually, I don't really need a remote control or filmic crosscutting. Old-fashioned association of ideas will do the trick as I slip from Nichetti and the popular cultural figure of the clown to "Yorick" (Sterne's pseudonym) and so to the courtly figure of the Renaissance fool or buffoon. Nichetti stands in a long line of twentieth-century filmic clowns—the Chaplin of *Modern Times* and the Tati of *Mon Oncle* prominent among them—who explore a problematics of belatedness in the context of industrial and technological dominance; but Sterne's own (belated) self-identification with the Renaissance fool looks back to a period before the Industrial Revolution and simultaneously founds a tradition in loiterly writing of the modern period. For loiterly narrators like to affect a Yorick-like persona of amiable eccentricity as a way of sharing the authority of the buffoon, whose criticism of authority and the social order was licensed by the pleasure he gave, through displays of verbal wit (that is, of acrobatic context shifting). Following Sterne, however, they also tend to combine this display of mastery with a clownish performance of failure. For, like critics unable to disengage themselves from the object of criticism, these clowns get hilariously caught up in whatever they engage with, as does the Little Man in the assembly line or Nichetti in the TV, giving a spectacular display of loss of control in the process. In this respect, the pratfall is paradigmatic. But, finally, both the clown and the buffoon are associated with sadness; and what I want to suggest is that, like them, loiterature proposes its digressive enactment of distracted attention as itself a mode of *diversion*, a therapy perhaps for the form of concentrated attention that's called brooding, melancholia, the *idée fixe*.

In *Tristram Shandy*, Sterne's particular form of the buffoonery of divided attention derives from the ironic (or paradoxical) structure of the discursive mode known as narrative. Narrative is definable interchangeably as a closed form that is nothing if it does not digress, and as a digression constrained by its dependence on structural closure. A story must have a beginning and an end, and some form of structural cohesion linking them. But a story that began with its beginning and proceeded directly to its end, without mediation—let's say: "John was unhappy, then he became happy"—would not be a story so much as a case of digression (in this case a digression of mood, an example of whimsy). For the bookends of beginning and end to become a true story, the mediation of a middle must be supplied: let's say, "John was unhappy, then he met Mary (or Paul), then he became happy."[20] But now, as a result, the story has a dilatory structure, in that the second clause ("then he met Mary/Paul") functions, or seems to function, as a digression from the topic of John's unhappiness (it introduces the possibility, for example, of there being a story about Mary or Paul); only the end reveals its cogency to that topic and thus restores a semblance of cohesion to the narrative, the causal link between middle and end enabling the end now to function as a structural inversion of the beginning rather than an example of caprice. A story coheres grammatically, then, only under the constraint of being dilatory, of not taking the shortest path (a straight line) between its opening and its conclusion. There's a requirement of what Peter Brooks calls plot, "the middle as detour, as struggle towards the end under the compulsion of imposed delay, as arabesque in the dilatory space of text."[21] Plotting responds to a double necessity, that of the story's holding *interest* for a narratee (through having a discernible "point"), and that of *holding* that narratee's interest, which, as I've argued, is a matter of stimulating, but then of maintaining, a certain kind of desire, the desire for narration.[22] Once aroused, though, desire is insatiable, and the narrator's temptation tends always to be to spin out the story. At the cost of extenuating the narrative's grammatical cohesion, the end to which the story tends (or sometimes only pretends to tend) is delayed by means of dilatory practices that both satisfy and sustain the desire for narration but also produce a form of divided attention, the narratee becoming split between one form of desire (the desire to know, corresponding to the question: How will it all turn out in the end?) and its other (the desire to prolong the pleasure, corresponding to a question formulated by Nicholson Baker: Will I ever want to stop reading [or listening]?).[23] This split is another form of the relation of difference and mutual alterity that links (the desire for) comprehension, as an understanding dependent on contextual closure, and (that for) comprehensiveness, predicated on the permeability of contexts and the untotalizable globality it implies. A felicitous narrative, of course, is held to tack evenly between end-directedness and the potentially endless exploration of dilating context(s), satisfying each desire only at the cost of frustrating its other, and risking pointlessness through complexity and overspecification at one extreme and the dreariness and monotony of an overly closed context at the other. Sterne's demonstration, though, was that there's a kind of teasing pleasure for the reader in witnessing a narrator's clownish failure to perform this feat of equilibrium, in watching him verge on pointlessness out of a compulsion to furnish circumstantial detail. Losing sight of the narrative *telos* of an ending, Sterne's narrator, Tristram, engages in a kind of long drawn out discursive pratfall, a loss of narrative control that is, of course, perfectly controlled by Sterne. In this process, it is demonstrated that pointlessness can have a cogency of its own and that a digressive failure of cohesion can be meaningful in its own way.

The trick of loiterly narrative is so to question the conventionality of beginnings and endings that the alleged story becomes all middle. Thus birth, as the conventional beginning of Tristram's "life and opinions," is cheekily preceded, in Sterne, by the famous account of the young man's conception, a conception that itself takes place under the sign of divided attention (his mother absent-mindedly distracting his father by choosing the critical moment to remind him to wind the clock). As a result, Tristram has acquired a distracted character that he might himself describe as whimsical; and his narrative's end-directedness suffers in consequence from the effects of his inveterate digressiveness. Indeed, Tristram is as undeviating in his narrative dilatoriness as his uncle Toby is single-minded in his obsession with fortifications and his father in the unpredictability of his opinions and systems.

For a long time, Tristram never quite loses touch with the story line he is committed to, that of his own life from conception, through birth, baptism, circumcision, and so forth; but as these events themselves attest, he is a figure for whom the accidental is not exceptional but the norm. Although he boasts of his skill at so ordering the digressions that divert attention from his story that they themselves constitute a mode of narrative progress,[24] the escalation of digressivity and the loss of control to which his inborn dilatoriness leads become inescapable at the point where he is forced to acknowledge that a reversal of interest, away from the end-directedness of narrative and toward the potential endlessness of reading and writing, has occurred. The narration has lagged so far behind the narrative, and the delay is in such geometric progression, that there is, by book 4, no chance of the story's ever reaching an end.

> I am this month one whole year older than I was this time twelve-month; and having got, as you perceive, almost into the middle of my fourth volume—and no farther than to my first day's life—'tis demonstrative that I have three hundred and sixty-four more days life to write just now, than when I first set out; so that instead of advancing, as a common writer, in my work with what I have been doing at it—on the contrary, I am just thrown so many volumes back (etc.). It must follow, an' please your worships, that the more I write, the more I shall have to write —and consequently, the more your worships read, the more your worships will have to read.
>
> Will this be good for your worships eyes? (4.13.285–86)

And indeed, whether by Sterne's design or the accident of his death, the last three volumes lose sight of the initial narrative altogether, relating a voyage through France in book 7 before revolving in books 8 and 9 almost exclusively around the figures of my uncle Toby, Trim, and the widow Wadman, so that the text ends, without resolving either the story of my uncle Toby's amours or that of Tristram's life, on the pirouette of a (literal) "cock and bull" story.

In spite of his concern for his readers' eyes, Tristram is anything but contrite. His narrative predicament is a natural consequence of his accident-prone character, which itself follows from, as it is illustrated by, his botched coming into the world (his distracted conception, the damage to his nose at birth, the misnaming at his baptism, his acciden-tal circumcision by a window sash). Lack of control and impotence, leading to digressive drift, are something like Tristram's birthright—and by extension (to the extent that he is a kind of everyman), the birthright of humanity. We're born to the pratfall—but the important point, in Tristram's view, is that one be consistent with one's nature, whatever the vagaries, whimsicalities, and deviations that may result: "in my opinion, to write a book is for all the world like humming a song—be but in tune with yourself, Madam, 'tis no matter how high or low you take it" (4.25.315). This harmoniousness with "nature"—an un-willingness to constrain it by compliance with artificial requirements—

is the secret of the consistency all the male members of the Shandy family display in the very whimsicality of their behavior, my uncle Toby obsessing over his fortifications, my father predictably unpredictable in all his views, Tristram himself undeviatingly digressive. And the word furnished by the English language for this characteristic (un)self-consistency is eccentricity, which implies, by its etymology, a characterological uncenteredness. Eccentricity redefines human subjectivity, in other words, as a reliable versatility, not a matter of substance and self-sameness but of always potential otherness and the normalcy of the accidental. Even the predictability of my uncle Toby's obsession is an uncentered one, as the wound to his groin inescapably symbolizes—and when the peace of Utrecht deprives him of an alibi for his hobbyhorsical messing around with fortifications, he readily turns his attention to the widow Wadman, who has been waiting all this time in the wings. The wager of *Tristram Shandy*, in short, is that a theory of versatility grounded (if that is the word) in uncenteredness— Tristram's damaged nose replicates the wound to Toby's groin—gives a better account of human subjectivity than centered or essentialistic accounts. For his associationism, Locke then is Sterne's philosopher; and by virtue of his amiable digressiveness, Montaigne a model both of humanism and of the human.[25] Moderns might well agree that phenomena of linearity, predictability, cohesion, and control can more readily be accounted for as an alienation of uncentered discursivity than the phenomena of divided attention and split subjectivity can be predicted from theories of the autonomy, integrity, and self-sameness of the self.

Not that Tristram's intent is polemical, however. He's quick to assure the reader that he has no satirical or critical target in writing as he does: his book is no more "wrote against predestination, or free-will or taxes" than my uncle Toby is a caricature of military men or Trim a representation of the duke of Osmond. "If 'tis wrote against anything, —'tis wrote, an' please your worships, against the spleen . . ." (4.22.301). Needless to say, this is disingenuous; *Tristram Shandy* has plenty of satirical and critical targets. But, thanks to the comprehensiveness of Tristram's galloping digressivity, abetted by my father's encyclopedic erudition and appreciation of counter-intuitive views, it *is* a capacious and tolerant work, one that makes room for the dottiest theories or ideas, even though they may come in at the same time for some affectionate mockery. And the claim that it was written against melancholia is one that can and should be taken seriously, partly for the positive implication that the book is "wrote" to give pleasure, and partly in view of the suggestion made throughout that the "againstness" of excentric writing's relation to melancholy might be taken in a two-sided or anaclitic (leaning against) sense as much as an adversative one.

Tristram's name, from Latin *tristis*, may or may not be a misnomer, but his person does suggest a certain proximity of the melancholy his name connotes and the digressivity he practices, especially as digressivity is associated, in a convoluted way, with Tristram's "other" name, Trismegistus (the sage, hero, or god who invented writing and, according to my father, was "born sideways," i.e. by cesarean section). Similarly, the reminiscence of the grave digger scene in *Hamlet* that's implied by the name Yorick, suggests a certain permeability of melancholy and "infinite jest." Tristram's intellectually eccentric father is much given to lamentation, notably over Tristram's fate. And finally, my uncle Toby's hobbyhorse is an *idée fixe* like melancholy but one that cures him of brooding over the "unspeakable miseries" (1.25.79), the "sharp paroxisms and exacerbations" (2.1.83) caused by his wound. Thus, it's suggested that melancholy, and eccentricity as an antidote to melancholy, lie within a hair's breadth of each other, as alternative ways of living the consequences of the same phenomenon of uncenteredness, each the other's other and, taken together, a manifestation of the two-sidedness of things in a three-way world. A morbid obsession with impotence, inadequacy, and death becomes, by the merest deviation, a joyous acceptance of the potential for diversion that's offered by a world in which the division of attention—and hence, distraction—is possible.

Narrative, as an enactment of divided attention, is thus the text's vehicle of diversion: "the history of a soldier's wound," as we learn early, "beguiles the pain of it" (1.25.79). As Toby is healed, first by telling the story of his wound and then led on—in the way one thing does lead to another—by the difficulty of telling it clearly, into the complicated building of his model fortifications, a construction that soon takes over and becomes an end in itself, so the narrator of Tristram's "life and opinions" beguiles both himself and the implied reader, diverting attention from the regrettable implications of his damaged, accident-prone existence through escalating digressivity and the entertaining spectacle of his narrative loss of control. Thus we come close to losing sight, simultaneously, of the slender narrative thread that constitutes the tale of Tristram's life and of the reasons for lamentation it might otherwise suggest. That we don't and can't lose sight of them completely is predicted, however, by both the oddly two-sided or ambiguous structure of the narrative discourse as a simultaneously dilatory and end-oriented phenomenon and the very condition of digression which is, as etymology proposes, a stepping away from — but a stepping away from that's sutured to that away from which it steps. Digression isn't only travel that doesn't need to leave home; it's also travel that can't quite manage to leave home, ever, step away as it might.

But beguiling narrative — or better still: beguiling narration as an alternative to narrative closure — isn't a bad phrase with which to characterize loiterature generally, the history of which I don't plan to write, although I *am* proposing that it can be thought to have had its modern beginnings in the revelation that was *Tristram Shandy* in Enlightenment Europe, and in the model of delight Sterne's book provided for subsequent generations. What was the need to which such a revelation responded? What forms of beguilement are attractive to the sensibility of post-Enlightenment modernity? And why? What do they step away from? Any account I can give of these matters in the chapters to come will be at best a digressive and unsystematic one. But Sterne, I think, drew attention, more than any of his predecessors, to a certain *lack of fullness* in existence, a dividedness that his text doesn't lament, however (and this is its real modernity) because without it, it would not have the beguiling power to digress.[26] Tristram means sad or sorry, but a shandy, in Yorkshire dialect, was a split or crack-brained fellow. Such divided consciousness, Sterne suggests, is less an occasion for pathos or regret than a matter for a certain wry mode of celebration and delight, as is the inevitable triviality — the insignificance, the vulgarity, and also the inability to "concentrate," notably on the higher things — to which it makes human existence subject. Two hundred years later, Frank O'Hara would not have disagreed.

On Stepping out of Line

ON NOT MAKING A BEELINE

> The straight-line distance between Fort Kearney and Omaha is two
> hundred miles at most, as the bee flies—as the Americans say. If the
> wind held, this distance could be covered in five hours. If there were
> no incidents, the sled would be in Omaha by five o'clock.[1]

Jules Verne has gotten his "American" idioms a bit mixed up, but no
matter. This passage from *Around the World in Eighty Days* is an emblematic one, since making a beeline, and doing so in spite of delaying
contingencies, is what the novel is all about. Phileas Fogg is making
a helter-skelter voyage around the world, intent on demonstrating for
a bet that the circumnavigation can be done in the amazingly brief
time (for 1872) of eighty days. He moves by the fastest possible route
between ports and railheads, without purpose except to meet deadlines
and make connections, never deigning to take note of the exotic land-
scapes and cultural diversity through which his itinerary cuts a swathe,
and patiently filling in time on long ocean legs or transcontinental train
journeys with rubbers of whist, as if he hadn't left his London club.

One fact is made clear about him from the start, the moment the
narrative reaches the exotic East: "As for seeing the town, he did
not even think of it, being of that breed of Britons who have their
servants do their sightseeing for them" (34). An interest in alterity
is incompatible with getting there fast, and indeed, throughout the
journey (and with only one major departure from the rule), dealing
with otherness—an activity clearly as indispensable to the text's own
narrative interest as it is to Fogg's successful circumnavigation—is
left to Passepartout, the loyal manservant who (in the way of these
Giovanni-Leporello pairings) is as curious, of course, as his master
is single-minded. But it's Passepartout's trickster-like skills (as an ex-
acrobat and ex-firefighter) that resolve difficult situations—rescuing an
Indian widow from *sati*, cutting short an attack by marauding Sioux
on a train—and extricate Fogg from engagements with recalcitrant

others whose interests don't coincide with his own and who therefore have the potential to impede his stately but speedy progress. Making a beeline, it turns out, does not absolve one from the necessity of engaging with otherness, of mediating relations, however much one may seek—like Fogg marrying the English-educated Indian widow— to assimilate them to the sameness of one's self-defined project.

"If the wind held," we learn, Fogg's party could make it to Omaha (by sail-driven sled) in five hours. "If there were no incidents," they would be there on schedule at one. These insistent conditionals point to the most evident stakes of Fogg's wager: not so much the money (although he stands to win a small fortune), as a demonstration of the irrelevance of contingency to the maintenance of a schedule. Such respect for the discipline of a schedule over the natural forces of accident and incident makes *Around the World* an important document of modernity. But so too does its equation of natural accident with colonial resistance—those vaguely mentioned, pesky "incidents"—to Western technological mastery and political domination. Fogg and his fellow clubmen have just read the *Morning Chronicle*'s hypothetical eighty-day schedule of circumnavigation:

> "Possibly eighty days!" exclaimed Stuart, trumping a winner in his excitement. "But not allowing for unfavorable weather, headwinds, shipwrecks, derailments, etc."
>
> "All included," said Fogg, continuing to play—for the discussion was no longer respecting the whist.
>
> "Even if Indians and Red Indians [les Indous et les Indiens] tear up the rails?" cried Stuart. "Even if they stop the trains, plunder the carriages, and scalp the passengers?"
>
> "All included," repeated Phileas Fogg; laying down his hand. "Two winning trumps." (19)

One can speculate about what the two winning trumps stand for: European technological and moral superiority, perhaps (both matters of single-mindedness)? It's more important to see, though, that the possible impediments to the voyage, as they are exemplified in Stuart's scenario, are themselves of two kinds: natural forces of delay and disorder and recalcitrant colonial subjects unwilling to submit to European designs and who are assigned, by implication, to the same category of natural obstacles as the headwinds and derailments. "Progress," as exemplified by Fogg's fast-forward, is conditioned on the control of natural forces that include colonial others, and it's not an exaggeration to say that Fogg's imperturbability and indifference to otherness are part of a geopolitical game plan, like keeping one's cool when others are giving way to excitement in the game of whist. Fogg's colonial policy— the policy of attending to otherness only to the precise degree that's necessary to assimilate it to the requirements of a strictly scheduled European beeline—has little to do with making money (after all, Fogg spends almost as much on his adventure as he stands to gain) but everything to do with control: the reduction of alterity to sameness isn't a means to an end but an end in itself.

The symbolism of Fogg's marriage to the beautiful and thoroughly assimilated Aouda at the end of the novel confirms such an interpretation of his project. But the end also shows that he wins his bet by a kind of unplanned (and thus uncontrolled) twist that introduces unexpected elasticity into the supposedly rigorous schedule. Traveling eastward (toward the British colonies), Fogg and his party will turn out, at the end, to have unconsciously gained an extra day en route: they return to London within eighty days by London's count, but they have in fact incorporated an extra day's travel time—an extra day that vindicates everything (natural delays, the resistance of colonial others, Passepartout's *flânerie* and touristic interest in sights and sounds) for which the strict schedule published by the *Morning Chronicle* made no allowance. So if the strict disciplining of the natural through scheduling, which is at the heart of Fogg's character as well as of his project, does win out in the end, it does so only by making a kind of inattentive concession to the category of the natural itself: the other of its beeline project, here exemplified by cooperative rather than recalcitrant astronomical facts. And in that, this novel of breathless haste, this narrative of end-oriented suspense, makes a nod of its own to the leisurely mode of writing that I call loiterature. I'm not being paradoxical just for the sake of paradox in making *Around the World* a loiterly text in spite of itself: there's good reason to think that no writing can be so speedy as not to qualify in some degree for membership in the category of the loiterly (and thus, for considering loiterature to be in that sense typical). But that said, the matter of degree can't be ignored.

Against Fogg's beeline we might set, then—as a more exemplary case of loiterature—a travel narrative that sets out *not to make a beeline*, or to put it even more accurately, to turn a "B" line into an opportunity to take time in order to explore, in leisurely, readerly fashion, a world of otherness. François Maspero's ironically titled *Roissy Express* begins with playful reference to jet travel and world adventure, a kind of updating of the universe of Verne's *Around the World*.[2] Two travelers plan to take the B line of the RER, the regional system of fast trains that serves the Paris suburbs, in order to get to the international airport at Roissy:

> They have arranged to meet at 9 A.M. on the northbound platform at Châtelet–Les Halles, deep underground. Their first stop will be Roissy–Charles de Gaulle international airport, their launch pad into the wide-open spaces of their great adventure. They will be away for a month. For a month, then, farewell Paris. (3)

Where are they headed? Kinshasa? Rio? Around the world? No. At the airport,

> [t]hey write their last postcards. . . . Finally they have to go — it's boarding time. They make their way towards the stop for the shuttle that will take them back to the SNCF railway station. They want to get to Roissy-village. (6)

Roissy village? "Have you ever been to Roissy village?" the text asks slyly (Connaissez-vous Roissy-village?). Well, obviously not. Who has been to Roissy village? Who notices, let alone *visits*, the village of Roissy, in their rush to or from the airport on the B line? There is an overlooked, domestic form of otherness, named here by Roissy, that contrasts with the exotica Europeans either gape at, like Passepartout, or ignore, like his master, as they rush by, intent on concerns of their own.

Maspero's contention is that this familiar but unexplored alterity is worth knowing, but that to know the other, whether familiar or exotic, takes time, since haste is the reason it is ignored in the first place. In a kind of parody of *Around the World*, he and his friend (a photographer, Anaïk Frantz) have set aside a month, in the course of which they plan to explore the different stations of the Roissy line, line B, at the rate of (roughly) one station per day. At each station, they will get off and look around them, without preconceived plans or hard-and-fast schedule, meeting the inhabitants of the Parisian *banlieue* and experiencing for themselves something of how these people live. For to Parisians, the suburbs (*la banlieue*), and particularly the working-class suburbs to the north and east of the city, with their large immigrant populations and their infamous mass housing developments, are terra incognita, as remote as Africa: a vague space "where the savages are" (4), and associated mythically with delinquency and drugs, the sole topics of media reporting. The colonies are no longer distant, as they were in 1872; in 1989 they are at the very gates of the city; but European colonial policy remains much the same: either assimilate the other to oneself or—which has a similar effect—distance it by making it the object of an exoticizing gaze, and in either case *ban*ish it to the periphery (the *ban*lieue) of attention, where it will not interrupt the beeline of progress.

In *Roissy Express*, then, it's a bit as if Fogg had become Passepartout but a Passepartout of the nonexotic: the familiar, the near-at-hand, and the overlooked. A Passepartout, also, who has a Passepartout of his own in the person of his photographer-companion Anaïk, who is charged officially with making a photographic record of the trip and unofficially (gender *oblige*) with making contact and striking up friendships with the *banlieusards*, while François does the intellectual labor: taking verbal notes, reading guidebooks, and writing up the history of the neighborhoods they pass through. The two modern Passepartouts, moreover, are free to devote themselves full time to their "nonchalant sort of stroll" (13): they're not, like Fogg's manservant, condemned to gaping through train windows at exotic landforms, architecture, flora and fauna, or to fitting in a few hours of flânerie while awaiting the departure of the next ship. And, as a result, what they discover from their haphazard investigation is the very opposite of Passepartout's ready amazement at the other's inexhaustible strangeness.

In the case of the Parisian *banlieue*, the exoticizing perspective belongs to the media, with its litany of delinquency and drugs. Taking their time, trusting to chance, walking long distances in search of an elusive hotel, talking with people encountered on the street or sitting at their window, having lunch with friends or friends of friends (letter carriers, local "geographers," workers in youth centers), François and Anaïk discover the simple ordinariness of the other, the perspective in which the life of the *banlieue* (etymologically related to *banal* as well as *banish*) is not exotic but everyday. "Il faut prendre le temps de respecter les autres," is Anaïk's summing up (Respecting others entails taking time [translation modified]; 106); and in taking time, one finds out, finally, that as ordinary as the life of the other may be it's still not the same as one's own: the other is *familiar* but not (as Fogg might wish) assimilable. You might say it is an "inner" other, as opposed to "external" alterity that one can exoticize, which is why one doesn't need to travel far in order to find it. It's the other of those who travel without really leaving home. But it's also the reason why one needs to take one's time, for only an exoticized, distanced other (however geographically close it may be) can be perceived through the windows of a passing train. The sense in which the other is familiar takes much longer to find out than the easily grasped, but literally alienating, sense in which the other is strange. So the relaxed rhythm of François's and Anaïk's "nonchalant sort of stroll" is appropriate: "they weren't looking for anything exceptional. They weren't looking for events" (15).

Taking one's time, not running the "Paris-Dakar race" (15), not looking for events but patiently getting to know the (already) familiar in its ordinariness, poses a narrative problem, of course. Readers expecting a narrative of "events" and excitement need to be weaned onto another, more "nonchalant," style, one that takes its time, makes no beelines, is always ready to turn away from a given direction in order to explore something other. Such a style, always ready to interrupt itself, is inevitably episodic (asyndeton, the figure of discontinuity, is its rhetorical mode), and, veering easily (i.e. *without* a sense of discontinuity) from topic to topic, following associative drifts or the promptings of memory, it is digressive: it is organized, that is, by relations of resemblance and contiguity, metaphor and metonymy rather than the formal unity required by argument or the narrative of event. Such a style is more concerned with the, often obscure, "coherence" of experience—in this case the experience of travel (one of the West's favorite metaphors for the human subject's encounter with contingency, as we saw in Verne)—than it is respectful of patterns that are more strictly designed and thus "cohesive." In loiterature, there is always time to explore a byway, and often it's not clear which road is a byway and which represents the beeline—the main road, the most direct route—since when you're "not looking for anything exceptional" there is no particular goal to attain and no schedule for achieving it.

Such a style seems somehow *natural*—or at least more natural than disciplined argument or the tightly controlled narratives, like *Around the World*, that we nevertheless tend to get so caught up in. It's more in tune with the complexity of things and the tangled relations that join them. As opposed to the heady satisfactions of method, system, argument, and intelligibility, it offers the pleasures of errancy: that sometimes delightful and surprisingly refreshing sense of getting lost. For the end-directedness of suspense and the goal-oriented consistency of single-mindedness, it substitutes a kind of relaxed openness, an endless availability to otherness that means one can never *arrive*, since no point can ever be "the" point. But, frustrating as it is to seekers after event, linearity, cohesion, consistency and conclusiveness, such a style also involves frustrations of its own, for it turns out both that digressivity is escalatory—one digression leads inevitably to another—and that it can never be quite digressive enough: there are constraints and limits.

Thus, if the pattern of François's and Anaïk's progress down the B line of the RER is simultaneously episodic (one station, then the next, day by day) and digressive (departing each day from the station for unknown adventures off line), the line itself still runs like a connecting thread through their narrative, one from which they never completely depart. And Paris also anchors their errancy; it's understood that they will not return to Paris for a month, but they will nevertheless return: they can't wander forever through the suburban spaces of non-Parisian otherness. This "time out" quality of loiterly writing, its failure to detach itself completely from a linearity from which it departs only to return in due course, is as characteristic a feature as its digressivity and errancy. Such writing functions in this sense like the "extra day" in *Around the World*, I mean that it's a relaxation of the rigors of scheduling that is itself *scheduled in*; it's a part of an overall pattern of discipline to which it contributes, by making it livable. That's one reason why one can define loiterature as a distinctively "modern" genre even though it has some very obvious premodern ancestors: it is of the age of discipline and scheduling. And that is why its supposed naturalness needs also to be carefully redefined: it's not something that can be opposed to the constraints of culture—Freud's "civilization and its discontents" (a title that more literally translates as "discomfort in society")—but rather the form that the natural takes when it is incorporated into culture, like a pet cat or dog admitted to the house on the understanding that its animality is cute so long as it doesn't "go too far" and eat the houseplants or foul the living room carpet.

It's this inability to go too far, then—rephrased as an inability to go far enough—that François and Anaïk soon begin to lament. Loiterly writing's capriciousness isn't capricious enough. For it quickly turns out that the two travelers haven't allowed themselves sufficient time to pursue the multiplicity of leads they've stumbled on, and their note taking (like Tristram Shandy's life in Sterne's novel) is fast outstripping their ability to write the notes up. So, if "respecting others entails taking time," the problem is that there can't ever be enough time to do so adequately. "How can we take it all in?" asks François, and Anaïk laments that she has never found herself forced to take photographs so quickly (105). "We shouldn't linger," says François, remarkably,

> "but for every question there's a flood of answers we haven't got time to look for, and which always prompt other questions. To talk properly about les Beaudottes, for example, we'd need to stay there a long time. . . . So I take notes, and more notes, and soon I'll have no more time to look around me." (106)

The problem is theoretically insoluble, since alterity, once you take the time to "respect" it, turns out to have its own othernesses, and every digression can only lead to further digressivity, by virtue of an inbuilt escalatory principle of limitless generation that I'll call the etcetera principle in this book. Practically, though, the loiterly solution turns out, in this instance at least, to consist in resignation to the inevitability of constraints on one's loiterliness, a resignation that takes the form of taking time out from the time-constrained pleasures (and anxieties) of digressivity, themselves a time out from existence in the beeline mode. The anxious conversation just lapses, as Anaïk and François themselves lapse into the *dolce far niente* of a warm spring Sunday afternoon by the canal de l'Ourcq:

> Swimming just below the surface, its nose barely poking out of the water, a coypu scurries silently from one hole in the bank to another, as if there were nothing in the whole world except him and his mysterious little affairs. Families laze on the dirty grass. Our travelers close their eyes against the orange light. . . . Behind them, two bare-breasted women sit near a bush doing singing exercises, their faces raised in ecstasy towards the sun. On the other bank, just opposite, the anglers are out in force: one eye on the float, the other on the breasts. Lots of cyclists ride past on the path just a meter away. It feels faintly like a weekend at the time of the Front Populaire. It's Sunday. They eat apples and yoghurts. (107)

After all, the coypu, the anglers, the singing exercises, the cyclists, the apples, and the yoghurts are also part of life in the *banlieue*, and their triviality, their familiarity, are as significant, in this book, as the most eventful situation (rescuing an Indian woman from *sati* or fighting marauding Sioux) might be in another, and just as important as finding out more about les Beaudottes (a housing development). Significant and important *because* trivial and familiar and so, generally overlooked. The travelers are losing nothing by taking time out from their too hectic, far too fast, month-long excursion on the B line, for in loiterature taking time out is always the condition of knowledge—knowledge of an other too humble and too familiar not to be forgotten in the hustle and bustle of the "fast lane." The canal, in other words, is to les Beaudottes as les Beaudottes is to the B line or to Paris. But time out is also the condition of pleasure: the pleasure of relaxing the constraints of discipline and rediscovering the simpler apples and yoghurts satisfactions of the body and of nature—a "nature," by the canal de l'Ourcq, that's duly contained by culture, of course. The pleasure, too, of escaping from single-mindedness into the agreeably divided attention—"one eye on the float, the other on the breasts"—that is, the openness to otherness presupposed by the ability to digress.

So we can say that the transvaluation of the trivial is what loiterature is about. Trivial here refers generally to an other that is so familiar that it is thought insignificant and normally receives little or no attention, and more specifically to manifestations of the natural in culture: bodily needs and responses, sexual and other "animal" urges, everything that culture has only half tamed or hasn't succeeded in fully controlling, everything that it classifies therefore as other than itself. The transvaluation of the trivial thus describes both a mode of knowledge and a form of pleasure, a knowledge and a pleasure, however, that should not be confused with those of modernist "defamiliarization" as touted by the Russian formalists. The effect of loiterature is to retain, not to abolish, the sense of familiarity that attaches to the overlooked other of the trivial; and any sense of estrangement it produces is due to the reversal of conventionally hierarchical values to which it subscribes— a coypu is as interesting as les Beaudottes, which is as important as the most prestigious monuments. By insisting on the importance of that which is thought to be unworthy of attention, loiterature implies, furthermore, not only the unexpected otherness of the ordinary but also the generalized ordinariness of all others, including the most remote and the most strange, and so a kind of universalized triviality. If the familiar other is only a digression away from our daily beelines, and if one digression leads inevitably to others, then the exotic itself may in turn be only a digression or two away from home and so, potentially familiar too.

A GENRE AND ITS OTHERS

In defining loiterature as a writing that takes the time to know the other and as the genre that transvalues the trivial, I've made it the object of a classificatory practice (it's one of several subgenres that make up the literary) and simultaneously described it as a practice that calls into question the hard-and-fast distinctions—between sameness and otherness, between familiar and distanced otherness, and between the trivial and the significant—on which classifications depend. I like to use the word "paradigmatic" to refer to loiterature's fondness for descriptions and lists, its ways of spinning out the narrative and at the same time clogging it so that its movement is slowed down. Here, at the outset, though, I want to say that genre itself (like loiterature), as a case of the paradigmatic (of classificatory listing), is exactly the phenomenon that both mobilizes and contests the classificatory practices without which we could neither think nor engage in social interactions.

By the word *paradigmatic* I intend on the one hand something like what the word means in linguistics, where it refers to a set of items (say adjectives, or the forms of a given verb) that can be grouped together (or listed) by virtue of a principle of substitutability: although different, the items are equivalent in that they have at least one feature in common and are therefore in a crucial sense alike. For "good" I can substitute "bad" (for example, "a real bad dude"). This principle of equivalence and substitutability governs all lists and inventories, and it will quickly be seen that my method in this book is to demonstrate the genre of the loiterly, as a category, by listing examples of writing that have at least one feature of loiterliness in common, different as they may be in other respects. I've been browsing my way through a shelf of books that I assembled and grouped over the years for this purpose. Thus, my study does not have the cohesive structure of an argument so much as it reads like an inventory: it is coherent rather than cohesive, and such "method" as it has is episodic, digressive, and descriptive. As an inventory, it is radically incomplete: my shelf does not contain anything like all the books that might be read as loiterly, nor do I discuss half of the books that are on my shelf. But I figure I've grouped enough texts—maybe more than enough!—to demonstrate that they can be grouped, and I rely on my readers to come up with further texts that might be included in the paradigm.

In Thomas Kuhn's scientific usage of *paradigm*, though, which has given the word its common currency even among literary people, the paradigm is not a list but something like a conceptual model, which has the enabling function of making work (Kuhn's "ordinary science") possible: it's a germ or an idea (Kuhn is strategically elusive in his definition) that has the potential to be endlessly elaborated—until it is replaced by another paradigm.[3] In describing loiterature as a genre, I also intend a Kuhnian sense of the paradigmatic in which a genre is one possible model (in this case a model of "literature" as a whole) but not an exclusive model, not "the" (one and only possible) model. The concept of "paradigm" is useful only by virtue of the real or possible existence of at least one other paradigm (if there were only one scientific paradigm, we would not need the concept of paradigm, since "science" would do). It must also be possible to "shift" between paradigms— to get from one paradigm to another by some kind of mediatory transition, much as one shifts gears in a car: science would not have had a history if it had not, according to Kuhn, been a history of paradigm shifts. (And similarly, words can shift paradigms, as anyone who has ever verbed a noun—"Stop eyeballing me like that!"—or nouned an adjective—"I just can't get the tacky out of my behavior!"—is aware.) Paradigms have an identity, then, that depends on there being other paradigms, and the relation between paradigms is a digressive one, in the sense that one can move fairly easily from one to another by a process that involves both continuity and discontinuity, so that work governed by one paradigm finds itself governed, soon after, by that paradigm's other.

From the digressivity of paradigms two consequences flow. One, any paradigm must have within it the elements of difference from itself (Derrida would say "traces") that make possible a shift from that paradigm to its other(s); that is, no genre is pure. And two, by virtue of the relation of continuity that links any given paradigm to the whole field of other paradigms, that paradigm (or genre) can function as a model (albeit not *the* model) of the totality. The paradigm is a site of alterity in the sense that its others (other paradigms) and its Other (the field of paradigmaticity) are *familiar* to it. It's not just that you can get "there" from "here" or even that "there" lies close to home; "there" is already "here," the other is already at home in the paradigm.

Combining the paradigm as list with the paradigm as model, we can then understand a genre such as loiterature as a list that is potentially able, at any point, to digress by paradigm shift into another list. Loiterly texts are listable, but no loiterly text is purely loiterly: *Around the World* and *Roissy Express*, which I've just used as exemplary loiterly texts, could just as well have opened a study of travel narratives, for example. And in a moment I'll be looking at loiterly texts that could be listed also under the heading of documentary film (Varda's *Sans toit ni loi* [*The Vagabond*]) or philosophical dialogue (Diderot's *Rameau's Nephew*). Before long, the reader of this book will encounter texts that I list here as loiterly but that could be classified under headings like memoirs or autobiography, "excentric narrative," novelistic fiction or flâneur realism, the meditation (religious or philosophical), the picaresque and the cynical, the lyric, the diary, "pointless stories," or criticism. Consequently, at any given point in my enumeration of loiterly texts, I could veer off into another enumeration: Varda or Colette could send me into an examination of other modes of feminocentric fiction, whether or not they display the sense of *ça ne se dessine pas* (the failure of things to take shape) that I'm inclined to think is characteristic of feminist loiterature; Nicholson Baker's *The Mezzanine*, which I read here as a meditation in tandem with Descartes and Marcus Aurelius, might easily start a drift toward Volney or Lamartine, Michel Serres or Montaigne. And such "proximate" genres, of course, have proximate genres of their own, so that in following the thread of the loiterly I could eventually find myself drawn into an inexhaustible rhizomatic field of tangled connections between all the listable genres that, actually or potentially, constitute the literary (and beyond that, the discursive). I've resisted that drift, like François and Anaïk giving up on the complexity of the suburbs (one has to "draw a line"). But I hope I will have demonstrated to anyone patient enough to read even a small chunk of this book both the openness to generic alterity of the genre of loiterature itself (a genre definitionally attentive to alterity, as I've tried to suggest) and the ease with which it merges with its others.

However, there is one proximate relation that I'd like to call particular attention to: the relation between loiterature as a literary genre and the genre of knowledge known as "cultural studies," which shares with loiterature an interest in the ordinary and the everyday and so a certain transvaluation of the trivial, and in addition displays an openness to other epistemological modes that's comparable to loiterature's openness to other modes of the literary. Cultural studies is a form of critique that is usually traced, as it is in Raymond Williams's *Culture and Society, 1780–1950*, for instance, to philosophical modes of social criticism that arose in the wake of the Enlightenment and under the impact, most notably, of the Industrial Revolution.[4] But loiterature, to the extent that it's a distinctively modern genre, also has its beginnings in the Enlightenment and can be understood as one historical response among many to the emergence of a new, bourgeois world of work, with the redefinitions of leisure that it entailed. So it may not be fanciful to look, in particular, to the loiterly subject—attentive to the trivial and the familiar, given to digression as an (implicit) critique of the beeline civilization of modernity, favoring asystematic, not to say random, and "nonchalant" modes of exploration over disciplined and systematic inquiry, and carefully avoiding grand claims ("they weren't looking for anything exceptional. They weren't looking for events")—as one possible predecessor of the cultural critic, and more generally of what I will call a critical intellectual.

In reading Baker's *The Mezzanine* in terms of the problem of "philosophizing the contingent," in looking to the ancient figure of the Cynic as a model for modern and contemporary practices of doglike social criticism, and in chapters on Charles Baudelaire, Roland Barthes, and Meaghan Morris as (widely diverse) figures of the critical intellectual, I will be drawing attention to both an epistemological and a critical dimension of the loiterly genre of writing, a dimension that's coexistent and perhaps consubstantial with its pleasurable side. But I'll also be trying to suggest a certain sense in which contemporary cultural studies, with its commitment to the everyday, the popular, the noncanonical (if not the trivial *per se*), and with its cultivation of informal, counterdisciplinary, and sometimes flâneur-like methods in the face of the rhizomatic tangle of culture, can be viewed as an academic revision of insights—about "how things are" and the prose of the world—that were earlier formulated, and are still being formulated, in parallel fashion, in loiterature.

If loiterature's relation to cultural studies can be described in "like" sentences, then one needs "not" sentences to describe its more distanced relation to two other genres of alterity (one literary, one epistemological) that describe otherness as significant by virtue not of its familiarity but because it appears as exceptional, disturbing, or disruptive.[5] These are the genres of history, with its emphasis on events and eventuality, and of the sublime, attentive to the transcendent. Of course, we now have histories of *longue durée* and of ordinary life; but it remains true that eventfulness, the stuff of historical narrative, is at the opposite pole from loiterature's dailiness. And similarly, loiterature's attention to the trivial contrasts markedly with, and can be viewed as commenting ironically on, the concept of sublimity. Finally, where both history and the sublime are faced with a problematic of representation (how to capture change in narrative structure? how, in Lyotard's formulation, to "present the unpresentable"?) loiterature's mode is anamnestic; it is a discourse of reminding.[6] Quite obviously, one does not need reminding about the impingements of history and sublimity on one's life, although one may wish they would go away; but the familiar is always in danger of being overlooked, just as— with our attention fixed on the "higher" things—we tend to forget the presence of nature in culture, of the animal in the human, and the dependence of all our aspirations toward the ideal on the fact that we're possessed of—and possessed by—a body. Thus, there's something a bit impudent or provocative in loiterature's vocation to remind us of such overlooked facts. It's the writing of im-pertinence. ("The important thing," Rameau's nephew points out, "is to evacuate the bowels easily, freely, pleasantly and copiously every evening").[7]

But, of course, loiterature also connects with the genres from which it seems most remote. With history, it connects through its own dependence on narrative, even as it extends it through digression, a topic that I will return to at some length in what follows. With the sublime, loiterature connects through the writerliness that results from its practice of digressivity, which disrupts the syntax of story or of argument and distinguishes loiterly writing, much as sublimity itself is divorced from the useful and the commonsensical, from so-called utilitarian or practical uses of language, the genres of communicational "exchange" by means of which people attempt to "get somewhere." Writing as an "intransitive" practice of language (to use Roland Barthes's term)[8] has been theorized continuously in France since Mallarmé, but the theory, through Bataille, Blanchot, Artaud, Jabès, and Sollers to Cixous, Derrida, and Lyotard, has constantly understood such writing as a practice of sublimity. It's about achieving a form of impersonality that frees a fluid, multiple subjectivity from the constraints of what in the United States is called "identity," and—such freedom being ultimately unattainable—it's conceived as a kind of heroic failure, an asymptotic affair of endless approach à la Beckett, a matter of glimpses and inter-mittency the contradictory nature of which is signaled by Lyotard's now famous oxymoron: the presentation of the unpresentable. I mentioned earlier (chapter 1) that Blanchot's term for this "worklessness" of the work (its failure to write its way to sublimity) is actually *désœuvrement*, a word that might normally translate as "idleness,"[9] and if I were writing about loiterature in French, "littérature désœuvrée" is what I would call it. The difference is only that the pathos of failure that attaches to the term in Blanchot is quite alien to loiterature, which prefers to make failure the occasion of a successful "performance of failure" in the manner of *Tristram Shandy*, that is, a buffoonish simulation of loss of control in the form of an inability not to digress. (It's true that one might think the buffoonery a mask for loiterature's own version of unattainable sublimity, the inability of digression to escalate to a degree of digressivity that would detach it from the linearity and directionality on which, in the last analysis, it depends.)

Jean-François Lyotard views the sublimity of writing as the only alternative we have to what he understands as the absolute incompati-bility of genres: the fact that a given sentence may have "force" in genre A but either another force altogether or no force at all in genre B.[10] But loiterature mixes genres "easily, freely, pleasantly and copiously," as if the achievement were quite natural and in no wise extraordinary. More particularly, it views genre switching—dependent on the possibility of genre mix—as an ever-present potential in any given generic situation: a well-calculated sentence can deftly deflate the power of genre to determine the force of sentences by reminding us that genre A isn't the only genre on the block and that its authority, therefore, is relative to that of genres B, C, D, and so forth. This antisublime practice of genre switching is exactly the secret of loiterature's im-pertinence; and it's also the reason for its interest in the otherness of the trivial, since the trivial, as that which is overlooked, can stand for that which, in any generic situation, has to be repressed for the genre's authority to exert itself, the presence of "traces" of otherness (other genres) that make transition possible, via digression, to some other generic context.

Finally, this ever-present possibility of genre switching by a subtle or not-so-subtle "reminder" of generic alterity is also the condition of what Lyotard himself once called "the strength of the weak,"[11] and—as Lyotard also suggested by drawing his examples from the ancient cynics and sophists—the secret of social criticism, a practice at some remove from the flight toward the "impersonal" and the "inhuman," the escape from social conditioning that motivates the sublime. The secret of loiterature's critical genre switching can be encapsulated as the insight that the context in which we may presently find ourselves is never the only possible context: the story we are being told or the genre we're in isn't the whole story or the only genre, and there are other, competing stories or genres that one can be, im-pertinently, reminded of, thanks to "divided attention" (chapter 1), to the detriment of the authority exercized by the story (genre) in question. I'll look later at the critical practice of cynics, ancient and modern; but for now it's enough to note that loiterature's interest in the familiarity of the other has as its corollary a critical awareness of the cogency of the im-pertinent. If loiterly digressivity, like contemporary cultural studies, is an epistemo-logical mode, then—the mode of knowledge of the other as ordinary and the ordinary as other—and if it functions as a pleasurable relaxation of narrative and argumentative single-mindedness, in contradistinction to history's eventfulness, it's also a translation of sublimity's writerly relativization of the power of genre into an instrument of critique. And as such, it's grounded in the perception that, whatever the context that may frame a given interaction (whatever its genre), there's always another context (another genre). And you can get there from here, it's only a short step away.

But it has to be a step out of line.

PARASITES

The potentiality for stepping out of line has as one of its main figures the parasite, although the parasite's "slot" can be filled by anyone of so-called marginal identity, who both is and is not a member of a given community and so figures a certain "otherness within." As an idle and unproductive figure in the world of work and general busyness, the parasite may also be viewed as a potential troublemaker, especially when there are grounds for associating the term *parasite* with communicational "noise," as in French.[12] The parasite disturbs the conventional order of things, as the representative of everything that is other to it. But the parasite also—as in the classical figure of the *parasitus*—makes the party "go." Otherness, when it is seen as forming part of a given community, stands for all the mediations that are other than the community's business but without which its business could not get done; it's the intermediary through which social interchanges inevitably pass; and in that sense the parasite is indispensable.

Any figure cast in the parasite's role may consequently experience hostility and rejection as an alien presence or undesirable other or be welcomed and appreciated as one who relieves life of some of its daily dreariness. I've already used, and will use again, the example of domestic animals, as representatives of the natural within culture, who are admitted to the house under the condition of being cute or "spirited" but consigned back to nature (through death or banishment) if their animality begins to appear too alien or destructive of order. Diderot puts the ambivalence inspired by the parasite this way, à propos of Rameau's nephew:

> I don't think much of these queer birds myself, though some people make boon companions of them, and even friends. They interest me once a year when I run into them because their characters contrast sharply with other people's and break the tedious uniformity that our social conventions and our politenesses have brought about. If one of them appears in a company of people he is the speck of yeast that leavens the whole . . . (35)

If the parasite is to sociability as nature is to culture, that is, the trivial element or "speck of yeast" that nevertheless "leavens the whole," then the parasite is both alien and indispensable; and if loiterature—through its interest in the trivial, its concern for otherness, its genre switching, and the general ease with which it demonstrates the undecidability of same and other—displays an affinity with the parasite, then it has an interest in being considered the life of the party, rather than a "queer bird" that no one thinks much of.

The problem being, obviously, that the line between the status of "outsider" parasite (the alien) and that of "insider" parasite (the indispensable figure of mediation) is difficult to draw. Agnès Varda's 1985 film, *Sans toit ni loi*, which is about a community's hostility toward, and complicity with, but ultimate exclusion and destruction of a parasite figure, is instructive both about the difficulty of drawing such a line and about the limits of the loiterly genre that such a line might represent.[13] The film is sympathetic toward the rather pathetic if far from likable personage of Mona, while, through its adoption of a pseudodocumentary mode of portrayal, through interviews and conversations *about* her, it distances itself from her and sides with the culture that excludes her. In this way it is free to follow Mona's wandering existence with a loosely episodic and quite digressive structure of its own, and to present a satirical picture of the community by straightforwardly reporting (without either endorsing or judging) the opinions about Mona that members of the community express (the technique known as giving them enough rope to hang themselves with). Most of the men, encountering a solitary and vulnerable woman, become predatory; then—when their sexual advances are rejected—savage and symbolically violent: "Les rôdeuses," says one, "toutes les mêmes. Dragueuses, fainéantes" (All the same, these prowling women. Cruisy, good-for-nothing bitches). The women, who are frequently, if not universally, complicitous with Mona, are also shown to be velleitary and unwilling to break with convention as she has done: "I'd have liked to be free," says one, dreamily; and another: "When you're married, you're caught for life" (*coincée pour la vie*). But neither acts on this assessment of her own situation, and none of the women Mona encounters is able to offer her more than a symbolic solidarity, a small handout, a few hours of friendship. In these two ways, then: its formal looseness and its disenchantment with the, in this case, gendered power structure of conventional society, the film has loiterly attributes that connect it to Mona; but it is unlike loiterature in its third personing of her, its pursuit of a project of social commentary that isn't Mona's, and its distancing of its own perspective from hers.

Thus, at the start, an authoritative voice-over (spoken by Varda?) says: "Je sais peu de choses d'elle, mais il me semble qu'elle venait de la mer" (I don't know much about her but my impression is she came out of the sea). As the natural and the unknown, but also as the alien (a sea creature on dry land, among the vineyards of the Var— later it becomes clear from her accent that she is also a northerner among Provençaux), she is doubly distanced. From that moment, we watch, and listen to reports of, her solitary errancy and vagabondage: she lives on handouts and what she can either beg or steal, works occasionally at odd jobs but is allergic to extended employment, seems a wild and unsociable thing—*farouche* (untamable, but etymologically akin to *ferocious*)—while showing unmistakable signs of a need for affection. She is like some animal prowling the outskirts of a human community that it fears and which in any case will not let it in. She is the parasite as a figure for the natural, then, but also as stranger; and we watch her solitude, and the community's rejection of her, intensify as if governed by a quasi-tragic sense of fatality, until finally she freezes to death in a ditch, dying alone while surrounded—as she knows and once or twice mentions—by thousands of empty beds in houses that are themselves unoccupied or too large for their occupants. In light of this refusal of hospitality, what we most clearly see but without being able to understand—for such is the perspective of the film—is the simple, stubborn fact of her alien existence. To the truck driver who is explaining that hospitality is scarce during the winter since no one is around (Y a personne), she points out that "Il y a moi" (I'm here).

So, in the film's analysis, there is a kind of irreducible incompatibility underlying the fact of Mona's alien existence, coming out of the sea, and the community's inhospitableness, its unwillingness or inability to integrate her. Her death is the outcome of that incompatibility; but what is its cause? That question is not so easy to answer. The episode in which she is taken in by a solitary immigrant worker, only to be thrown out on the return of his coworkers (referred to with unconscious irony as "les autres," the others), suggests that Varda may be allegorizing, inter alia, France's difficulty in integrating communities of Islamic culture. But the incompatibility arises also from the radicalness of Mona's own refusal to conform. Once a secretary-typist ("sténo-dactylo," one who takes dictation), with her high school diploma (the "bac") and a knowledge of English irregular verbs, which she recites to herself to pass the time—significantly enough, the one she recites for us is "to catch, caught, caught"—it's as if she had rejected writing as a cultural *techne* that submits her to "dictation" in favor of a supposedly more natural orality associated with foreignness and irregularity. Her alien life, in other words, is a certain "recitation" of the irregular, the opposite of being *coincée* (caught) for life.

Consequently, she's impatient of half-measures and compromise positions—whence her disagreement, for example, with the young goatherd couple who take her in and invite her to join them in working the land. "Yours isn't the only way of being marginal," she retorts when the ex-philosopher turned *berger* (Mona has a "paternal" name—specifically referred to as "le nom de ton père"—which is Bergeron) vaunts his own life as a rational compromise (he gets to go "on the road" twice a year when the flock has to be moved, and he leads a life isolated from the mass of society, into which he is nevertheless integrated by his participation in the productive exchange economy). Not for her the potato patch he wants her to till; so she steals some goat cheese and moves on. It's as if, in rejecting writing, she has also refused the possibility of being a subject of writing, a position that entails compromise: the ability to play a part in the social world but bought by a loss of freedom, the "subjection" of one's agency.[14]

And it's here that Mona parts company with loiterature, which is overwhelmingly a first-person genre. She cannot or will not write; she must therefore be written *about*. (I'm borrowing Marx's famous ironic comment in the *Dix-huit Brumaire* about the peasant class as the dupes of Napoléon III's regime: "they cannot represent themselves, therefore they must be represented.")[15] Varda's film itself, with its memorable opening image of sand ridges that look like lines of text, is the cinematic writing that writes (about) Mona, which is why in the end it turns out to side with the culture of dictation she is fleeing and the community that rejects her. The connotations of parasitism are intimately bound up, as we've seen, with the practices of *hospitality*, a word which—through the Latin *hospes*, both host and guest—has *hostility* as its close kin. *Sans toit ni loi* thus leads me to suggest that the boundary marking the limits of loiterature is the thin line separating hospitality from hostility on the part of the host, and on the part of the guest subjection to law (loi) from homelessness (sans toit). In remaining attached, as Varda's film does, to the *techne* of writing, with all the compromises it entails, loiterature as a literature of the other nevertheless ensures that it remains within homebound limits, those within which a certain hospitality applies, unlike Mona, who puts herself beyond the reach of hospitality by her unwillingness to be a writing subject and hence a subject of writing.

That's why loiterature's crucial figure is not Mona Bergeron, rebellious daughter of her father, but Rameau's nephew, the queer bird (but also the leavening speck of yeast) who is the Great Rameau's cynical, dissolute, scampish, but irresistibly likable kin. Between uncle and nephew, figure of authority and wayward namesake, the relation remains fraught, embittered as it is for the nephew by his recognition that the staid uncle enjoys an identity and a status—that of "genius"—that the livelier but less single-minded artist can't lay claim to. But the disparity of nephew and uncle is mitigated in this case by the dialogic relation the text sets up between the parasite figure of the nephew ("He") and "I," the philosopher figure who clearly understands himself to be a fully integrated member of society, despite his criticism of its ways. "I," as we've already seen, can be quite disdainful of "He" and keeps him at arm's length. But the I/he third personing is counterbalanced by the philosopher's willingness to enter into the first-person/second-person exchange of a conversation with the intriguing fellow (at least when he has nothing better to do). And it's belied by the fellow feeling and even identity that the two philosophers—one officially so named, the other a "popular intellectual," full of astute observations about the ways of the world—turn out to share.

In particular, each of them views himself, albeit from a different angle, as a latter-day Diogenes, the nephew because, as he puts it, the place for his statue would be somewhere "between Diogenes and Phryne. I am as impudent as the one and I am fond of consorting with the others" (37), and "I" because, in nominating Diogenes ("the philosopher who has nothing and asks for nothing," 22) as the one person who is not constrained by social hypocrisy and the "universal pantomime," he is patently, if immodestly, thinking of himself. Each figure, therefore, is the other's other, and although *Rameau's Nephew* is not formally first-person writing as so much loiterature is, its dialogic representation of the I/he couple as joint components of a single split subject—the subject whose other is familiar because "inner" as well as external—qualifies it, no less than its freely digressive conversational form (a loose, colloquial, down-home version of the classic philosophical dialogue), as a canonical work of loiterature—that is, if loiterature can give rise to "works" and admit canons. And by the same token, the parasite—nephew to his uncle, and accepted into dialogue by a genuine philosopher—is perfectly at home in the hospitable space of the café de la Régence, where the encounter takes place. Indeed he is so integrated into the community of the Régence that it is he who light-heartedly welcomes the philosopher, as if it were "I," not the nephew, who was the outsider: "What are you doing here, among this lot of idlers?" ("ce tas de fainéants," 36). ("Fainéante," remember, was one of the words that signified Mona's rejection: and when *she* enters a café, the atmosphere is electric, as the assembled males eye an intrusive but vulnerable female, and the café idlers identify one who is far more outcast than they.) The café, in short, is the space of hospitality that makes it possible for the dialogue of philosopher and parasite to take place.

Like the bowel movement the nephew considers the "most important point," the conversation of "He" and "I" ranges "easily, freely, pleasantly and copiously" (52) over a wide range of topics. But it has three main themes: the nature of the parasite, the character of cynicism (a parasitic practice), and finally the nature of art, in particular the art of music and especially art viewed as a technology of the natural (my phrase). It's the relevance of these three themes one to the other—a loose relevance, for their cohesion is never demonstrated and the connecting threads are never draw together—that legitimates the conversation as a philosophical dialogue; through them it treats three aspects of a single problem that's encapsulated in "I"'s baffled comment: "I like you better as a musician than as a moralist" (112). But this problem, with its suggestion of potential but unrealized unity and its acknowledgment that the pieces don't quite fit together, identifies the conversation's affinity with a loiterly preference for the dynamic of inexhaustible otherness over cohesion and closure.

The problem of the parasite, as it emerges from the dialogue, is that his indispensable "leavening" function as social mediator and general go-between (concretized here by the demand for the nephew's services as an "arranger" of love affairs) makes him a figure of falsity: he represents person A to person B, then person B to person A, espousing each interest in turn but never, of course, forgetting to put his own interests over A's or B's. Thus he becomes a master of acting, mimicry, and flattery: skilled in all the arts of representation, he tells others what they want or need to hear but without necessarily believing it himself. And because, as intermediary, mimic, and flatterer he is never himself, in the long run he loses track of his own identity: although he knows what his interests are (basically, eating as well as possible and sleeping as comfortably as possible), he doesn't know who it is that those interests serve. "Devil take me if I really know what I am" (79).

Without a firm identity, however—without single-mindedness as opposed to endless versatility—how is it possible to be genuine, like Rameau le Grand? Our Rameau is condemned to be "always someone's nephew" and never the uncle; mediocrity is his assigned status in life. But if that is so, if his identity is weak, and if also "pantomime" is universal— "the beggars' pantomime is what makes the whole world go round," the two philosophers agree (122)—then why is the pantomimic parasite so *isolated* a figure, a figure of fun (both in the sense that he is uniquely entertaining and in the sense that "I" speaks for the majority in regarding him as a queer bird)? And finally, most surprising of all, how is it possible for such a *man without qualities*, lacking identity and addicted to the mimicry of others, to be simultaneously a truth teller? For the flatterer and go-between is also a scathing social analyst, and the point of the anecdote that gets spun out through most of the conversation is that Mlle Hus's resident flatterer and *pique-assiette* has been ignominiously evicted for having inadvertently uttered a truth. Not, to be sure, the truth about Mlle Hus's acting but a social truth nevertheless (he compared himself and his two neighbors at Mlle Hus's dinner table to a prick between two *coglioni*).

The parasite's proclivity for the truth isn't simply im-pertinent with respect to his own (lack of) character, as flatterer, mimic, and *entremetteur*. It's also a social impertinence: to tell the truth about a hypocritical society in which pantomime is universal is to strip away the hypocrisy twice, once by denouncing it and then by contravening it. Only another philosopher, such as "I," can tolerate it. For such a practice is prototypically that of the cynic philosopher, of Diogenes as "I" likes to understand him, an exceptionally clear-sighted and outspoken member of a society addicted to self-deception, who owes his position as a critic of such a society to the position of marginality he maintains with respect to it. The scandal of the nephew, then, in "I" 's eyes, is that in this case the "Diogenean" position is occupied by one whose style of life, marginal as it certainly is, is outrageously out of synch with his access to truth, since he's willing to denounce hypocrisy but not to contravene the social law of universal pantomime. The nephew prefers the company of prostitutes to the practice of virtuous abstinence; and he daily prostitutes himself—in order to stay alive–as a flatterer, messenger, go-between, leader of *claques*, and social entertainer. His advice to the young would be not to cultivate the sterner virtues but to get rich so as to enjoy the advantages of power; and were he in charge of educating the philosopher's daughter, he would not bother with grammar, history, geography, and the like, all laced with "a great deal of ethics" ("I" 's educational recipe, 57), but teach her the *useful* arts, the "essential things," as he says: dancing, singing, music (the arts of entertainment).

Like an ancient Greek or Roman, "I" believes, on the other hand, that a philosophical position implies a way of living, and vice versa. So how can it be, he worries, that in the case of the nephew, so much moral turpitude coexists with a philosopher's clear-sightedness and outspokenness? "I was dumbfounded by such sagacity and such baseness, such alternatively true and false notions, such absolute perversion of feeling and utter turpitude, and yet such uncommon candour" (51). But as far as the nephew is concerned, philosophizing is one thing but staying alive is another, and he has a clear interest in the latter: thus he is as prepared to justify every form of opportunism as he is lucid in analyzing falsity; they are for him quite separable activities. His position, in short, is a cynical one, but not cynical in the sense that "I," thinking of Diogenes, would wish. He's cynical according to a sense in which philosophical analysis (an interest in truth) does not necessarily imply any corresponding commitment (the love of virtue). The nephew cheerfully acknowledges the existence of universal hypocrisy and as cheerfully participates in it because it is in his interest to do so.

As Peter Sloterdijk argues in his *Critique of Cynical Reason*, the existence of cynicism in this sense is a thorn in the side of Enlightenment philosophy, the more so as it is (without having been an invention or product of the Enlightenment, as Sloterdijk sometimes seems to imply) closely related to, and is indeed a form of, the practice of ideology critique that is at the heart of Enlightenment philosophy.[16] It both depends on the ability to recognize ideology ("hypocrisy," "pantomime," self-interested self-deceit) and challenges the assumption that error and prejudice will disappear once they are identified and denounced. It does so by demonstrating that participation in ideology isn't necessarily incompatible with, or abolished by, the possession of what we would nowadays call a "raised" consciousness: one can be consciously "hypocritical" as well as unconsciously so. But the most delicate point of all, for philosophers like "I," is a point Sloterdijk ignores but which from the perspective of loiterature I consider crucial and will return to at length (see chapters 6 and 7, "Learning from Dogs"). The existence of nephew-like cynicism casts doubt on the moral purity and ethical virtue of critical practices in general, including Diogenean ones, by demonstrating that critical consciousness does not, in and of itself, imply ethical purity. It may therefore be that the purest ideology critics are *unconsciously* ideological and thus hypocritical without realizing it because inattentive to the degree to which the criticism they mouth may be made in their own self-interest. From what margin is it possible, after all, to criticize social ways without in some sense demonstrating, by one's very act of criticism, one's own membership in the society under criticism? The only alternative would be Mona's—but in renouncing writing Mona has renounced the conditions of subjecthood, which include on the one hand the possibility of having one's say in society (e.g. critically) and on the other the subjection of what one says to "being written" by the social.

This is perhaps the truly modern realization, that criticism is inevitably contaminated by what it criticizes; and as I will put it later on, it's what we can "learn from dogs." It implies that, excluding Mona Bergeron's (self-destructive) rebelliousness, a limit-case, there is no pure, that is, *natural* position, outside of culture, from which a critique of culture might be launched. The apparently natural positions from which we criticize the cultural are themselves part of culture, not of nature, and so they are suspect as critique; they *represent* (themselves as) the natural and are consequently subject to the same suspicion as all representations, of being ideologically positioned, that is, self-interested. "I," in *Rameau's Nephew*, as it happens, does not draw these conclusions but merely records his disapproval of the nephew as a moralist. Rather, the conversation shifts finally to the topic of music, on which it turns out that "I" and "He" can enthusiastically agree, in their preference for Italian opera over the French tradition.

But it's symptomatic that, in their analysis, the separability of the natural and the cultural, on which the possibility of criticism depends (the question being only that of their complete separability, as assumed by "I," or their messy involvement with one another, as demonstrated by the nephew's cynicism), turns out to be what music, in its moments of *sublimity*, overcomes and denies. There is (metrical) recitation (déclamation) on the one hand—a technology and as such cultural—and, on the other, the natural tones of speech. Music, though, we learn—and it is clear that both characters are interested exclusively in melody (leaving harmony to the uncle)—is the product of a convergence between the "line" of speech and the "line" of the declamatory: it is speech declaimed or a declamation that is natural. "It is the animal cry of passion," says the nephew, "that should dictate 'la ligne qui nous convient,'" the line that is pleasing to us, suitable in our eyes: the "cultural" line (105). In short, the problematics of criticism, with the unfortunate question of cynicism that it raises, is left behind when one turns to the phenomenon of the aesthetic, and in particular of sublimity, in which the natural and the cultural are fused.

The sublime is thus opposed to the *systematic*, those "unintelligible visions and apocalyptic truths" (35) for which Rameau le Grand, the author of a famously abstruse treatise on harmony, is mocked, both by "I" and by "He" (e.g., 99). The implication is that the uncle was a musician of genius not because of but despite his theorizing, so removed from the natural; whereas the nephew, mediocre as a musician, is superior to the uncle in that he has a developed sense of the sublime (consonant, of course, with his gift of mimicry, as the artistic reproduction of a natural model) and so never loses touch with nature. "Sublime, I tell you!" he enthuses of an aria by the now-obscure Duni, an Italian composer working in Paris (98), and "I" concurs: "if this kind of music is sublime, then that of the divine Lully, Campra, Destouches and Mouret, and even, between ourselves, of your dear uncle, must be a bit dull" (99). But the sublime is opposed, also, to the whole area of the *critical*, in which (appropriately enough) "I" and "He" do not agree. "How is it that with a discrimination such as yours and your remarkable sensitiveness to the beauties of musical art, you are so blind to the fine things of morality, so insensitive to the charms of virtue?" (107). That is "I" 's problem in the face of "He," the problem of cynicism, and it's a problem that remains unresolved to the end of the dialogue, thereby establishing the dialogue itself—the text of *Rameau's Nephew*—as a mode of writing that is unsublime, by virtue of the dialogic fissure that runs through it, that is, the separability of the natural and the cultural, on which the debate about the nephew's cynicism rests, but also the very possibility of being critical.

If we revert now to the question of genre, it is possible to see that Diderot is foreshadowing Lyotard in theorizing the sublime as that which transcends generic difference, such as that between the natural and the cultural, the kind of difference that grounds not only criticism but all cultural conflict (the "différend"). The *critical* debate between Diderot's protagonists is in fact about whether the difference between nature and culture is itself a "natural" difference, as "I" appears to assume (since he believes the two to be separable in an absolute sense), or whether it is a generic, and therefore "cultural," difference, as the nephew's cynicism (in the "natural" mode I criticize my culture, in the "cultural" mode I conform to it) appears to demonstrate. And along with the philosopher's belief in the natural difference of categories and their absolute separability goes the belief that one's social behavior should be aligned on the position of (philosophical) truth that one adopts, and that *le vrai* and *le bien* are inseparable. Conversely, the assumption that the categories are generic entails the knowledge that they are not fully separable and that, for instance, the "natural" is itself a cultural category, along with the conviction that philosophical truth telling (*le vrai*) can be conveniently (because generically, not naturally) distinguished from ethical issues (*le bien*). "He" and "I" are united in their recognition that, in the sublime, *le vrai* and *le beau*, the true and the beautiful, can be(come) one and the same, abolishing the distinction between the natural and the cultural. But their conversation takes place in a café, not an opera house, and in the world of the café, they are disunited about the question of criticism and the relation of *le vrai* to *le bien*.

Loiterature, I want to claim, corresponds neither to the sublime nor to the "Enlightenment" philosophical position (involving the absolute separability of nature and culture) defended by "I." Like that Enlightened position, loiterature is a critical discursive phenomenon: not the fusion of the categories, but their separability grounds it. But as a literature of the parasite, it understands reality, nephew-fashion, to be a cultural matter and categories therefore to be generically constituted: as cultural categories, "nature" and "culture" can be differentiated but they cannot be completely severed one from the other, as "I" would like to think. And loiterature demonstrates its generic understanding of the constitution of reality by its conformity to two consequences that flow from such an understanding: the possibility of digression and the familiarity of the other. If generic categories are contexts that can be differentiated but not separated, then slippage between contexts is always possible and digression, as the mode of such slippage, demonstrates their continuity. So too does the parasite as a figure, in various guises, of the "inner other." Digression and the parasite thus together illustrate the cogency of the loiterly axiom that, yes, you can get there from here. So *Rameau's Nephew*, as a piece of literature, is dialogically constituted as a digressive conversation between two philosophers who are each the other's other; and its setting is in a place of hospitality where otherness is welcomed as familiar rather than alien, the café.

But as critical literature that does not recognize the possibility of an outside of culture that would be nature and remains, unlike the sublime, in an area where generic differences hold, loiterature must also recognize the possibility of nephew-like cynicism, which also depends on the difference between genres and on the possibility of getting from one to another (I can shift, when it is convenient to me, between a "naturally" grounded *critical* position with respect to "culture," and a position of absolute cultural *conformity*, as if the position were independent of my critical position). Loiterature, as a critical writing, must therefore also understand *itself* as being, at least potentially, cynical in the shifty sense that so baffles "I." Now it criticizes, now it conforms, and it does not view those two positions as incompatible. It knows how to step out of line without stepping out of *line*.

This observation may permit us, finally, to make use of *Rameau's Nephew*, where the problem of cynicism emerges, to establish some sort of historical limit for loiterature as a modern genre. It suggests that loiterature emerges as a particular form of "public sphere" discourse, with its characteristic setting in the coffeehouse, its characteristic openness to dialogue, and its no less characteristic hospitality to otherness. What particularizes loiterature as a public sphere discourse, though, is its hospitality to a form of otherness—the trivial, the familiar, the everyday, the antisublime, and even the low life—that I've consistently linked to the parasitic (often overlooked but mediatory and thus indispensable) presence of nature within culture. What I want to suggest now, however, is that such attention to the trivial is itself dependent on the historical emergence of a specific form of "idleness": you need to have plenty of time to spare if you are going to turn your attention to matters that are generally considered unworthy of attention. The new idleness is not aristocratic leisure—which was a way of life in itself, defined as *otium* (not working for a living) in opposition to *neg-otium* or trade. Idleness as defined in a bourgeois context (that is, in relation to the world of work and the productive economy), was something that had previously been associated only with the lowest of the lower classes, not respectable artisans or hard-working peasants but shifty vagabonds and loiterers, like the *pícaro* in whom so much (pre-)loiterly writing took an interest. This idleness is most simply defined as the ability to waste one's time—but an ability that, when it becomes a middle-class practice, also becomes something of a privilege.

As a privilege, it's somewhat suspect, of course, and in a number of ways. The bourgeoisie isn't supposed to be privileged, and it feels ambivalent about the privileges it enjoys. Within the middle class, a privilege that tends to assimilate one to low-life types is dubious in another way again. Such a privilege needs to be able to claim both that it isn't really a privilege (more in the nature of a reward, perhaps?) and that *as* a privilege it doesn't in fact identify one with those parasitic types that wasting time is associated with (there is, as Mona pointed out, more than one way to be "marginal"). It's the association of the privilege of wasting time with the privilege of work that performs this double trick. The middle-class privilege of leisure, as a perhaps perverse but pleasurable indulgence, is a *second* privilege that's superadded to a *first* privilege, which is that of being, at least potentially, a direct participant in the productive economy, so that there can be no danger of one's time-wasting being confused with a Mona-like rejection of social order.

Until relatively recently, that meant being a man, and it still means being an adult. It excludes the unemployed and any others who have idleness thrust upon them unwillingly, such as prisoners, say, or invalids, for whom the empty passage of time is not a pleasure but an imposition and a burden. The range of applicability of time-wasting as a bourgeois privilege goes, on the other hand, from the idle existence of younger sons of wealthy families to the working stiff who gets a half-hour lunch break and a couple of weeks of vacation per year. The middle-class artist and the middle-class intellectual, who are regarded as not really working even when they're at work (because, for them, they are working even when they're not at work), fall squarely into the category of the privileged idler. But all who work can claim the right to relaxation and a little time out; and if they choose a loiterly mode of employing their spare time, their employment ensures that they not be confused with the loiterers on the social fringe that they may nevertheless associate with. Thus even Rameau's nephew himself belongs in the café de la Régence, in part because he makes a philosophical contribution to the analysis of society. And more cogently still, it's OK for "I" to enter the café and consort with the nephew for a bit because even a hard-working philosopher needs to take a break from time to time. Each case—the nephew's and the philosopher's—entails a shuttle between categories, genre shifting: something like the "yes, but . . ." of the cynic. And taken together, they define the double shuffle of loiterature, which by virtue of its interest in alterity has something in common with both.

So there's a space, then, for the philosopher in the café where the parasite hangs out. "What, you here?" says the nephew to "I." "Are you wasting your time, too, pushing the wood about?" ("Wood pushing" was café slang for playing chess.) "I," of course, denies the time wasting, but concedes the point as he does so: "No, but when I've nothing to do I enjoy for a moment watching those who push well" (36). And conceding the point while denying it is perhaps what loiterature is most significantly about. Of course it's a privilege, in the workaday world, to *have the time* to write, or to read, and to write or to read such *trivial* (time-wasting) stuff, just as it's a privilege to be able to take time off from hard philosophizing and go watch the chess players in the Régence for a bit. But—like the study break, for example—the privilege has to be justified. Thus, I only come here "for a moment," "when I have nothing better to do," that is, when gainful employment permits: I may look like a parasite and act like a parasite, but I'm not really a parasite; I'm exercizing the rightful privilege of those who work, which is to consort with parasites and to take an interest in the trivial. And at the same time, the trivial isn't necessarily all that trivial, especially to a philosopher. There may be something to be learned from watching the wood pushers push wood, and certainly there's something to be gained from talking with a "queer bird" like Rameau's nephew. Thus the trivial, in entering the domain of my attention, gets transvalued and ceases to be trivial at all.

So loiterature, like "I," likes to acknowledge its affinity with parasites (here I am having a conversation with one, queer bird that he is). But equally it likes to maintain a certain separability between "He" (the likable scamp, with his provocative views) and "I" (respectable, well-dressed citizen and family man). Change a letter, and lo, from being that dubious thing, "loiterature" (which keeps suspect company), I can become literature again. I'm simultaneously a slightly slummy genre (acquainted with the lower classes, immigrants, *piliers de cabaret*, and the like) and worthy of being read by the nicest people (witty, urbane, entertaining, educated, middle class). I can even lay claim to being a *model* of the literary. Between those two things, and others like them, I shift. But shifting is what I do best. It's not in being one thing or another that I am most myself but in my ability to be always already something other than what I supposedly am. Good luck, then, in reading me.

3 Loiterly Subjects or *Ça ne se dessine pas*

Lately I've been thinking some more about Jacques Tati (see chapter 1). That persona of his, Monsieur Hulot or mon Oncle, is a good first approximation of the loiterly subject: amiable, eccentric, well-meaning, avuncular, but out of synch with the patterns and rhythms of modernity and hovering a bit anxiously on its edges. He is neither rejected by modern life (which just doesn't have much of a place for him) nor explicitly and trenchantly critical of it (although everything about his personality and position expresses mute, implied criticism). My Uncle Toby is his ancestor, and Jacques Réda is a cousin, put-putting along the freeway on his moped while lost in his own beatific and dizzying personal ride to "the sources of the Seine." The loiterly subject does not share Mona's intense anger, but one can imagine him—he *is* usually male—like Rameau's nephew (although not so readily impertinent), with straw in his hair on occasion, or like Passepartout, as adept at getting into trouble through "misplaced" curiosity as at getting himself out of it again (through skill, charm, sophistry, or sheer good luck). All these uncle and nephew figures suggest a somewhat marginal membership in the social "family," and there is something solitary about most loiterly subjects—or there would be if they didn't have friends among those of their own ilk or drawn to them like Diderot's "I" to "He" and if they didn't form a kind of family group of their own, the community of those who are marginalized from (in) the community of the established. Thus they seem always to have someone—usually but not necessarily a fellow idler, eccentric, or entertainer—with whom to pass the time of day; and like the court buffoon addressing the prince or Diogenes cutting Alexander down to size, they hobnob sometimes on equal terms with the great.

If dividedness of attention (the permeability of contexts, the proximity of difference, the familiar otherness of the self) is the condition that makes digression possible (chapter 1), and if digressivity is in turn a condition of the possibility of stepping away (chapter 1) but also of stepping out of line (chapter 2), the loiterly subject, who is always on the cusp of a context and *its* other, becomes a socially marginal figure to the extent that social centrality is defined in terms of stability, permanence, and closure—the virtues of single-mindedness and discipline that eschew digressivity. Thus, he is also on the cusp of a dominant social context and its other, always on the periphery of things, the legendary nonparticipant bystander, a bit out of step with respect to the march of the majority, and swimming not exactly against the current but not with it either. I want to devote this chapter to three historical avatars of this personage, choosing them from different moments in the story of European modernity. I'll consider Gérard de Nerval's self-representation in *October Nights* (*Les Nuits d'Octobre*, 1852) as an amiable flâneur, Colette's semi-autobiographical representation of a "new woman," Renée Néré—she of the chiasmatic and oddly bigendered name—in a loosely episodic novel, *The Vagabond* (*La Vagabonde*, 1910), and, finally, Neil Bartlett's engaging study, in *Who Was That Man?*, of the difficulty for a contemporary gay man of piecing together a community of those banished by homophobia to society's fringe.[1] But these figures should be taken more as indicative than as exemplary. There were and are many more ways of being loiterly than these, and loiterly subjectivity is in any case protean and not easily reduced to illustrative examples.

That said, Renée Néré's go-nowhere name with its bigendered indeterminacy draws attention to something these different forms of loiterly writing do have in common. Nerval writes in the capriciously digressive manner of mid-nineteenth-century journalistic and literary flâneur realism; Colette effects a graft of loiterly writing—episodic, impressionistic, easily interrupted, and easily diverted—onto a novelistic plot (will Renée marry her Big Noodle or not?); Bartlett invents a mode of investigation, I hesitate to say historiography, that's modeled on the enthusiasm of the collector, the ever-alert curiosity of the maker of scrapbooks and personal bulletin boards, and ultimately the *disponibilité*, the openness to experience and encounter, of the sexual cruiser. These are different forms and modes of the loiterly, but they correspond in each case to a self-conscious gesture of refusal that has as its target the disciplinary (disciplined thought, argument, narrative, or writing), represented in Nerval's case by the Sorbonne examiners of his narrator's nightmare, in Colette's by the Balzacian novel, and in Bartlett's by the normal narrativity of mainstream historiography, which has no place for what does not fit its chosen plot (the silenced, the marginalized, the forgotten). And in each case, this option of refusal implies that the writing assume a certain formlessness—and uncertainty of identity—that corresponds to the unstable subjectivity of those whose life is led on the periphery.

It's a formlessness that's made, on the one hand, of a certain restlessness, a ready availability and motility, corresponding to digression's proclivity to resolve into permanent digressivity (*permanente Parekbasis*): the inability to stop digressing that seems to follow from a first stepping away from or out of line. But it has to do also with a certain sense of precariousness and an awareness of the failure of things ever to fall into shape or achieve closure, an awareness that can be, as the "other side" of the loiterly subject's freedom (itself hedged and limited by the rules of the majority), a source of anxiety and disturbance. Thus, Nerval's narrator doesn't only have nightmares about the Sorbonne but gets arrested for lack of provable identity; Renée Néré is permanently tempted by the security of marriage even as she rejects it as servitude; Bartlett worries over a gay cultural identity that seems to have to be "made up as we go along."

Renée Néré projects this experience of shapelessness onto her music hall comrades, the *artistes* with whom she works, in part unaware of the extent to which her own only slightly more favored existence, as a former member of the respectable classes *déclassée* as a result of divorce, shares the precariousness for which she pities them. They are fringe figures who eke out, as she sees it, a vague and shadowy existence, one engagement at a time, now happy to be employed for a time in a "legitimate" theater, now filling in as best they can by working for the despised cinema. *Ça ne se dessine pas* (It's not coming together, I'm at a loose end) they say of their desperately vague prospects, employing in turn a strategic vagueness of their own that's protective of their pride: "Things aren't shaping up too clearly. . . . This is the vague circumlocution my wandering companions use to cover hard times, 'restings,' money troubles, and destitution" (65, translation modified). What Renée shares with them, as a middle-class but unmarried woman, is her own fringe status with respect to employment: there is next to nothing a respectable woman can do to earn a living as an independent person in 1910, just as—in the declining years of the music hall before World War I—her companions (and she among them) must compete for fewer and fewer and steadily less remunerative jobs. It is not really surprising that the loiterly failure of things to shape up should find its explicit formulation in the context of an early feminist consciousness, whether Renée's or Colette's.

But this *ça ne se dessine pas* experience extends easily enough, also, to Nerval's attempt to make remunerable copy out of the experience of missing a train and finding himself at a loose end, an experience clearly symbolic of the writer's more general sense of belatedness and alienation in mid-century Paris and of his near-unemployability as one thought to be mad. As for Bartlett (who thinks a good income is a prerequisite for being gay), the *ça ne se dessine pas* doesn't derive from economic precariousness but from sexual marginality and a fragmented identity. But there is little cause in all this for more than momentary pathos and discouragement, even on Renée's part: each writer, each loiterly subject, is confident of the advantages he or she enjoys with respect to freedom from disciplinary constraint, a stable and protected existence or a mainstream identity; each is as celebratory of the loiterly subjectivity as he or she is conscious of the price to be paid in insecurity, anxiety, and even persecution.

Freedom is one of those advantages, relative though it may be; access to a certain kind of knowledge is another. If Nerval's narrator did not find himself *anuité*, as he puts it—stuck for the night, having missed his train like a true loiterer—he couldn't take us on a guided tour of Parisian night spots and the low life that frequents them. If Renée had remained a married middle-class woman, or were she to marry again, she wouldn't have access to the lives of the music hall *artistes*, nor could she report that knowledge to middle-class readers. Bartlett's whole enterprise is defined as the pursuit of knowledge: knowledge of an already recognizable "gay" community in 1890's London, of which only shreds and fragments of evidence have subsisted—and much of it has to be intuited with the skills of a cruiser—because it was effectively silenced, forced underground, by the spectacular trial and condemnation of Oscar Wilde, an habitué of that community. In each case the texts affirm the existence of "fringe knowledge" that is inaccessible to more disciplined subjects, who are too close to the seat of power and the cultural mainstream, but is available to loiterly subjects by virtue of their own peripheral position, with its advantages and drawbacks. Such fringe knowledge is defined as knowledge of the social fringe, of which those whose lives are lived closer to the social "center" are necessarily ignorant, knowledge of an other that is scorned, not only by disciplinary subjects but also by the disciplinary modes of knowledge (Nerval's Sorbonne, the narrative historiography that Bartlett implicitly rejects, the mainstream bourgeois novel) to which loiterly subjects are so unsuited.

However, in a way that's totally characteristic of loiterature, whose ultimate loyalty always goes to the seat of power, the texts generally make this fringe knowledge available—through their access to publication—to those who are deprived of it by their disciplinary blinders and the comfortably closed world of experience they inhabit. Unlike the silenced fringe dwellers they frequent, the loiterly subject is at home on the fringe but can also claim certain bourgeois privileges on occasion, including the ability to write and the claim to be read. Thus, their texts are all, in some sense, reports to the bourgeoisie (and/or the straight world) on the lives of the fringe classes (artists, unmarried women, gay men, as well as proletarians and subproletarians), on the nature and existence of the bourgeoisie's own familiar other, an other of which it is perfectly ignorant although access to it (as the loiterly subjects daily prove) is only a step away. They are also, though, affirmations (implicit and sometimes explicit) of the epistemological value of informal and artisanal practices that are, at least officially, excluded by concepts like discipline and method: Renée refers to them as *métier* (knowing the tricks of the trade); Nerval, too, associates them with the artistry of street entertainers and wandering showbiz folk (saltimbanks, in the terminology of his age), while Bartlett associates them with the *nous*, the flair, the intuition, the empathy—as well as the openness to encounter—that a good cruiser needs in order to turn tricks. Such is the skill he deploys among the documents in the British Library, poaching with gay intent on the national archive, just as the cruiser, with no less gay intent, poaches on the public streets.

I'll be suggesting intermittently in this book that the loiterly subject approaches knowledge in the manner of a reader, that reading—especially loiterly reading—can be understood as the "other" of disciplinary examination (identified by Foucault as the characteristic practice of disciplinary society[2]), and, finally, that the appropriate place from which to do such reading (in particular reading that is critical) is the periphery. Whereas examination implies objectivity, and hence the separation of the (examining) subject from the (examined) object, reading is a practice that implies the continuity of subject and other: the text that I read is other than I, yet I discover and reinvent myself through my encounter with it. Reading is thus both a peripheral activity and one that knows a few tricks denied to methodical and disciplined "examining" subjects of knowledge, in that it is situated at the cusp where contexts meet and intermingle, much as the loiterly subject has a foot in the world of the straight and the mainstream but one also in the experience of the fringe, on (and from) which the loiterer can report to the established.

But a peripheral subject (one who knows the mainstream as well as the periphery, that is) is able to read in two directions. The loiterly subject is not only one who reports on life at the margins for the benefit of those who inhabit the center, but is also in an excellent position to acquire a relativized knowledge of life at the center of things (where people are too single-mindedly absorbed in what they are doing to be able to read their own existence) and to report (to all who read) on the deficiencies of that life, which are of course those of self-enclosure, blindness, and the exclusions and marginalization—the ignorance of the other—that these give rise to. Renée Néré, who knows the tribulations of marriage intimately and prefers the *ça ne se dessine pas* of fringe existence to them—Renée who comments more generally on the subjection of women in turn-of-the-century France—is a case in point. Although her writing reports on the precariousness of existence on the periphery, it simultaneously indicts the world of respectable society for the pain and injustice that it inflicts. Nerval and Bartlett work more circumspectly and by implication; but it's evident that the very fact of reporting to a disciplinary society on what its own disciplinary practices prevent it from knowing implies, in itself, an important critique of that exclusionism and indifference to alterity, not to say the actual persecution of otherness, on and through which such a society is constituted. Any loiterly subject is thus, potentially, either an *empathetic* reader of the social other (what is situated at the social fringe) or—whether by implication or more directly—a *critical* reader of mainstream society's own self-absorbed indifference to, and ignorance of, otherness. And any loiterly subject may—like Baudelaire (to whom I return in chapter 8)—become a double reader and do both of those things, because he or she is not fully identified with either group.

One reason, then, why things don't shape up clearly for a loiterly subject is that peripheral consciousness, readily able to shift both its loyalties and its *visée* or target, is an essentially mobile consciousness—indeed it's a consciousness of mobility. Peripheral consciousness, furthermore, as the site of the loiterly subject's social to and fro between established and fringe communities, is experienced in addition as a historical peripherality, that is, as a shifting relation between the present moment and some (half-forgotten) past or (not yet realized) future moment, a temporal fringe in which the subject might be, or might have been, more at home. And, finally, such consciousness is experienced geographically, as a relation between the dominant here (and now) and a closely proximate space that, again, might represent for the loiterly subject a region of greater comfort, freedom or sense of community, the sense of being at home. The motility of loiterly and readerly subjectivity is thus, simultaneously, social (a to-and-fro between dominant and marginalized class attachments), temporal (a sense of the intermingling of temporal moments), and spatial (a sense of the close proximity of here and elsewhere). As a kind of traveler who moves between social, temporal, and spatial contexts, the loiterly subject scarcely needs to move at all, or to move very far, in order to enjoy both the privileges and the ingloriousness of loiterliness. Such a traveler not only knows how to travel without leaving home but—in a sense—can't travel any other way, for, to the fringe dweller (independently of where he or she may be), distance is not the relevant concept; proximity is.

Nerval seems to view this kind of consciousness of proximity (social, geographical, and temporal) as one of the fruits of experience: "Avec le temps," his opening sentence runs, "la passion des grands voyages s'éteint. . . ." (With time, one's passion for long voyages fades). Notice the strategic ambiguity of the opening adverbial phrase, which means "as a result of time's passing" but also "when it comes to dealing with time." To his narrator a nocturnal stroll through the busy quartier des Halles in the very heart of Paris or a short excursion to Meaux and then Creil in the near countryside will do just as well, if not better, than a "grand voyage," these being sites of temporal otherness with respect to the Parisian modernity of 1852 and the important thing being to remain mobile, not to lose the loiterer's characteristic ability to "travel" (in time as well as in space, in the mind as well as with the body). As a woman, Renée Néré can scarcely stroll the streets, of course: her mode of travel without leaving home will be the *tournée*, a circular trip as an actress through the French provinces, from theater to theater and from seedy hotel to seedy hotel, that brings her back in due course to Paris.[3] And Bartlett's figure of travel without leaving home is sexual cruising, that is, a practice of *disponibilité* that makes the most familiar streets a potential site of encounter, a potentiality that already transforms their familiarity into something other, so that the proximity of the dominant world and its peripheral other is here particularly close, so close that proximity isn't the word.

But what I've already suggested of Nervalian strolling is also true of touring in Colette and cruising in Bartlett: each is also a mode of time travel, a way of experiencing the proximity of the past or the future to one who lives on the fringes of the present. The Nerval narrator's missed train is a sign of his general belatedness in mid-nineteenth-century Paris, a city that had already undergone vast historical trans-formation and was, in 1852, about to be subjected to even more radical modernization at the behest of Baron Haussmann. For a nostalgic subject who has witnessed the political collapse of the Second Republic and recalls his country childhood as a time of bliss, the past is thus situated just a short step in either direction from the new Strasbourg railway station (now the gare de l'Est), whether back in the old city (still working class in this pre-Haussmann era, and where pre-1848 "socialist" customs survive) or in the Valois region lying just to the north of the city, where development has not yet destroyed the old rural way of life. Renée, a "new woman," is in the reverse historical situation: far from being belated, she has arrived a little too early in a society that isn't yet able to accommodate her need for freedom and independence, and the future is her terrain of predilection, a future that is already, as her own sensibility demonstrates, impinging on the present. During her tour of the provinces, she both experiences the backward tug of Paris (of convention, tradition, marriage—what she summarizes as "the leash") and enjoys a degree of self-empowerment that gives her the courage to refuse the Big Noodle's offer of marriage on her return and turn toward an open future. And cruising, in Bartlett—whether street cruising or library cruising—is a response to his sense, as a 1980s Londoner, of both separation from and connection with the gay male community of the 1890s, which was intimidated by the scapegoating of Oscar Wilde into virtually disappearing from the scene but has left recognizable traces of its existence and its gayness, so that Bartlett can imagine walking a contemporary West End street and being cruised by a young man of the gaslight era. Historical interruption thus corresponds for him to Renée's anticipation and Nervalian belatedness; but it has the character of the rhetorical figure of asyndeton, which is one of the modes of digression (one interrupts oneself in order to pursue another line of thought, so that there is both discontinuity and continuity);

so that if historical asyndeton defines gay male culture as digressively constituted ("making it up as we go along"), cruising becomes a fundamental practice of gay community-construction because, as an act of mutual recognition across barriers of otherness, it counters the effect of historical interruption.

Different though they are as temporal experiences of the fringe, Nervalian belatedness, Colettian anticipation, and Bartlettian asyndeton or interruption have similar effects in that they produce a sense of the side-by-sideness of different moments in time. This side-by-sideness permits movement and exploration, but it can't be resolved; whence finally the loiterly subject's experience of endless deferral and so, of inconclusiveness. Cruising does not resolve the effect of interruption because each trick leads to another one. And texts like *October Nights* and *The Vagabond* end, very symptomatically, without concluding (a missed otter hunt in Creil echoes and follows from the missed train in Paris, Renée refuses her suitor without rejecting outright the possibility of her choosing marriage and security another time), the rhetorical effect being not interruption, in these cases, but its corollary, suspension. Either way, in a world governed by digressivity, there is no closure that can't be reopened through another shift of context, another movement of consciousness, another slippage in one direction or the other, of peripheral loiterly subjectivity. And that is ultimately why things don't gel and *ça ne se dessine pas*. There's a lack of fullness and firmness—in French, *un manque*, as in *un train manqué*, a missed train—which means that every *visée*, every aim misses its goal (*manque son but*), overshooting or undershooting it. There's always a loose end, more to be explored, thought, or said, another direction to take, an unforeseen swerve or clinamen, the possibility of which makes the very idea of stability, or even a settled path or firm destination, let alone a definitive point of arrival, unthinkable.

I like to appropriate Walter Benjamin's term, *Erfahrung*, as a word for the loiterly subject's experience. Benjamin uses it, famously, in his essay "The Storyteller," where it serves to designate the content of the true storyteller's tale.[4] It means experience, but a traveler's experience (from *fahren*, to travel), an experience both of "la passion des grands voyages," of course, and of what subsists of that passion when it has faded, a sense of motility that makes travel without leaving home— strolling, touring, or cruising—a modus vivendi in its own right. *Erfahrung* is differentiated, therefore, without its being possible to disentangle it completely, from the word *Erlebnis*, referring to the experience of those whose life (*Leben*) is lived on the spot rather than under the sign of movement. *Erfahrung* in that sense is to the mobility of the periphery as *Erlebnis* is to the stability of the center; and that is why it can also be differentiated (but again not necessarily distinguished in an absolute way) from *Erkenntnis*, knowledge. For *Erfahrung* is also a kind of knowledge, a way of informing oneself and others, but it's more the knowledge of experience than the knowledge that results from method. It's the knowledge one picks up along the way, the knowledge of the wayfarer, always informal and never complete—like François's and Anaïk's knowledge of the *banlieue* in *Roissy Express*—not the knowledge that is an outcome of methodical thought or disciplined investigation.

Erfahrung, then, is knowledge of a kind that knowledge itself—let's call it foundational knowledge—*can't have*, because it's the knowledge one derives from the consciousness of lack, lack being the reason why things never come finally together and there's always a loose end. It's knowledge that has learned not to trust itself as knowledge (because it is always incomplete), but which can't trust foundational knowledge either (because it is always exclusionary). If one understands desire as a dynamic of insatisfaction "grounded" in lack—the more desire is "satisfied," the more it desires—and if power be understood as a dynamic that produces stability by denying the effects of lack, one might say, then, that *Erfahrung* is knowledge that knows itself, not as one of the forms of power but as one of the forms of desire. The loiterly subject is a creature of the periphery because knowledge, for such a subject, is less infected by power than it is traversed by desire.

So let's miss that train with Nerval. I don't plan to provide exhaustive readings of these texts of strolling, touring, and cruising, although each certainly merits a more careful discussion of its individuality. My purpose—more a *visée* that might be missed than a goal to be single-mindedly pursued—is to make use of the texts, following a somewhat digressive method of my own and assuming them to be interlinked, so as to follow out some of the more general aspects of the *ça ne se dessine pas* of loiterliness. These might be loosely listed as the issue of an identity that's split because (socially, historically, geographically) it is peripheral; the fraught relation such a peripheral subjectivity maintains with the representatives of disciplinary power; its recourse to nondisciplinary—artisanal, artistic, informal—practices of expression, investigation, and knowledge, together with the fringe knowledge that results; and, finally, the relation between such practices and the structure of desire and between the structure of desire and the formation of a community of the marginalized—a community composed not of a group of disciplined individuals but of peripheral subjects whose consciousness implies the recognition, not simply of alterity but of self-alterity, the inexhaustible otherness of self. And this last theme will bring me back, briefly, to the loiterly subject as reader.

STROLLING

In *October Nights* an originary lack (i.e., *un manque*) is figured as a missed train (*un train manqué*), and the outcome of this critical delay, after three days and two nights of dallying in Paris and the neighboring Valois countryside, will be a missed otter hunt. Between this failed departure (*départ manqué*) and the missed ending, the narrative is structured (if that is the word) by accumulated delay and repeated lack in a way that is foreshadowed, *en abyme*, from the start: having missed his first train because of a lackadaisical approach to scheduling, the narrator also misses the second, having become involved while waiting in the pleasures of flânerie with a friend encountered on the boulevard. The two are thus *anuités*, as they say, "adjourned for the night" with time on their hands, and their response is to fill this potentially endless, Shandyan time of deferral with further flânerie. On the first night this takes the typically Parisian form of strolling the streets in search of a likely place for a late-night supper, interminably putting off the decision until they end up in a low-class dive in the Halles ("chez Paul Niquet"). Thus is launched a narrative in which events, observations, conversations, and subjective impressions follow one another in an aimless, nonteleological and nonhierarchized way—nothing is more important than anything else, nothing advances the narrative toward what is in any case its anticlimactic conclusion. But this, the narrative also implies, is also the condition of a gain, for which the name will be *realism*: knowledge of a reality that is not available to disciplined travelers who catch their trains or to readers of less loiterly writing.

Engaged in a story that borders on pointlessness, however, the narrator has a problem to deal with: how to attract and maintain his audience's attention for an account that seems to have no point except its own insignificance. His solution will be an art of temporization, a technique characteristic of paid-by-the-column feuilleton writing which Nerval had already demonstrated, con brio, in "Les Faux-Saulniers" (1850). Temporizing is the check-is-in-the-mail tactic: in lieu of what the audience expects and wants (in this case an ending-oriented story leading to the closure of, as Nerval puts it, either a wedding or a death), a substitute satisfaction is provided, but of such a patently inadequate kind that it generates a whole series of such substitutes. The audience becomes prey to the "just one more" or the "bowl of cherries" syndrome: pointless and deficiently pleasurable as any given narrative moment may be, it offers just enough "satisfaction" to keep the reader reading. There is always hope (which always proves vain) that the next moment will bring a more substantial satisfaction. This is a narrative practice known to us these days through much radio and TV programming; and it has the characteristic feature of producing a strict equivalence between the experience of unstructured, now-this-now-that temporality and that of desire, structured by lack, as Lacan has it, into an endless metonymic chain of substitute "satisfactions." The narrator is manipulating his readers' desire, so as to lead them into a world of the fringe—of fringe people and fringe knowledge—to which they would not otherwise have access, a world in which life is "other."

It is worth noting, therefore, that the narrator has rather deliberately chosen to put himself in this situation. If one is invited to an otter hunt in Creil, one can take the northern railroad direct (even though it describes a long curve that Nerval ascribes on other occasions to real estate speculation: modernity is efficient, but not direct enough to abolish time altogether).[5] It is quite willful, therefore, to choose, as this traveler does, to take the Strasbourg road to Meaux, with the idea of *strolling* through the Valois, traveling by coach to Dammartin, through the forest of Ermenonville on foot for three hours, following the course of the Nonette to Senlis, and from there by coach again to Creil (chapter 22). This is a way of traveling without leaving home—the narrator insists from the start on the proximity of the Valois to Paris—while nevertheless generating something (an *Erfahrung*) to narrate by taking the longest and slowest route. But as a narrator, too, this willful loiterer has deliberately opted for the difficulties of temporization over the easier, and expected, method of telling a suspenseful story. In this, he says, he is emulating a prolix orator, described censoriously by Cicero, who cannot say that his client left town without describing him waking, rising, setting forth, taking the right side of the via Flaminia and crossing the bathhouse square—and never reaching the port. He has also been inspired by an account of London nightlife by Dickens: "How fortunate the English are to be able to write and to read chapters of observation completely unalloyed by fictional invention. . . . Our neighbors' sense of realism is content with truth in the absolute" (1). But Londoners, the narrator grumbles, are in any case much freer than Parisians: they have a house key ("La clef de la rue" is the title of the Dickens piece) and so can wander their city at night without fear of having to affront a censorious concierge. Our narrator is simply taking for himself *la clef de la rue*, and—since after the first night his story shifts to the country—*la clef des champs* as well.

But these are provocative options, and deliberately so. Expressing disapproval of the hated "portier" as a figure of social authority is not the only risk, therefore, that the narrator knows he is taking. Like Nodier in *Le roi de Bohême et ses sept châteaux*, he imagines the unfriendly review his trivial narrative is likely to draw from an idealist critic (the kind whose doctrine is that "truth lies in falsity," 21). More alarmingly, he is arrested at Crespy by a gendarme who discovers that the man who culpably misses trains also absentmindedly leaves his travel passport at the hotel in Meaux, and who is unconvinced by the story that one might travel from Paris via Meaux to an otter hunt in Creil. Why travel east to reach the north? Such a loiterly traveler is clearly suspect, and in the nightmare that attends his night in prison he is hauled before what can only be described as a disciplinary tribunal that reminds him of sitting for the baccalaureate *en Sorbonne* ("the president looked uncannily like M. Nisard; the two assessors resembled M. Cousin and M. Guizot, my old teachers"). They hurl epithets at him: "Realist! *Fantaisiste!* Essayist!" until finally he cracks:

> *Confiteor! plangor! juro!* . . . —I swear to renounce these works accursed of the Sorbonne and the Institute: from now on I shall write only history, philosophy, philology and statistics. . . . You seem dubious. . . . Very well, I'll write virtuous bucolic romances, I'll try to win poetry prizes and prizes for good morals, I'll write children's books and aboli- tionist essays, didactic poems . . . tragedies! (25)

His crime is that of being simultaneously realistic and unserious and thus of escaping in two different ways the constraints of discipline; in another register, Nerval's passionate apologia in *Aurélia* for the rights of madness against the strictures of psychiatric medicine is foreshadowed here.

For this narrator is no examinee and even less an examiner, and his conversion to disciplined knowledge and structured plots takes place—revealingly enough—only in a dream. A simple observer, an impressionist, he has views, like his friend, *de omnis rebus scibilis* (about all knowable things), but his attention span is short and his interest is easily diverted. Like Dante and Virgil, the two friends descend into the night world of Paris: we catch glimpses of various cafés, goguettes, and dives and snatches of slangy, trivial conversation. Brief streetscapes open up ("adultery, crime, and weakness jostle without recognizing one another through the deceptive shadows," 10; "on the right are the leech sellers; the other side is taken up by Raspail pharmacies and cider stands," 11; "what a lot of cauliflower in this street," 14). The initiatory motif of the descent into the underworld hints at the forbidden character of this exploration and also informs us that the nature of true knowledge is at issue, although Nerval's mystic concerns are under wraps here in favor of the practice of flâneur realism. This is not incompatible with the fact that, as the external action shifts to the Valois, the focus of the narrative comes to fall predominantly on the contents of the narrator's mind as the privileged locus of travel without leaving home (for in loiterly texts, the question of the flâneur's identity is always, covertly or overtly, at issue, in view of his self-definition as a man given over, like Baudelaire's "homme des foules," to the exploration of alterity). Thus the nightmare of the third night is preceded on the second by a bad dream in which Fichtean gnomes hammer at the narrator's brain in an attempt to rearrange the deranged structure of his consciousness. But there is also a wonderful page of pure visual impressionism, as the narrator wakes after his disturbed night to sit by the Marne and await his morning coffee, in that absent mood we all know so well:

> People are beginning to come across the bridge; it has eight spans by my count. The Marne is *marneuse*, of course; but at the moment it has a leaden sheen ruffled occasionally by currents from the mills, or, further away, the playful swoop of swallows.
> Will it rain this evening? (20)

The major encounter of this section, however, symmetrical to the fellowship of the narrator with his friend in the first part of the text, is with a group of saltimbanks or strolling entertainers, two Savoyards passing respectively for an Italian tenor and a Spanish dancer, and an alleged "monstre" or freak, a "merino woman" who hails from Venice and whose woolly hair, the narrator speculates, is a genetic throwback to African ancestry. These folks stand, obviously, for the strangeness of the real in its most everyday manifestations (the flâneur's stock-in-trade) and doubtless also for the tricks of art, since their art—like the narrator's—consists of unstructured, episodic entertainment (first an aria, then a cachuca, then the freak), and appeals to an audience as idle as its performers are shiftless. But they are also archetypal fringe dwellers; and as the narrator of *October Nights* has a flâneur for his friend, partner, and philosophical alter ego, so the flâneur's own artistic counterpart turns out to be the wandering street entertainer, whether saltimbank or conjurer. For the friend was already described in these terms:

> He will stop for an hour at the door of the bird merchant's store, attempting to understand the language of birds. . . . No group gathers around some work site or bootblack seller, no fisticuffs occur, no dogfight happens, without his distracted contemplation taking it in. The conjurer always borrows his handkerchief, which he sometimes has, or the five-franc coin, which he doesn't always have. (2)

The hint of complicity here is unmistakable. If the conjurer engages in sleight-of-hand, the flâneur-narrator is a trickster too, in his way: his art of narrative temporizing "deceives" desire as the *escamoteur* deceives the eye, and both practice the art of programming the reader's or spectator's idle attention from turn to turn or from moment to moment. Not surprisingly, we will find Colette's narrator-protagonist, Renée Néré, among music hall *artistes*, an *artiste* herself, waiting her turn to take the stage after the performing dogs, the *chanteuse*, and the acrobats.

TOURING

While Nerval's narrative starts with a missed train, *The Vagabond* begins with Renée arriving early at the theater and finding herself "prête trop tôt," ready too soon. She has time on her hands as well, but for reasons and with historical implications diametrically opposed to those of Nerval's flâneur. The latter, in his contempt for schedules, shows himself a belated figure, behind the times; Renée is a "new woman," too early because she is struggling for emancipation from domesticity in a society that, as yet, scarcely has a place for her. Consequently, existence in time is, for her, experienced as a matter of deep insecurity, not only financial but also ontological: "Why are you there, all alone? and why not somewhere else?" she asks herself (4), and later comments anxiously, "How quickly everything changes, especially women" (88). Her problem is not that she is suspect as a loiterer but that she needs steady and honorable work; and if going on tour figures for her what strolling through the city and its near countryside represents in Nerval, the act of travel without leaving home, that phrase now has a more negative ring, signifying the inability her anxiety betrays to escape the law of domesticity that still (in 1910) imprisons women. For her life in the theater involves difficult compromises that are figured implicitly by her métier as an Apache dancer (the woman brutalized by the male, and performing fluttering steps of attempted escape), and explicitly by the tour through the provinces she undertakes, circling back in due course to Paris: "tourner," for her, is "tourner sur place," "revolving on the spot like my companions and brethren" (67).

There she is, then, ready too early. The consequence is a split identity, but one less metaphysically described than the Fichtean problematic Nerval evokes. Her alternative is between an absurd and lonely existence in pure time ("Why are you there, all alone? And why not somewhere else?") and the personage she sees in the mirror and calls her "conseillère maquillée" (painted mentor; 3), that is, her entertainer's persona garishly made up for performance, a seductive self devoted to entertaining the crowd whose work is the condition for the freedom the lonely self finds at once so precious and so burdensome. It is Renée's need for diversion from this intimate dialogue that accounts for the aspect of the book that most resembles the genre of flâneur realism and situates it as loiterature, despite its novelistic plot: Renée is a steady-eyed, nonjudgmental observer of the backstage existence of music hall performers, their poverty, courage, and pride, their makeshift conditions of life, their colorful language and sometimes easy morality, but also their hard work and devotion to their art—their life of instability that prompts her comment: "How quickly everything changes. . . ." *Déclassée* as she is by her employment, Renée shares the flâneur's traditional sympathy for the life of the underclass, along with the loiterly subject's ability, as an educated member of the middle class, to represent its color and pathos for a similarly middle-class audience. In this too she is a creature of compromise.

The compromise of her existence becomes a crisis of choice, however, on the occasion of the love affair that introduces narrative interest and plot: will Renée's affair with Dufferein-Chautel, affectionately known as "le Grand Serin" or the Big Noodle, end—as Nerval would phrase it—in marriage? One of the few employment choices available to a "dame seule" is work in the theater, as Renée explains: "What would you have me do? Sewing, or typing, or streetwalking? The music hall is the job (le métier) of those who never learnt one" (134)—of those, that is, who have been excluded from the privileges of discipline. Renée, in short, is exploiting for employment purposes the seductive art she learned as a wife (knowing how to use her tears of pain, for instance, to make herself look beautiful). But for that very reason, her theatrical art jeopardizes the freedom of which it is also a condition, exposing her not only to the sexual advances of men (which she knows how to handle) but, more dangerously, to the temptation to return to the security—as well as the pain—of a conforming position in the patriarchal order as a married woman. This temptation is represented by the marriageable Dufferein-Chautel ("he looks married already," 102), who is drawn to her by her stage performance, with his "ridiculous name, the sort of name for a member of Parliament or an industrialist, or a director of a discount bank" (100), but also with his ready assumption of male authority. Renée knows that she will not necessarily be reduced, as in her previous marriage, to being a kind of go-between in her husband's extramarital affairs; but she is also aware that marriage "turns so many wives into a sort of nanny for grown-ups" (137). Her little dog Fossette (the reference is to a fetching dimple) stands for the strength of the impulse in her to revert to the life of a "submissive bitch, rather shame-faced, rather cowed, very much petted, and ready to accept the leash, the collar, the place at her master's feet, and everything" (120).

Renée has only a choice of compromises: freedom with insecurity or security with the leash—*and* the opportunity to write. Once a quite successful novelist, Renée's new loiterly, "too soon" existence is one in which, paradoxically, she has no time for writing, since earning a living means being subject to constant distraction and interruption:

> It takes up too much time to write. And the trouble is, I am no Balzac! The fragile story I am constructing crumbles away when the tradesman rings, or the shoemaker sends his bill, when the solicitor, or one's counsel, telephones, or when the theatrical agent summons me to his office for a "social engagement at the house of some people of good position but not in the habit of paying large fees." (12)

Consequently, her eventual return to writing, coinciding with her return to Paris, her rejection of the Big Noodle, and her implied acceptance of the loiterly life that is defined by interruption, is—as Nancy Miller has pointed out—the key to the book.[6] Her return is also a renaissance (as her name foreshadows), since the writing to which she returns is not the writing she left behind her in her bourgeois existence. It is the writing, as Miller eloquently proposes, of a "feminist" (and I would add "loiterly") subjectivity, one that has renounced the illusions of the bourgeois self and knows itself "subject to change." Miller rightly emphasizes that the letter of rejection for Dufferein-Chautel that Renée brings back to Paris with her is described as "unfinished" (214). But *because* it is unfinished, and corresponding as it does to the anticlimactic ending of the missed otter hunt in Nerval, this letter cannot signify a resolution of Renée's identity problematic. It means only that, for now, she has chosen between her two compromises and opted for the one that associates independence and freedom with, on the one hand, insecurity and, on the other, the deployment of "feminine" attractiveness, the conditions of her "too soon" existence.

My proposal is that the writing she returns to incorporates a similar compromise and is epitomized in the novel itself: it accommodates the problematic split in Renée's identity in the (mixed) genre of the "loiterly novel," exactly that impure "alloy" Nerval sought to avoid, a compromise between pure observation in the digressive, interrupted flow of a narrative of temporality, and fictional invention, sentimental interest, and the seductions of plot. Such writing indicates that Renée's renaissance derives from her discovery and acceptance of the implications of being "no Balzac." Writing need not ignore interruption but can accommodate to it and incorporate it; it need not have the monumental character of the *Comédie humaine* but can be a matter of *désœuvrement*, of that "crumbling" of the edifice that loiterature seeks not to resist or to deny but to assume and deploy as a tactic of digressivity—a tactic whose success depends, however, on obtaining the pleasurable assent of its audience.

Part of the compromise Renée invents involves plot, then, but another part involves finding a place in her writing for triviality. Early in the piece, she is tongue-tied when she seeks to represent herself to Dufferein-Chautel, hesitating between her "own *personal* language," which she describes as that of "a one-time blue-stocking," and "the slovenly, lively idiom, coarse and picturesque, which one learns in the music-hall, sprinkled with expressions like: 'You bet!' 'Shut up!' 'I'm clearing out!' 'Not my line!'" ("Tu parles!" "Ta gueule!" "J'les mets!" "Très peu pour moi!", 77–78). This is exactly the linguistic alloy of writerly distinction and colloquial vulgarity that we discover in the writing of *The Vagabond*, but it is Renée's dancing, as an art of the body ("Nothing is real except making rhythm of one's thought and translating it into beautiful gestures," 41), that has taught her that it is possible to make art out of the trivial. And as Renée becomes aware when she dances for a society gathering (i.e., in exactly the circumstances she evoked when complaining of the interruptions that constitute the life of an *artiste*), dancing embodies a compromise between the freedom of a woman's body and an art intended to be seductive to the powerful (and specifically to Renée's own former set):

> Is not the mere swaying of my back [un coup de reins], free from any constraint, an insult to those bodies cramped by their long corsets, and enfeebled by a fashion which insists that they should be thin?
>
> But there is something more worth while than humiliating them; I want, for one moment only, to charm them [les séduire]. It needs only a little more effort: already their heads, under the weight of their jewels and their hair, sway vaguely as they obediently follow my movements. At any moment now the vindictive light in all those eyes will go out, and the charmed creatures will all give in and smile at the same time. (41–42)

By the time she is ready to negotiate her *tournée* with the theatrical agent who stands as another figure of the social (here economic) conditions of Renée's independence (and who is, of course, the personage mentioned in the earlier passage about interruptions), she has lost her linguistic inhibitions—"I have found my voice again and the art of using it, and the right vocabulary [i.e., a suitably salty one] for the occasion" (92)—and it is not accidental that what is at issue here is a contract. Renée's loiterly art will be subject to a contractual obligation—the aesthetic obligation to be "charming" to the bourgeoisie—in a way that is modeled by the financial haggling that governs the limited freedom of her "escape" to the provinces on tour and defines her every experience—social, linguistic, and artistic— as peripheral.

There is a name that might be given to the set of compromises Renée finally opts for, including the compromise formation that is her writing; it is *métier*. In order for a woman to be free of the domestic leash, she must be employed, and *métier* names the only kind of employment for which, as a middle-class woman, she is suited: not the discipline of the factory floor or the professional disciplines of knowledge, but "le métier de ceux qui n'en ont appris aucun," a job one can learn by doing it, under a sort of (pre- or extra-disciplinary) apprenticeship system. For *métier* also names the artistic know-how one can acquire with hard work and under the guidance of a strict mentor, like Renée's partner Brague, from one's actual, "hands-on" contact with the world of the theater: in rehearsal, from observation of the audience, and from watching one's fellow performers. But *métier* finally, in the music hall and perhaps the theater generally, is the art of crowd pleasing, the tricks of the trade that bring the audience back every Saturday night for more. It designates the theatrical seductiveness Renée must deploy as well as the means of livelihood that ensure her relative independence. In that sense it confirms what Renée's tour also teaches her, that although one can travel without leaving home, it is the impossibility of ever quite leaving "home"—and everything that word implies, for a woman—that governs the degree of travel one can achieve. "I am going away," she writes to Max at the end; but she thinks: "I am escaping, but I am still not free of you, I know it. A vagabond, and free, I shall sometimes long for the shade of your walls" (215). Just as Nerval's belatedness permits him the relative freedom of peripheral existence and the ability to step somewhat out of line but does not free him from the censorious judgment of authority (in the form of *portiers*, examiners, or police), so Renée's anticipatory situation lengthens her leash and allows her to be something of a "vagabond, and free" (within the limits of a *tournée*) but not to step away, absolutely, from the condition of domesticity to which she remains, inescapably, chained.

CRUISING

How, then, to "lose oneself in the city"? And what has that to do with knowledge? *Who Was That Man?* has an interesting epigraph drawn from Benjamin: "Not to find one's way in a city may well be uninteresting and banal. It requires ignorance, nothing more. But to lose oneself in a city. . . ." I would draw out the implications of this epigraph as follows: if Renée Néré experiences her freedom as solitude and is consequently forced into a compromise with the society that limits that freedom, her problem grows out of ignorance—ignorance, that is, of any community to which she is connected—the community, say, of other independent women attempting to survive on their own terms. Knowledge of such a community—by definition a community of peripheral subjects—is unlikely, however, to be a disciplinary knowledge, if only because discipline begins by separating its subjects in space, like soldiers on the parade ground, so as to turn them into autonomous individuals. Because it seeks, on the one hand, to promote "self-reliance," and, on the other, to instill conformity, discipline is anticommunitarian, even through it is the distinctive trait of those who exercise social dominance.[7] And community is therefore likely to be the experience, and the source of identity, of those who are excluded from a disciplinary subjecthood, that is, of those who frequent or inhabit the social fringes. But it is crucially dependent on knowledge, on the part of such peripheral subjects, that they are not, like Renée Néré (or as she believes herself to be), alone.

The model for such people is therefore, in Bartlett's book, the sexual cruiser, seen as one who seeks identity, as knowledge of "self," in a community formed through identification with *others*, through "losing one's *self*" in a "city." Identity here is not a matter of individuality but of connectedness, in which both self and other, being mutually defining, exist only as members of a community. "I've come to understand," Bartlett writes, "that I am connected with other men's lives, men living in London with me." But he adds: "*Or with other, dead Londoners. That's the story*" (xx). The story, in other words, is not only that personal identity—in this case, for gay men—is indistinguishable from belonging to a community but also that the community extends into the past. Historically, gay identity emerged in London simultaneously with the constitution of a community of gay men; that is why a Londoner living in 1986 is connected with men who lived in 1895, the date of Oscar Wilde's trial. And the reason it is important to establish this historical connection, as the book does, is that in producing Wilde *individually* as a homosexual the trial functioned—in typically disciplinary fashion (i.e. as a kind of examination)—precisely to obscure his membership in a community, and hence to deny the existence of a specifically gay identity as a communitarian phenomenon. But both the identity and the community were henceforth phenomena of the fringe, having the characteristics of loiterly subjectivity: its motility, its *ça ne se dessine pas*.

London's present cruising grounds were already cruising grounds a century ago, and the streets have a memory. "What if I rounded the corner of Villiers St at midnight," Bartlett writes, "and suddenly found myself walking by gas-light, and the man looking over his shoulder at me as he passed had the same moustache, but different clothes . . . would we recognize each other?" (xx). In this question of recognition lies the kinship of the historian and the cruiser as subjects of knowledge: the power of recognizing the self in the other makes both historian and cruising man—or, of course, woman—into constructors (for the historian, reconstructors) of community. And recognition is crucial because the social conditions of cruising are such that it cannot be a systematic activity: there is no way of identifying gay men unless they identify themselves; they are not available, as "gay men," for the kind of disciplinary examination by which "homosexuals"—a noncommunity—are identified. Cruising can only discover, through recognition, a *covert* community in a *random* way. For similar reasons, the historical cruiser is forced to be an unmethodical searcher, looking for "evidence" (and hoping to recognize it) wherever and however it might turn up. His knowledge is fringe knowledge because it is knowledge of other subjects who are themselves on the social fringe.

In this unpredictability sexual and historical cruising have much in common with the activity of "collecting"; and like collectors, cruisers of knowledge are also driven, obsessive figures, creatures of desire, always in search of one more "item." Because their work is driven by desire, there is no end to it and they are therefore never in a position to systematize finally or definitively what can appropriately be called their "findings," which remain just that: collections of "trouvailles." Between gay cruising literature like John Rechy's *Numbers* or Renaud Camus's *Tricks* and loiterly history like Walter Benjamin's *Passagenwerk* (a collection of quotations) or Georges Perec's *Je me souviens* (a collection of memories that have the specific quality of being both trivial and nonpersonal, or collective), there are consequently "recognizable" structural and epistemological similarities that imply a generic relationship. Bartlett's book—the record of intense cruising not in Villiers St. but in the British Library—lies somewhere between the two groups, that is, at the heart of the genre that identifies the pursuit of (fringe) knowledge with cruising and collecting, with desire rather than power.

There is therefore in this genre a deliberate rejection of a certain narrative structure that is itself a structuring of history, and of the implications of such a structure. Two narrative models are available to gay people, as Bartlett points out (23–24). One is the coming-out story,

with its firm narrative structure of "before" and "after," a beginning and
an end mediated by a crucial event that has the status of an emergence
of truth. A coming-out story can be either individual or collective,
and Wilde's coming out—more accurately his involuntary "outing"—
functions as both. But the closed structure of such a narrative makes
it exclusionary, and Bartlett's study of the 1895 trial demonstrates that
the outing of Wilde had as its unacknowledged purpose to silence gay
voices that were beginning to be heard, to force back into invisibility
and oblivion the community of gay men that had begun to emerge—
of "gay men," not just of men with homosexual desires, a distinction
that hangs significantly on their communitarian invention of signs
of recognition, such as Wilde's green carnation or the moustache in
Villiers St. But the cruising story, the obsessive collection of scraps
of forgotten history, makes use of just such signs of recognition in
order to undo the effect of exclusionary and scapegoating stories
constructed by the powers that be. Thus, Bartlett notices that men such
as Arthur Symonds and Edward Carpenter were already, long before
him, engaging in the "inspired queenly assemblage of fragments" of
gay history (227), and I, in turn, have just pointed out that such
cruiser-historians form part of a larger epistemological community of
(re-)collectors of the past that includes Perec and Benjamin.

The point, then, as Bartlett indicates, is that "it never is in all the
papers" (125): the official story always needs supplementation by the
collector, looking for the forgotten but telling scraps. "What I want are
details, details are the only things of interest" (159). "I read texts with
the dogged energy that I usually reserve for cruising; I became excited
by the smallest hints; I scrutinized every gesture for significance;
sometimes I simply stood close and waited for a response" (28). The
outcome of working principles such as these is a book whose pages
often seem to reproduce the bulletin board in the author's room: "On
my wall a handsome face is pasted up next to a fragment from a novel,
next to the latest report of an arrest or a persecution" (96); quotations
from a range of nineteenth-century sources, personal observations
about gay life in modern London, and analytic commentary coexist
on the page; a chapter on flowers as recognition signals includes the
story of one Private Flower who was arrested for "cottaging" in the
1830s. Bartlett puts together a portrait gallery of men's faces and a
glossary of historical gay slang omitted from the OED; he rejoices
that at the Wilde trial "the prosecution assembled one of the most

extensive and glamorous collections of details about our life" (99), but he also assembles counterevidence of the energy and vividness of gay life in the years between the trial of Boulton and Parks (alias Stella and Fanny) in 1870 and the Wilde trial, in the form of a year-by-year "calendar" of quotations and cuttings that extends over twenty-five pages.

A scrapbook such as this, says Bartlett, is "the true form of our history" (99). Because "our past is continually lost" (59), it is necessary to make good the omissions; "because the clues change" (63) and recognition is therefore always aleatory, no truth claim can be made or conclusions safely drawn. The scrapbook "embodies in its own omissions how we remember and forget our lives. We are always between ignorance and exposure" (99); but in doing so it nevertheless demonstrates that "the past is still with us" (82). Like the cruiser hunting familiar streets that harbor memories of dead Londoners, the scrapbook's demonstration of the proximity of past and present represents another sense in which the loiterer's experience consists of traveling without leaving home. Such *Erfahrung* is exhilarating—but its dependence on recognition also makes its epistemological status dubious, as Bartlett emphasizes. After all, as Oscar Wilde's "composing" of a new identity after 1895 demonstrates, gay men are given to "making it all up as we go along" (170–71); moreover, in a way foreshadowed by Wilde's story "The Portrait of Mr. W. H.," the whole enterprise of the "recollection" of gay culture and community raises the question whether it is perhaps all a fantasy, fueled only by desire. "My father always said, if you're not sure if it's the real thing, then it isn't" (189). And collecting, as an activity of knowledge, has exclusionary implications of its own: it takes place "within a specific economy" (186) of class and privilege and is dependent on one's having "discretionary income" and (something Bartlett does not specifically mention although it is everywhere implied) time and leisure. Who can otherwise afford to spend an idle bank holiday weekend ("I wasn't working, and it was the first good weather of the year") and then return to the library, as Bartlett describes himself doing (125–26)?

But what matters here is not the incompleteness of the scrapbook method, or the dubious objectivity of an epistemological "hunt" motivated by desire, or the dependency of this activity on specific social conditions. What matters is the dubiousness of claims to completeness and objectivity and of narratives that mask their socially positioned status with implied or explicit truth claims. It is in *not* making such claims, and in making its specific position of enunciation readable in historical, economic, and cultural terms by its careful exploration of the conditions of gay male life as Bartlett knows them in modern London, that this loiterly narrative makes its own epistemological point. In so doing, it makes the point for loiterature in general, whose doubtful reliability in matters of information and whose class ties to the bourgeoisie and its history scarcely need to be indicated. It is not that such features are invalidating but that their visibility—the ease with which loiterly writing foregrounds the connection of its knowledge with desire, for example—questions the assumptions by virtue of which they might be invalidated. Such assumptions are those of disciplinarity, whose epistemological reliance on examination presupposes the separability of (examining) subject and (examined) object and excludes the relevance of desire. Claims to dispassionate objectivity rest on such assumptions of separability, assumptions which themselves derive from a concept of individual identity as autonomous, unconnected, not dependent on the alterity of a community in which it is possible to "lose oneself/one's self."

But when Bartlett writes simply: "It's quite true, I am other people" (205), he is echoing flâneur knowledge that goes back at least to Nerval's "I am the other" (a phrase he scribbled on a portrait of himself), or to Baudelaire's definition of the flâneur (itself derived from Poe) as "l'homme des foules," the man of the crowd (see chapter 8). As visible as are the class differences in Nerval's account of Parisian low life and Colette's *reportage* on the backstage life of the music hall, there is also a sense of community in these texts—of the community of society's misfits, underlings, and rejects—that draws a line from Nerval's preoccupation with alter egos (the Parisian friend, the saltimbanks), through the comradeship celebrated in Colette's novel, to Bartlett's "I am connected with other men's lives." That statement is embroiled in gendered blindness, of course, just as those of Nerval and Colette are embroiled in the limitations of class, but all of them can be rephrased as: I am connected with other lives.

As I foreshadowed earlier, the name that's available for practices of knowledge that are grounded in connectedness and recognize an affinity with the structure of desire—practices exemplified by Bartlett's recourse to cruising and collecting but easily seen to be at work in

Nerval and Colette—is reading. Reading is the mode through which community is constituted, where community refers to the forms of connectedness available, not to disciplinary subjects (isolated by their individuality, as subjects and objects of the practice of examination), but to peripheral subjects conscious of the constitution in and through alterity of their own subjectivity, subjects who are thus always on the cusp of another context and defined by constitutive relations of proximity and motility. Thus loiterly knowledge, as it is exemplified by the texts of Nerval, Colette, and Bartlett, is, on the one hand, readerly knowledge (defined by its antidisciplinarity) and, on the other, knowledge on which the constitution of community, among fringe dwellers, depends.

But, as I've also already foreshadowed, loiterly reading can also be critical reading, when it is turned in the direction of the society to which the loiterly community is itself peripheral. That which is established and disciplined, self-absorbed and exclusionary, is subject to implicit and sometimes explicit relativization from the perspective of its own fringe consciousness, where subjectivity knows itself as split, mobile, and other-constituted (that is, as unable really, by virtue of *ça ne se dessine pas*, to know itself at all). The later chapters of this book (in the sections on learning from dogs and on loiterly intellectuals) are about the conditions of critical reading, which are essentially those of loiterly subjectivity. Baudelaire, in particular, the hero of chapter 8, is a figure in whom one can see an awareness forming, over a period of time and against considerable psychological resistance, that the condition of social criticism, for a modern flâneur poet, is peripheral positionality and loiterly subjectivity, which means acknowledgment of his own belongingness to a community of peripheral subjects and acceptance of his own subjectivity—he is a belated reader of what he designates a culture of impatience—as that of a desiring subject. The central paradox of critical reading, which appears to have been a major sticking point for Baudelaire, is that one cannot be critical of the desire inherent in the culture of impatience without simultaneously acknowledging that the belatedness that makes such a critique possible is itself a desiring position. To read, then, is to open oneself to the possibility of being read in turn; and to wish to escape that condition is to seek to become a disciplinary examiner, not a reader. Such is the wisdom, as we shall see, that one can learn from dogs, and it is the wisdom of the critical intellectual.

But the sign of such wisdom is the sense of connectedness that is at work in the community of the peripheral and the marginalized. Critical reading, in this sense, can't be dissociated from the community-building reading that Neil Bartlett figures as cruising and that Baudelaire explores in his great poem, "Le Cygne." That's why, as a preface to the studies of loiterature as social criticism that follow in the latter part of this book, I've emphasized here the solidarity, in Nerval, Colette, and Bartlett, of the loiterly subject's critique of mainstream society and of the same subject's need for an alternative community of the peripheral. It's in their readerly construction of communities of the peripheral that peripheral, loiterly subjects are able to mitigate something of the solitude they feel as subjects who—like contemporary critical intellectuals—belong fully to neither group but shuttle restlessly between them, in the awkward and constantly shifting position of the mediator. The privilege they enjoy of being able to travel without leaving home is bought at the expense of being nowhere fully at home, but it is that sense of their homelessness that also makes them, simultaneously, critical readers of social dominance and empathetic readers of the marginal.

Toward a Poetics of Digression

Changing the Subject (or the Etcetera Principle)

Permanente Parekbase (endless digression) was Friedrich Schlegel's famous definition of Romantic irony,[1] and from Laurence Sterne (see chapter 1) to Nicholson Baker (chapter 5) narrative digression has been one of the more artful practices of modern writing. Yet we lack a poetics of digression, and in rhetoric the topic has been largely ignored since Aristotle, digression being considered neither a trope nor a legitimate rhetorical practice but an error, a wandering away from the subject at hand. But like other practices with which it has some common features—asyndeton (interruption), anacoluthon (inconsistency), parenthesis, description—it is less an error than a relaxation of what are regarded as the strictest standards, not of relevance or cogency, but of cohesion. It is for that reason that the possibility of digression (from which loiterature derives its most characteristic effects) poses something of a problem and a threat to proponents of views of discourse that assume its being under the control of a cohesive subject and susceptible, therefore, to strict rules of ordering.

Modern narratology, with its stress on the grammaticality of story and on the figure of the narrator as the controlling instance whose function is to filter information, determining what is relevant to the story and what isn't, is a field that typically makes such an assumption. No narrative construction can be so cohesive, however, as to be totally closed to the possibility of supplementarity (no story is the whole story[2]), and it is on this fact that digressive practices depend, demonstrating as they do so that the narrative subject is less a controlling instance than a site of split—subject(ed), that is, to instances that the subject may itself acknowledge as forms of alterity.

Digression, in other words, exemplifies what I will call the etcetera principle, which states that, whereas contextuality is a condition of all discourse, no context is ever the whole context: there is consequently no message that does not admit of there being a second or other message, and indeed, by continued application of the rule, a third, fourth, and fifth, to infinity. The proponents of coercive systems and disciplinary molds, with their pretensions to universal control, are made uncomfortable by the etcetera principle because it implies that there can be no law without a loophole; and digression, which demonstrates that there is no situation, however constraining, without its etcetera—its loophole or escape hatch—is therefore a key device in the hands of practitioners of oppositionality. Theirs is an art, precisely, of the unexpected swerve, the clinamen that, diverting atoms from their predicted path, changes everything. The swerve, however, is necessarily defined by that from which it departs, just as predictability is always subject to diversion; and so it is the close embrace of these two, apparently contradictory but in fact complementary, conditions that the etcetera principle ultimately expresses.

For the word *etcetera* has the function of conferring formal exhaustiveness and closure on any inventory—but it signals simultaneously that the inventory, as it stands, is in need of supplementation precisely because it is not complete. The closing gesture turns out in this way to be a marker of lack, and vice versa. That narrative is subject to the etcetera principle in this sense—that the closed structure of story, marked by the cohesive linking of a beginning and an end, is in permanent tension with the proclivity to *di*-gression that is the characteristic feature of *dis*-course[3]—is a primary assumption of this essay.

The oddity, though, is that although it interferes with predictable *pro*-gression of narrative toward its closure, *di*-gression is not necessarily regarded for that reason as *trans*-gressive. There is a certain legitimacy of digression, which derives from the fact that it is sensed to be discourse's "pente facile," its *natural* proclivity against which laws of grammaticality and cogency have to struggle to impose themselves. So legitimate was it once that, according to Randa Sabry, in the earliest Greek rhetorics the digression (*parekbasis*) actually had its assigned place in the *dispositio* (or *taxis*).[4] We might compare it, therefore, with subordinating practices that are currently regarded as similarly legitimate, such as the parenthesis or, especially, the footnote. These—parenthesis, footnote, and digression—are practices that mark certain discursive material, not as illegitimate, then, but as secondary: secondary yet in some sense relevant, not fully cohesive but admissible. They consequently have the curious feature that, in so doing, they simultaneously *draw attention* to the supposedly secondary material, subjecting it to a certain emphasis.

Material that is specially marked as secondary is, in short, material that is specially marked. It's like the etcetera that closes a list only to open it up: an initially hierarchizing gesture tends on second thought to have a dehierarchizing effect and thus introduces a degree of tolerated but controlled disorder into a supposedly orderly text. Digression introduces forks in the textual road that require us either to hesitate, to opt for one path or the other, or (as Yogi Berra recommends) to attempt to take both. And one fork can always fork again. Canny readers know therefore to look at least as carefully at the so-called margins of a text as at its main argument because parenthetical passages and footnotes may contain revealing second messages; and the same is true of digression. Freud's footnotes, which are themselves given to breeding further footnotes by a kind of galloping digressivity, are infamous in this respect and have been rightly subjected to much dehierarchizing reading in recent years. That digression escalates in similar fashion, unless it is carefully controlled, is an equally common experience. Writers who do not wish to offer their readers the wherewithal to deconstruct their "main" message—that is, to challenge its main-ness— have consequently learned to be chary of concessives and wary of the syntax of discursive subordination, for these are the places where, in what feels like the "natural" pursuit of an argument, the argument can overturn itself.

Just so the tribunals of Athens, at the time when digression was an acknowledged and expected part of the orator's speech, employed an officer of the court whose function was to control its use and to ensure that digression did not *go too far* [5] (Peter Schickele, in his radio show "Schickele Mix," honors the tradition by employing a "hot air detector" that emits a loud buzz when his professorial meanderings become "too" digressive, "too" pedantic, or "too" long-winded). A certain degree of digressiveness, in other words, is regarded as "only natural," but—just because it represents an emergence of the natural within the order of the cultural (a courtroom, a classroom, the literary work . . .)—it must be limited and controlled. For when the Greek orator "moved forward" and "departed" from his argument—as the words *parekbasis* or *digression* etymologically imply and as, to digress, I too sometimes do in class, professorially abandoning the lectern and with it my prepared notes to tell a related story or to "embroider" my material as a way of *bringing it to life* for my students—when the orator digressed, then, bodily relations (a matter of proxemics) suddenly impinged on what were supposed to be purely intellectual deliberations (a matter of rationality), a potential for emotion and feeling threatened the court's carefully maintained performance of dispassiveness, and desire became a factor—indeed a constituent—of would-be rational argument.

Cultures have a stake in the control of desire to the extent that it represents the natural, that "other" against which the cultural is defined and which is consequently an essential component of its identity, its permanent "second message." Desire, like nature itself, cannot be ignored, it must be at one and the same time acknowledged (and so legitimated), and prevented from *going too far* or *taking over*. (All "let's not open the floodgates" arguments are arguments that acknowledge desire and seek to control it.) Power might well be defined, culturally speaking, as the ability to take the stance of defending culture by identifying (and controlling) others as subjects of desire, in the sense of subject *to* desire (unable to control it for themselves). Thus, a major theme of the pervasive misogyny that serves as an alibi for patriarchal social formations is, for example, the alleged inability of women to control their desire.

To the extent that the natural is the inevitable second message of all discourses of culture and desire figures the natural; and to the further extent that digression represents for discourse both the danger of the natural and the inevitably diversionary force of desire, discursive power will similarly take the form of the ability to keep digression, alleged to be a kind of "necessary evil," under control. Within the discursive economy digression has, so to speak, a status comparable to that of household pets in the domestic economy, which are admitted to the house as representatives of nature on condition that they be tamed and trained but are of interest and give pleasure to the extent that they can always potentially get out of control and eat Dad's favorite slippers or run up the drapes. Note, however, that a pet that bites the letter carrier or suffocates the baby is likely to be summarily "put down": in these exemplary confrontations of nature and culture, nature has "gone too far," and its representatives are accordingly suppressed. The animals, indeed, may eat slippers or run up drapes once too often as well and be taken on a one-way trip into the country—consigned, that is, back to nature where they "belong." Yet we need their presence, as we enjoy digressions, not only as reminders of that nonnaturalness that defines us, against them, as cultural subjects, but also as very necessary mitigations of the law of culture, with its potential (if it, in turn, were to go too far) for alienation. The category of the "controlled natural" functions in the social order as something like the loophole in the law of culture.

I am arguing, then—to draw together the threads a bit at this point—that if Bataille was right and transgression and the law are intimately bound up with each other such that the law requires transgression as that which confirms its status as law, there is a type of practice, the digressive, that perhaps offers a model of how the law can be more effectively subverted, since in it something that does not manifest itself as a transgression nevertheless has the power to put the law into question, and potentially, even to "get out of hand." What a culture defines, and permits, as "only natural" or a "natural indulgence" is therefore a crucial area because it is at one and the same time a cultural *necessity* and a site wherein cultural constraints can be—not overturned, undone, or even evaded—but e-luded (in French, *dé-joué*), the "play" they allow being exploited in a way that is itself often "play"-ful, but may have significant consequences. If digression is seen not as revolt against the law but as the *manifestation of another law*—the so-called law of nature—and of a law that can only be respected because without it the law of "culture" has itself no purpose or legitimacy, then the tolerance that is extended to digression has its ground in culture's conscience of its own self-constitution as that which has no grounding except as the negation of the natural. Digression is culture's inevitable reminder that its law is not unique and so not necessarily as legitimate as one might like to think.

But cultural tolerance must simultaneously have its limits, since a manifestation of the natural that was allowed to get out of control would no longer provide culture with the "foil" against which it defines itself but would become transgressive; it might even threaten to *abolish* culture, overwhelming it and blotting it out of existence. (It is the threat of such an extinction of culture through natural manifestations of disorder that have gotten out of hand that is thematized in Paul Auster's novel *In the Country of Last Things*.) It follows that from the side of culture the tolerance accorded to digressiveness must be balanced by control of its tendency to go too far, while from the side of the natural the practice of digressiveness can help to ensure that such tolerance is extended to it by a certain performance of harmlessness. The natural as a cultural category simultaneously harbors fearful potential to destroy culture and is subject to marginalization, inattention, and neglect—a kind of careless surveillance like the control we exercise over our pets—because as the "other" of culture it is so easily relegated to the domain of the secondary and the unimportant.

Narrative texts in the Shandean tradition that *flaunt* their digressiveness are therefore, like animals that make a practice of running up the drapes, playing quite a delicate game. They give pleasure by flirting with the potential for transgression that lies in the fact that there is no law without its loophole (in this case the law of good narrative, with the expectation it fosters of a well-constructed story), but they must—as Cocteau put it—know "jusqu'où on peut aller trop loin" (how far one may overstep the line). They must respect the (of course, undefined) limit beyond which flirtation with the possibility of transgression becomes transgression *tout court* and amusing or titillating manifestations of the force of desire threaten to unleash cultural anarchy or chaos. For this reason, digressive narrators are careful to perpetuate the ancient tradition of the court buffoon or fool, as the figure whose critical function was protected, as well as constrained, by the institution of royalty: Sterne's move in claiming the authority of Yorick is in this sense foundational, and the cultivation of "eccentricity"—whimsicality or hobbyhorse riding—is part of the same tradition. At the same time, such narrators like to signal their playfulness, like Gregory Bateson's puppies whose play is framed by the proposition: "This bite is not a bite." And, of course, they take advantage of the tolerance accorded the category of the trivial, as an ambivalent zone that allows manifestations of the natural (especially those associated with the body, its needs, functions, and desires) to be resignified as unimportant or secondary. In sum, texts that flaunt their digressiveness both take advantage of and contribute to the careful fostering of a belief that is colluded with on all sides because on it the power of culture really depends, a belief in the unseriousness of clownery, the insignificance of the trivial, and the pointlessness of departures from "the point" or of playfulness with respect to structure and to the principle of cohesion and order.

These are moves that activate in the audience the cultural response of pleasure and so protect the practitioners of digression from reactions of anger and retribution; but the pleasure is not simply that of witnessing the control of desire. It is also that of participating vicariously in a certain testing of the limits that separate pleasurable manifestations of the natural from those that are threatening or dangerous. The shift of frame that would transform the trivial-insignificant into the trivial-threatening, the playful bite into an aggressive act, and a clownish narrator into a figure of rebellion seems always imminent; and this sense of potential shift of frame suggests that the etcetera principle has qualitative implications as well as quantitative ones. For, if *this* digression is accepted, then other digressions may follow, and will indeed follow—but the next digression may well prove to be the famous "last straw," the one that goes too far. The ultimately transgressive digression is in this way already implicit in the very first, perhaps imperceptible and in any case tolerated, swerve from discursive rectitude; and the need for pleasure (the relief from cultural alienation) that such a swerve subserves harbors within it, therefore, a danger of disorder and discursive collapse. Narratives that flaunt their digressiveness work at the limit-point between pleasure and something more threatening and thus have a certain modus operandi in common with what is called teasing; their dynamic is such that it can at any moment "tip the balance" and go "over the edge." The social frames that legitimate such narratives as pleasurable and insignificant are what they simultaneously test to the limit.

They do this by pitting what might be called theory against the ordering principle of narrative. Let me explain what I mean. If the (ideal) narrative subject, or narrator (etymologically, one who knows), is the paradigm of a controlling or masterly subject, as narratology seems to assume, the split subjectivity exemplified by digressive narrative might well—in deference to the terminology of *clivage*, *fêlure*, or *brisure* and the thematics of supplementation and drift that command the vast corpus of poststructuralist speculation—be termed a *theoretical* subject, the subject whose knowledge is that it is constituted by an unknowable other or unconscious, that is, by an alterity that is the principle of digression. In this sense, theory (as the sphere of digressiveness and the etcetera principle) would constitute the "second message" that is repressed by, and returns within, narrative discourse as the discourse of control. And certainly digressive narrative (think of Montaigne and Burton or De Quincey and Proust) tends "naturally" to be theorizing discourse, and very frequently its theorizing becomes self-theorizing. It is as if an act of digressing away from narrative strictures—the requirement of storytelling—poses the question of its own condition of possibility—how is departure from rectitude possible? and what does it signify?—so that the content of digressive discourse tends to consist of speculation about its own discursive status, which is that of split subjectivity.

This, as it happens, is a fortunate circumstance for my present enterprise of beginning to formulate a poetics of digression, since it means that the paucity of reflection about digression in the rhetorical tradition can be overcome by supplementation from another tradition, that of the "reading" of digression that is performed in certain digressive texts. I propose in what follows to look briefly at the theory of digression that is performed, figured, and proposed—that is, in various ways made readable—in three such narratives, Xavier de Maistre's *Voyage autour de ma chambre*, an early short story by Samuel Beckett, "Ding Dong" (from *More Pricks than Kicks*), and Paul Auster's novella, *City of Glass*. To read the self-theorizing performed in such narratives may well be one of the few ways to do a "critical" (i.e., discriminating) reading of texts that tend, to the extent that they are composed of digressiveness, to block the hierarchizing (the discrimination of what is significant and what is insignificant) that is characteristic of our disciplinary practices as professional readers. Their well-judged drift in the direction of episodicity and fragmentation, their studied cultivation of aporia (in the etymological sense of pathlessness), do not only challenge the directionality and closure of narrativity; they also challenge the discriminatory power of "critical" reading. But they simultaneously invite a reading, or a metareading, by posing the question of what is at stake in their challenge to the power of critical reading.

My own "critical" claim in what follows is therefore that what is important in my three narratives is not so much the pleasure their digressiveness affords a "casual" reader (which I also am) as the theory of digression that they, quite incidentally (in affording that pleasure), make available to be read. I claim further, and will try to demonstrate, that there is a significant degree of overlap between the three theories they offer, which I understand as exemplifications and specifications of the etcetera principle. The three texts cohere, albeit loosely, as though they were digressive departures one from the other, and taken together they can therefore be read as enacting not only digression's tendency to escalate into further digression, but also its proclivity to test the limits that require it, while tending constantly in the direction of maximum disorder, to fail in its subversion of a culture of which it is inescapably a part. Digression *changes the subject* in more senses than one; but if it substitutes for social identity the knowledge that subjectivity is constituted by self-alterity and experienced, therefore, as digressive drift, it does not permit the digressive subject to attain ultimate freedom from the constraint of a social identity: a subject of digressive writing remains a writing subject and, as such, attached, by however tenuous a thread, to the order of culture.

Xavier de Maistre starts the drift by proposing a theory of second messages and the split subject. In Beckett, the second message becomes a factor of aporia and produces a form of subjective paralysis—etymologically, a "coming loose" or "coming unstrung"—that simultaneously alludes to a desired inertia and signifies the impossibility of its attainment, for this paralysis is a state of suspension that derives from digression's oxymoronic pull toward a state of stasis, on the one hand, and a need to move or even a desire to progress, that is, to move on, on the other. In Auster's text the inclination of digression toward inertia is pursued to the limit as we follow a writer-detective in his decline from making sense and pulling things together toward fragmentation and dispersal as his identity fuses with that of a character named Stillman. All these texts thus figure narrative as a form of *busyness* that is inhabited by a second message that is its tendency to inertia, worklessness, or *désœuvrement*, and they identify digression as at once the site and the indicator of narrative's proclivity to fall into disorder, a fall that is a pleasurable indulgence in de Maistre, but in Beckett an aporetic torment, and in Auster a drift that ends in obscurity, as digressive disjunctiveness escalates toward its limit.

Digression is thus revealed, in the end, to be a factor of entropy, that is, of the disorder that results *naturally* within discourse from the fact of its existence in time (which in turn appears as the ultimate condition of possibility of the digressive). But the incipient disorderliness of split subjectivity that de Maistre treats as an occasion for urbane wit becomes in Beckett the unattainability of a paradise of stasis, while—confirming the proposition that digressive narrative tests limits that it does not go beyond—Auster demonstrates that digression's enactment of the etcetera principle is at one and the same time that which allies it with disorder and that which, finally, prevents writing from crossing the brink into chaos, because—the etcetera being inexhaustible—going too far can never go far enough. If digression is the equivalent in the order of discourse to the category of nature in the order of culture, the loophole that it represents in the law is itself subject to a law: the law of loopholes. And the law of loopholes is that they are, in turn, constrained by the very order that they disturb.

Changing the subject can be said to have been one of the historical tasks of the nineteenth century. Between the time of Rousseau and the time of Freud, the deed was done: the dominance of the classical, or "narrative," subject was displaced by a new prominence of the modern, "theoretical," subject (which does not mean, far from it, that the former was or is "dead"). In this historical task, *Voyage autour de ma chambre* (1794) made the modest but not insignificant contribution of exemplifying very early the *changeability* of the subject, enacting the dynamics of subjectivity in terms of digression (following Sterne) and contributing to the poetics of digression a theory of second messages: that of "the soul and the beast." The first step in changing the subject was necessarily to perceive that subjectivity is changeable and to ask how that might be; thus de Maistre's demonstration of the digressiveness of the subject, combined with his theorizing of digressivity, constituted a significant move toward the historical emergence of the "theoretical" subject.

A major textual mode in *Voyage autour de ma chambre* is that of the inventory, and this recourse to list structure (a "paradigmatic" device of text construction that is also characteristic of description[6]) can be thought of as a device of loose cohesion, less strict by far than the "syntagmatic" cohesion of story or the cohesion of logical argumentation. Sentenced to forty-two days of house arrest for duelling, the narrator responds to this disciplinary measure by an affirmation of freedom, writing an account in forty-two chapters of his mental divagations during that time. These are figured as a voyage around his bedchamber in parodic imitation of the exhaustive accounts of more celebrated travelers, such as Cook and his companions Banks and Solander (chap. 38) or those whose narratives of an ascension of Mont Blanc or Etna include "the slightest circumstances, the number of travelers and mules, the quality of the supplies and excellent appetite displayed by the party, and every stumble of the mounts."[7] We are treated in this way to an inventory of furniture (the armchair, the bed, the desk), of the pictures on the wall, of the books on the shelves, and each item is an occasion for detailed praise and commentary, for these material inventories are only a pretext for, and the figure of, the text's overall project, which is to give a portrait of the narrator's personality by making a mental and psychic inventory of his subjectivity. That is why, of all the pictures on the wall, it is his mirror that is treated as the most engaging because it offers everyone who looks at it a self-portrait, "a perfect picture to which no objections can be made"; and this observation is the occasion of some speculation about the possibility of a "miroir moral," or psychological mirror, which is dismissed as being as useless as other mirrors (since no one would perceive the truth portrayed) but which nonetheless figures clearly, *en abyme*, the text's own project (see chap. 27). We learn, then, in no particular order, of the narrator's opinions on various and sundry matters, of his delight in daydreaming and indolence; of his distractedness, his sensibility, his love for Madame de Hautcastel, and his fondness for his dog; of his occasional brusqueness with his no less faithful servant; of his dreams; and so forth.

But the crucial point is not so much in the portrait's contents as in the fact that the portrayal is an unsystematic one. The topics that compose it are allowed to emerge (unlike the inventories of furniture, pictures, and books) in random order, arising as a matter of indirect or associative consequence—that is, as digressions—from the narrator's commentaries on the supposed subject at hand, the traveler's inventory of his room.[8] There is a reason for this reliance on an unsystematic approach to the inventorying of the narrator's personality; and it lies in his knowledge of the double constitution of his psyche: "Never have I more clearly realized that I am *double*," he writes as he is about to be released, his voyage ended but incomplete (113). For in confinement, he has been imaginatively freer than he will now be "under the yoke of daily business," and he regrets his unfinished inner travels, while knowing at the same time that "solitude resembles death" and looking forward to starting another kind of journey when he steps outside again. "Yes, I remember this house,—this doorway,—this staircase; I thrill in anticipation." This contradictoriness, which necessarily implies the impossibility of there being a coherent account of the narrator's personality, means that the complexity of his psyche cannot be accounted for by a procedure of analytic or rational abstraction but only by a process of inventory, a process that must furthermore be willing to accommodate itself to incoherence by permitting deviation and digression (*now* I want to stay in and complete my journey; *now* I want to go back to life outside . . .). The loose cohesion of the digressive inventorizing text thus corresponds to a perceived incoherence of the "double" subject.

If it is a product of doubleness, the very incoherence that resists abstraction or summary can be accounted for theoretically, however; and that is the function of the "system" that is ambitiously introduced to us in chapter 6 as the key to all the narrator's ideas and actions, and hence to the book itself: "mon système de l'âme et la bête" (my soul and beast system, 26). The ambitious word *system*, commonly employed in the period in the sense of a theory, is used here with more than a tinge of irony, in spite of the many further references to it as the book progresses; for the reader quickly comes to realize that the narrator's pride in his theory is not fully justified by its explanatory powers and that it is more like a Shandean hobbyhorse than a developed philosophical "system." But it is a notable, and notably early, statement of a pre-Freudian intuition that consciousness ("l'âme") does not exhaust the psyche, and that there is an other of consciousness, "the beast that is joined to our soul. It is really this substance that is our *other* and plays such strange tricks on us" (27). Notice, then, that the *other* is neither Platonic nor Cartesian in conception, that is, not radically separate from the soul—the narrator specifically dissociates himself from the former doctrine and implicitly from the latter, for the relation of "l'âme" and "la bête" is not to be construed, he says, as that of soul to body. Rather, the two are conjoined in a relation of split, such that the "other" and the "soul" are mutually dependent, each the other's other, one would be tempted to say, if the narrator—bent on emphasizing the originality of his discovery—did not reserve the word *autre* exclusively for "la bête" and describe it also as "a veritable individual, enjoying its own separate existence, tastes, likes and dislikes, and will." So it is as if the soul is understood as the mind's capacity for attention and consciousness while the beast represents inclinations of the subject that are not available to conscious control. It has, so to speak, a mind of its own.

This split but double control exercised over the subject by "l'âme" and "la bête" accounts in particular for the absent-mindedness that is so characteristic of the narrator; but distractedness, in turn, accounts for digression in its most primary sense of straying from the path.

> One day last summer I set out to go to court. I had been painting all morning and my soul, indulging in a meditation upon painting, left it up to the beast to get me to the king's palace. (29)

A lengthy account of this meditation on the pleasures and powers of painting follows. And then:

—While my soul was pursuing these reflections, the *other* was up to its own business, and God knows where it was heading!—Instead of betaking itself to the court as it had been ordered, it drifted so far to the left that at the point when my soul caught up with it it was at Madame de Hautcastel's door, half a mile from the royal palace.

I leave the reader to reflect on what would have happened if it had entered such a fair lady's house quite unaccompanied. (30)

There is some anticipation here, in the joke at the end, of the Freudian topography (ego and id) of the psyche; but the two salient points for my argument are that digression, figured as a "drift to the left," is treated as the work of "la bête," a manifestation of alterity in a split psyche, and that the alterity is not understood as a matter of successive control of the whole psyche by different instances but of a shared and simultaneous division of powers. Language, obviously, can follow the path of only "l'âme" or "la bête" at any given time, but digression will occur whenever these paths diverge, the soul going off into sublime speculation (while the beast tramps on), or the beast straying from its orders and swerving to the left, only to be "caught up with" in time by language, returning from its flight in company with the soul to record the impulses of desire. The simultaneous regime of the two instances combined with their tendency to split apart means that language, which cannot follow both at once, is engaged in a constant to and fro, diverging with the one or catching up with the other and each of them forcing it into digression.

The implication, then, is that all the discontinuous, digressive moments that constitute the text of *Voyage autour de ma chambre* should be read as coexisting simultaneously in the psyche, of which, taken together, they constitute a synchronous portrait. The digressivity of the narration does not imply a narrative having the temporal linearity and cohesion of a story (first X, then Y, then as a result Z) but a nonlinear simultaneity of split impulses that disrupts the diachronic syntax of narrative. When the digression about "l'âme et la bête" that began in chapter 6 ends at chapter 10, we learn therefore (the device is, of course, borrowed from Sterne), that in fact the voyage around the narrator's room begun in chapter 4 has never been discontinued:

while my soul, withdrawing into itself, was pursuing the tortuous twists and turns of metaphysics in the last chapter,—I was leaning comfortably back in my armchair . . . ; and as I swung to the right and left and moved forward, I had gradually reached a position near the wall. (35)

To which the narrator adds this comment: "That is the way I travel when I'm in no hurry."

One might well read this last phrase as referring only to the mode of travel that consists of leaning back on the legs of a chair and inching forward in zig-zag fashion, since that is a clear figuration of digressive narrative. But the reference is ambiguous and can also be taken to mean that it is the subjective split of soul and *other*—such that one engages in the twists and turns of metaphysics while the other moves the chair—that constitutes the narrator's way of traveling when he is in no hurry. If so, the passage does not insist simply on the simultaneity of split psychic instances that discourse can represent only in linear order. It also figures digressive narrative as the introduction into linear discourse of a certain double directionlessness: it advances, under the control of the beast, but twisting to left and right as it goes, and it is free to lose itself, with the soul, in the tortuous twists and turns of reflection. It is in this way that digression introduces into narrative linearity a tendency to inertia, which de Maistre calls "indolence," that makes it not only a way of traveling without leaving home but also a way of moving while staying still, a mode of travel for those who are not busy, and are "in no hurry." It is as if the inevitable movement of narrative, in its linearity and directionality, were understood to be *slowed down*—its *affairement* infected with *désœuvrement*—by digressiveness, as a manifestation of the simultaneous but diverging vectors that constitute, and split, the psyche.

It was, of course, as a mode of travel for the indolent that the narrator extolled his invention of bedchamber voyaging from the start:

> Would the most indolent person hesitate to set forth with me in order to obtain a pleasure that will cost neither trouble nor money? Courage, then, let's be off . . . ; we will travel in short stages, laughing along the road at voyagers who have seen Rome and Paris;—no obstacle will stand in our way, and giving ourselves over cheerfully to our imagination, we will follow it wherever its good pleasure takes us. (18)

But if the injection of indolence into travel, and of *désœuvrement* into narrative hurry and busyness, is understood here and throughout the *Voyage* as a form of pleasure, another key passage nevertheless suggests

a more thoughtful interpretation and seems to imply that the directionlessness of digressive narrative has a direction of its own. Xavier
de Maistre could not have known the second law of thermodynamics
any more than he could have read Freud, but his text demonstrates
insight into the idea that, where the directionality of story structure
is determined by its movement toward closure, the only direction
pursued by digressive narrative, with its much looser cohesion and
its injection of "indolence," can be the direction of time itself, that is,
the entropic tendency toward inertia and ultimate stasis. As if to hint
that digression's subversions of narrative linearity and the dispersal and
disorder it introduces into discursive cohesion can be understood as
a stage on the way to the ultimate dissolution of things in death, the
narrator describes armchair travel as a halt, agreeable and tempting,
but a halt on the way to the "exit."

> Thus, when I travel in my bedchamber, I rarely follow a straight line; I
> go from my table toward a picture . . . ; from there I set out obliquely in
> the direction of the door; but even though it is certainly my intention to
> reach it, should I encounter an armchair on the way, I make no bones
> about it and ensconce myself forthwith. An armchair is an excellent
> item of furniture; and in particular it is of the greatest utility to a
> contemplative man. (23)

At the exit point of the narrative, the narrator will still be hesitating
deliciously between the pleasures of armchair travel and the delights of
the world of "affaires" outside; and the text will end in this way without
closure, as if armchair travel and its haphazard inventory of the psyche
might go on forever. But the passage I have just quoted is followed by
a brief meditation on the pleasures of armchair reverie by a cosy fire,
which ends with this sentence: "The hours slide by you, and fall silently
into eternity, without your being aware of their sad passing" (23). A
pleasurable indulgence in disorder, digressive narrative is nonetheless
haunted by knowledge of entropy's alliance with the ultimate dispersal
of all things into the inertia of death, nature's final victory over *all* the
forms of culture.

A not dissimilar in-betweenness—but coded negatively (as torment)
rather than positively (as pleasure) characterizes the representation of
digressivity in Beckett's "Ding Dong" (1934), where the dialectics of
inner and outer lives, of freedom and constraint, of inertia and activity

define digressive subjectivity as the product of a painfully unresolved, and unresolvable, oxymoron: an inability either to move forward or to rest. Thus, digression is associated not with the cosy pleasure of the fireside and of the inventory of a psyche but with a curious form of metaphysical paralysis that arises from having the ability to approach a desired stasis without ever achieving it, so that the halfway situation represented by de Maistre's armchair becomes purgatorial. For Beckett's characters are caught somewhere between a necessary movement they cannot escape and an immobility they desire; and simultaneously, they vainly await the release of what is referred to in "Ding Dong" as the *internus homo* from "the faint inscriptions of the outer world" (38).[9]

Belacqua, the first of Beckett's seekers after escape and the protagonist of all the *More Pricks than Kicks* stories, is a restless figure whose mode of living digression has little in common with that of de Maistre's narrator, in spite of their common love of indolence. As his name, after a character in the *Purgatorio*, suggests,[10] his position between the desired inner and the unquittable outer world is not a delightful hesitancy, and these conditions—associated respectively (as in de Maistre) with motionlessness and movement—determine instead a ceaseless, tormented to and fro, "very nearly the reverse of the author of the Imitation's 'glad going out and sad coming in' " (37). The indolence in which he is "bogged" is attractive; but equally "the mere act of rising and going, irrespective of whence and whither, did him good" (36), for he is pursued by what he calls the Furies "and is able to stay put only at their good pleasure," obliged to resort constantly to motion in order to escape them (37). Entropy's tug in the direction of inertia, represented by Belacqua's "sinfully indolent *nature*" (36, my emphasis), is counterbalanced by an equal and opposite negentropic pull in the direction of the *city*, a place whose cultural status is associated not, as one might expect, with order, but with the disorder of haphazard motion. Digression, which names the outcome of this tension—the to and fro between an inner place that is not inner enough and an outer space that is not ordered enough—also names the haphazard movement imposed by the city. It is the purgatorial punishment, the torment of disjunction, that is inflicted on Belacqua, in lieu of the pleasurable drift from topic to topic of which de Maistre writes.

It's not odd, therefore, that all this movement is experienced by the sufferer as a torment of waiting. That's what is specifically purgatorial about it. Belacqua thinks of his existence as a kind of pause, variously described as a "moving pause" or a "Beethoven pause" (38). Like the long passages in remote keys which in Beethoven seem unable to resolve into the peace of a return to the tonic, such a busy pause is the opposite of stasis: it is a suspension. And it is this suspended state between inner and outer, immobility and movement, the freedom of chaos and the constraint of order, that defines the peculiar form of paralysis ("coming loose") that makes Belacqua not only a Dantean figure but also something of a Joycean Dubliner, a victim of "hemiplegia."[11] Constantly making choices—whether to go in or to come out, whether to move or to stay put, whether to move in this direction or that—but making choices in a world in which there is no reason to prefer any particular option over its alternative, results in aporia. No place can ever be the right place (since it must eventually be moved from), and no movement can ever be in the right direction (since no direction can lead to stasis). So many pathways are plausible that none imposes itself as necessary. Belacqua's world is aporetic, therefore, in the strictest etymological sense: it is bafflingly pathless.

One form such aporia takes is illustrated by the incident of the cinema queue. A Dantean line of people are awaiting admission to a cinema ("the Palace") in Pearse Street, like souls queueing for paradise. But the world in which they wait is subject to accident and disturbance: "All day the roadway was a tumult of buses, red and blue and silver" (41); and when one such bus runs over a little girl who has been sent out for milk, the crowd is "torn by conflicting desires: to keep their places and to see the excitement" (41). Keeping their places means continuing their passive wait, gradually inching toward stillness in the dark; seeing the excitement means turning back toward the external event, which is a distraction from the desired ingress but also from the endless wait, and so an "excitement."

Similarly, when Belacqua moves through the city, in the peculiar directionless way that is described as his "gress" or "gression" (that is, the product of a series of digressions), he is a prey to a dilemma equivalent to that of the cinema crowd. The haphazardness of his motion makes him peculiarly apt to receive impressions of all the random diversity of the city, and that is "not the least" of its charms—but it is also "very nearly the least."

Not the least charm of this pure blank movement, this gress or gression, was its aptness to receive, with or without the approval of the subject, in all their integrity the faint inscriptions of the outer world. Exempt from destination, it had not to shun the unforeseen nor turn aside from the agreeable odds and ends of vaudeville that are liable to crop up. This sensitiveness was not the least charm of this roaming. . . . But very nearly the least. (38)

This wonderful passage describes, perhaps, in the figure of Belacqua, the characteristically loiterly nineteenth-century genre of "flâneur realism," which Beckett's text resembles more than a little, as it follows Belacqua on one of his typical gresses through Dublin. But the Beckettian twist is a bitter one: it describes "flâneur realism" as an aporetic and purgatorial genre, caught—so to speak—on the horns of its own digressiveness, which simultaneously conforms to the confusion of the outer world and foreshadows, but does not realize, a more charming form of charm: the charm of total inertia. Such narrative, like Belacqua himself as the text describes him, thus has a "strong weakness for oxymoron" (38); it is the narrative equivalent of the hopelessly adulterated drink Belacqua likes to "overindulge" in: "gin and tonic-water."

But if Belacqua's mode of locomotion figures digressive narrative as a form of flânerie, all stops and starts corresponding to the oxymoronic tug of stasis and movement, the actual moment of digression corresponds to another form of aporia—that of having to choose, like Buridan's ass, between equally preferable and therefore equally unenticing paths, such that no path can be the path. This is the moment that specifically defines Belacqua's purgatorial predicament—his "moving pause" or waiting game—as a paralysis in the sense of an inability to move. Thus he emerges, in a parodic symbol of birth, from "the underground convenience in the maw of College Street," and squats—in approximation of the fetal, waiting position assumed by his namesake in Dante—at the foot of Thomas Moore's statue, "not that he had too much drink taken but simply that for the moment there were no grounds for his favouring one rather than another" (38–39).

> Yet he durst not dally. Was it not from brooding shill I, shall I, dilly, dally, that he had come out? Now the summons to move was a subpoena. Yet he found he could not, any more than Buridan's ass, move to right or left, backward or forward.

It is only the appearance of an apparently arbitrary "sign"—which happens to be the sight of a kind of Belacqua twin, a "blind paralytic" being wheeled home in one direction from his day's begging—that enables Belacqua finally to "ma[k]e off at all speed in the opposite direction" (40). Digression is thus defined here, not (as earlier) as the product of a contradictory tug between movement and stasis, but as a divergence in the path of two paralytics, one blind, one sighted, but equivalent in that each alludes by his paralysis to a desired inertia that is simultaneously suggested, and prevented, by the disorderly, pathless world of contingency, accident, and turmoil. For Belacqua's direction takes him into busy Pearse Street and the incident of the bus accident and the cinema queue; and it is from there that he will find his way to yet another point of temporary rest, this time in the "very grateful refuge" provided by a public house (41).

Since the blind paralytic is simultaneously making his way to his "home in the Coombe" (39), the implication is that all digressions tend ultimately toward a place of rest. Indeed the pub, Belacqua thinks, is "the only place where he could come to anchor and be happy," and he is persuaded that "all the wearisome tactics of gress and dud Beethoven would be done away if only he could spend his life in such a place" (42). The pub, in short, is a paradise, or at least one of the antechambers to paradise. For in the pub Belacqua is sold tickets for "Seats in heaven . . . tuppence apiece, four for a tanner" by a "woman of very remarkable presence indeed," (with features "petrified in radiance," in short, by a Beatrice figure, 44–45).

The problem with these figurations of an end—the pub, the tickets to heaven—is, however, that they are just figurations, not paradise itself but its signs. After some grumbling and hesitation, Belacqua buys the tickets, but is done out of his change and feels that he has been "[sold] a pup" (46). The coming to rest in the pub, similarly, is only temporary; there is a closing time ("they closed at ten," 42) that does not signify closure, for it means only that Belacqua will be ejected into the street again. *This* grateful place is not *the* desired place; and already at the point when "Beatrice" appeared, Belacqua had in fact, "having come briskly all the way from Tommy Moore," found himself again "sitting paralyzed and grieving in a pub of all places, good for nothing but to stare at his spoiling porter, and wait for a sign" (43).

What kind of sign *is* her appearance, then? Simply one of the many, like the Bovril sign in College Street, that lie "on all hands" and function only to produce digressions (39)? Or a sign of possible, eventual closure, an end to Beethoven pauses and directionless gress? As the woman departs, Belacqua remains staring into his now "dead" porter.

Now the woman went away and her countenance lighted her to her room in Townsend Street.

But Belacqua tarried a little to listen to the music. Then he also departed, but for Railway Street, beyond the river. (46)

Life has its mild comforts, there is tarrying and listening to the music while one's porter goes, entropically, flat. But the parting of the ways here—she to Townsend Street, he to Railway Street—repeats the disjunction of Belacqua and the blind paralytic at Thomas Moore's statue and seems to signal, therefore, that all signs are contingent and there is no end. It is, in short, the "old story" of "torment in the terms and in the intervals a measure of ease" (36)—a phrase that enables us, incidentally, to situate Xavier de Maistre in Beckett's universe and Beckett's pessimism with respect to de Maistre's urbane self-indulgence. If digressiveness in de Maistre is a pleasurable way station, a "measure of ease" on the way to dissolution and death, in Beckett it defines something more like a "torment in the terms," a purgatorial waiting game without much hope of exit, while one's porter nevertheless goes flat and dies.

Taken together, then, *Voyage autour de ma chambre* and "Ding Dong" define between them the dynamics of digression as being, like Belacqua, oxymoronic because the phenomenon is itself the site of a disjunction: always headed toward dissolution, chaos, and inertia, but always held back from the brink and unable to go, as Xavier de Maistre might put it, "too far" or as Samuel Beckett would say, "far enough." Always *controlled* in short, always pulled in the direction of order and cohesion by the negentropic constraints of a cultural order, or a syntax that, like narrative syntax, seems inherent in the very use of language and prevents it from falling into absolute incoherence. Yet, these constraints cannot be dispensed with if only because they are part of the very definition of the digressive, as that from which it departs, that against which, like the Maistrean beast with respect to the soul, it represents a desiring drift to the left. For Belacqua's desire, too, pulls him in the direction that the directionlessness of digression seems to indicate, the direction of stasis, and makes him glad coming in and sad going out; and in this perspective digression might well be defined as the oxymoronic product in discourse of an endless tug between the ordering power of language (or culture), and the disruptive influence of desire, with its natural proclivity for an inertia it can never achieve, and so its ceaseless leftward veering.[12] The figure for this oxymoronic product—both orderly and disorderly, neither orderly enough nor disorderly enough—is the city.

Given this oxymoronic situation, only two alternatives (both ideal) to the in-betweenness of digression suggest themselves: a language disentangled from the tug of desire or desire untrammeled by its involvement with language, that is, culture freed of natural interference or nature uninfluenced by the order of culture. An earthly paradise of order or the inertia of complete chaos—such are precisely the alternatives envisioned in Paul Auster's *City of Glass* (1986), *imagined* alternatives to a fallen *reality* figured by the Tower of Babel—alternatives too that turn out in the end to be identical. For, as a "great philosopher" (Heraclitus?) is cited as having said and as the yoyo is held to demonstrate, "the way up [to paradise] and the way down [to chaos] are one and the same" and the oxymoronic in-betweenness of digression itself thus constitutes an aporia.[13]

The Tower of Babel, here, is another city: New York. It has two main aspects, which also turn out to be aspects of the same problem. Language is one of them. In the fragmented, disarticulated, schizospeech of young Peter Stillman, who has been subjected to a barbaric linguistic experiment by his father, language has become a broken (or, etymologically, paralytic) thing, moving as Peter himself moves "like a marionette trying to walk without strings" (25). "In the dark," as he puts it, Peter knows the language of God, but human speech is for him a false and haphazard instrument; and his father, also called Peter Stillman, will later develop a theory of postlapsarian language, "severed from God" (70), in which "[n]ames became detached from things; words devolved into a collection of arbitrary signs. . . ." (70).

It was in an attempt to restore to language its original purity that Stillman undertook the famous experiment on his son, and he continues to pursue this quixotic effort. But now he wanders aimlessly in the streets of New York—a city that suits his purpose admirably, he says, because it is a "junk heap," "the brokenness is everywhere, the disarray is universal" (122)—scavenging broken and disused objects and following "haphazard itineraries" (94) whose trace on the street grid nevertheless spells out the truncated message OWER OF BAB (which seems to be the "broken" form of the words TOWER OF BABEL). His purpose is to invent, like some new Adam, names for these nondescript objects that will correspond to their reality and thus, as Mallarmé might have put it, to begin the poetic task of "remunerating" (restoring) the deficiency of languages.[14] The cure of young Peter's linguistic deficiency depends on Stillman Sr.'s ability to recreate an Edenic language—but meanwhile the son is an image of entropic brokenness and the father a figure of wandering digression.

The second aspect of the digressive world of Babel also manifests itself in Peter Stillman Jr., who, just as he cannot speak the language of God that he knows only in the dark, does not know his own real name: his linguistic difficulty is also a problem in identity. What he knows is that he is not Peter Stillman and that he has had to be taught "how to be Peter Stillman" (29). He might equally be Mr. White or Mr. Green or Mr. Sad, or Peter Rabbit. His identity, in other words, is alienated—subject to alterity—and has become haphazard in the way that a language arbitrarily disarticulated from reality is subject to the associations of chance. The problem of the otherness of identity is worked out more fully, however, in the figure of Quinn, both as a character and in his relation to Stillman Sr., for it is clear that Quinn and Stillman are a split pair, each the other's alter ego, like the more famous couple of Sancho Panza and Don Quixote; and the novel can be read as an account of the surmounting of this alienating duality, the history of the becoming-Stillman of Quinn, as an identity cure parallel to Stillman's attempted reform of language. But, as Stillman's name indicates, this resolution of the alienation of identity is to be achieved by Quinn's arriving at a state of inertia that abolishes difference. Where Stillman's aim is to reform language by returning it "upward" to an original paradisal state when there was no difference between words and the world, Quinn's becoming-Stillman will be a "downward" movement of the yoyo, following the entropic direction suggested by linguistic digressiveness and ontological dispersal rather than attempting to counter it. It will be a descent from the disorder of Babel toward the inertia of chaos.

Whereas the etymology of Stillman's name is patent,[15] Quinn's is glossed in a conversation he has with Stillman, who points out that it is the perfect postlapsarian name. It recalls "twin"—and then "it flies off in so many little directions at once":

> "I see many possibilities for this word, this Quinn, this . . . quintessence . . . of quiddity. Quick, for example. And quill. And quack.

And quirk. Hmmm. Rhymes with grin. Not to speak of kin. And pin. And tin. And bin. Hmmm. Even rhymes with djinn. Hmmm. And if you say it right, with been. Hmmm. Yes, very interesting. I like your name enormously, Mr. Quinn. . . ." (117)

This jerky little analysis seems to respond to the same kind of disjointed associative mechanisms that account, in part, for Peter Stillman Jr.'s schizoid speech. And, although his control of language is good, Quinn has indeed the wholly dispersed identity his name suggests: he is ontologically a marionette trying to walk without a string in the way that Peter is a figure of linguistic disarticulation. Thus, at the beginning of the novella, Quinn is given to taking walks through the city, "never really going anywhere" but feeling "always as if he was leaving himself behind" (8); and his response to this condition consists at first in writing detective novels, under the pseudonym of William Wilson,[16] and identifying with his own hero, who (in the context of Blanchot's *désœuvrement*) has the significant name of Max Work. This is an attempt to put the Humpty Dumpty of his identity together again, and to cure his ontological dispersal in an "upward" direction—but to do so, ironically, through vicarious identification with another.

Not surprisingly, when a "wrong number" gives Quinn the opportunity actually to impersonate a detective himself, he does so with some alacrity, assuming in the process the name of Paul Auster. For detectives, he explains, are people who, like writers (with whom they are "interchangeable," 15), "pull things together," "make sense of them"—the detective is the agent of an upward impulse toward order. What the novella actually traces out, however, as indicated already by the accumulation of names and pseudonyms with which Quinn now identifies, will be the disintegration of his detective persona through a gradual coming together of his already multiply split personality with that of Stillman as a personification of inertia. Once again, it is his desire for a unified identity that engages him in dispersal, and it doesn't take much ingenuity to realize that the addition of Peter Stillman to the group formed by Quinn, William Wilson, Max Work, and Paul Auster makes up a fivefold identity and that the unmentioned sense of Quinn's name is therefore that "he" is dispersed among a set of quintuplets. The solution to this problematic identity lies, however, not in returning to some condition of pure or undivided selfhood, but in pursuing to the limit the implications of his dispersal.

That is why there is for Quinn a particularly significant digressive moment, when he chooses, at random, the downward rather than the upward path. Stillman Sr. has been sent to prison for his cruelty to his son, but he is now to be released; Quinn's assignment is to tail him from the moment of his arrival at Grand Central so as to prevent him from doing further harm to the boy. But at the station two Stillmans appear, one drab, dazed, and seedy—an incipient bum—and the other "his exact twin" but with "a prosperous air about him," elegantly dressed and fitted out (90).

> Quinn froze. There was nothing he could do now that would not be a mistake. Whatever choice he made—and he had to make a choice— would be arbitrary, a submission to chance. Uncertainty would haunt him to the end. At that moment, the two Stillmans started on their way again. The first turned right, the second turned left. Quinn craved an amoeba's body, wanting to cut himself in half and run off in two directions at once. (9)

Shades of Belacqua. . . . But Quinn at first follows the prosperous Stillman to the left, then doubles back and follows the shabby twin to the right, thinking that this is more likely to be "the madman" (91) and opting indeed in this way, as it turns out, for the downward path to still(man)ness. He thus conforms to the implications of digression's affinity with disorder by choosing the direction of entropy rather than negentropy; yet the yoyo doctrine suggests that the other choice would not, in the end, have been wrong, except in the sense that no digressive option can be right, the implication of digression being that all choices are equal and lead in the direction of inertia. Whatever choice one makes—and one has to make a choice—it is arbitrary, a submission to chance, and in the end they all come down to the same thing.

His blind choice made, Quinn takes to the streets, following the shuffling old man as he pursues his "haphazard itineraries," "ransacking the chaos of Stillman's movements for some glimmer of cogency" and, like the good detective he is trying to be or like Belacqua again, "looking for a sign" (105). But the sign, when it comes— once more as in Beckett—merely confirms the unreliability of signs. It is the message OWER OF BAB, which might (or might not) be a purely accidental happenstance. The detective and the flâneur, in Walter Benjamin's famous analysis of these two nineteenth-century figures, have much in common; but Benjamin situates their commonality in the surveillance he perceives the two figures to exercise: his flâneur, in other words, is assimilated to the detective.[17] In Auster it is the other way round. Here it is the detective's very skill in the adequation of his thought to the mind of the other—the skill of Poe's Dupin— that determines his becoming the other, his gradual abandonment of the task of surveillance in order to become the flâneur himself, in the latter's role as a loiterly, digressive, and disreputable figure, the opposite of one who "pulls things together" and "makes sense of them."

Thus, when Stillman finally disappears, becoming "part of the city . . . a speck . . . a brick in an endless wall of bricks" (141)— Melville's Bartleby is in the intertext—Quinn is left wandering the city again in a haphazard itinerary that is now his own—an itinerary that the text reproduces in fully inventorying detail, deploying verbs of digres- sion such as "turning," "cutting right," "shifting course," "veering left," "angling," "swinging around," "sliding" and "hooking," in an account of aimless drift that goes on for two pages (163–65). Finally, Quinn camps permanently outside the apartment he believes to be occupied by Stillman Jr. and Mrs. Stillman, reducing eating and sleeping to a minimum, taking shelter like a Beckett tramp in a garbage can, and like Stillman "melt[ing] into the walls of the city" (178). He winds up in the empty apartment writing—again like a Beckett character— in his notebook and gradually slipping into the "growing darkness" (199) (a darkness that recalls the dark in which Stillman Jr. heard the language of God, as well as the "Henry Dark" who is one of Stillman's own pseudonyms) as the space in his notebook dwindles and his time diminishes toward a timelessness of stasis.

The stress here on writing suggests that some revision is necessary in Quinn's earlier confident assessment of the interchangeability of the writer and the detective. There is, it now seems, writing and writing: some writers, like detectives, pull things together and make sense of them, but others, like bums, record Humpty Dumpty's fragmentedness and dispersal. These are the writers whose writing is the trace of an aimless shuffling through the streets, like Quinn's notes in his red notebook on Stillman's haphazard itineraries—the same notebook that serves, after Stillman's disappearance, for the jottings that record scattered impressions of Quinn's own "gress" or "gression" through the city. These fragments do not "make sense"; they are a random inventory, not unlike Stillman's collection of anonymous objects, of the human trash in the junk heap of New York. For example,

> There are the women with their shopping bags and the men with their
> cardboard boxes, hauling their possessions from one place to the next,
> forever on the move, as if it mattered where they were. There is the man
> wrapped in the American flag. There is the woman with a Halloween
> mask on her face. There is the man. . . . There is the man. . . . There is
> the woman. . . . There is the man. . . . (168)

As the novella progresses, and Quinn takes refuge in the Stillman
apartment, we learn that his entries now consist mainly of "marginal
questions" (197–98)—scarcely the wherewithal of sense-making. And
the notebook's final sentence, the only remaining fragment that is
quoted, turns out to be not an effort to pull things together but an
homage to the etcetera principle: "What will happen when there are
no more pages in the red notebook?" (200). For this is writing that,
instead of making sense, is content, at the price of its own cohesiveness,
to be at one with the infinite diversity of the world.

> Quinn no longer had any interest in himself. He wrote about the stars,
> the earth, his hopes for mankind. He felt that his words had been severed
> from him, that now they were a part of the world at large, as real and
> specific as a stone, or a lake, or a flower. They no longer had anything
> to do with him. (200)

The principle of such writing is no longer identity, therefore; and
the subject has been changed. A desired but unattained exhaustiveness
is at stake—the etcetera principle—which is why it is painful for Quinn
to realize that his supply of stationery will run out before the world—
and hence his writerly subjectivity—does. "He wanted to go on writing
about it, and it pained him to know that this would not be possible"
(200). The notebook will inevitably run out of pages, and writing must
cease before its inventory of the world is done; its only conclusion is
etcetera.

The abandonment of identity implied by Quinn's "bum" writing
as opposed to his "detective" writing also comments eloquently on
the third theory of writing presented in the book. After the detective
theory and before the bum's practice, a speculation about writing as a
means of reconstructing dispersed identity is proposed to Quinn by the
writer Paul Auster, whom he visits in the hope that he will prove to be
the detective Paul Auster from whom he has derived his own alias (and
who might, therefore, be capable, as a "real" detective, of making sense
of Stillman and his mysterious disappearance). Auster's theory takes

the form of an essay on *Don Quixote* that can be mapped without too much strain onto *City of Glass*. According to Auster's view, the author of *Quixote* is not Cervantes so much as it is Cid Hamete Benengali, who is himself a composite of Sancho, the priest, the barber, and the bachelor Samson Carrasco (all figures who represent with respect to the knight something like Quinn's surveillance function with respect to Stillman, and who produce Cid Hamete, in turn, as quintuplets). His (their) idea had been to cure Quixote's madness by recording "each of his absurd and ludicrous delusions, so that when he finally read the book himself, he would see the error of his ways" (153). This is a view of writing as the production of order out of disorder—the cure of "madness" like Quixote's or Stillman's by making *sense* out of it—and, at the same time, as the reduction of difference to identity.

But the trouble is that Auster has a second theory—or his theory has a "second message." It is possible that Don Quixote is the true author and "orchestrated the whole thing himself" (153), setting up the Cid Hamete group for reasons of his own. Quixote wasn't really mad, just indulging in an elaborate hoax. In terms of *City of Glass*, this would make Stillman (not Quinn) the author figure, not really mad at all but having a crazy wisdom like Quixote and drawing Quinn into an adventure that offers him something like a means of salvation—a salvation that involves, however, not the writing of sanity and identity but the writing of the diversity of the world, the writing of inventory and the etcetera principle, the writing of a dissolved subjectivity and of a certain madness. Which of these two readings (of *Quixote*, of *City of Glass*) is actually the case? There is no way of choosing, and it is clear that the conversation with Auster thus represents the novella's second disjunctive, digressive moment, another parting of the ways at which an impossible choice must be made, but this time by the reader: a choice about the nature of the writing—Quinn-like or Stillmanesque? Cid Hamete-ish or Quixotic? a factor of order or of "madness"?—that lies on the page. A choice that cannot be made, since again the upward path (in this case, detective writing) and the downward path (i.e., bum writing) are, *in the end*, one and the same. For it is here, precisely that the figure of the yoyo is introduced (156).

The novella is pinned in this way on its own aporetic moment, which signifies the fundamental joinedness of detective writing and bum writing, of sense making and the making of an endless inventory, options between which hesitation and choice are nevertheless inevitable. And just as Quinn is left, after his conversation with Auster, with the impression of having heard a "joke that stopped short of its punchline" (155), so too the novella ends without having been able to follow Quinn's becoming Stillman to the point of his, or its, going over the brink—the ultimate brink—beyond which would lie absolute inertia, the total abolition of difference. Quinn can, of course, only metaphorically be said to "become Stillman," if only because at the end the text continues to maintain a difference between the Stillman who has disappeared and the Quinn who survives, or dies, or disappears too—"[a]t this point the story becomes obscure" (200), melding into a darkness of its own. In similar fashion, the novella itself remains a well-written text—containing, for example, some of the most perfectly constructed sentences outside of the work of Beckett and with an intricate thematic and compositional structure—never losing its affinity with the detective writing of which it is a kind of pastiche even as it tails Quinn's own descent into bum writing. It does not take us into chaos; it explores the mutual entailments of chaos and order as an orderly exploration of the world of disorder that is itself as much an homage to pattern as it expresses a longing for release into inertia.

What emerges from a study of these digressive texts appears to be a vision of discourse, of human subjectivity, and of culture itself as sites neither of perfect order nor of absolute chaos but of a symbiotic and oxymoronic embrace of the orderly and the disorderly, such that what defines them is a problematics of disjunction and aporia. For it is the need to make choices under conditions that produce choice as aleatory that defines the condition of culture, and so the position of the subject as well as the nature of discourse, when they are viewed from the perspective of digression. We cannot not make choices that imply some principle of discrimination, but we cannot know that our choices are anything other than digressions, that is, "departures" from the cohesiveness, the coherence, and the correctness for which we aim. And it is the city—as a place where the busyness of our choicemaking selves combines with the entropic drift toward inertia that is implied by digression—that exemplifies, at least for writers like Beckett and Auster, this simultaneously oxymoronic and disjunctive condition (a fact that perhaps suggests a special relevance of the phenomenon of digression to the historical circumstances of "modernity").

In such a culture, texts that flaunt and theorize their own digressiveness are inevitably in an ambiguous situation. On the one hand they present themselves, at least implicitly, as *paradigmatic* of (to borrow another Beckett title) "how it is." On the other hand, they figure as *exceptional*, accidental, and secondary in the view of an official culture that insists on dichotomizing the oxymoronic and on favoring the values of order, cohesion, system, and rationality— of informed choices—as absolutes that make manifestations of the disorderly seem merely insignificant and negligible. Such texts, I have argued, are treated not quite as transgressive, since they are endowed with a certain half-acknowledged legitimacy, but as always tending in the direction of a transgression of cultural law even as, in their enactment of a supposed natural order of things—a nature controlled and circumscribed by culture—they provide us with pleasure and relief derived from our sense of a certain relaxation of cultural constraints. In that ambiguity, I suggest, lies the reason why digression has not been a favored topic in the more authorized traditions of Western thought: its "truths" are too uncomfortable in a culture that emphasizes, as ours does, the ordering power of human discourse and thought. But therein lies the reason also why we ought now, perhaps, to give the topic a more careful consideration than I have been able to do in this brief introductory sketch.

Time Out: Meditation and the Escalator Principle

So essential to the productive economy are the small pleasures of "fugue"—napping in class, calling in sick, walking the dog—that time out is sometimes actually institutionalized and scheduled into the regulated hours of work. We take annual vacations at predetermined dates and go to lunch each day at the appointed hour. To the extent that it tells a story, Nicholson Baker's novel, *The Mezzanine*, tells the story of such a period of scheduled time out.[1] A young office worker on lunch break leaves his place of employment on the mezzanine, takes the escalator down to the street, walks around a bit, buys some lunch and a pair of shoelaces to replace those that have just broken on him, sits in the sun with a copy of the *Meditations* of Marcus Aurelius in his lap—and takes the escalator back up to work.

This, from the point of view of conventional literary expectations, is an impoverished and trivial scenario. But the poverty of narrative interest is an indicator, perhaps, that Baker's text seeks ways to give pleasure and earn authority other than those that are characteristic of narrative. What are these ways? How do they relate to the requirements of narrative interest? Can we understand them as something like a narrative equivalent of "time out," providing a break from the goal-orientedness of story in the way that lunch hour provides a break from the requirements of economic productivity?

The triviality of Baker's narrative suggests, in turn, a hypothesis that has more to do with philosophical questions than with narrative as such. What kind of text treats the trivial as significant? How does it go about establishing the importance of the (supposedly) trivial? What modifications does this suppose in conceptions of knowledge and in the evaluations on which our recognition of knowledge rests? Is there something like an *epistemological* "time out" that might have philosophical, educational, or critical interest?

This chapter is an attempt to find a passage between these two sets of questions: the question of textual pleasure as a counternarrative practice, and the question of the transvaluation of the trivial and its consequences for knowledge. In so doing, I will be led to explore a thematics of passage in Baker's own work, which, I will contend, substitutes for the principle of narrative, which inevitably tends toward closure, the principle of meditative genres of thought and writing, which is the idea that one thing leads not to an end but to another. This idea defines the practice of digression as it is governed by the etcetera principle (chapter 4); but it emphasizes the continuity entailed in digressive moves rather than the disjunctive effects—digression's tendency toward disorder—that were prominent in the previous chapter. The escalator, as we shall see, is the text's figure for this meditative principle, which is also the principle of mediation.

But the escalator is also the means of transport that takes us down from our orderly offices into the relatively unconstrained world of the street, where we walk around a bit before taking the escalator back up to work. What forms of connectedness does it imply, what to-and-fro passages does it authorize, between counternarrative practices and narrative constraints? Between philosophizing the insignificant and more majestic modes of thought? Between arts of fugue and the world of productive work? That is the question (the set of questions) that underlies this chapter as a whole.

THE ESCALATOR PRINCIPLE

In *U and I*, an essay on John Updike that bears the motto: "It may be us they wish to meet but it's themselves they want to talk about" (Cyril Connolly), Nicholson Baker—talking about himself, then—takes issue with Updike for a remark about a descriptive passage that "would clog any narrative":

> What he meant to say, I thought, I hoped, was that Edmund Wilson's passage was simply no good, not that one's aim was to avoid clogging narratives with description. The only thing I *like* are the clogs. . . . I wanted my first novel [*The Mezzanine*] to be a veritable infarct of narrative cloggers; the trick being to feel your way through each clog by blowing it up until its obstructiveness finally revealed not blank mass but unlooked-for seepage-points of passage.[2]

(I've omitted from the second sentence a long descriptive clog about the signs of impatience Baker gives "when, late in most novels, there are no more [clogs] in the pipeline to slow things down"—a clog that is further clogged by a parenthesis that compares picking at the price sticker on the back of a book as one reads with the delight, shared by Updike and Baker, of "picking a psoriasis lesion." Welcome to Nicholson Baker's world, and let us note immediately that unclogged narratives, going straight to the point, have no time for the trivial whereas Baker might have said of the trivial what he says of clogs, that it is the only thing he likes. His work effortlessly realizes the potential for aesthetic and philosophical transvaluation that lies within the trivial, and hence implies a positive valuation of "having time.")

Linked associatively (not narratively or logically) to this passage, the following paragraph digresses, or appears to digress, into the description of a clogged sewer pipe that turned out to be obstructed by tampons: "their strings caught on a tufty invading root and expanded to the full extent of their puff, about thirty of them. Earthworms took up residence in them [producing] an Edenic scene in the lower garden near the standpipe: around the probe . . . was a roil of roots and black tampon fruits and pinkly prosperous earthworms" (74). "And why shouldn't this clog clog some narrative of mine?" Baker asks rhetorically, omitting to specify that it has just done so. "To the worms it was not obstructive, it wasn't revolting, it was life itself. It is life itself." And he goes on, in another parenthesis, to compare their owner's use of tampons to Elvis Presley's profligacy with scarves in his decline, "barely touching them to his neck before flinging them mechanically out to the audience as souvenirs."

Rhetorical appeals, especially to "life itself," are pretty dubious, but it's worth noticing that, if narrative clogging is Baker's pleasure, his intent has something to do with representing an alternative, worm's eye view of what life is—a complex "roil" that resists narrative and can only be approached descriptively, with the aid of connections and associations that are essentially metaphoric in kind (Wilson's clogged narrative and the blocked sewer; a price sticker and a psoriasis lesion; Presley's scarves and an excessive consumption of tampons). My problem is how to approach such luxuriant writing critically, especially when criticism is habitually so invested in narrative, with its speed and selectivity, and has so little time for the trivial. Loiterly writing, of which Baker's is exemplary, is anticritical in its very principle (that is *its* critical function): it blocks critical gestures with the same glee that it delights in clogging narrative structures. The temptation is therefore simply to quote Baker's prose in extenso, transmitting the pleasure his sentences give. But criticism is by definition discriminatory; it works—like narrative—by hierarchizing (this is significant, that is secondary), and its aim is not to be comprehensive but to comprehend. As Roland Barthes points out in *The Pleasure of the Text*, a theory of pleasure is inevitably inadequate with respect to pleasure itself, and it is in part a theory of the pleasure that Baker's text gives, not pleasure itself, that this chapter aims to deliver.[3] You have been warned.

What is at issue in Baker's clogging of narrative is a certain reversal of proportion and emphasis between narrative structure, with its reliance on story and its beginning-middle-end grammar of closure, and the paradigmatic or listing dimension of discourse that spins out a narrative enunciation in time, employing devices like description, parenthesis, asyndeton, digression, so that the supposedly secondary comes to occupy the foreground of attention, and the hierarchizing distinction between the relevant and the pointless, on which story depends, begins to lose its own cogency. Baker, he says, gets "that fidgety feeling" (73) in reading novels and starts to pick at the price sticker as the fiction moves toward closure and allows less occasion for clogs. It isn't delay in getting to the point but the failure to delay, too hasty point making, that makes him itchy. Barthes's theory of textual (really, readerly) pleasure has been unfairly reduced to the sentence that describes the erotic site in text as comparable to the place at which a garment "gapes" (and we will come in due course to the matter of textual gaping). Of more immediate relevance here, both to Baker's writing practice and to his readerly fidgets as closure approaches, is the passage in *The Pleasure of the Text* (29–30) in which text is described as a kind of "time out" in what Barthes calls "the warfare of ideologies" (whereby Barthes means something like instrumental uses of language). Textual pleasure is like the relaxed moments that are so precious to the combatants in warfare proper when there is time to linger over a beer or a quiet conversation; one does not want such moments to end. And Barthes goes on to account for this "withdrawn" position of texts with respect to ideological discourse by referring, precisely, to their paradigmatic dimension. In them, discourse undergoes a process of "progressive extenuation"; the story is spun out and language is stretched—and a stretched text will eventually come to gape.

Like all Barthes's dichotomies (the readerly and the writerly, the text of pleasure and the text of *jouissance*, etc.) this one—between closed, point making, ideological discourse and extenuated or spun out, pleasurable text—should be understood as merely heuristic, and it is certainly not part of my own intention to absolve loiterly texts of an ideological function. Pleasure, too, has its place in the "pole-mological space" of culture.[4] It's evident, too, that story structure, headed for closure, and paradigmatic lingering, enacting the etcetera principle, are mutually dependent and inevitably co-occur. But in texts of pleasure it's nevertheless paradigmatic extension that predominates: in them, time, constructed in narrative configurations as end-oriented, becomes more episodic and extendable, as the vehicle of a readerly pleasure that might, ideally, never end. Baker puts it this way, in a later passage in which Updike is again upbraided for a hasty judgment, this time of Nabokov (accused by Updike of failing to generate narrative suspense): "[R]eally, the only suspense a book needs, as Updike by now must know, having tolerantly motored through dozens of much more experimental bad novels [than *Glory*] for our benefit, is not 'What will happen next?' but simply 'Will I ever want to stop reading?'" (121).

Let's not forget, though, that the defense of clogging with which I started had a point of its own, which was the revelation of an alternative view of things. "[T]he trick," Baker says, "[is] to feel your way through each clog by blowing it up" until it reveals "unlooked-for seepage-points of passage." The submerged pun, here, suggests that the trick of clogging is so to "blow up"—distend or extenuate—narrative discourse that its end-oriented linearity is "blown up" in the sense of exploded. But the point of the explosion is to substitute for linear narrative syntax a "roil" of *other* connections, like the tangle of worms and tampons in the sewer, connections made possible by the discovery of unexpected "seepage-points." What is an "infarct" to the narrative is "life itself" to those worms. To obstruct the unidirectionality of narrative opens it up, then, to the unlimited potentialities of textual multidirectionality, such that, through unlooked-for seepage-points, it can move, at any moment, in any number of possible directions (which are "digressive" with respect to the narrative but not necessarily, for that reason, incoherent or irrelevant). And because the points of passage are "unlooked for," the alternative view of things that emerges contrasts pleasurably with the predictability of conventional narrative structures.

In *The Mezzanine*, this exploded aspect of clogged narrative is simulated on the page by a riot of footnotes that divide the reader's attention at various seepage-points and induce the exquisite pleasure—and anxiety—of hesitation. One can't quite decide whether to continue

following the text (and miss the relevant material in the note) or
to plunge into a luxuriant note (and risk "losing track" of the text's
direction). These notes, in other words, enact both the pleasure and
the frustration that digression induces because they stage as an actual
alternative a certain nexus between a simplifying sense of order and a
dehierarchizing disorder, between simply following a given direction
and the "pathlessness" (aporia) that is a product of multiple options.
Or so it would be if "text" could be straightforwardly identified with
narrative in this novel and "footnotes" viewed as departures from
a simple story line. But Baker's narrative, such as it is, is already
thoroughly clogged and his footnotes are themselves expansive and
subject to digressions of their own, having the same "Will I ever want
to stop reading?" quality as the text "proper." The option they stage is
therefore not between linear "narrative" and disjunctive "digression,"
but between something like the continuity of an *already* extenuated,
distended narrative text and supposed discontinuities that are in fact
scarcely distinguishable from the extenuations that are the natural
product of the spinning out process itself. The supposed alternative —
an ultimately false one — is between a text that is "blown up" in the sense
of extended and a text that is "blown up" in the sense of exploded.
This is exactly the difference (that does not admit of distinction)
between Barthes's text of pleasure and his text of *jouissance*; and Baker's
footnotes are points of seepage that have the particular quality of
enacting the erotic moment of Barthesian "gape." But points of seepage
are everywhere in his text and the gape corresponds only to the moment
when the continuities of seepage have become so stretched that they
are perceived as discontinuities.

Digression, as the seepage of thought that disturbs its linear progression, enacting textual extenuation as a phenomenon that baffles
the distinction between continuity and discontinuity, is, then, the
pleasure that Baker's writing luxuriously explores, in the text, in the
footnotes, and in the relation between the two. As in Perec or Proust,
digression's counternarrative affinity with the paradigmatic dimension,
the dimension of lists and listing, is itself associated with memory, as
the faculty that both realizes mental continuities and, on occasion,
interrupts them with sudden disjunctions, or "second messages."[5] (In
ordinary conversation, "Oh, that reminds me of . . ." is both a way of
keeping the discourse flowing and a device for *changing the subject*.)
Just so, washing the face is described in *The Mezzanine* as a pleasurable

moment of memory-induced gape, in which "sudden signals of warmth flooding your brain from the nerves of the face, especially the eyelids, unmoor your thinking for an instant, dislodging your attention from any thought that had been in progress and causing it to slide back randomly to the first fixed spot in memory that it finds" (95). But the gape itself, "dislodging" and "unmooring" as it is, nevertheless becomes an experience of continuity here; it is a "slide" of the mind into randomness that is halted when one hits on a "fixed spot" and commences another "progress"—a progress that is, of course, liable to interruption in due course from further slides.

Whereas some digressive writers tend to explore the implications of the disjunctiveness and pathlessness inherent in digression and its power to "change the subject," Baker is generally more concerned, then, with the continuity digression also implies, a continuity-in-disjunction that induces metaphors like "seepage" or the "slide" of memory and derives from the fact that digression is not a random occurrence but a mediated, and so motivated, phenomenon whose dislodgings, un-moorings, interruptions, and disjunctures can therefore never be ab-solute. If metaphor is Baker's characteristic mode and the principle vehicle of his digressive style, it is because metaphor inevitably implies similarity in difference and difference in similarity, since the terms of metaphor are by definition unlike, yet assimilable to, each other. In-deed, the more apparently unlike they are, the more vivid and effective is the perception of their similarity.

But both memory and metaphor thus pose the problem of me-diation as the slide through "randomness" that connects two fixed points. The mediations are so fine, subtle, or complex that language, a differential system, cannot represent them, and their multiplicity is experienced as chaos, a kind of swoon of the analytic consciousness as it slides "randomly" between the points that it is able to grasp or fix on. The multidirectionality of pathlessness that is prized in a clogged or blown up text such as Baker's is thus ideally realized in those between-moments of slide that the text itself can't represent because they elude the descriptive powers of language. To speak of a "roil" of earthworms in a sewer pipe is both to designate, and to give up on, a problem of description: "'I found your problem,' the rooter called up nonchalantly, and beckoned me down to an idyllic scene in the lower garden near the standpipe: . . . 'Best cut the strings off,' he advised, and wrote 'sanetery napkins' on the invoice—our vocabulary always lags reality" (*U and I*, 74). Baker has no intention of "cutting the strings off" his writing, which aims rather to be all strings, and his vocabulary, fortunately, does not lag reality quite as egregiously as the rooter's. Indeed, the characteristic quality of his writing lies most obviously in the precision and close detail, the manic myopia and brilliant accuracy of his descriptive style, which borders on something that could be called descriptivitis (or perhaps paradigmomania). But, as the rooter says, there's the problem. For no description can ever be complete; it is always obliged to imply an "etcetera," corresponding to what memory forgets and language can't, or doesn't, say. Baker's prodigiously precise descriptions, characteristically adduced in support of a metaphoric relation between two terms, thus function, in the end, as mere gestures—gestures in the direction of making explicit all those mediations that can't be said—and hence as signs that the descriptions themselves require supplementation. It is, in other words, for the reader to supply the slides of memory, the leap between the metaphoric terms, without which the text is incomplete but which description itself, however comprehensive it seeks to be, can never fully furnish. The instance of reading is thus an enactment of the textual "etcetera" and the site of all the mediations on which the text depends but which it can't provide, and without which it fails as a vehicle of pleasure.

"Metaphor," it is frequently pointed out, is etymologically cognate with "transport": it gets us smoothly from point A to point B, a mediator of distance. In modern Greece, "metaphor" designates a literal means of transportation, say a bus or a shuttle. Reading, as the site where textual mediation is realized, might therefore be appropriately described as a vehicle of local transport, of travel without leaving home, in which one moves, metaphorically, on the spot. As the flâneur reads the life of the streets, making the connections that attempt to make sense of urban experience, the reader is a flâneur of texts, and the reader's pleasure is that of the mediating slide, the experience of continuity in discontinuity and discontinuity in continuity. As a child, the narrator of *The Mezzanine* informs us, he was fond of boats, cars, trains, and planes but was "more interested in systems of local transport" (35) such as (and here a long, carefully detailed, descriptive list intervenes, which I can only summarize) airport luggage-handling systems, conveyor belts at the supermarket checkout, those connecting the store's interior to the parking lot, milk-bottling machines, marble chutes, Olympic bobsled or luge tracks, the "hanger-management

systems" at the dry cleaner's, laundry lines, the barbecue-chicken display at Woolworth's and rotating Timex watch displays, or finally the
cylindrical roller-cookers on which hot dogs slowly turn. But one
further system of local transport—something like the list's "etcetera,"
similar to the other items although already their other—remains as
the one from which the adult narrator still derives pleasure. It is the
escalator, which "shared qualities with all of these systems, with one
difference: it was the only one I could get on and ride" (36). As the
best metaphor of metaphor of them all, then, it is the escalator that
furnishes the governing figure of *The Mezzanine*, which is framed by
an account of an escalator ride and also uses the escalator as the vehicle
of its own metaphoric self definition, the figure *en abyme* of textuality as
it is conceived in this text. So I will say that *The Mezzanine* exemplifies a
particular variant of the etcetera principle that can be called the escalator
principle.

Where the etcetera principle is a principle of open-endedness, its
maxim being that there is always an etcetera, the maxim of the escalator
principle is that one thing leads to another, and it is a principle of
mediation as seepage—one thing leads to another, as the escalator
takes us from one floor to the next, by slow and gradual intervening
"steps." But in the principle of seepage, as we have already seen, there
also lies a potential for *escalation*: being "blown up" incrementally—
sufficiently slowed down and delayed, clogged in their movement
toward a goal or destination—the steps of discourse are capable of
exploding narrative linearity into pathlessness and multidirectionality.
The "long hypotenuse" that is an escalator (59) seems at first blush an
unlikely candidate as a figure for the multidirectionality of an exploded
text: it is more obviously suggestive of linear narrative progression
from a beginning to an end via a succession of intervening steps. But
Baker's ingenuity as a master of metaphor is more than adequate to
the task of suggesting, via a single image—that of the escalator—that
there is a continuity between mediation as the vehicle of a smooth ride
from point to point and mediation as the instrument of an explosion
of linearity.

The crucial point in this respect is that the escalator is a set of gradually moving steps or graduations. Although there's no engineering reason why it shouldn't be a simple inclined conveyor belt, historical and
cultural reasons have caused it to imitate a staircase (and Baker discusses
his youthful belief that one should therefore advance on an escalator

"at the normal rate you climbed stairs at home," 100). In spite of its step-by-step structure, its motion however is conveyor-belt smooth: one can glide locally on an escalator from point to point, "in the pose of George Washington crossing the Potomac" (99), even though one is in fact advancing by *degrees*. But as a visual phenomenon—and again because it is made of steps that move—the escalator is not the vehicle of a smooth ride so much as it is an object that dazzles the eye, which is unable to maintain the distinction between successive steps on which linearity depends:

> Grooved surfaces slid out from underneath the lobby floor and with an almost botanical gradualness segmented themselves into separate steps. As each step arose, it seemed individual and easily distinguished from the others, but after a few feet of escalation, it became difficult to track, because the eye moves in little hops when it is following a slow-moving pattern, and sometimes a hop lands the gaze on a step that is one above or below the one you had fixed on; you find yourself skipping back down to the early, emergent part of the climb, where things are clearer. It's like trying to follow the curve on a slowly rotating drill bit, or trying to magnify in with your eye to enter the first groove of a record and track the spiral visually as the record turns, getting lost in the gray anfractuosities almost immediately. (59)

This effect of dazzle, it is clear, is for Baker a pleasurable one (cf. "I love the constancy of shine on the edges of moving objects" [3] and, in *U and I*, "[t]he only thing I *like* are the clogs" [73]). But it arises here, on the one hand, from an effect of "escalation," and on the other from the fact that the eye shares a deficiency with language in that it can only view differentially (it moves in "little hops") what is nevertheless experienced as a continuum, whether it be the slide of memory between two fixed points in the progress of thought or the slow upward climb of an escalator. The escalator blows up (magnifies) the mediating slide of metaphor or memory and slows it down; but it still blows up (explodes) the sense of linearity by making it impossible to track its moving steps.

So the confusion of the eye that seeks to track the steps of the escalator in linear fashion is a figure for the "randomness" associated with mediating slides and imitated—in similarly blown up, slowed down fashion—by the multidirectional text. The eye hops here like that of the reader encountering a footnote and unsure whether to follow the textual continuity or to skip to the foot of the page, where disjunction is more clearly (but still deceptively) signaled. If the escalator is a "climb," a *gradus* (as in *Gradus ad Parnassum*, the title of old handbooks of rhetoric), the movement of escalation nevertheless reveals how it is that linear *pro*-gression, from point to point, is not incompatible with, and in fact can be seen to generate, clogging, seepage, and blowing up — the delights of *di*-gression and multidirectionality. And the principle of escalation, it emerges, is the *gradual* which functions here like the pun on blowing up in the passage from *U and I* with which I began, in that "an almost botanical gradualness" is on the one hand the secret of the smoothness of the escalator's step-by-step ride, and on the other what baffles the eye, confronted with this "slow moving pattern."

If an escalator ride is therefore, as Baker puts it, failing to resist the obvious pun, "the vehicle of my memoir" (37), it is because memoirs necessarily invoke memory as the mediating principle that holds things together and simultaneously disjoins them, and with it metaphor as the mediating principle of continuity in discontinuity and discontinuity in continuity that governs the associative working of memory as it produces a clogged and blown up text. *The Mezzanine* isn't completely bereft of narrative structure, but its adherence to the escalator principle means that it coheres loosely, in the extenuated manner of the paradigmatic dimension, rather than tightly or syntagmatically (or metonymically), in the linear fashion of story structure or logical argument. Like lists and collections, it groups within the limits of a text a set of different items that are linked by perceptions of similarity and are themselves subject therefore to the etcetera principle. The list we just encountered of systems of local transport, in which the escalator functioned as an etcetera, might serve, therefore, as the text's structural emblem; and lists are indeed vital to this text's discursive texture. But metaphor is in turn the principle of lists, not because all lists group items that are specifically related by the figure of metaphor, but because the metaphoric phenomenon of continuity/discontinuity underlies the associative structure of the paradigmatic, which is why no inventory of paradigmatic relations can be securely closed. The "that reminds me" of memory can always intervene.

But, to repeat, *The Mezzanine* is not particularly preoccupied with the open-endedness of the inventorizing process. It even assigns quite significant limits to its own escalatory potential by limiting its narrative to a period of time out, the "fixed interval" (102) of absence, or at least withdrawal, from the workaday world that corresponds to lunch break and is enjoyed on other occasions by commuter-train passengers, or escalator riders. Where a Beckett or an Auster (chapter 4) thinks digression as an approach to disorder, chaos, and inertia, Baker's text links it back to the domain of discipline, work, and order from which it departs. Accordingly, its concern is less with the etcetera principle as such and more with connections, points of passage, or seepage, that is, with the baffling question of mediation as the escalator principle phrases it: how is it that one thing leads to another? Because of this textual preoccupation with passage, I want to describe Baker's "memoir" as a meditation, taking advantage of the etymology that links the words *mezzanine* and *meditation*—from the Latin *medius*, halfway, middle—with mediation itself, and understanding meditation as the genre of thought/discourse that is defined by the gradual, a genre in which step-by-step progress is consequently capable of exploding into multidirectionality.

WRITES OF PASSAGE

I entered a bookstore and asked, already thinking of writing this essay: "Do you have the *Meditations* of Marcus Aurelius and the *Meditations* of Descartes?" "Depends," said the clerk. "Do you know who the author is?" It was a difficult question to answer tactfully, but I realized on reflection that it is not an irrelevant question to ask about meditations, which seem to be generically concerned with the possibility of self-knowledge on their author's part. "Who am I?" is, always implicitly and sometimes explicitly, their preoccupation; and a single meditation, however long drawn out, is rarely adequate to answering that question, so true is it that self-knowledge is subject to a law of limitless supplementation, whether in the linear sense of "one thing leads to another" or in the more escalatory sense that any given step may explode and lead in any number of possible directions. It's symptomatic, therefore, that the texts grouped under the generic heading of "the meditation" (singular) most often bear a title in the plural: *Meditations*. And it's because of this potential for explosion of the meditative process that the classical tradition of meditation has been a tradition of discipline. Whether the meditation is conceived as an "imitation of Christ" (Thomas à Kempis) or as an application of the "method of rightly conducting the reason" (to coopt the long title of Descartes's *Discourse on Method*), the problem of meditators and their advisers has been to prevent the mind—like the eye attempting to track the grooves of a record or the steps of a moving escalator—from getting "off track." Following an exemplary guide, keeping to the highway (*method* is from *meta-hodos*, a direct route or main road), are the standard precepts for meditators.

A reason why the question "Who am I?" tends to arise is, however, that meditating is a "time out" activity, when one is typically reduced to "one's own resources." Marcus Aurelius meditated at night, after heavy days spent administering the Empire or combatting Germanic tribes in the region of the Danube. Descartes had his famous *poêle*, the warm room in which he withdrew from the distractions of the world. I get reflective myself or start to woolgather when I've run out of reading matter on long journeys, or there's no one to talk to and nothing to look at, or the in-flight movie is more than usually vapid. "One's own resources," of course, are not in fact one's own, and thinking is a cultural, not an individual, matter; but the phrase "one's own resources" does describe a certain freeing of the mind from its habitual constraints that occurs when one finds oneself "at a loose end" and one thing begins, consequently, to lead to another. Religious or philosophical attempts to discipline the meditating mind are, in essence, attempts to take advantage of this freeing of the mind from its habitual concerns, without permitting the loose-endedness of the meditative moment (like tampon strings in a sewer pipe) to clog things up, with all the consequent "dangers" of the experience's becoming haphazard, random, multidirectional, and open-ended.

French has an expression, *de fil en aiguille*, which is used, like "one thing leads to another," when mediating connections are too complex or subtle to be easily tracked (as in the slide of memory). And it has another, *avoir de la suite dans les idées*, which refers to people who are unusually single-minded or dogged in their pursuit of a goal. One might say that disciplined meditations attempt to channel the *de fil en aiguille*, multidirectional potential of "one thing leads to another" into a single-minded "one thing leads to another" that has *de la suite dans les idées*. We don't know how Marcus Aurelius conducted his nightly meditations—presumably with considerable consequentiality—but what we have inherited, in the "book" of private jottings he left whose original "title" (more like a filing label) was, symptomatically enough, *To Myself*, is a jumble of *sententiæ*; and these can easily be taken to emblematize the potential randomness of meditative rambling to which reduction of the mind to its "own resources" can lead, by virtue of the "that reminds me" slide. Descartes's *Meditations*, by contrast, are the prime example of the logically controlled if not end-oriented philosophic meditation; their full title, *Meditations on First Philosophy, in which the Existence of God, and the Real Distinction of Mind and Body, Are Demonstrated*, clearly indicates both the directionality of the argument and the ease with which it lends itself to summary, always a key indicator of systematic as opposed to comprehensive thinking. But it is in Descartes also that one finds the emblematic sentence: "I who know that I exist inquire into what I am" (*Meditation* 2).[6]

My hypothesis, of course, is that the two extremes of meditative reflection are never absolutely separable and that the most haphazard of rambles show some degree of *suite dans les idées* (Aurelius's recurring stoic themes, for instance), while the most logical of meditative progressions can have moments of (acknowledged or unacknowledged) *de fil en aiguille* looseness. If that's so, the meditation can be described as the genre of nonnarrative writing ("argument") that demonstrates a nexus, between carefully controlled linear order and the looseness of paradigmatic cohesion that looks like disorder, that corresponds to the nexus of story structure and textual "extenuation" or "escalation" in narrative. *The Mezzanine* situates itself intertextually as much closer to the "Marcus Aurelius" end of my hypothesized spectrum than to the "Descartes" end, since it is the emperor's *Meditations* in the Penguin Classics edition that the narrator takes with him to read on his lunch break. But it does so, in a way that's highly characteristic of the loiterly tradition, by positioning the intertextual other as classically noble or sublime, and itself, therefore, as modern and trivial. (Similarly, Nerval alludes to Dante in *October Nights,* and Barthes to Chateaubriand in "Soirées de Paris," as magnificent foils to their own unpretentious jottings; see chapters 3 and 9 respectively.) Baker's narrator finds Aurelius alienating: "I was nearly ready to abandon it entirely, tired of Aurelius's unrelenting and morbid self-denial" (124). And if my hypothesis of a meditative continuum between randomness and discipline is correct, this distancing from Aurelius and his "self-denial" may also hint at a way in which *The Mezzanine* is closer to the modern and self-affirmative writer par excellence, Descartes, in spite of the latter's insistence on method.

The link with Descartes has to do crucially, I think, with a connection between meditation and the process of growing up that exercises both the philosopher and Baker's narrator. "Today," Descartes writes calmly in a programmatic sentence of the First Meditation, "since I have opportunely freed my mind from all cares and am happily disturbed by no passions, and since I am in secure possession of leisure in a peaceable retirement, I will at length apply myself earnestly to the general overthrow of all my former opinions" (79–80). It's not just Descartes's undisguised enjoyment of "time out" that links him to the narrator of *The Mezzanine*, nor is it merely his clear linking of the meditative process with a project of self-knowledge. It's also the fact that, in Descartes, self-knowledge is so clearly linked in turn with a procedure of discarding "opinions" that have outlived their usefulness—a process, that is, of maturation or coming of age that also informs *The Mezzanine*.

This kind of preoccupation refers us again to the close connections between the religious and the philosophic traditions of meditation, the way in which the imitation of Christ and the right conduct of reason can be oddly related, both through the religious and pedagogical concept of discipleship and through the initiatory theme of becoming "a man." The meditation (meditations) is a capacious genre and its history, because of the crisscrossing of religious and philosophical traditions in the story of its emergence, is a tangled one. Aurelius's "philosophic" example furnished a model for the Christian practices of meditation that proceeded to develop the imitative scenario, or set of scenarii, of discipleship. But these in turn, as Amélie Rorty in particular has shown, structure the Cartesian meditation, which straddles philosophy, theology, and even religious mysticism, reconciling them through its mind/body dualism.[7] An epistemology that depends on a demonstration of the existence of God grounded the scientific revolution. But the demonstration itself depends on self-knowledge (a methodical, step-by-step examination of "what I am" who know that I exist) and is simultaneously addressed to a reader positioned as a disciple whose own coming of age, as emancipation from prejudice, is also at issue: "I would advise none to read this work, except such as are able and willing to meditate with me in earnest, to detach their minds from commerce with the senses, and likewise to deliver themselves from all prejudice; and individuals of this character are, I well know, remarkably rare" (Descartes, 73). That there is consequently some preoccupation in the *Meditations* with a problematics of *passage* is indicated, further, by the explicitly mystic moment, at the heart of the book, in which meditation—the step-by-step progress of "clear and distinct" ideas—yields to mute contemplation, the contemplation of an infinite divinity whose existence mediates the two parts of the *Meditations'* overall structure, the step from uncertainty and systematic doubt to the possibility of epistemological certainty.[8] For example, Descartes writes: "But before I examine this with more attention, and pass on to the consideration of other truths that may be evolved out of it, I think it proper to remain here for some time in the contemplation of God himself . . . as far, at least, as the strength of my mind, which is to some degree dazzled by the sight, will permit" (110). Readers of Baker may recognize in this moment of "looseness" that has been so deliberately structured into the firm progress of the *Meditations* not only a thematics of "blowing up" (examining "with more attention") and of seepage ("other truths that may be evolved out of it"), but also, and more particularly, a thematics of the dazzle induced by the inexhaustible mystery, the *de fil en aiguille* "untrackableness" of mediation. But they may sense further that the problematics of passage that's defined here by the question of a partially unknowable God as mediator of the "steps" of thought mimes a question of maturation that underlies the "Who am I?" of meditation, a question that takes the form: How and when do I *become* an 'I' worthy of philosophical and religious examination?" For it's a concern of Descartes that, to write the *Meditations*, he choose the precise moment of maturity that makes him worthy to give an account of the steps of thought that have led him, via self-knowledge and the knowledge of God, from the virtualities of doubt to their mature realization in epistemological certainty. The continuous process known as maturation needs to be marked, in other words, by a coming of age that divides the process into steps, a before and after.

In social life, the ceremonies of coming of age are called rites of passage; and what I'm proposing is that Descartes's *Meditations* and Baker's *The Mezzanine* (and here is the place to mention also the endlessly proliferating autobiographical writing of Michel Leiris) have in common the fact that they are not so much rites as "writes" of passage. I mean by this that in them the very *fact* of writing itself celebrates a coming of age, a point of passage into maturity that justifies self-examination and sanctions it as worthwhile. But such self-examination is itself necessarily an ongoing process, and it's the *act* of writing that furnishes the modality of this further coming of age. Writing in this second sense is the instrument of a meditation that is itself a rite of passage, whether it be conducted in linear, step-by-step fashion and, as Descartes puts it, "by degrees" or whether it be carried out, as in Baker, according to the principles of "escalation."

Accordingly, Descartes writes in Meditation 3, "holding converse only with myself, and closely examining my nature, I will endeavour to obtain by degrees a more intimate and familiar knowledge of myself" (95). I don't know whether the title of Baker's second novel, *Room Temperature*, refers quietly to the *poêle* in which, the *Discourse* tells us, Descartes liked to "remain the whole day . . . with full opportunity to occupy my attention with my own thoughts" (10), but it *is* in this text, whose meditative character is even stronger and whose narrative interest is even further reduced than that of *The Mezzanine*, that the interest of Baker's writing in self-exploration becomes fully explicit. "I certainly believed, rocking my baby on this Wednesday afternoon, that with a little concentration one's whole life could be reconstructed from any single twenty-minute period randomly or almost randomly selected."[9] Here too it is specified that such a reconstruction involves a backward slide of memory: it is a matter of making "connections . . . that would proliferate backward" (41) in such a way that "everything in my life [might seem] to enjamb splicelessly with everything else" (92), a procedure that is significantly different, as the narrator points out, from proceeding "serially, beginning with 'I was born on January 5, 1957,' and letting each moment give birth naturally to the next" (41). *The Mezzanine*, in its own counter-narrative deployment of proliferat- ing enjambments generated, in the perspective of memory, from the account of a brief period of relaxation in the narrator's day, does not proceed differently from what is outlined in *Room Temperature*. But where, in the second novel, it is paternity, I suppose, that figures the passage to maturity, *The Mezzanine* situates itself explicitly, as does Descartes, in relation to the general issue of coming of age.

Meditation, for Descartes, is indeed a matter too serious and its stakes too high (given the sensitivity of the post-Reformation church to departures from strict orthodoxy) for it to be undertaken lightly. Although he has been aware for several years, he writes, of the necessity of ridding his mind of false opinions, he has consequently waited to fulfil this task "until I had attained an age so mature as to leave me no hope that at any stage of life more advanced I should be better able to execute my design" (79). As a getting of wisdom, meditation, as it turns out, is dialectically related to experience, through which one achieves a maturity sufficient to guarantee the validity and success of the meditative enterprise. But this indispensable prior experience without which there is no maturity is simultaneously, and by definition, a matter of living in error, so that while the *fact* of embarking on meditation marks the moment of passage from immaturity to maturity, it remains for the *act* of meditation still to realize this crucial passage, by achieving the displacement of error in favor of truth. The alternation in Descartes's biography of periods of travel with time out for quiet reflection (in Germany and later in Holland), as if travel in the world and meditation, as a form of travel without leaving home, were each other's natural complements, clearly enacts this Cartesian dialectic of error and its correction, experience and meditation. But meditation, in its textual embodiment, is itself dialectical in that it both celebrates and enacts the achievement of a maturity that is simultaneously already attained and still to be reached when meditation begins.

In a not dissimilar way, maturity in *The Mezzanine* is already achieved, justifying the "memoir," and yet still in abeyance, continually in process through meditation. The narrator situates at age twenty-three the moment of his having achieved adulthood and calculates that up to that moment he had spent seventeen years accumulating childish opinions. It follows, he thinks, that the moment of his coming of age inaugurates another period of seventeen years during which he can hope to accumulate enough adult opinions for these to outweigh eventually his old, immature views. That moment, which I calculate he will reach at age forty, will be the moment of his true Majority (47). The problem, though, is that we don't learn the age of the narrator when he undertakes his memoir; it is specified only that the events of the lunch hour he is remembering took place two years after the crucial moment when, at twenty-three "[his] life as an adult began" (47). Whether the narrative perspective is that of Majority attained or of Majority still to be reached, is—as I suppose a general perception of the nature of maturity requires—strictly undecidable. If the autobiographical "pact" holds, identifying narrator with author, one can calculate from the author's biography on the back cover, which conveniently conforms to the conventional narrative order of "Nicholson Baker was born in 1957" and so on, that Baker himself will not have turned forty until 1997, which confirms, in contradistinction to the Cartesian case, the incompleteness at the time of writing of the process of maturation that would put the stamp of Majority on the text.

The closure of Cartesian meditation, its completedness as opposed to the open-endedness of meditation in Baker, is thus a significant difference between the two coming of age texts. So, too, is the treatment in each text of what coming of age itself implies as a measure of human potential. For Descartes it means nothing less than the achievement of epistemological certainty, the assured knowledge that "man" can know himself and his world, and have some knowledge of God. But Baker's narrator, who is repelled by the high-mindedness of Marcus Aurelius, similarly situates his own coming of age at a considerable distance from Descartes. To begin with, the moment one achieves maturity isn't necessarily discernible, although "luckily, I *can* remember the very day my life as an adult began" (47). The event, furthermore, had nothing obviously momentous about it. At twenty-three, the narrator discovered, not a method, but a trick, specifically a way to apply deodorant when one is fully dressed. Delighted with this achievement, he then took the subway and spent his commute reflecting on the advantages of slicing toast diagonally rather than straight across and on the many styles of buttering that exist. A short while later, he has his revelation:

> I realized that as of that minute . . . I had finished with whatever large-scale growth I was going to have as a human being, and that I was now permanently arrested at an intermediate stage of personal development. . . . I was set: I was the sort of person who said "actually" too much. I was the sort of person who stood in a subway car and thought about buttering toast. . . . I was the sort of person whose biggest discoveries were likely to be tricks to applying toiletries while fully dressed. I was a man, but not the magnitude of man I had hoped I might be. (54)

Becoming "a man," in short, does not necessarily signify achieving the exalted status Descartes attributes to humanity as the site of a mind capable of thought, and hence, in the chain of argumentative steps, of establishing the existence of God and therefore of knowing truth with certainty. The self-knowledge that marks maturity may be something like knowledge of arrested growth, that is, of permanent immaturity. In that case, becoming a "man" means discovering that one is not the "magnitude of man" one had hoped.

The historical difference between early modern "man" and the human subject of later modernity and postmodernity is demonstrated here. Let's hypothesize that, at least since Descartes, the meditation has functioned generically as a means of mediating transformations in the nature of knowledge. What meditation mediates, then, is epistemological mutation, the passage by which new knowledge comes to replace old, so that the personal coming of age it celebrates counts, from one angle, as the successful achievement of one's "education," the getting of wisdom, while from another angle meditation functions as a teaching device through which disciples are created and the new knowledge one has achieved can be disseminated and replace old "prejudices." In order to get wisdom and complete one's education, one needs to reject what one has been taught (Descartes has a long passage in *The Discourse of Method* that is critical of what he learned from the Jesuits at La Flèche) and to fall back on "one's own resources," working "by degrees" from there to new certainties that then justify publication, as a step in the education of others. Thus it comes about that the forms of knowledge Descartes achieved through meditation are now part and parcel of what is taught as a matter of course, to moderns; and it is these that post-Cartesian meditators like Baker are implicitly resisting in the process of their own coming of age—a coming of age which, in turn, entails publication of the new results attained through meditation. The process of achieving knowledge only to make of it a teachable doctrine continues, although what counts as knowledge may thus undergo severe modification over the course of time.

If meditation in Descartes is a linear, goal-oriented "method," it is because at its end (and hence presupposed from the beginning) lies the (fore)knowledge that new knowledge is attainable. If in Baker it becomes a pathless and apparently random inventorizing, however, it is because the (fore)knowledge that controls the enterprise is that knowledge is beyond humanity's reach and that arrested growth is the best we can hope for. We can manage some cute tricks, but the highway of method is no longer for us. What has most crucially changed in this historical process is the understanding of the "self" itself, to whose resources the meditator is reduced as a rule of the genre. For Descartes, the self is self-contained, individual, and knowable because it both exists as the site of thought and is distinct from everything else in the world except God, with whom it is linked through its defining faculty, the power of thought. It follows that the *cogito* must be an exercise in mental detachment: "corporal objects" being difficult to know with certainty, whereas "we know much more of the human mind, and still more of God himself" through the powers of cogitation, it is evident that in the pursuit of truth one should "abstract the mind from the contemplation of sensible or imaginable objects, and apply it to those which, as disengaged from all matter, are purely intelligible" (111). And Descartes's readers in turn, as we've seen, are invited to "detach their minds from all commerce with the senses, and likewise to deliver themselves from all prejudices" (73).

If the self is no longer knowable, though, the Cartesian follow-through from self-knowledge to a state of epistemological certitude about God and the world is no longer possible and the meditative process, still pursued as fact, is short-circuited as an act—it can no longer achieve the maturity that is its goal and becomes, instead, the process that confirms us in the knowledge that we are "not the magnitude of man" we might have hoped. Historically, it's the emergence of what could be called the "theoretical subject" (see chapter 4) that transforms Cartesian meditation from a royal road to truth into a prejudice that, in turn, needs to be corrected through a meditative return to the self and its now diminished possibilities of "knowledge." At about the time of Rousseau, the modern subject emerged in Europe, not as a self-contained and individual self but as a mobile and multiple consciousness constituted by alterity. Such a subject can believe itself to be autonomous, self-controlling, present to itself and capable of self-knowledge only as a consequence of suppressing what will come to be called the unconscious, the site in which constitutive alterity lodges. This is the "split" subject; otherness for it cannot be a matter of absolute alterity, but is rather a product of difference, the implication of which is that neither the subject nor its other—conceived in a mutual relationship such that each is the other's other—can lay claim to the Cartesian ideal of full selfhood, as that which would be individual and immediately present to itself. For, instead of enjoying self-presence, its existence is "subject" to mediation by alterity. But mediation, in turn, implies temporality—nothing that is dependent on an intermediary "step" can exist as a timeless "essence"—and the mediated self is consequently not only incapable of self-possession because constituted by alterity but also time bound and historical. It has a temporal existence that is, like its ontological structure, split and experienced, therefore, as a matter of continuity/discontinuity, or of "enjambment."

Where the Cartesian self is figurable as an island, the mediated subject, therefore, has the temporal structure of, say, an escalator or a toilet roll, whose apparent continuity is split (but not interrupted) by grooves or perforations, but whose discontinuity doesn't permit of "clear and distinct" separations such as those on which Cartesian step-by-step thinking depends. Furthermore, for the mediated subject, digression from linearity is always a possibility, for the reason that discontinuity is always inscribed in its continuity. The linear consequentiality of which the Cartesian self is assured by virtue of its unmediated self-presence being no longer either guaranteed or easily achieved, the split that constitutes the subject can become a gape, and escalate into multidirectional multiplicity. Perhaps Rousseau is the figure who historically dramatizes the moment when the Cartesian self begins to yield its sway to the theoretical subject, and it's symptomatic that as an autobiographer, Rousseau, whose *Confessions* begin as a more or less orderly chronological narrative in the "I was born on January 5, 1957" mode but finally disintegrate into obsessive and paranoid ruminations about the power of others, was led to devise, in the *Dialogues* and the *Rêveries*, more episodic and open-ended modes of self-exploration. Soon thereafter, Xavier de Maistre's meditative *Voyage autour de ma chambre* (chapter 4) began to develop an early theory of the digressive subject not as an individual but a "dividual," a divided "self."

A subject whose existence is mediated cannot expect to know itself through philosophizing in abstracto, far from the cares, passions, involvements, and prejudices of the historical world. To the extent that such a subject *can* achieve a degree of self-knowledge, it can only be through an exploration of its own connectedness. Thus, the one sentence in Marcus Aurelius that comes as a stunning revelation to the narrator of *The Mezzanine* is one in which, in absolutely anti-Cartesian fashion, a necessary connection between philosophizing and historical contingency is casually implied. "Manifestly," Aurelius writes (and it is the "manifestly" that is so magnificent), "no condition of life could be so well adapted for the practice of philosophy as this in which chance finds you today!"[10] And the narrator comments:

> Wo! I loved the slight awkwardness and archaism of the sentence . . .
> as well as the unexpected but apt rush to an exclamation point at the
> end. But mainly I thought that the statement was extraordinarily true
> and that if I bought the book and learned how to act upon that single
> sentence I would be led into elaborate realms of understanding, even
> as I continued to do, outwardly, exactly as I had done, going to work,

going to lunch, going home, talking to L. on the phone or having her over for the night. (124)

Thus is defined the mode of philosophizing, grounded in the triviality of the merely contingent ("merely," that is, from a Cartesian point of view), that characterizes meditation in *The Mezzanine* as a radically anti-Cartesian pursuit. The assumption is not that thought is grounded in detachment from everyday life, but that there can "manifestly" be no point of departure for philosophy other than the "condition of life . . . in which chance finds you today!"

There is a problem, though. The book, once bought on the strength of this crucial sentence, turns out to be disappointing because it gives no answer to the question of *how* to make the practice of philosophy responsive to the chance circumstances of life, how to enter "elaborate realms of understanding" while getting on with the business, or the busyness, of going to work, going to lunch, going home, talking on the phone, and having a lover over for the night.

> Chance found me that day having worked for a living all morning, broken a shoelace, chatted with Tina, urinated in a corporate setting, washed my face, eaten half a bag of popcorn, bought a new set of shoelaces, eaten a hot dog and a cookie with some milk; and chance found me now sitting in the sun on a green bench, with a paperback on my lap. What, philosophically, was I supposed to do with that? (125)

This sentence, which—incidentally—offers a good account of the narrative content of *The Mezzanine*, defines the narrator's problem as that of loiterature generally, the transvaluation of the trivial, a problem to which Aurelius' high-minded *sententiæ* offer no solution. This is also, for what it is worth, a crucial problem in, and perhaps the defining problem of, contemporary cultural studies, faced as it is with the question of what it means for intellectuals to take seriously, as an object of knowledge, the ephemera and the banalities of everyday or popular culture. But already to pose the problem itself implies a criticism of the traditional practice of philosophy, the grandeur of whose concerns it is that defines the trivial as synonymous with the insignificant. That is, perhaps, why the narrator sunning himself on his green bench recalls Diogenes, who made sunning himself in the agora itself a philosophical practice, critical of the belief in more "elaborate realms of significance." The answer to the question of transvaluing the trivial may lie, then, less in rethinking the allegedly trivial than in a revaluation of the practice of philosophy, a revaluation that itself depends on a criticism of conventional understandings of the status of knowledge.

Such a redefined philosophy, in other words, would have to be something more modest than the pursuit of "elaborate realms of understanding" and less portentous than Aurelius's "thing about mortal life's being no more than sperm and ashes" (124). Reflecting on and finding meaning in a broken shoelace, it can be familiar and approachable. Rather than driving relentlessly forward, like a systematic argument of the Cartesian type, it might be more like what *U and I* calls a "veracious stochasticism" (99), governed more by chance than by method, and more subject to the loiterly etcetera principle than inclined to hasten toward closure. Such a philosophy might be a philosophy adapted to the limitations of modern humanity, "not the magnitude of man I had hoped," a humanity subject to historical contingency whose modernity consists of being "up to the minutiæ" (*U and I*, 110) as much as up to the minute. Its narrating subject can therefore be something as apparently simple, if in fact inexhaustibly complex, as a young man sunning himself on a bench and whose only degree of maturity lies in the discovery of his permanent arrest "at an intermediate stage of human development." Unlike Aurelius's grim pronouncements, such a philosophy might even be a source of pleasure. But it remains in the long tradition of the meditation, of which Aurelius was the distant ancestor.

PHILOSOPHIZING THE CONTINGENT

That philosophizing the contingent is a possible function of writing—indeed "the function of art"—was the view of Walter Benjamin. In *The Origin of German Tragic Drama*, he wrote that the object of "philosophical criticism" is to demonstrate this function, "to make historical content, such as provides the basis of every important work of art, into a philosophical truth."[11] This is an important sentence because it locates "truth" in a mediating function—that of the critical reading as the means by which philosophical "truth" emerges from history—and because it depends, therefore, on an understanding of the incompleteness of the work of art "in itself," that is, its subjection to a version of the etcetera principle, its connectedness to a form of alterity figured by the reader. For Benjamin, therefore, temporality is of the essence: indeed, an actual time lag must intervene, causing a "decrease in effectiveness" of the work's initial historical embeddedness, so that it becomes a "ruin," for it is only this entropic ruination of the work, making it into a readable allegory, that enables its philosophical "truth content" to be restored by the critical reader.

But supposing the work is always already a "ruin," as Blanchot's concept of *désœuvrement* implies? Its philosophical readability, in that case, would be a given from the start, or at least would not depend on a long historical time-lapse. Nothing resembles a ruin more than a would-be "work" that remains incomplete, condemned to a state of arrested growth; and some writing—that, for example, of the loiterly tradition to which Baker's belongs—does not even aspire to the status of work but seems to have no ambition other than to be a kind of ruin, already marked by temporality from inception. In either case, the function of "discipleship," if it is understood as the reading of the ruins that are, in short or long term, by default or by profession, what writing is, acquires an emphasis and a significance that differs markedly from the construction of the disciple as an imitator—a mere follower—that is familiar from the philosophical and religious tradition of the classical meditation. The disciple as reader—as an agent of signification—becomes the indispensable supplement called for by the work's own inadequacy to its task.

If, as I suggested, Baker's writing has some affinities with contemporary cultural studies in its concern with the problematics of philosophizing the contingent, its general adherence to the meditative tradition (that is, its yoking of the questions of culture and history to the meditative question of "Who am I?") and its emphasis on the readerly function (as the site of memory's mediating slide as well as of philosophical supplementation) aren't particularly characteristic of academic practices, which haven't typically been prone to acknowledge either the embeddedness of knowledge in subjective positioning or its dependence on phenomena of mediation. I want to reflect a little, therefore, in these final pages, on the ways in which Baker's text seems to understand the conditions of cultural knowledge as a philosophizing of the contingent, that is, on the condition of subjectivity and the condition of readability. But I am interested, too, in what this text conveys about the conditions under which meditative knowlege as a philosophizing of the contingent can be regarded as a mode of criticism, and not only of the ambitions of traditional philosophy. It's because the book's writing is both the vehicle of its knowledge construction and the modality of its critical functioning that I'll be led to return at some

length, and with some risk of repetition, to the questions of narrative
clogging and explosion—those of "escalation"—with which I began.
But it's the thread of *connectedness*—the connectedness of subjectivity
and the connectedness of reading, but also that of the critical gesture
and its object—that itself links together the various topics I want now
to traverse, producing them in their turn as items in a kind of list or
paradigmatic chain, linked by a relation of discontinuity but continuity.
And such connectedness, I submit, is an inescapable theme of modern
writing but more particularly of writing in the loiterly mode that itself
explores a paradigmatic or listlike view of things, because at its heart is
the connnectedness that defines the modern or theoretical subject, the
mediated subject as opposed to the detached Cartesian self.

"Patty was at work" is the second sentence in *Room Temperature*,
the first of which ("I was in the rocking chair giving our six-month-old
Bug her late afternoon bottle" [3]) establishes the narrator's meditative
situation. In *The Mezzanine* also, the relation of meditation to the
world of work is a fundamental preoccupation, since it is the workaday
world that defines the historical contingency the narrator would like
to philosophize, as well as the object of his critical attention. And the
two are inseparably connected, as is suggested both by the way the
lunch hour, with its "sunlit noon mood" and its explosive sense of
freedom (106), is scheduled into the working day, and by the way the
"long hypotenuse" of a mediating escalator triangulates the noonday
relaxations of walking in the city (eating popcorn, buying shoelaces,
sitting in the sun) with the employments of an office that lies, on the
mezzanine floor, but a half-"step" away. In comparable fashion, too, the
corporate bathroom, to which three of the novel's fifteen chapters are
devoted, blurs the distinction between work and lunch. "Is a lunch hour
defined as beginning just as you enter the men's room on your way to
lunch, or just as you exit it?" (71). Urinating "in a corporate setting" can
have a critical function as well as figuring the connectedness of trivial
relaxations and powerful modes of social organization, and I'll return
to this bathroom episode in due course (and also to the significance
of learning to tie shoelaces, having a shoelace break, and going out
to buy new ones). But it's enough for now to note that meditative
"stochasticism," however "veracious," can't be completely divorced
from the orderly filing system of the "Pendaflex" world of corporate
business, so that the connectedness that distinguishes the modern
subject from the Cartesian self is also the connectedness implied by

the relation of mutual alterity—the split—that holds between work and lunch, criticism and its object. And the model for this kind of connectedness, I suggest, is the inseparability of linear narrative from its explosion into multidirectionality through clogging, of the escalator as the principle of *gradus* and steady progression and the escalator as principle of escalation. The escalator, in short, connects meditation and work, criticism and its object, as well as narrative and the clogged text of meditation.

As a figure of connection, the escalator also quite naturally figures, as we know, memory, the principle of continuity and discontinuity in the temporality of a mediated world. And as we have also noticed, it is the problematics of memory that introduces paradigmatic disorder into narrative's syntagmatic ordering structure. "Reconstitut[ing] the events of that noontide for this opusculum," the narrator of *The Mezzanine* is, a little like Marcel in *A la Recherche du temps perdu*, a man remembering the more immature man of memory that he once was, and he knows that "the determinism of reminding often works obscurely" (60)—that memory is not easily subject to the controls of logical argument or linear narrative. Among the intertextual precedents his writing evokes, an allusion to Proust is consequently inevitable:

> Incidentally, if you open a Band-Aid box, it will exhale a smell (as I found out recently, needing a Band-Aid for a surprisingly gruesome little cut) that will shoot you right back to when you were four— although I don't trust this olfactory memory trick anymore, because it seems to be a hardware bug in the neural workings of the sense of smell, a low-level sort of tie-in, underneath subtler strata of language and experience, between smell, vision and self-love, which has been mistakenly exalted by some writers as something realer and purer and more sacredly significant than intellective memory, like the bubbles of swamp methane that awed provincials once took for UFOs. (109)

I couldn't bring myself to abbreviate this dense passage (although I *have* spared my reader the two footnotes that, in attaching to it, themselves enact the "obscure determinism of reminding"). But from it emerges, broadly speaking, both a certain solidarity with Proust—based on a common reliance on the dimension of memory and the shared knowledge that the triggers of memory are trivial, so that it is through memory that the contingent acquires (philosophical) significance— and a certain mistrust of the obscurer workings of what Proust calls "involuntary memory," but is here characterized as low-level tie-ins. For a writer who loves clogged sewer pipes to refer slightingly to hardware bugs and the bubbling of swamp methane in this connection certainly seems contradictory. But the contradiction is the sign of a certain ambivalence, and the narrator's preference here for "subtler strata of language and experience" that can be captured by intellective memory has much to do with the nature of his philosophical project, which is not conceived, like Proust's, as a quest for *individual* redemption—the rediscovery of an essential self in the dispersed multiplicity of the subject—or even as a quest for *redemption* at all. Baker's project could be described (too pretentiously) as something like an exploration of cultural modernity, one to which the personal dimension of memory is indispensable but in which the obscurer reaches of reminiscence, in which the purely personal resonates too strongly like a merely accidental hardware bug, are somewhat suspect. For a writer whose private meditation is also, albeit implicitly, a gesture of social criticism, the subjectively personal must also be recognizably "veracious" to the reader whose mediating role in the philosophizing of the contingent is no less indispensable than is the writer's personal memory. That is one of the conditions of the embedding of knowledge in subjectivity. Baker's project, in this sense, is in fact more like that of Perec's *Je me souviens*, which is a random collection of collective memories stored in the privacy of a single remembering mind, the "je" of the title.

The Mezzanine's narrator is, in any case, quite conscious of the fact that his writing is a form of cultural study (whereas academic cultural studies has emerged most obviously from philosophical scrutiny of the commodity, in Benjamin for instance, Baker's favorite turf, I would say, however, is the area of technological gadgetry and industrial design). It is the narrator's ambivalence about the role played in his study by the personal in the form of "kid-memory"—as if a state of "arrested growth" were not understood to be the condition of knowledge for us moderns—that is curious. His ambivalence about the personal vibrations of memory is not dissimilar, perhaps, from the shyness of academic cultural studies about its own literary origins and affinities, the desire in each case being to distance a certain project of knowledge from the prestige of authorship and from authority claims grounded in exceptional personalities and precious essences. The narrator indicates, for example, that a history of social change is readable in the "disorienting" changes that have occurred during and since his childhood in everyday objects, like "gas pumps, ice cube trays, transit buses, or milk containers." But, he adds,

> the only way we can understand the proportion and range and effect of these changes, which constitute the often undocumented daily texture of our lives (a rough, gravelly texture, like the shoulder of a road, which normally passes too fast for microscopy), is to sample early images of the objects in whatever form they take in kid-memory—and once you invoke those kid-memories, you have to live with their constant tendency to screw up your fragmentary historiography with violas of emotion. (41)

In other words, the exploration of self and the recourse to one's own resources that is characteristic of the meditation as a genre is thought by the narrator to interfere, by introducing "subjective" connotations through memory, with a philosophic investigation of everyday culture, an investigation that would not need to be such a "fragmentary historiography" if only impersonal documents were available.

What the narrator admits, slightly grudgingly, as a *pis-aller*—the fact that personal memory necessarily intervenes as a form of documentation when other documents are unavailable—might however be viewed more positively. If the everyday is that to which official institutions of knowledge, like schools and libraries, pay no attention because it is "trivial," then a philosophical approach to the significance of the everyday might not want to deny its personal connotations and investments but rather to acknowledge and incorporate the "violas of emotion," as part and parcel of its constitution. Many academic practitioners of cultural studies, aware for example of the degree to which their scholarly interest in popular culture is embedded in childhood interests and enthusiasms (not necessarily outgrown), might cheerfully accede to the proposition that forms of knowledge marked by conditions of immaturity (arrested development) are necessarily part and parcel of a historically modern epistemology. *The Mezzanine*, in any case, includes an interesting social history conducted through a remembered, child's-eye view of the changes in the delivery of milk to households (including a stirring hymn of praise to the designer of the contemporary milk carton, 42–43).

It also includes many less developed observations that—childlike as they may be (and precisely because they are childlike in their ability to notice what usually passes unnoticed)—compensate for this "undocumented" character of daily life. Remarks on things like the etiquette of signature placement on office get-well cards (31), the mechanical ingenuity lavished on bathroom gadgets (72–73), or the courtesies of whistling in men's bathrooms, themselves provide raw material for future social historians. Their function in this text is not so much to *demonstrate* the social significance of trivial phenomena (as in the case of milk delivery) as it is to cause in the reader a certain shock of pleasurable recognition ("Yes, that's true") combined with awareness that one had never attended to things that, in one's own childlike fashion, one had nevertheless noticed. The realization that one might nevertheless attend seriously to them—that Baker's description furnishes material for a future historiography, for instance—is the first step in the transvaluation of the trivial or the philosophizing of the contingent. Reflecting, with or without "violas of emotion," on the potential significance of these previously unremarked details, the reader becomes a disciple of the narrator's teaching. But the teaching itself is not demonstrative (like Descartes's) and insistent on imitation but consists only—somewhat in the mode of Jacques Rancière's "ignorant schoolmaster"[12]—of drawing our attention to matters on which we might profitably reflect for ourselves. After the condition of subjectivity implied by the role of memory, this transfer of responsibility for signification onto the reader is then the second condition for philosophizing the contingent.

An example is the prevalence of perforation in contemporary material culture. The narrator writes that

> People watch the news every night like robots thinking they are learning about their lives, never paying attention to the far more immediate developments that arrive unreported, on the zip-lock perforated top of the ice-cream carton, in reply coupons bound in magazines and on the 'Please Return This Portion' edging of bill stubs, on sheets of postage stamps and sheets of Publishers Clearing House magazine stamps, on paper towels, in rolls of plastic bags for produce at the supermarket, in strips of hanging file-folder labels. (74)

(Like the escalator in the list of systems of local transport, toilet rolls go unmentioned, as the etcetera of this list, because they are in fact the point of departure of the narrator's outburst). We look in the wrong direction if we want to learn about our lives; we attend to versions of political—that is, narrative—history rather than to the more "fragmentary historiographies" in which the "rough, gravelly texture" of the everyday becomes visible, a texture, we recall, like that of the shoulder of the road that becomes apparent only when we slow down—when the narrative becomes clogged.

The narrator does not explain why the prevalence of perforation is more important than the events recounted on the TV news, but his text functions as the slowing down mechanism that brings it into view. As readers reflecting on the significance of perforation, we may then be led to see that its prevalence signals, or at least emblematizes, a culture of mediation—less one of ideas "clear and distinct" and progress "by degrees" than of connectedness, enjambment, slides, and escalation. Perforation figures perfectly the effect of split, or continuity/discontinuity, that is produced by the phenomenon of mediation; and a perforated strip such as a toilet roll is itself in metaphoric relation (that is, a relation of continuity/discontinuity, similarity and difference) with those systems of local transport that work on the principle of the divided conveyor belt, such as the luggage carousel in airports and of course the escalator. Furthermore, the list of examples of perforation, from the zip-lock top to strips of hanging-file labels, doesn't merely illustrate the ubiquity of perforation in modern culture but is itself, metaphorically—as a list—an *example* of "perforation," the listed items being in exactly the relation of continuity/discontinuity, of similarity and difference that perforation figures. Lists are like unfolding toilet rolls or forms of local transport on the principle of the conveyor belt: the reader glides along them somewhat as one rides an escalator, in the stance of Washington crossing the Potomac, entering at zip-lock tops and exiting at strips of hanging-file labels. The implication of the unnoticed ubiquity of perforation is that we live in a culture of mediated connectedness that is "structured" (i.e., unstructured) like a list, or a set (a list) of lists, while our attention is illegitimately solicited by, and given to, the constructions of narrative history.

The Mezzanine, of course, offers no explanation of the significance of this alternative but obfuscated, listlike way of comprehending ourselves and the world, corresponding to the grainy texture of the everyday over which we travel too fast and unheedingly. But it teaches us, by its narrator's example, to attend to the paradigmatic dimension and to perceive the reality of the world it brings into view, and in its own writing it enacts the characteristics of the world it describes, so that reading it, in the role of disciple, becomes a pedagogical experience, an induction into a world constituted by lists. Here, then, is the philosophizing significance of its loosened narrative texture. The novel lists, for example, the class of events that correspond to the particular form of deceived expectation that makes breaking a shoelace so frustrating (13–14); it lists the events—from learning to tie one's shoelaces to ordering a rubber stamp with one's address on it so as to pay one's bills and "deciding that brain cells ought to die"— that count as major events in one's life and constitute the gradual process of coming of age (16); it lists, as we have seen, the systems of local transport that resemble escalators; it lists the items (from escalators to ice grooved by a skater) that make up the class of "grooved surfaces" (76), and the moving surfaces (escalator handrails, turning LPs, propeller and fan blades) that shine, glint, and dazzle (3); even the narrator's plot summary, already quoted (125), is a nonnarrative listing of events. Several of these lists "enjamb" on one another: the escalator and the shoelace, in particular, make it easy to connect, in a relation of continuity/discontinuity, a list of items that are associated with these objects from one point of view with a list of items that resemble them from another. The text teaches us, in short, that the world is listable as well as narratable—it can be constructed paradigmatically as well as syntagmatically—and we are left to wonder at our relative blindness to the alternative vision the text so convincingly embodies in its own perforated, continuous/discontinuous texture. So let us look a little more closely at how this texture is constructed.

It depends essentially on metaphoric relations, and the principle of the list is metaphor. But associations can arise also, by metonymy for instance, between items without obvious physical or functional resemblance, such as doorknobs and ties—and the father whose habit it was to drape the latter over the former (27). An associative list of this kind—from doorknobs to ties to father—has a greater looseness of texture than a list constructed metaphorically; the list in this case begins to "list" like a boat becoming unmoored (Baker's word for the effect on one's thought processes of washing the face).[13] Associative drift of this kind can move a passage from a consideration of milk containers (themselves part of a list of objects that have undergone disorienting changes in the narrator's lifetime), to a description of making iced coffee and a discussion of the ice-cube tray, which itself "deserves" (and so gets) a "historical note" (45); or, by a combination of metonymic association and metaphor, from the beauty of grooved surfaces via a discussion of record-cleaning systems to a description of street-cleaning machines (65–67). "Listing" in this way, the text becomes what is called digressive, as the escalator or toilet roll-like linearity of the relatively ordered metaphoric list moves in the direction of a more "stochastic veraciousness" and the textual texture begins to gape and, by "unlooked-for seepage-points of passage," to move toward explosion. It becomes apparent, finally, that there is no difference that is absolute, none that cannot be bridged by resemblance or association, metaphor or digression, which merely represent poles of the continuity/discontinuity continuum, so that the writing mimes—not narrative or argumentative selectivity, with its teleologically oriented principle of "strict" relevance that aims at comprehension—but something like a potentially limitless, descriptive comprehensiveness. Between the poles of comprehension and comprehensiveness, of strict textual cohesion and the explosion of linearity, however, there is again only a relation of continuity/discontinuity, of gradual passage and of glide, since a plot summary can take the form of a list, and a list can itself "list," drifting toward digression in such a way that cohesion is gradually loosened toward breaking point. Loosened, though, without the sense of relevance ever being completely destroyed, with the result that a true disjunction never occurs. Indeed, it cannot occur.

The text's play with footnotes mimes this failure to achieve disjunction. The narrator cannily adopts a classical definition of digression as potentially disjunctive while defending the digressiveness of "essay-like" footnotes on the grounds of the comprehensiveness they permit:

> Digression—a movement away from the *gradus*, or upward escalation of the argument—is sometimes the only way to be thorough, and footnotes are the only form of graphic digression sanctioned by centuries of typesetters. And yet the MLA style sheet I owned in college warned against lengthy, "essay-like" footnotes. Were they *nuts*? Where is scholarship *going*? (They have removed this blemish in later editions.) (122)

His own footnotes, of course, are often spectacularly essay-like, consisting of developments many paragraphs long and containing their own expansive lists and digressive drifts. The distinction between textual *gradus* and footnoted digression is further subverted by typographical means: "footnote" typography (in smaller font) frequently invades the text proper, not only in indented quotations but also in numbered lists, which consequently look like footnotes incorporated into the text. Finally, it becomes impossible to sustain the apparently clear difference between text and footnotes, so cheerfully digressive is the text "proper" and so substantive and relevant—or alternatively so undistinctively trivial—is much material that is relegated to the notes. There is on the one hand no distinct *gradus* and on the other no "movement away" from the *gradus* that might be thought qualitatively different from the movement away from itself that occurs in the text "proper." The value of footnoting to the text, then, is essentially that, as the only graphic representation of digression "sanctioned by centuries of typesetters," it makes for a visual representation, on the page, of the explosion of linearity that is achieved, both in the text proper and in the notes, by the narrator's paradigmomania, the desire for comprehensiveness that produces the whole text as a "veritable infarct of narrative cloggers."

Take, as an example, one double page (14–15). The narrator is in the midst of recounting the episode of his broken shoelace, and there is a perhaps atypically long and uninterrupted stretch of pure story telling, especially on page 15. But, starting on the previous page (13), this account has been clogged by a list of occasions that resemble breaking one's shoelace, and it is the fourth item on this list (attempting to staple when the stapler is out of staples) that occupies the greater part of the textual space of page 14. It does so because it is itself clogged with carefully detailed descriptive accounts of the act of stapling, of reloading a stapler, and of toying with the leftovers from that operation, the first of these accounts being further expanded, in an indented paragraph, by an analytic retailing of the "three phases of the act" of stapling, each described with intense precision. But the mention of staples also gives rise to a footnote that digressively develops a metaphor relating staplers, locomotives, and phonograph tone arms by comparing the three stages of their design history, from "cast-iron and upright" through "streamlined" to "the great era of squareness." Note that description here is functional rather than merely amplificatory to the extent that the metaphoric point would be obscure without it; but this passage also contains a lengthy parenthesis that begins by comparing the devices in terms of their relation to "their respective media of information storage," and it proceeds with another list, this time of the kinds of documents that get stapled (the "kinds" being themselves specified in further lists) before comparing, over five lines of print, old staple marks in paper to the traces of TB vaccination on arms. The whole comparison collapses, moreover, with the remark that locomotive design in France and Japan is reverting to aerodynamic forms, the hopeful prediction that staplers are about to follow suit, and the regretful observation that CDs have made the "inspirational era" of the tone arm a thing of the past. (Another of Baker's footnotes, on page 82, is completely self-erasing, ending with the comment that "it is irresponsible of me to bring [the matter] up.")

By the time one has read one's way through the long illustrative list of happenings, A through D, that resemble a shoelace break, interrupting oneself at the footnote in order to digest the design history of staplers, locomotives, and tone arms, returning to the list only to embark on an interpolated description of the three phases of the act of stapling, one returns to the narrative with a mind multiply distracted and ready to understand the narrator's later comparison of his own head to an exploded popcorn, "composed of exfoliations that in bursting beyond their outer carapace were nevertheless guided into paisleys and baobabs and related white Fibonaccia . . ." (106). Reading has become an exercise in learning to redirect one's attention from the linear requirements of narrative, and to do so in a way that does not exclude narrative constructions but attempts to take into account all the fascinating paisleys and baobabs, the trailing "strings" that narrative tidiness ordinarily has no time for, cutting them off or hastily clearing them out of sight.

Baker's exploded text thus stands in relation to narrative as the messiness of everyday life to the artificially and expensively ordered paradise of the office: this is in each case a relation of continuity in discontinuity. "We came to work every day and were treated like popes—a new manila folder for every task, expensive courier services; taxi vouchers" (I abridge a long list of examples of corporate excess). "What were we participating in here?" asks the narrator (92–93), drawing attention in the first instance to the high profit rates of corporations that make such extravagance possible. But this luxurious "every day" of the work week nevertheless has within it a more ordinary *everyday*, the interest and value of which become evident in memory, that is, when one has left the job and its "problems, although they once obsessed you . . . turn out to have been hollow. . . . But coterminously . . . the nod of the security guard, his sign-in book, the escalator ride, the things on your desk, the sight of colleagues' offices, their faces, . . . the features of the corporate bathroom, all miraculously expand; and in this way what was central and what was incidental end up exactly reversed" (92).

In a similar way, the "lived workweek" itself has a syncopated, "Hungarian 5/2 rhythm" (92) that organizes the relation of work to time off, and of the respective values that attach to each. For, finally, the orderliness of the office contrasts with the home life of its workers who

> return . . . and stand sweating in front of the chest of drawers, some hanging open, no ball bearings at all, and put the briefcase and the bag from the convenience store down on the floor and begin to pull handfulls of change and stubs of Velamint packs out of our pockets. . . . We walk around in our underpants and T-shirt waiting for the Ronzoni shells to boil. Can this disorganized, do-it-yourself evening life really be the same life as the clean, noble Pendaflex life we lead in office buildings? (93–94)

Everything tells us that yes, as linear narrative is not discontinuous with exploded textuality, so the "every day" of work and the messiness of the everyday combine in a single, albeit unevenly accented, rhythm. Pendaflex files (which themselves exemplify the continuity/discontinuity of toilet rolls and escalators) are not therefore fully remote from—they might belong in the same list of classificatory devices as—a chest of drawers with its drawers hanging open (and perhaps a few socks draped over them like ties over a doorknob). The philosophic genre of the meditation, itself "disorganized" in this case and generically "do-it-yourself," exists here to teach us to attend to that relation, and perhaps to question the disproportion of the 5/2 ratio that the disciplined, organized, and anti-do-it-yourself working economy imposes, with its values of efficiency, productivity, and progress.

The critical function of *The Mezzanine* as a philosophical meditation is not limited, however, to the questioning it encourages. In clogging the linearity of narrative so that those 5/2 proportions are reversed, much as memory reverses the relative importance of the official values of the office and its everyday realities, meditative writing takes a kind of explosive revenge that is figured graphically in the device employed by the narrator when, attempting to "urinat[e] in a corporate setting," he finds himself intimidated into retention by the proximity of a colleague. The trick consists, like that of the escalated text, in converting the blockage in plumbing into a liberating explosion. "When someone takes his position next to you . . . imagine yourself turning and dispassionately urinating onto the side of his head. Imagine your voluminous stream making fleeting parts in his hair. . . . Imagine drawing an X over his face . . ." (84–85). It always works, the narrator comments, and in this particular case it works explosively. "I gave [the urine] a secondary boost from my diaphragm, and it blasted out" (85).

It's in the bathroom, too—the liminal space, as we recall, between work and lunch—that he recommends another, parallel form of revenge. Angered by the cynicism of managements that allege self-serving and hypocritical reasons for economizing on paper towels by installing hot air machines, claiming greater hygiene and efficiency and forgetting that one doesn't wash only one's hands at the sink, he advises a tactic that combines the explosive pleasure of face washing, generous use of the perforated toilet roll in lieu of the absent towels, and the satisfaction of clogging the plumbing:

> You go into a stall and pull yourself a huge handful . . . and return to the sink with it. As soon as you dampen it with water, it wilts to a semi-transparent purse in your fingers. You move this dripping plasma over your face; little pieces of it adhere to your cheek or brow; then you must assemble another big wad to dry off with—but ah! now your fingers are wet, so that when you try to pull more toilet paper from the hundred-thousand-sheet roll, the leading end simply dissolves in your fingers, tearing prematurely [like a broken shoelace]. Deciding to let your face air-dry, you look around for a place to throw out the initial macerated flapjack, and discover that the wastebasket is gone. So you drop it in the corner with other miscellaneous trash, or flip it vengefully into the already clogged toilet. (90–91)

Two things are worth noticing here. One, the frustration produced by managerial parsimony and the revenge that consists of clogging the toilet are coterminous; their meeting place is in the toilet roll. Two, managerial economy provides the means, through its own (false) economy, as well as the motivation, by the frustrations it induces, for the vengeful pleasure of making a satisfying mess in the hygienically clean and tidy corporate bathroom, in the same way that narrative economy supplies the means of its own subversion through the simple device of escalation, clogging it with details and blowing up the clogs. In the connected world of mediation, power structures provide the means of their subversion, but the pleasures of oppositionality can in turn, and conversely, only be opportunistic, turning manipulative means into unlooked-for devices of momentary release and revenge.

Another occasion on which frustration and an experience of release combine is the breaking of a shoelace. I suppose the reason why learning to tie your own shoelaces is so widely regarded as a major step toward adulthood (it is first on the narrator's list of the coming of age events in his own life) is that, under the guise of achieving independence, it transparently figures instead the disciplinary principle that self-imposed constraints are more economical than, and achieve the same outcome as, externally imposed training, supervision, and punishment. In an economy of production it is much more efficient for me to go to work daily of my own accord than to have to be rounded up each morning by, say, a posse of fellow workers or the police. We are encouraged, then, to learn to tie our own shoelaces. And the fact that shoelaces come undone, and sometimes break under the strains that are imposed on them, furnishes an appropriate metaphor for the inevitable weak point in any disciplinary system, the place where untidiness and messiness enter the well-ordered picture. And with them enters the "noise" that, according to Michel Serres, hints at the possibility of an alternative economy, an economy not of production but of the freely given and of parasitism.[14] The snapping of a lace, frustrating as it may be, also induces a sense of relief—the same sense of relief one's foot experiences when shoelaces come undone: "My left shoelace had snapped just before lunch. At some earlier point in the morning, my left shoe had become untied, and as I had sat at my desk working on a memo, my foot had sensed its potential freedom and stepped out of the sauna of black cordovan to soothe itself with rhythmic movements over an area of wall-to-wall carpeting under my desk" (11). Laces come untied, of course, because, as the narrator points out, the knot that constrains the foot is not a true knot but something more dubious, like an ideological construct or a mystification, "an illusion, a trick that you performed on the lace-string by bending segments of it back on themselves and tightening other temporary bends around them: it looked like a knot and functioned like a knot, but the whole thing was really an amazing interdependent pyramid scheme. . . ." (17).

So the frustration attendant on breaking a shoelace is not unlike the irritation one feels when some cherished belief or practice one has always held to be natural is suddenly revealed to be ideological. One *ought* to be relieved, and one *is* relieved, but one misses a certain order of things and its constraints because they had become familiar and habitual. And so, meekly, like the narrator of *The Mezzanine*, we retie our loose laces (13), and if they break we go out in our lunch hour and buy ourselves a new pair, armed with which we return to our appointed place (at the office, in the factory, in the classroom, in the home), happy to lace ourselves again into the familiar constrictions. The time of the broken shoelace, between the relaxation of constraint and its reimposition, is "time out," something the system knows how to foresee and provide for, accommodating itself to the inevitability of noise by incorporating the noise into its workings so that any possibility the disturbance might suggest of an alternative order of things is held in check. The corporation can't foresee broken shoelaces but it can schedule lunch breaks and it can encourage us to use the latter to repair the former. And so, like the narrator returning to the office at the end of his "sunlit noontide hour," I put down my copy of *The Mezzanine*, which I've been reading for the nth time with undiminished pleasure, and return dutifully to pounding out laborious sentences in the capacity of a professional critic. My task is to "theorize" pleasure; that is not the same as experiencing it. Lunch break is over.

The Greek word *lysis*, from which we derive *analysis*, *dialysis*, and *paralysis*, refers to a looseness or loosening (as of the straps of a sandal), and it's to this loosening of discipline that the meditation, with its extenuated, step-by-step, spinning out of text, owes both the pleasure it gives and its ability to mediate change. Some meditations are *analytic*, however: they take things apart, like Descartes, with a view to putting them together again methodically, into a new and improved and possibly tighter system. Already in ancient times, the Greek word *analysis* was associated with disciplinary concepts like examination and investigation (*historia*, whence of course *story*). *Paralysis*, though, etymologically suggests a coming unstrung, a relaxing of the nerves such that one goes limp, like a puppet without its strings, and a truly "paralytic" meditation would be one that so explodes the constraints of narrative (or argumentative) ordering that a state of textual *inertia* ensues, from which there could be no return. I have looked in chapter 4 at some texts in which the discontinuities inherent in the effect of continuity/discontinuity produced by mediation tend strongly toward actual disjunctiveness and hence approach (but do not reach) a state of paralysis.

But *The Mezzanine* might be described as a "dialytic" meditation, in which the loosening of disciplinary constraints serves the function of permitting new and more pleasurable connections to be formed and an

alternative view of things to be glimpsed without the separation from
the world of discipline—here figured by the corporate office—ever
becoming absolute. The connection is always there, just an escalator
ride away. Our narrator is a fellow who asks for his half pint of milk
in its zip-lock container to be stapled into a bag so that he can walk
with one hand free and with it slightly do childish things, like slapping
a mailbox as he passes. "I liked other people to see me as a guy in a tie
yet carefree and casual enough to be doing what kids do when they drag
a stick over the black uprights of a cast-iron fence" (8). That childish
stick against the uprights, recalled by an older but still not fully adult
narrator, is playing yet another continuity/discontinuity game, one that
is quite comparable to the fun of riding an escalator. But the non–stick
wielding hand doesn't only hold milk and one or two other items,
including the rest of his lunch and a paperback Marcus Aurelius. It also
grasps the new pair of laces the guy in a tie has bought and with which
he is returning, up the escalator, to his office. Like blood in a dialysis
machine, he remains connected; for a time he has left the constraining
environment of the "usual channels," but now he is returning to them,
duly refreshed.

Lessons in Crittercism

Learning from Dogs, 1 (Home Truths)

Being asked what he had done to be called a hound, [Diogenes] said: "I fawn on those who give me anything, I yelp at those who refuse, and I set my teeth in rascals."— Diogenes Laertius

Let's go back to those campus dogs in Frank O'Hara's Ann Arbor poem (chapter 1). They were animals that had been turned loose by their student owners on graduating or on leaving town at vacation time. They roamed freely on the campus and scavenged for a living, until finally a cleanup campaign was launched by the authorities and they were eliminated from the scene. It's axiomatic that institutions of learning are intolerant of alternative occasions for education, and the species I'll call canine philosophers have never been welcome in the eyes of the established and the tenured. For institutional authority has every interest in maintaining contextual closure, but what humans can learn from dogs is precisely an art of digressing as a critical practice.

In recent years, North American universities have undergone a form of democratization that has made women and so-called ethnic, racial, and sexual minorities a sizable part of their population. By virtue of their extra-academic provenance, such people are apt to play a critical role in the modern academy not unlike that performed in fourth-century Athens by those canine philosophers, the Cynics. The welcome they have received has therefore been somewhat ambivalent. A change of perspective is refreshing, another contextualization of things can be instructive—but one doesn't necessarily want it to bring about change or to divert well-settled lives from their established path. The newcomers have thus been received *on sufferance*, a bit as one might take a stray dog into one's house. If its presence doesn't disturb things too much, it can stay. Let it challenge the traditions too radically, and it will discover that tolerance has its limits. If it actually bites, it is out.

For their part, and again like a stray animal brought into a house, the academic newcomers themselves feel strange and out of place. They've learned the codes of academic discourse, but it's a lingo that doesn't necessarily sit well with the kinds of things *they* might like to say, things having to do with extra-academic knowledge (an other context) and which may be critical, therefore, of the self-enclosure inherent in disciplinary modes of knowing and the ivory tower of scholarship. Such people may feel they have something in common with the kind of dogs that populate the modern literary tradition from Cervantes on, dogs who have to face the fact that they've somehow acquired an unexpected talent, that of speaking as humans do. What, given this unlikely competence, are the dogs to *say*? My two-chapter study of literary "dogs' lives"—fictional biographies and autobiographies of dogs (most frequently talking dogs)—is therefore dedicated to all those who, like campus dogs promoted to the faculty, find themselves occupying the particular critical niche reserved for canine philosophers as talking dogs. My questions will concern their own dubious position, but also, and more particularly, what the resident humans, as supposed noncanines, can learn from them.

Talking dogs, after all, who have shared living quarters with humans, can be expected to deliver some telling *home truths*—truths that humans, with their cultivated way of life and their various gentilities, may tend to have forgotten but that canine observers are quick to see. But also, and perhaps more fundamentally, there is something that humans can learn, not simply from what talking dogs may say about them and their way of life, but from the very existence of such hybrid creatures as talking dogs. Talking dogs can be seen to enact a problematics of *mongrelization* that might, at first glance, seem to be the special worry of street curs. But it quickly reveals itself, instead, to be emblematic: are humans so very different from dogs that may have learned a few tricks, including that of speech? In our own makeup, too, there's a baffling coexistence of nature and culture, of the animal and the nonanimal, an odd mongrelization that makes *Homo sapiens* a very dubious species indeed.

In this chapter, I concentrate on dogs as tellers of home truths, leaving the question of mongrelization—the problem of canine "spottiness"—for chapter 7. But the two questions, which concern on the one hand the problem of plain speaking (can speech ever be "plain" or "unvarnished"?) and on the other the problem of who speaks when a dog speaks, are really aspects of the same dilemma, which is the basic dilemma—or at least the very condition of possibility—of cynical philosophy. And the dilemma, or condition of possibility, of cynical philosophy is in turn that of social criticism in general: it is the problem of the position of the critic with respect to the object of criticism, and of the odd, but inescapable, mutual intrication that affects the relation of critical subjects to their object. One can't criticize the culture of which one is oneself a subject without one's own self, and hence one's criticism, being in some degree *disqualified* by virtue of their involvement in the culture that is declared deficient. When a dog talks in order to cast critical light on human culture, can the dog's speech represent in any sense the point of view of a dog (a nonhuman, nonspeaking animal)? Or is such speech inevitably a discourse that participates in the general conversation of the humans whose culture the dog wishes to criticize? And if the dog's criticisms are inescapably part of the culture they criticize, how is it possible for them to be taken as plain and unvarnished—as home truths—and not in some sense affected, inflected, by human motivations?

In short, to speak, even if one is a talking dog, is inevitably to be ventriloquized by the language one speaks and the culture that mediates all discourse, including discourse critical of the culture. A cynic philosopher is one who speaks and acts doggishly, as etymology suggests (Greek *kyon*), but the cynic is nevertheless doing so *as a philosopher* and with a view to making a philosophical point, even though the point is about the delusions under which humans labor in culture. And literary talking dogs of course constitute a particular, and particularly vivid, example of speech as ventriloquism, to the extent that their speaking is subject to the prior condition of authorship: without Cervantes there would be no "Coloquio de los perros," and J. R. Ackerley in the "Tulip trilogy" (which is my main text on the present occasion) makes no attempt to conceal the evident fact that it is he who is making use of his dog Tulip for the purposes of a misanthropic project that is not Tulip's but his own. Even as they enunciate doggish home truths from which humans can learn, talking dogs are uncomfortably aware of a human voice that is speaking through them.

For philosopher dogs, this critical problem of the ventriloquial and hence cultural character of one's criticism of culture has a particularly poignant edge, which stems from the fact that the cynic philosopher's principal target can be classified under the general heading of hypocrisy, or in more modern terms, of "false consciousness." False consciousness, like hypocrisy (in one sense of the term), is a state of unconscious error: it derives from our ability to mistake a particular context that happens to be culturally dominant for the only context; and it is open to correction, therefore, by the basically very simple act of changing context, by means of a pointed digression. I've told the story of Diogenes and the plucked chicken, which exposed the philosophical forgetfulness of the trivial in Plato's definition of the human species as a "featherless biped" (chapter 1). Similarly, when Alexander condescendingly asked the doggish philosopher how he could be of assistance to him, as the latter sunned himself tranquilly on the agora, he was stunned to be asked (as one might ask some ordinary person) kindly to step out of the way and stop blocking the sunshine. The problem, though, is that the new context in which the philosopher places the situation may itself be subject to false consciousness, that is, to the unconscious error of assuming a given context to be the whole context. The forgetfulness of which Alexander stands condemned may equally be the error of the critical philosopher. For to ask Alexander to step out of the sun is not, in the end, something that a dog would do, even if a dog could speak (or it is something that a dog might conceivably do only if it could speak as humans do). It is, however, something that a Greek philosopher might do, with a view to making a philosophical point: in order to enjoy the pleasure of cutting Alexander down to size, it is necessary first to participate to some degree in the cultural illusion of Alexander's greatness—whereas, to a dog, Alexander is, always and only, just another human, indistinguishable from the rest. So Diogenes's plain speaking, the home truth he delivers as one might deliver a blow (the great Alexander, when all's said and done, is just another man whose body blocks the light), is in the final analysis anything but plain speech: it is, through and through, speech for rhetorical effect. And the cynical philosopher thus stands guilty of a form of hypocrisy of his own.

There is worse, though, for hypocrisy isn't always unconscious, and false consciousness can be actively simulated. In his *Critique of Cynical Reason*, Peter Sloterdijk has coined a helpful terminological distinction between the plain speaking of the cynic philosopher, whom he calls a *kynic*, and the practice of *cynicism* in its more modern sense, which Sloterdijk defines as "enlightened false consciousness."[1] This is the cynicism that takes advantage of the phenomenon of false conscious-ness by simulating it for the advantage of the cynic: it is a pretense of false consciousness, then, and it entails a shift of context that is not dissimilar from the critical, plain-speaking, philosophical cynicism that Sloterdijk calls kynical. For, like Pontius Pilate washing his hands of the death of Christ, cynics "step away from" beliefs they (act as if they) subscribe to and stand apart from them, inhabiting (as it were) another context, like ironists, and disculpating themselves by a certain disavowal of responsibility: "Is it my fault if people are so deluded?" The cynical gesture, then, is a digressive one, like that of the kynic, and it is potentially even a critical one—but this particular form of hypocrisy consists of denying the connectedness between the cynic's position and the false consciousness it simulates, a connectedness that is axiomatic by virtue of the theory of the permeability of contexts. Cynics thus fail to perceive the sense in which they are responsible for the effects of that false consciousness, even as they subjectively distance themselves from it. Thus the cynic, in the end, is neither openly critical of false consciousness nor in any sense self-critical. The ideology of cynics is an ideology of distinction, consisting in the belief that their enlightened superiority as connoisseurs of other folks' forms of false consciousness somehow protects them from falling into false consciousness in their own way and on their own behalf. Yet that belief is itself a form of false consciousness.

For the kynic, the problem posed by cynicism lies in the fact that, in a digressive gesture, the kynic dissociates her- or himself from false consciousness much as the cynic does. The kynic, it's true, rarely indulges in cynical handwashing; rather than being coolly dissociated from human follies, she or he is made angry and indignant by them. But kynics do enjoy the pleasure of distinction that derives from the agreeable sensation of being wiser than the mass of deluded humanity; and they aren't necessarily above exploiting the delusions of the masses for personal advantage, enjoying a reputation as a particularly acerbic critic, for instance, or even making a career (as I suppose Diogenes did) out of the practice of kynicism. It's never clear, in other words, that kynical practices, as the criticism of false consciousness, aren't in some sense and to some degree "tainted," not only by a false consciousness of their own but also by cynical self-advantage; and that thought is a demeaning one for kynics who would like to believe in the plainness of their plain speaking, and to be able to deliver home truths without running the risk of someone's pointing out to them a few home truths of their own.

Such a problem haunts in particular those literary dogs' lives—such as Cervantes's "Coloquio de los perros" and Bulgakov's *Heart of a Dog*—that are particularly conscious of the problem of mongrelization and which are inclined, therefore, to pose the problem of being a talking dog as a question of genealogy. Authorship as a ventriloquial human presence in the dog's speech is figured in these cases by the dogs' dubious ascendancy, an ascendancy of which the ability to talk is itself the sign, or the symptom. Bulgakov's Sharik is a street-cur who becomes a dog-man by receiving the pituitary gland of a criminal, implanted by a surgeon guilty of the ideology of distinction. And Cervantes's pair of *pícaro* dogs, Cipión and Berganza, worry that they may be descended from a witch — information they receive from another witch, one Cañizares, whom they know to be a hypocrite of the cynical, not the kynical, kind. I amplify this point in chapter 7.

In the two texts I want to concentrate on now, however, these genealogical questions aren't raised. In J. R. Ackerley's Tulip trilogy and Barbara Bush's *Millie's Book*,[2] we're dealing not with *pícaro* dogs, whose lives are a series of shifts and digressions, but with domesticated animals whose literary function lies in the area of telling home truths — with this important difference, however, that in one of them the relation of authorship to the canine persona is kynical in kind — the author activates the dog as a critic of humankind — whereas in the other it is cynical. Indeed, one of the more cynically manipulative documents of recent years emanated, during the Bush years, from a White House that was disingenuously presenting itself as just a home; and I'll begin my exploration of canine literature, therefore, with a kynical reading of the cynicism of *Millie's Book* before going on to contrast it, in the matter of the telling of domestic verities, with the three texts by Ackerley that form something of a modern kynical canon. That Ackerley may himself be cynically exploiting Tulip in a way not essentially different from Barbara Bush's clearly cynical exploitation of the White House dog Millie is a question I'll leave in abeyance for now, the better to point a contrast between cynical rhetoric in the one, and the rhetoric of kynicism in the other. But it's telling, I think, that although genealogical motifs are backgrounded in the case of these house dogs, another motif, present in both texts, does raise the issue of parenthood, and hence the possibility of cynicism, from another angle.

The participation of the cultural critic in culture doesn't only make the critic a kind of mongrel; it also implies that the critic is engaging, willy-nilly, in cultural reproduction, an issue that surfaces therefore, in texts devoted to telling home truths, in episodes in which canine motherhood and the act of giving birth — that is, the matter of biological reproduction—are represented. This is the case in both *Millie's Book* and the Tulip trilogy. The degree of gentility and the degree of frankness with which each text deals with the gynecological and obstetric facts are good indicators, as we shall see, of the respective degrees of cynicism and kynicism with which each text makes its cultural contribution. But the equal rhetoricity of each text—kynical frankness being as much a rhetorical effect as cynical euphemism—serves to remind us that kynicism and cynicism have more in common than my borrowing of Sloterdijk's distinction might at first seem to imply, and that what links them is their connectedness to the culture of false consciousness that each, in different ways, seeks to dissociate itself from.

If canine philosophers teach us to digress, then, the single most salient lesson we budding kynical critics stand to learn from their example, as it's represented in the literary tradition, is a lesson in humility. One can't digress from culture, whether kynically or cynically, without participating simultaneously in the ways of culture.

MILLIE, OR HER MISTRESS'S VOICE

Who is the author, or (to put it another way) what is the genre of *Millie's Book*? Is it autobiography (Millie's life told by Millie) or is it biography (Millie's life told by someone else)? The title itself is unilluminating on this point, the force of the genitive in *Millie's* being unclear and the word *book* generically unspecific. In the bookstore where I bought my copy, I first nosed unsuccessfully around the "Biography" section and then dug about, equally fruitlessly, under "Fiction" (where I was rewarded, though, by encountering a number of "dogs' lives" by writers ranging from Cervantes to Woolf and Kafka, who were less cagey than Millie's author about acknowledging their authorial status).

It's true that Millie is a fictional dog only in a relatively sophisticated sense, so I found her book finally in another part of the store altogether, where books intended for animal lovers are shelved under rubrics like "Dogs," "Cats," and "Horses." By classifying the book in terms of its *readership*, the store had made a canny move (to which I'll return). But I thought they had nevertheless committed themselves finally as to authorship by shelving *Millie's Book* alphabetically at *B* for (Barbara) Bush. Imagine my discontent, then, on reading the first line of text, to discover that Millie, unlike most literary dogs, has a middle and last name of her own (Millicent Kerr Bush) and is also, therefore, a "Bush." The store's shelving practice was of no help. Furthermore, the byline to the title, which reads in full: *Millie's Book as Dictated to Barbara Bush*, seems to constitute a fairly clear claim to authorial priority on Millie's part, *if* one is prepared, that is, to assume that dogs can speak (and dictate) but not write. The text proves to be in doggy first person, too—except that the style, content, and diction are so undoglike and gushy that new doubts quickly arise as to who dictated to whom (or alternatively, who is ventriloquizing whom). Take as an example this passage about one of the smaller and more intimate White House gardens:

> I think of the spot as the sort of place a First Lady who is a grandmother might wheel a baby carriage and sit in the shade and enjoy her own back yard, in a quiet, secluded spot. And very especially it would be a good place for four year olds to have a "tea party," or watch the goldfish in the little pool—or for their mother or grandmother to read about *Peter Rabbit* or *Winnie the Pooh*. (76)

Is this Barbara Bush's reverie, or is it Millie who is somehow daydreaming herself here into the role of First Lady and doting grandmother? (In either case, "back yard" is a particularly condescending touch.)

One's doubts about Millie's authorship grow even stronger when one looks more closely at the front matter. The cover illustration shows a tall, whitehaired, grandmotherly woman, wearing pearls and a blue tailored suit, and holding a spaniel—but in a position more reminiscent of a ventriloquist's dummy than a dog. Both the human and the animal look uncomfortable but especially the latter: maybe it suspects it's being made use of, for a photo opportunity if nothing else? There's a whole slew of dedications, too, including a particularly fulsome one to George Bush, that are attributed to "Bar and I," seemingly giving Barbara equal billing with Millie; and another slew to some "special" people (where "special" seems to mean "little" in the Oscar Awards sense of production and technical folk), that are signed by "мкв" alone, as though she were only a secondary author. But just when one is willing to decide that the author can only be Barbara Bush, it turns out, most intriguingly of all, on the following page that all "author proceeds" will be donated to the Barbara Bush Foundation for Family Literacy— which seems to put *both* Barbara B. and Millie B. in the back seat.

Don't worry too much for now about the difference between "family" literacy and the ordinary kind (the foundation thinks kids should learn to read at home, around the goldfish pond), or whether "proceeds" from authorship differ significantly from royalties or profits. By the rule of follow-the-cash, responsibility for authorship is here being "donated" to an *authorizing* instance that happens to be part of the conservative Republican apparatus. The privileges, proceeds, and responsibilities of writing have receded progressively, in other words, from Millie's own tenuous claim, to the strong likelihood of Barbara Bush's having had a hand in the matter, and on to the Barbara Bush Foundation for Family Literacy; and by the same token authorship has become increasingly faceless as well as increasingly political. But, of course, the name Bush unites all three authorial entities, as if it were being claimed that membership of a family is the only thing that really matters. And, recalling the way the word *family* is stuck a bit incongruously to the word *literacy* in the foundation's title, and noticing that the date of copyright (held, by the way, by the foundation) is 1990, one is reminded that, in preparation for the 1992 elections, "family values" had become a slogan of the Republican Party, which used them as a major platform plank. It is, in fact, to the not innocent promotion of "family" that the book is dedicated, yet someone is washing their hands of responsibility for that promotion, ventriloquizing it through poor Millie, and "donating" authorship and its "proceeds" to the lofty purpose of encouraging literacy. That's the kind of hypocrisy that gives cynicism a bad name.

All the coyness over authorship falls into place when one realizes that Millie's voice and vision are being recruited in the service of a politically motivated depiction of the White House—as the site of an exemplary (Republican) family enjoying its equally exemplary home life—in which the text's author(s) don't believe but which they think its readers will swallow. It's not just that the Bush family leads such a sanitized existence, although that's suspicious enough; it's more that the book's breathless account of life in the Bush White House so thoroughly depoliticizes the practices and processes of government (something that can be thought to connect with, in particular, the privatization of social issues implied by the collocation of family and literacy in the foundation's title). But the clue that really triggers suspicion is, of course, that Millie's attention and style are so overworked by the ideological task to which they are bent that she scarcely has time to sound like a dog at all. Even her doggie hobbies, like chasing squirrels and digging in flower beds, are mentioned mainly because of their repercussion in the White House bureaucracy.

Most of the time, though, her attention is fixed unwaveringly on the invariably amiable doings of the Bush clan, its distinguished guests, its devoted and of course beloved staff, its multiplicitous grandchildren and apparently limitless circle of "dear friends." A secondary interest is in the anecdotal history of various White House rooms and spaces, portraits and furniture, and gardens. Ladylike in her interests, she's ladylike too in her manners, seeing and hearing no evil and careful to give no offense. From her narrative you wouldn't know that people are capable of duplicitous or hypocritical behavior, or of getting divorces and committing adultery, any more than you'd learn that the presidency of the United States is a political office serving powerful interests. Thus, the grandmotherly picture of tea parties and storybooks by the pond is matched by the President's innocent fondness for pitching horseshoes:

> There is no happier sound [says Millie] than the clinking of a horseshoe as it hits the post. The Prez invited sixteen departments in the White House to field a team for the first tournament. It is now up to thirty-two teams and growing. (77)

(Imagine the joy in the departments when the memo arrived "inviting" them to field a horseshoe pitching team!) What one learns from Millie, in short, is that life in the White House has no seamy side; it's a kind of happy pastoral. Berganza's capacity for *murmuración*, in the "Coloquio" (chapter 7), is a talent that has passed her by.

So learning from dogs, in this case, would have to mean something like learning to be, like Millie, a ventriloquist's dummy or a patsy. I mean that the appropriation of the dog's perspective—which is common, obviously, to the literary genre of dogs' lives as a whole—isn't just blatant, here, to the point of implausibility. It's also deeply condescending to the book's audience: the book's project, as my bookstore understood, lies in its targeting of a supposedly gullible readership, from which the cynically "absent" author(s) are distancing themselves by washing their hands of responsibility for the gushy text that's attributed to Millie. As the vagueness of the book's title implies, it's addressed to a class of infrequent readers to whom the word *book* is supposed to be sufficient generic specification; and these readers are further supposed to be dog lovers in need of ideological instruction in what it means to constitute a family. In spite of the foundation's fervor about families reading together, it's particularly striking in this connection that the White House family itself is so busy being an exemplary Republican family that they never in fact have time to set the example of actually reading. The idyllic scene of reading by the pond is imagined as desirable but seems not actually to happen; the Bushes do display real interest in press coverage; and some shelves of books are visible in the background of a photo representing, in the foreground, an almost obscenely familial Kennebunkport bedroom, with the President and Mrs. Bush presiding, patriarchally if a bit sleepily, over a sprawling bedful of grandchildren, plus Millie. But that's it. It's quite evident that the interest of the text, addressed as it supposedly is to relatively illiterate readers, isn't in encouraging them to read or even to read *en famille*, so much as it's in depicting for them, as a model to admire and emulate in preference to their own supposedly unkempt and unseemly mode of life, the genteel, middle-class family life of the Bushes. The reason one should learn to read, in other words (from the point of view of the Barbara Bush Foundation), is so that one can learn the value of family values, as opposed to the evils of, say, single parenthood (or worse). But since no family could ever be quite as cute, amiable, and conflict-free as Millie's humans appear to be, and the model is so exemplary as to be inimitable, the real reason for learning to read must be so as to acquire proper respect for one's betters and a suitable sense of one's own inadequacy with respect to the hegemonic model. (It's a version of the star system, in other words: the home truth about the Bushes the book wants us to swallow is that they are the stars of family life.)

So it's ironic, in this respect, that dogs have a family life of their own and one that rarely measures up to the irreproachable gentility of the Bush clan as it's represented in *Millie's Book*. Indeed, it much more closely resembles the life of the text's imagined audience. The generic interest of the domesticated subgenre of dogs' lives in motherhood, as part of their anxiety over the question of who speaks when a dog talks, thus produces some surprisingly awkward difficulties for *Millie's Book* when it embarks on the story of Millie's pups. For, alas, their father's role is confined to that of stud, and the puppies themselves, instead of forming a snug, wriggly brood around Millie like the Bush grandchildren around the President and the First Lady, are ignominiously separated from their mother and shipped off all over the country. What kind of an example of family values is that? The narrative, therefore—which I suppose can't resist mentioning Millie's motherhood because the photos of her with the pups are very cute—deploys considerable energy in euphemizing the conditions of their birth and upbringing. More cuteness than ever is mobilized to prevent any possible connection being made between Millie's case and the lives of "welfare mothers," those putative readers of the book who might even live—Washington being the city it is—not too far from the White House itself. She's made to express regret at not seeing the sire more often (at least they're still "in touch"); much fun is had with Barbara Bush's squeamishness and general incompetence in obstetric matters; and the breakup of Millie's progeny becomes an amusing count down game, its possible implications being conjured out of sight in a flurry of praise for the various "dear friends" (not Millie's friends, of course, but the Bushes') who take the pups in. In this way a danger is averted, that of the book's intended readers recognizing a picture of their own powerlessness in Millie's inability to hold together her family as the Bushes do theirs. And it's averted by making her completely oblivious of the contrast between the conditions of her life and those that enable the White House humans to be such exemplary figures. She's offered as a model, in other words, not of ideology critique (the specialty of canine philosophers), but of ideological self-mystification. And that is what makes her the object of a cynical project.

A dog with more street smarts than poor Millie (to whom the meaner neighborhoods of Washington DC are manifestly off-limits) would certainly not have missed such a golden opportunity for *murmuración*: the double standard that prevails between dogs and humans with respect to their family arrangements presents a worthy target of kynical irony. But Millie isn't street smart, she's the model ideological subject, the subject of ideological hegemony, as cynics—anxious to imagine themselves as non-dupes, absolutely exempt from all forms of self-mystification or false consciousness—are obliged, by the logic of distinction, to imagine such a subject, that is, as a complete, unmitigated, totally uncritical, dope. And that's the sense in which she's a model for the projected readership of the book. Over the gates at Auschwitz a motto reads: ARBEIT MACHT FREI (work makes you free). The Nazis certainly didn't believe such a doctrine themselves, nor did they much care whether the inmates believed it. Their interest lay in its being believed by the general population, and as Sloterdijk points out, it was already a cynical doctrine in that sense when it emerged in the nineteenth century as an ideologeme designed to encourage the working class to acquiesce in its own exploitation (64).

It's a bit hard on Barbara Bush and the Foundation for Family Literacy, I know, to draw a parallel between *Millie's Book* and the gates of Auschwitz. But cynicism is never innocent, even when its vehicle is genteel rather than brutal, and the parallel with nineteenth-century capitalist hegemony holds quite nicely in the case of the Republican Party's promotion of "family." All cynicism wears a kind of self-disculpating smile, "as crooked," Sloterdijk says, "as the comma between yes and but" (143). This is the smile of belief in its own distinction: *we* are the only true humans, everyone else can be manipulated like some stupid mutt.

LEARNING FROM TULIP

J. R. Ackerley's project, though, is a project of human/canine indistinction, best illustrated by the story of his domestic arrangements with a female German shepherd named Queenie in life, but renamed in literature either Evie or Tulip. Where Millie's position in the White House family is that of a pet (and in what's alleged to be "her" book that of the instrument of an enterprise that doesn't really concern her), Ackerley—after living the life of a middle-class homosexual man in Edwardian and between-wars England—settled for fifteen years into a relation of shared domesticity and some semblance of real equality, bordering even on sexual intimacy, with Tulip, and it's the story of that commingling of man and animal that he tells. It gave him more satisfaction and happiness, although the relation was dominated by Tulip's possessiveness and jealousy, than any of his human connections over the years had done. "Unable to love each other," as he once put it with characteristic misanthropy in a letter, "the English turn naturally to dogs"[3]; and the summary of his love life that he gives us in *My Father and Myself* is a personal confirmation of that judgment: "[it] may be said to have begun with a golliwog and ended with an Alsatian bitch; in between there passed several hundred young men, mostly of the lower orders and often clad in uniforms of one sort or another" (MF&M, 110). So this is a family story of a clearly different order than Millie's, one that challenges hierarchical distinctions between animal and man, and in so doing produces home truths of a kind to shock the genteel inhabitants of the White House and their circle of acquaintance.

Which, of course, is Ackerley's goal. The story is true, but the tone of its telling, as my quotations will already have shown, is deliberately provocative; it has the characteristic impudence of the kynic. Gentility isn't the modus operandi here, it's the target. I don't mean that Ackerley was out to deflate cynicism as such; the object of his criticism, writing as he did in the last years of Empire and the immediate postwar years, was old-fashioned British hypocrisy of the unself-conscious, uncomplicatedly self-deluding, sort, a fear of the sexual and a blindness to the body (more generally an obliviousness to the category of the natural), that made life in Ackerley's London, "enormous, puritanical and joyless" (MF&M, 134), a deprived and dreary affair. Kynical insistence on triviality—the doglike side of human make-up—is thus Ackerley's response to the false consciousness of his hypocritical contemporaries.

But he had also a second, related target, which was the failure of communication that he had experienced in his own (hypocritical) family, a failure that made his relation to his own father a strained and difficult one, the son concealing his homosexuality while the father (as it turned out) concealed his extramarital love life and very probably a gay past of his own. The kynical response to this failure of openness is to insist, therefore, on another aspect of indistinction: the relative ease with which dogs and humans can communicate and get along, as witness the *entente* that prevailed between Tulip and Ackerley. Tulip is the only dog in my corpus who doesn't talk, in a literal sense. When it comes to *murmuración*, Ackerley is her willing mouthpiece, of course; but the thematics of the talking dog is in any case present, especially in the last of the three books, *My Dog Tulip*, where it's transferred onto the observation that, in spite of dogs' inability to speak, and in contradistinction to the sad shambles to which the lack of communication reduces relations between humans, not only can dogs and humans communicate, *as if* dogs could talk, but dogs are also able to teach us humans some valuable lessons in how better to be human. The condition of such successful communication, though, is necessarily (since dogs don't talk) a compensatory effort of attention on the part of humans, a willingness to acknowledge another perspective (the canine) and another possible contextualization of human affairs. Hypocrisy, however, is exactly an unwillingness on the part of humans to acknowledge the existence or possible relevance of such another, doglike, perspective, let alone any possible permeability between the two or consequent ability of humans to learn from dogs. Whence Ackerley's unremitting war on the blindness and premature closure of context entailed by hypocrisy, and his insistence in *My Dog Tulip* not only on the possibility but also on the necessity of our learning to digress—that is, to attend to dogs and so learn from them.

As the two bookend texts of the trilogy, *My Father and Myself* thus concentrates on the study of hypocrisy and lack of communication in the family, while *My Dog Tulip* tells the story of Ackerley's having learned to learn, *en famille*, from Tulip. Each text is autobiographical, with a human first-person subject; but the autobiography is conducted in each case, as the titles suggest, through the exploration of another ("my father" or "Tulip") and in a perspective, therefore, of relationality. A failed relation to the father is thus set against the counterexample of the intimacy with Tulip, the intensity of mutual attention between dog and man, and Ackerley's success in learning something from Tulip, both about dogs and about humans. Mediating these extremes of failed and felicitous relations is the book of relationality itself, a fictionalized autobiography, *We Think the World of You*, that explores in particular the mediations between the human and the canine, that is, the permeability of the two contexts. Homosexuality, a topic introduced in *My Father and Myself* by the picture of Ackerley and his father sitting in a Paris park contemplating a large dog turd, is the key to Ackerley's own alienation from hypocritical middle-class morality and hence openness toward the canine context; in the plot of *We Think the World of You*, it mediates therefore between the world of a working-class heterosexual family and the Ackerley character's final domestic arrangements with the dog Evie, as if being gay gave one a head start in the direction of "caninicity." But Evie, dog that she is, is also, and symmetrically, a very "human" character in this novel. Not that she's capable of hypocrisy and not that she baffles understanding as the human characters do; but she's intimately involved in the intricate thematics of imprisonment and possessiveness that also governs the antics of the humans and defines a disabused and somewhat Proustian psychology of love, where love means what humans and animals do to those they "think the world of."

Taken together, then, these three books about learning to learn from dogs form a general introduction to kynicism, as the form of canine philosophy we might like to call "crittercism."[4] Kynicism 101 and 102 involve, respectively, a study of the damage done to human relations by hypocrisy and a preliminary exploration of the mediations that make human and canine contexts permeable. The advanced course is about learning from dogs as an antidote to hypocrisy, something like "Crittercism for Majors." What is obviously missing from the trilogy is the graduate seminar, which would be about kynical spottiness and the home truth that the teller of home truths has some personal home truths to acknowledge, including the possibility of there being something cynical in the makeup and modus operandi of the kynic. But on that topic, we'll need the input of Cervantes and Bulgakov (chapter 7). Ackerley likes to confess his own deficiencies and trivialities as part of his campaign against hypocrisy; but his value and interest for us beginners in the field of canine philosophy lie in the relatively straightforward and unexamined quality of his kynicism. The theoretical complexities can await the topic of mongrel lives in chapter 7, while we concentrate here on the relatively elementary kynicism of home truths and the art of telling them.

Kynicism 101

In *My Father and Myself*, the art of domestic truth-telling goes like this:

> I was born in 1896 and my parents were married in 1919. Nearly a quarter of a century may seem rather procrastinatory for making up one's mind, but I suspect that the longer such rites are postponed the less indispensable they appear and that, as the years rolled by, my parents gradually forgot the anomaly of their situation. (MF&M, 11)

Notice, of course, the irony and the cheeky tone, especially of the first sentence with its casual inversion of the conventional chronological ordering of events. But notice, too, the double theme. There's a seamy side to middle-class respectability: not content with marrying almost a quarter century after the birth of his son, Ackerley's father was to go on to maintain a secret mistress and a second family until his death, while as a young guardsman he had engaged, it seems, in forms of homosexual prostitution. The candor of the narrator's tone contrasts with this history of hypocritical concealment. But it contrasts too— this is the second theme—with the alienated relations hinted at here in the words "I suspect." His parents having never discussed with him the matter of their marriage or any other family skeletons, Ackerley is left to speculate about their significance. And the alienation between his father and himself was to recur, or be passed on, to what Ackerley refers to as his "baffled sex life" (MF&M, 210), so that the overall picture painted in *My Father and Myself* is one of general "failure . . . personal inadequacy . . . waste and loss" (MF&M, 198), with the result that there's little in the end (except honesty) to distinguish the object of criticism from the critic himself.

The lucid analysis of family dysfunction is completed in this way by a merciless self-analysis on Ackerley's part, displaying his driven and anxious life as a middle-class homosexual man (in a place and at a time when for such men sexual satisfaction was hard to reconcile with emotional bonding), and going on to analyse his sexual dysfunctioning as a sign of subconscious guilt in an environment of fierce homophobia. The outcome of such fierce honesty is the production of a sort of "domestic" ethnography, bringing to light by dint of candor and attention to the allegedly trivial a whole *terra incognita* of deprivation and pain that's normally excluded from view by the power of convention:

> Let anyone keep a candid, detailed diary for a year, noting down *everything* that happened to him (sic) day by day, in his life, in his mind, and a book would emerge more fascinating, however clumsily written, than if he had been anthropologizing among Pygmies or sliding about on Arctic ice. (MF&M, 215–16)

This is a recipe for a form of loiterature, not only as a sort of "cultural studies," but more particularly as a project of anamnesis, bringing to life a concealed underside of everyday British life that enables it to be seen (once the effects of habit are countered by the practice of comprehensive attention) as no less harsh and deprived than that of supposed savages.

Tulip's explicit presence in this first volume is restricted to a brief mention and a long appendix; but it seems clear that the whole ethnography of hypocrisy and miscommunication is contextualized, in the final analysis, by a possible alternative view of human relations suggested to Ackerley by the dog's capacity for emotional transparency and wholehearted affection, her willingness to "bestow" herself on him. In a sentence that foreshadows Bulgakov's dog-man Sharik, Ackerley speculates therefore that "the Ideal Friend I no longer wanted, perhaps never had wanted, should have been an animal-man, the mind of my bitch, for instance, in the body of my sailor" (MF&M, 218). The problem here, however, is that what's ideal in this idealization isn't, as one might expect, that the canine element in the composite lover stands for unimpeded communication between equal partners; it has to do instead with something that could be called the Fido factor, an ancient strand surviving from the pre-talking dog tradition of canine representations that enables the middle-class Ackerley to imagine for himself a working-class lover without a mind or will of his own and completely defined by doglike devotion. Thus the sentence goes on to speak demeaningly of "the perfect male body at one's service through the devotion of a faithful and uncritical beast."

So this is a dream of unconditional attachment, that is, of control and possession, at some considerable distance from the idea of being able to learn from dogs thanks to the superior ability to communicate that can exist between dogs and humans. In this appendix to *My Father and Myself* we're much closer to the world of *We Think the World of You*, in which love is analysed as a struggle for unconditional possession of the other, than to that of *My Dog Tulip*, in which it's treated as the ability to learn from the other. We're closer, in other words, to a human view of what dogs are or should be—the "faithful companion" myth—than we are to a view of the human that might be inspired by attempting to imagine a dog's perspective on it. Tulip here is a prop to Ackerley's misanthropy rather than an object of attention in her own right: he who makes no bones about being critical of his fellow humans places the dog on the other side of a human-animal divide where it's her function to be uncritical of him and to be possessed by him for purposes that are exclusively his—to serve, that is, as a stooge. The weakness of kynicism always lies in the fact, well illustrated here, that it can only take the side of dogs in the context of an altercation between humans, so that (a) the critics are consequently uncomfortably close to the criticized, and (b) dogs-as-they-really-are (an impossible concept, I know) are left out of the picture. (And as we've already seen, that is why kynicism can be uncomfortably close to cynicism.)

Kynicism 102

Ackerley's evolution was to be in the direction of an interest in dogs-as-they-really-are and hence in the question of what we can learn from them. But the thematic interest of *We Think the World of You* remains on the human side of the divide. Homosexuality is identified as the factor that can lead to the love of dogs, and the bulk of the novel's plot consists, therefore, of following the intricate chain of triangulated situations that leads the narrator, Frank, from his involvement with Johnny to an involvement with Johnny's dog, Evie (English class relations, exacerbated by homosexual desire, here replacing middle-class hypocrisy as the novel's exemplification of humans' inability to communicate with one another). The dog, though, whose ability to communicate contrasts with the comedy of mutual incomprehension in which the narrator gets embroiled among humans, is nevertheless treated as a quasi-human character herself to the extent that she participates in the triangulations of desire, the novel's ironic twist lying in the fact that Frank, who initially desires to imprison Johnny in jealous love, ends up being possessed and imprisoned by the jealousy of Evie. This exacerbation of her Fido-like capacity for uncritical love thus serves as a form of poetic justice, visiting revenge on Frank for the demeaning dream of perfect control over a man-dog lover that is expressed by Ackerley, in his own name, at the end of *My Father and Myself.*

The novel, then, is a brilliantly satiric as well as an unblinkingly self-ironic account of how humans behave when they "think the world of" one another—a kynical account of jealousy and rivalry, pettiness, possessiveness, and self-involvement. Evie's owner, Johnny—a recently married petty criminal whom Frank is pursuing sexually—goes to prison; and Evie is looked after by his parents, who pen the large and energetic animal in a tiny yard, so that she's imprisoned in her turn. Seeking to stay in touch with Johnny through his relatives (who have visiting rights), Frank finds himself involved in a series of emotional triangles, in each of which the self-absorption resulting from his jealousy makes it impossible for him to understand the "point of view" of anyone else: "Incomprehensible people! What was one to make of them?" (WTTWOY, 103). Since Johnny's working-class family, in turn, can scarcely understand Frank's own middle-class sociolect, we're once again in a world of failed relations in which only Evie will give Frank the "feeling . . . of being . . . communicated with" (WTTWOY, 49).

From rivalry with Johnny's wife over Johnny (triangle #1), Frank first shifts, to a jealous relation over Evie (a Johnny substitute) with Johnny's parents and, in particular, with the envious and apparently homophobic Tom (triangle #2). On Johnny's release, the initial triangle (#1) mutates, therefore, into a rivalry between the two men over the affections of Evie, and for a while (triangle #3) a genuine *ménage à trois* develops, with Frank enjoying the combined benefits of Johnny's body and Evie's "faithful and uncritical" mind, somewhat according to the Ideal Friend recipe of *My Father and Myself.* But in a new stage, which leaves behind the solution envisaged there, Johnny finally drops out of the picture (returning to his wife Megan) so that Frank remains (triangle #4) as the object of a fiercely possessive jealousy that develops between Evie and his cousin Margaret. It's a situation he delights in, even though—as Margaret gets discouraged and retreats from the scene—he's left, in the end, totally and exclusively dominated by the dog's possessiveness. She scares off all other animals and, unable to read Frank's mail, tears it to shreds as it falls through the letter slot. "We live entirely alone. Unless with her I can never go away. I can scarcely call my soul my own. Not that I am complaining, oh no . . ." (WTTWOY, 158).

This portrait of himself as a willing prisoner is Ackerley's self-portrait as Fido, content now to give "constant, single-hearted, incorruptible, uncritical devotion" (MF&M, 217) of his own to an almost human mistress in the "person" of Evie. Such a reversal of the roles of dominator and dominated, one might think, marks a kind of advance on the situation envisaged at the end of *My Father and Myself*, since Ackerley—or at least his surrogate, Frank—is now able to project himself into the canine role, an acknowledgment of the permeability of the human and canine contexts and a step in the direction of learning to see the canine "point of view." But it's still the canine role as perceived by humans, that is, framed by concepts like domination, possession, and control. It's still a matter of imprisonment, however willingly accepted, and as such it derives from the triangulated human erotics that, as the whole book shows, produces love as the desire to confine the other.

That said, there are some glimpses in *We Think the World of You* of a genuinely alternative "point of view." Frank realizes as soon as Evie is released from the house of Johnny's parents that his inability to understand them—"perfectly ordinary people"—was conditioned by his own self-absorbed and jealous desire: humans *could* communicate if only they weren't so desperate to possess and control one another. And the "critical turning point" (WTTWOY, 34), when Frank's affection begins to switch from Johnny to Evie, occurs therefore when he first takes Evie for a walk and *lets her off the leash*. Indeed, it will be through a series of such walks that the relationship between man and dog develops through the novel. On these occasions, when the pair are alone and triangulated possessiveness is less an issue, the text's characteristically ironic tone gives way to lyrical passages describing the dog's delight in her freedom. Here an antidisciplinary thematics is foreshadowed that will invest Ackerley's kynical critique of human hypocrisy in *My Dog Tulip*. For, if dogs can be as possessive as humans, humans can also learn from dogs how to be free—on condition that they first free their dogs from the constraints of so-called discipline and training (which Ackerley reads in *My Dog Tulip* as evidence only of the terror humans have of the trivial, the sexual, and the natural; evidence, that is, of the hypocrisy that leads us to wish to forget our own doglike natures and to deprive ourselves of freedom). Walking with a dog can be a stage toward realizing the self-inflicted impoverishment of our own lives, for which our need to exert control over dogs is a correlative; for on walks the "natural" equality of human and dog, the potential reversibility of the relation of authority that prevails between them, can emerge. Thus, it may for once be the human who follows the dog's lead, stopping or moving according to canine priorities (and, one might add, loiterly principles): a fire hydrant to sniff at or urinate on, the compulsory halts for defecation or for socializing with other dogs, and so on.

If the dog-as-human can be a possessive "bitch" (Ackerley is capable, especially in this novel, of truly nasty misogyny), the human-as-dog can learn the benefits of digression, then, first as the joy of being released, to some degree, from the "leash" of culture, but second as the recognition that there *is* another perspective on life than that enforced by culture, a perspective from which we're not divided but to which we can have ready access, thanks to the actual indistinction of the two orders of the human and the canine that's obscured only by the hypocritical human ideology of distinction. The condition of our learning to be free is, in other words, the education of our attention so that it doesn't remain enclosed in a purely human, or "distinguished," context but can take in the nonhuman, canine context, from the point of view of which it's sheer folly to train dogs to conform to the conditions of human culture when that culture could itself learn from them, if only it wanted to, something that would be of immeasurable benefit.

Advanced Kynicism

That there's another context than the hypocritically self-enclosed human context, and that dogs are both able and willing to teach us that fact is thus what *My Dog Tulip* indefatigably teaches. But the fact is that "human beings are extraordinarily ignorant about dogs" (MDT, 136); Ackerley consequently takes his own case as exemplary, reverting to the mixed genre of autobiography through biography that he employed in *My Father and Myself* but framing it this time as the Bildungsroman of an education in attention. The story of how he learned to allow Tulip to teach him, not to see dogs from a human point of view, but to see human life from a canine angle is the story of a correction of vision that compensates for the alienation and bafflement recorded in the earlier narrative. Tulip's privilege in all this was that, as an animal "so infinitely superior to anything else in the domesticated species that she seemed scarcely to belong to it at all" (MDT, 80), she was a better educator than other dogs. But her luck, then, was to find in Ackerley a human disposed by his own experience of bafflement to reward the bestowal of her heart by freeing her of inhibiting discipline and to respond to the intense attention she fixes on him—out of a desire to know his will (MDT, 92)—with an equally searching and anxious attention of his own.

For the problem in the relation between humans and dogs isn't so much the inability of animals to speak, as it's the fact that, "in spite of constant efforts to inform them," dogs remain blissfully "ignorant of the Expulsion from Eden" (MDT, 155). Out of a panic fear of sexuality and the body, humans therefore practice precisely the forms of disciplinary training that, in cowing their pets, make it impossible for dog owners to learn their dogs' lesson, which is that what's trivial or natural needn't be a guilty secret and can instead be a source of wisdom and strength. Dogs' inability to speak wouldn't matter at all, then— although it does make the effort to understand one another a matter requiring attention and care between humans and dogs—if humans could cure their own self-absorption and blindness and overcome the forgetfulness, the denial, the inattentive hypocrisy that prompts them to exercise tyranny over animals.

Tulip's educational efforts are fortunately supported by "the excellent Miss Canley," a vet whose own understanding is that "dogs aren't difficult to understand. You have to put yourself in their position" (MDT, 21). This key advice specifies the remedy to humans' extraordinary ignorance about dogs. It's Miss Canley who, suiting action to the word, shows Ackerley that Tulip's personality, understood from her own point of view, isn't "split," although she savagely resists all attempts to approach either of them when he's present while behaving meekly and cooperatively in his absence. She behaves in this apparently contradictory way only because she understands herself to be charged with protecting him. Similarly, following countless fruitless consultations with breeders and dog books, it's Miss Canley again who reveals to Ackerley the vital knowledge that "Tulip herself supplies the answer to the question of her readiness" for sexual congress (MDT, 85), by holding her tail to one side when stroked. But mainly it's from his own constant and careful observation that Ackerley learns, and it's on the score of its sustained interest in the canine point of view that *My Dog Tulip* contrasts most tellingly, therefore, with *Millie's Book*, where the concern is the cynical one of using a dog to teach a human-motivated lesson (having to do with the maintenance of inequality and power), not the kynical conviction that we need to learn from dogs.

The White House dog, for instance, never urinates or defecates, never uses her nose. But Ackerley has learned that "dogs read the world through their noses and write their history in urine" (MDT, 43), the latter being the principle medium of their socializing. Consequently, he devotes a twenty-five-page chapter ("Liquids and Solids") to matters connected with excretion, taking indignant swipes as he goes at the hypocrisy of regulations that require the control of what manifestly defies control (canine defecation in the street). Millie's impregnation occurs off-stage and almost invisibly; by contrast, the two central chapters of *My Dog Tulip* are devoted to a long, sometimes funny and sometimes touching, account of the difficulty of finding a suitable match for "breeding" from Tulip, the whole amounting to a satirical account of the folly of dog breeding and ending, of course, when Tulip, on her own initiative, chooses to mate with a "dirty, disreputable mongrel" (MDT, 104) who lives next door. Miss Canley applauds, knowing that inbreeding produces delicate and unhealthy animals. Barbara Bush's squeamishness about birthing, it will be recalled, was part of an effort to divert attention away from what might be learned from the conditions of Millie's motherhood; Ackerley watches raptly as Tulip performs, "with no help but unerringly, as though directed by divine wisdom, the delicate and complicated business of creation":

> Suddenly she stopped panting, her face took on a look of strain, she uttered a muted, shuddering sound like a sigh, a movement passed over her recumbent body, and she raised her great tail so that it stood out straight and rigid from her rump. Immediately a dark package was extruded beneath it, and to this, with a minimum of general effort, she brought her long nose round. Now I could not clearly see what she was doing, for her head interposed and obscured the operation; but I knew what was happening and I heard her tongue and teeth at work with liquid guzzling noises. She was licking and nosing this package out of herself, severing the umbilical cord, releasing the tiny creature from its tissues and eating up the after-birth. In a few seconds she had

accomplished all these tasks and was guiding her fourth child to her teats, cleansing it on the way. (MDT, 112)

The writing in this passage is neither euphemistic nor, at the other extreme, crudely realistic, but it's frank. It's precise, carefully observed, comprehensive. Not coincidentally, therefore—since I'm not claiming Ackerley's vision of animality to be ideology-free—this remarkable passage combines a celebration of the naturalness of Tulip's birthing behavior with an account of birth as "release," a liberation. It constitutes a peak in the emancipatory story of the education of Ackerley's own attention. (And his brooding over the fate of these pups, distributed in due course to inevitably inadequate homes, again contrasts tellingly with the glib account of the distribution of Millie's offspring in *Millie's Book*.)

If walking the dog, in *We Think the World of You*, is a moment of freedom when human and dog bond, that bond and that freedom are simply *assumed*, then, in *My Dog Tulip*, and the many walks the book describes—along the towpath, on Putney High Street, on various London commons—are consequently more like occasions for the learning that's predicated on the dog's freedom and the human's acknowledgment of a relation of equality between himself and the animal. It's on walks that Ackerley learns, from observation, the significance of smell for dogs and reflects on the folly of attempts to control their natural functions: an amusing passage in this chapter— itself constructed in loiterly fashion like a ramble—relates to the intractability of Tulip's eliminatory habits to the requirements of train schedules. The final meditation ("The Turn of the Screw") again falls into an almost rhapsodic form as it follows Tulip's rabbit hunting on Wimbledon Common and contrasts human intolerance and fear of the sexual (exemplified in part by a gay man driven to suicide) with the dog's enjoyment of freedom. Here it's London Transport bus conductors, "a powerful and capricious race" (MDT, 130), who are humorously cast as exemplary figures of humanity's need to control.

It's on walks, too, that the lesson of indistinction is drawn, of the close affinity between dogs and humankind, the commonality between the species that makes it not only possible but also desirable for us to learn the lessons dogs are able to teach us. Tulip takes to urinating where Ackerley himself has peed, and he comments: "I feel that if ever there were differences between us they are washed out now. I feel a proper dog" (MDT, 44). Tulip in heat, escorted by her entourage of male dogs, engages in sorties "as harassed as the attempts of film stars and popular celebrities to leave the Savoy Hotel undetected by reporters" (MDT, 90); and, sympathizing with her "courtiers," Ackerley comments: "I would have been after the pretty creature myself, I thought, if I had been a dog" (MDT, 88). The cross-species sexual attraction is shared by Tulip herself, who on occasion makes it clear, in rejecting her canine suitors, that her preference is for her human companion. Of course, all this is anthropomorphic, as Ackerley willingly concedes (MDT, 80). But the point is that Ackerley's anthropomorphic imagination doesn't just humanize the dog, as is customary, it extends also to "caninizing" the human. And if the point of this emphasis on what's doglike in humanity is partly to administer the necessary kynical reminder, in the face of human self-aggrandizement, of our primarily animal nature, it lies also (and this is what is most original and profound in Ackerley's work) in a deep conviction that we would be better and happier people if we could just acknowledge, instead of denying, the ways in which we're like dogs. We'd then not be prevented by hypocrisy from learning what dogs have to teach us, the lesson that the "natural" is neither dangerous nor disruptive, and beyond that the lesson of the lesson, which is that there's another point of view than our own (our context isn't the whole context) and that *Homo sapiens* can therefore improve their own lot, as well as that of dogs, by acknowledging their close relation (bordering on identity) to the species *Canis loquens* and learning to learn from canine philosophers such as Tulip.

These are the home truths to which a cynical philosophy, such as we saw exemplified in the self-serving domestic depictions of *Millie's Book*, has every interest in ensuring that we remain blind. A kynical project such as Ackerley's can be said, therefore, to be anticynical even though its designated target is plain old false consciousness, rather than Sloterdijk's more fancy "enlightened" kind. For cynicism has an interest in encouraging human deludedness, so as to take advantage of it, whereas the aim of kynical crittercism is to teach us that, deluded as we may be, we *can* move away from our deludedness, through simple attention to the existence of an other—and therefore, of course, always yet another—context. That is why the loiterly activity of walking the dog, as an exercise in learning to digress, can be an apprenticeship in kynicism.

Learning from Dogs, II (Mongrel Lives)

We are the missing link.—Midas Dekker, *Dearest Pet*

Of course, the real specialists in moving away aren't house dogs like Millie or Tulip (chapter 6). It's street dogs and strays, the *pícaro* dogs, whose life—consisting of one shift after another—is, or looks to be, the true model of kynical digressiveness. But then, the funny thing about the lives of these animals, when one reads about it in Cervantes or Bulgakov, is that such dogs, like the loiterly subjects they are, can't really do without a master.[1] Indeed, Cervantes's protagonists, Cipión (Scipio) and Berganza, seem positively obsessed with masters: adept as they are at moving away from "bad" masters, their interest, nevertheless, isn't in freedom as such but in finding a "good" master, so as to be able to settle into a comfortable home and enjoy warmth and food, peace and contentment to the end of their days. And that's a doctrine Bulgakov's Sharik would certainly share. If Diogenes thought humans would be wiser and happier if they had no more needs than a dog, it turns out that dogs are quite partial to the minimal creature comforts and are willing, if necessary, to do a little boot licking to obtain them. What does that tell us about kynicism and the practice of crittercism?

It tells us that critics are spotty animals, of uncertain allegiance, whose doglike attitudes are not unmixed with human weaknesses and so with complicity toward what they criticize; they exemplify Dekker's remark that, if we are looking for a missing link between the animal and the human, *Canis loquens* (aka *Homo sapiens*) fits the description. It also tells us that we should therefore be somewhat cautious about the motives of canine philosophers and other social critics, and cautious about taking their words at face value. There is an entertaining Biedermeier-era sequel to the "Coloquio de los perros" by E. T. A. Hoffmann, in which the narrator, returning home late and a bit *begeistert* from a smoking party, runs into Berganza who, at the end of a lengthy conversation, sums up his advice: "I tell you, friend, don't trust the spotty!" ("Ich sage dir, Freund, traue nicht den

Gesprenkelten!").[2] It's advice against human hypocrisy, as is underlined by the way his "traue" melds into a bow-wow-wow ("Trau-Hau-Hau-Au-Au!") as dawn deprives him of his power to speak. But, in spite of his persona as an honest fellow and his claim to be "black all over" ("durchaus schwarz," 176), Berganza's ability to speak and his putative human origins as the supposed offspring of the witch Montiela make him a somewhat speckled hound himself.

Consequently, his admonition has the rhetorical structure of the paradox of the Cretan: there is mutual interference between the content of the statement and the force of the utterance. In short, it is spotty advice, of which one should be suspicious precisely in proportion to the emphasis, indeed the vehemence ("Ich sage dir, Freund") with which it is proffered. But this is exactly the problem of all kynical critique when it comes to grips with the evidence that social criticism in general, and ideology critique in particular, is itself part of the social formation the critic is targeting and itself tainted with ideology. In the way the street hound is willing to sell out to a master for a bone and a place by the fire, and like the talking dog who—however it may strive to talk like a true dog—is inevitably spoken through by human language, the kynic is always open to the suspicion of cynicism, that is, of complicity with the hypocrisy he hates ("he" because, where house pets like Millie and Tulip are female, street dogs in the literary tradition are male). Indeed, it seems impossible to criticize hypocrisy without enacting it, so true is it of kynical criticism that it's governed by the maxim "it takes one to know one."

The *pícaro* dog's need for a master is thus uncomfortably relevant to the kynic's desire to be free of masters and to be able to speak freely and plainly, without concern for convention or consideration of the consequences. The kynic's avoidance of "theory" is a sign of this desire but also of the uncomfortable involvement with the structures of power that the desire leads to. If one can't engage in ideology critique without demonstrating some sort of ideological commitment of one's own, a possible alternative is to engage in unsystematic sallies (usually drawn from the domain of the everyday and/or the trivial) that don't commit one to a body of doctrine but do cause damage to other people's unexamined assumptions and intellectual positions by pointing to what they forget, leave out, or otherwise omit. Plato's elegant "featherless biped" is mocked by a chicken from the market, much as Alexander's greatness succumbs (momentarily) to his being asked to move out of the sun. The *nomos*, to put it more generally (and to theorize a bit) is shown to be vulnerable to the *physis* that it vainly attempts to conceptualize or to regulate. (When they asked Diogenes why he masturbated in public, to the scandal of good citizens, he asked why it is wrong to do in public something that is ignored when it occurs in private, and went on to say that he wished hunger could be dealt with so easily, just by rubbing your stomach.) Such thrusts are devastating, but they also make the critic a kind of hit-and-run *guerillero* whose interventions can only be negative because there is no positive ground (*physis* being inaccessible to knowledge except as it is constructed in and through *nomos*) on which to develop a position.

For that reason, the kynical critic is a kind of dog who is nothing unless he has a master to be critical of. Indeed, to the extent that his criticism is purely unconstructive, he's condemned to go from master to master (today Plato, tomorrow Alexander, next week *nomos* itself, the law) in order to have employment for talents that are purely negative. He is like the street dog who, if ever he found a "good" master with whom he could stay, would be forced to renounce his kynical, digression-prone identity altogether, but meanwhile has no option except to go from one "bad" master to the next, grumbling as he goes. Pedestrian by virtue of the triviality of interventions that exploit the invisibility of the everyday to official culture, he is pedestrian also in the sense that the digressive gesture of moving away that makes criticism a matter of recontextualization also implies endlessly moving on (see chapter 10). Mobility, in other words, is at the heart of the kynical modus operandi, but that is both its strength and its weakness, its refusal to have "a" master entailing a relation of dependence on masters in general. The kynic doesn't simply need a master; he needs for there to be plenty of them.

By the same token, the kynic becomes a mere nose tweaker, unable to engage in modes of criticism that might actually destroy their target (nothing revolutionary about the kynic) or even reform it out of existence (nothing progressive about the kynic either). For without the target there's nothing to criticize and without something to criticize no status for the critic. And nose tweaking being what it is (something that leaves its target intact and so can't safely be done too often to the same nose), it makes sense therefore for the kynic to tweak once, maybe twice, and then move away in search of further noses. He's exactly like the *pícaro* or the street dog, who moves from master to master and episode to episode, displaying pusillanimity in the presence of power in proportion to his dependency on power's good graces.

What are we to think, then, of a form of criticism that has no interest in abolishing what it targets or even in doing it real damage? A tweak-and-run criticism that gives a certain satisfaction but is strangely respectful of forms of power that it knows how to dismantle but can't afford to destroy, such power being also the condition of its own prestige? Isn't there something "academic"—in more senses than one—about such criticism? Whether it's a matter of sneaking respect for the authority whose nose is tweakable, or of understandable fear of the vengefulness outraged authority is capable of, there's inevitably a hypocritical quality to criticism that likes to stand up to the master but without wanting the criticism of the master to have any consequences—whether it be the consequence of the master's being abolished or the consequence of the critic's being punished. In short, in the way that the vulnerability of cynicism lies in its love of the hand-washing gesture, kynicism has a vulnerability of its own, which is its propensity to nose-tweaking, as a sign of secret complicity with structures of authority that are indispensable to it.

Such spottiness—the unfailing complicity with human targets that is detectable in doggish criticism—is cause for concern, in the literary tradition of mongrel lives, about the ancestry of talking dogs. Are they genuine dogs of authentic canine lineage, or can it be, as the gift of speech so disturbingly suggests, that their breed is impure and that from somewhere in their ancestry they've inherited a drop or two of hypocritical, cynical, human blood? To ask the question is, of course, to answer it. Thus, Cipión and Berganza are terrified that they may turn out to be the human children of a witch, turned into dogs as a result of a spell and faced, in consequence, with an alarming alternative: either they will turn back into humans sometime, thus confirming their (hypocritical, cynical) nature, or—as long as they continue to talk— they will be subject to persecution from the authorities, as being the offspring of the devil, whose monstrosity is proved by the evidence of their speech. As for Sharikov, in *Heart of a Dog*, he is too much of an oaf to worry in person about his ancestry; but we as readers know him to be a dog-man produced as the result of an insane medical experiment: the pituitary gland of a human criminal implanted at the base of a dog's brain, so that he becomes a kind of human, at least in his body and his ability to speak, but with the desires and instincts, the "mind," of the street dog Sharik. With respect to Cipión and Berganza, the direction of mongrelization is, so to speak, reversed, and where Cervantes's point is about the complicity of doglike critics with the human society they inhabit and belong to, Bulgakov is pointing symmetrically to the admixture of doggishness that's apparent in humans, including not only run-of-the-mill, successful Soviet citizens like Sharikov, but also those (like the sophisticated Professor, who rues the outcome of his experiment) whose ambitions are more lofty but illusory and Faustian. But the dog-master relation is central to both texts and both accordingly share an interest in the question of origins (where do talking dogs come from? what is their genealogy?) that covers for an anxiety about voice: who speaks—a man or a dog—when a talking dog speaks? Whether it's the human that's suspected of ventriloquizing the critical dog, or alternatively the dog that's thought to show up in the genes of the critical (questing) human, the problematics of mixture is the same, and Dekker's judgment—we have met the missing link and it is us—is vindicated.

Under such circumstances—missing-link critics, in the guise of *Canis loquens*, reproaching missing-link humans for *Homo sapiens'* inability either to be fully human or to achieve the naturalness of animals—criticism becomes a kind of baffled grumbling, for which Cervantes's word—it applies especially to Berganza but characterizes perfectly the text itself, as a record of the two dogs' conversation—is *murmuración*. *Murmuración* is something that canine critics do well, giving vent to indignation about how things are. But it signifies also something like impotent muttering (if possible behind closed doors), expressive of a wish for one's indignation not to be heard and suggestive therefore of the dogs' (Cervantes's) pusillanimity, born of their dependence on masters they otherwise criticize. But finally, too, *murmuración* signals the kind of bafflement (I borrow the word advisedly from Ackerley) that arises from consciousness of the perfectibility of a certain situation—let's call it the human condition—combined with the knowledge that criticism is powerless to change it, in part because of the imperviousness to criticism of those in power but also because criticism itself exemplifies the very faults that it would cure: hypocrisy, backbiting, pusillanimity, in short (as Bulgakov might put it) the doggishness of the human. It confirms what it would like to do away with. And so, if kynical crittercism fails morally, because it can't help combining the indignation of *mumuración* (Berganza's specialty) with the caution of *discreción* (Cipión's constant recommendation), its moral spottiness seems to be the sign of something existentially half-baked in the state of being human. Where Nicholson Baker (chapter 5) suggests that becoming a "man" is about discovering that one is "not the magnitude of man" one had hoped one might be, *murmuración* names the kind of critical response that corresponds to such a definition of the human.

For these existential reasons, then, *murmuración* finally offers only a Hobson's choice. In one direction, it leads to the cultivation of plain speaking (and the telling of home truths), in the other to the cultivation of bafflement (and the exploration of mongrel lives). A kynic can more or less ignore the spottiness of the critical position, as Ackerley tends to do, in the interests of getting on with the criticism. Or—like E. T. A. Hoffmann's Berganza warning the narrator not to trust the spotty— the critic can foreground spottiness and attempt to face, as honestly as possible, the moral paradoxes and existential problems entailed in enacting what one criticizes and criticizing what one enacts. In either case, the force of criticism is blunted, however, whether it be by the lack of critical consciousness entailed in kynical outspokenness or by the excessive selfconsciousness that reduces it to impotent muttering, the actual choice between outspokenness and baffled grumbling depending in the end, it seems, on historical conditions. Writing with considerable courage, but in the relatively tolerant climate of modern England, Ackerley can wage war on hypocrisy, a little like Diogenes (a free, male, Athenian citizen) in the ancient agora, by arguing the indistinction of the human and the animal. The fact that he does so from a speaking position replete with distinctions of class and even more egregiously of gender, is something that he feels able to be (or to appear?) oblivious of, give or take the odd passing irony, even though he is highly vulnerable to a *tu quoque* response that would point out the sense in which he is as hypocritical in his own way as the puritanical, self-censoring citizens whose hypocrisy he reviles. Similarly, the Greek Cynics seem never to have been forced to acknowledge the sense in which their freedom of speech was grounded in power structures (again of class and gender) that they might have criticized but very largely did not.[3] Their small-*c* cynicism must have been largely unconscious; and they practice kynicism, therefore, at what (in chapter 6) is called the undergraduate level.

Things are more complicated for Bulgakov, writing satirically of Soviet society, or Cervantes, writing within earshot, so to speak, of the Inquisition. Their tactics consist, in large part, only of anticipating and appropriating the *tu quoque*, assuming it by acknowledging the universality of spottiness and writing criticism that's self-critical while it nevertheless seeks, like Hoffmann's Berganza, to target the forms of spottiness, in each society, that don't even know, and so cannot acknowledge, their own spottiness. This self-ironizing strategy is clearly a dangerous one in societies as repressive as Bulgakov's Soviet Union or Cervantes's Spain, particularly as the self-criticism works indirectly, through textual self-reflexivity and *mise en abyme* that presuppose a degree of sophistication on the reader's part. One can only admire these authors' courage. But their method is also internally self-defeating, as a form of honesty about spottiness that does not absolve them from the charge of spottiness but even compounds the problem. For such "honesty" can easily be read as self-serving and self-protective, and so hypocritical and cynical. The distinction it assumes, in a self-justificatory way, between those spotty individuals who are capable of acknowledging their spottiness and those who are ignorant of it reeks of the ideology of distinction and looks suspiciously like a version of the cynical "nevertheless" or "yes, but": "As a spotty critic, let me tell you: don't trust spotty dogs such as myself. Do, however, let me go on making my criticisms of your own spottiness, since I have the grace and the wit to acknowledge how spotty I am. . . ." Welcome to the complexities of graduate level crittercism.

One can always say, of course, that there's a difference between practicing self-conscious hypocrisy as a matter of self-defense and engaging in enlightened false consciousness, as the cynic does, for one's own advantage. Or one might wish to distinguish between "top-down" cynicism, in the form of manipulation carried out (à la Barbara Bush) by the powerful, and "bottom-up" tactics (as Michel de Certeau might say[4]), involving at most something like opportunism. But the difference between self-defense and one's own advantage isn't itself a very clear-cut one, and opportunism is easily describable as itself a form of manipulation—one that depends on the disempowered nevertheless having access to some degree of power (no opportunism without an opportunity, so to speak). In other words, attempts to distinguish in this way between forgivable and unforgivable forms of cynicism themselves have an odor of cynicism about them, if only because they depend, precisely, on the hand-washing gesture of distinction in a world that does not admit of distinctions although it is full of differences. There's real discomfort about this issue, therefore, in texts like those of Cervantes and Bulgakov that thematize kynical spottiness in their accounts of mongrel lives. And in the end it's perhaps only that discomfort itself—rather than any supposedly up-front "honesty" about spottiness—that makes it possible to distinguish between spottily kynical texts and their more overtly, or less self-consciously cynical and more glibly self-disculpatory counterparts.

It's hard to read far into "El coloquio de los perros," in any case, without encountering signs of such textual anxiety. Care is notably being taken, as I mentioned and will demonstrate in a moment, to ensure that the text's report of the dialogue between two dogs not be taken overseriously. And the dialogical representation of two dogs, one of whom is given, broadly speaking, to *murmuración* in the outspoken sense while the other enjoins *discreción*, can be thought to have a couple of advantages, from the point of view of textual honesty on the one hand, and of textual discretion on the other. For the technique itself reflects a problematics of mongrelization and enacts it through the dialogical relation between the dogs; but it's also a self-defensive device without being a self-disculpatory one, because it ensures that neither dog can be taken as the author's mouthpiece. If Berganza's outspoken-ness should get the author into trouble, he can shelter (hypocritically) behind Cipión's ingrained respect for authority. But he can't be accused of cynical toadying via the personage of Cipión (this would be the disempowered equivalent of the cynicism of the powerful represented by *Millie's Book*, telling the powerful what they want to hear as opposed to telling the underprivileged how they should think), because there's always Berganza and his kynical frankness. At the same time, the device enacts the difficulties, moral and existential, of being a Diogenes, that is, a "perro murmurador," under the historical circumstances of Cervantes's Spain. It's a clever (perhaps too clever) textual setup for getting away with some nose-tweaking, on the one hand, and on the other, for enacting, and so acknowledging, the infinite complexity of the business of being a canine philosopher.

A WITCH'S BROOD

One evening, then, in the hospital of the Resurrection in Valladolid, Cipión and Berganza, the establishment's resident dogs, are overheard muttering confidentially from behind the shelter of a bed. Or such, at least, is the claim made by the ensign Campuzano, who's undergoing

sweat treatment for syphilis and whom we know (and know to mistrust) from his role in the previous tale in the *Exemplary Novels*, "El
casamiento engañoso" ("The Deceitful Marriage"), a tale of mutually
canceling cynicisms. Expressing perplexity and wonderment at suddenly finding themselves able to speak, the dogs are also conscious of
the dangers of being overheard. Both the fact that they can speak, which
is more likely to be thought a devilish phenomenon than a miracle, and
what they have to say to one another about their life experiences make
their conversation suspect.

Nevertheless, they decide that each will spend a night telling the
other his life story, and Berganza takes the first turn. Campuzano
listens in and, in the morning, transcribes their dialogue. Concerned
that he may have been hallucinating, though, Campuzano submits the
manuscript to his skeptical companion Peralta, who thinks the ensign
likely to have made the whole thing up. We, the novella's readers, thus
read along, so to speak, with Peralta, the reading position having been
constructed by this series of broad hints (the dogs' dubiousness, Campuzano's unreliability and medical circumstances, Peralta's skepticism)
as a maximally incredulous one. Finally, we learn that on the following
night Cipión also told his own story as planned, and that Campuzano
intends to write it down; but for now the text is interrupted and
incomplete. "Let's go off to the Espolón and refresh our eyes ("los
ojos del cuerpo")," Peralta suggests, his reading done, "for my mind['s
eye] has been well refreshed." And the two companions go off, ready,
after a night of imaginative indulgence and inconsequence, to while
away the day in correspondingly loiterly and insignificant pursuits.
Thus Cervantes can always claim, if advisable, that Cipión's story was
to have supplied any corrective Berganza's outbursts might require;
and that, in any case, the whole text amounts to just a frivolous and
implausible fiction.

Everything in this frame seems to have another side to it: the
dogs talk but worry about what talking means; Campuzano overhears
but disbelieves; Peralta disbelieves, too, but reads; and having read,
nevertheless evades passing judgment. . . . Similarly, in the dialogue
itself instability is the norm. Berganza's tale is itself a series of episodes,
closely resembling the picaresque genre, in which he moves randomly
from master to master, wandering from Seville into the countryside
and then into the outskirts and, in due course, into the city of Granada
before finally winding up in Valladolid. He undergoes many adventures

and makes many observations about human society, its trades and professions, its classes and ethnic groups, the many deceptions and self-deceptions humans employ in their daily struggle, their hypocrisy. Literary critics have themselves struggled, a bit self-defeatingly, to discover structural patterns and thematic coherence in this rambling tale. Not that patterns can't be perceived (they always can), but the real point of Berganza's life, governed as it is by the swings of Fortune's wheel, lies in its enactment of the unpredictable swerves of digression. All contexts are fluid; there's no situation that can't be reversed, no master who can't be replaced, no episode that doesn't lead to yet another. There's no stability or finality—so that the end itself, in which Berganza appears to have discovered peace and perhaps some kind of redemption, as he and Cipión help good brother Mahudes gather alms for the hospice, doesn't imply closure. For one thing, there's the projected sequel (Cipión's story); for another, Fortune's wheel may swing again.

The errant character of Berganza's life also affects his mode of speech. It has two main characteristics, one of which is digression. The Renaissance ideal of copiousness takes the form, here, of the canine narrator's sense that truth lies in detail and that it's more important to be comprehensive than to conform to rules of good order. "I must make haste," he says, "to say everything I can remember, even if it is all jumbled up and confused, because I don't know when this blessing, which I consider to be a loan, will be revoked" (196). The blessing in question is the gift of speech, which may run out before Berganza has exhausted the inventory of the fruits of his experience; but it might also be the canine gift for remembering—the kynical faculty of anamnesis, as the failure to forget other contexts—that's celebrated in the text's tolerance of the "jumbled and confused." It's true that such tolerance isn't shared by the censorious Cipión, who frequently urges his companion to get on with it and leave out the side issues; but to Berganza there's no such thing as a side issue. He knows the account of his life would be incomplete if he left out his ramblings, which he calls philosophizing, since for him "the things that happened then" and the "things that have come into my mind at this moment" (the moment of narration) are inseparable. If he didn't break off and enrich his narrative with speculation and commentary, "it would be neither complete nor of any value" (211). Thus the disagreement of the dogs over the question of digression stages a narrative predicament we've encountered before: narrative loses interest if it doesn't digress, but it verges on the pointless and the whimsical if, in the interests of comprehensiveness, it loses all structure. This text, though, thanks to Berganza, consistently "errs" on the digressive side—digressiveness is its point.

What to Berganza is philosophizing, though, is quickly identified by Cipión as *murmuración*. This second quality of Berganza's discourse— his tendency not only to hold up the story but to do so in a particular way, by dwelling on the disreputable or scandalous underside of things—is thus a partial synonym of the first. But it's an object of even stronger reprobation on Cipión's part (and Berganza himself, who defends digression quite vigorously, seems to agree that his grumbling is reprehensible). It's as if *murmuración*, as a kind of "wild" social criticism that comes naturally to dogs, is something that, however natural, needs to be actively repressed and kept under control, especially in view of the fact that it may be overheard. "That's the way, Berganza," says Cipión, ticking him off for the umpteenth time, "make a virtue of this cursed plague of grumbling [by calling it philosophizing], and give it whatever name you like, for it will earn us the name of cynics, which means growling dogs ("perros murmuradores"). Now for heaven's sake shut up and get on with your story" (212, translation modified). So, although *murmuración* and philosophizing come naturally to dogs, *talking* dogs—whose conversation takes place in the human world and within human hearing—are kynical philosophers, and kynical philosophers are better off keeping their opinions to themselves or at the very least broadcasting them discreetly ("murmuring" them) from behind the screen of a bed; and here it's not Berganza's practice but Cipión's opinion that prevails in the text.

Which means that, in a hypocritical world, the dogs, together with the text they inhabit, are given to a form of hypocrisy of their own, attempting to conceal their true, critical nature out of self-interested respect for powerful opinion that warns them to keep it under wraps. Berganza displays this self-interested, self-protective, and hypocritical side of his personality often enough. He's capable, as a good kynic, of attacking a dishonest *alguacil* when the official thoughtlessly shouts "Stop! Thief!" ("Al ladrón!" 224); but he's also in favor of saving appearances (214). He's willing to take a bribe of food on occasion, but refers to it as "gift" giving (215); and of course both he and Cipión agree that "fawning" is the way to get a decent master. Toward the end of the story, he speaks warmly of the need to turn a blind eye to evils one can't set right (247). That said, it's Cipión, however, as Michael Nerlich has pointed out, who stands in the novella for hypocrisy and false consciousness.[5]

Cipión has completely internalized the value of *discreción*: he doesn't just disapprove of digression as (kynical) philosophizing and of philosophizing as *murmuración*, he wants it kept to a whisper if it can't be suppressed altogether. Favoring in this way a certain pusillanimous, self-censoring circumspection in speech and behavior, he's the partner most obviously spoken through by ideological beliefs, losing few opportunities for preaching servility—his *predicar* is a counterpart of Berganza's *murmurar*—and constantly reproving his companion for giving way to digression and/or grumbling. It's symptomatic that only when Berganza speaks of the "duty of honest dogs" to serve their masters well does Cipión allow that the word *philosophy* might be appropriate ("for these are arguments that stand by their truth and good sense," 213). The narrative problem staged by the two dogs, of reconciling coherence and point with comprehensiveness and truth telling, is matched, then, by a critical problem that shares its structure, the problem of a canine modus vivendi that's contradictorily divided between ideological subjection (Cipión's major characterological trait) and kynical critique (Berganza's forte). But the text, which as narrative subscribes to Berganza's digressiveness (and by extension to the *murmuración* that is part and parcel of it), also adopts Cipión-like modes of self-censorship and hypocrisy as protective cover, in its recourse to a complex framing technique as well as in the dialogism of the relation it constructs between the dogs, with the upshot that it makes itself readable as the literary equivalent of *murmuración* in the word's complex sense: indignant muttering, muted outspokenness, self-censoring criticism, baffled grumbling.

But the point about the intrication of kynical criticism and hypocritical caution isn't made solely by the dialogical relation between the dogs. There's dialogism also within each dog, since the character of neither is actually consistent with his principles. I've pointed out how Berganza, who hates hypocrisy, falls into hypocritical attitudes of his own on occasion. Censorious as he is toward digression and *murmuración*, Cipión, for his part, frequently leads Berganza into digression by asking distracting questions: how to get a good master (204–5); and very prominently, what Cañizares's story means, at a point (238) when

Berganza has already moved on from that episode. Similarly he falls into *murmuración* from time to time, commenting on the wealthy who cultivate appearances and are "greater by reason of the shadow they cast than they are in themselves" (207) and then splitting hairs hypocritically about whether it counts as *murmuración* if you don't speak ill of anyone in particular. A bit later he happily joins in a joint *murmuración* about scholars who misuse their knowledge of Latin and Greek (213); and later still he again manages his trademark combination of *murmuración* with hypocrisy by adopting the device of left-handed praise (defending police officers and notaries on the grounds that "many, very many" of them are honest souls, 220). Cipión's sanctimoniousness, in other words, is such that it extends without difficulty to his engaging in what he is most censorious of when he encounters it in his friend (*murmuración*) while Berganza is also perfectly capable of falling now and then into the vice that he most strongly disapproves of, that of hypocrisy. Such is the spottiness of the kynical.

But, although neither Cipión nor Berganza is particularly self-critical, each does freely criticize the other, and neither is self-conscious about their inconsistencies of character. Spottiness and false consciousness are their faults, but they are more ingenuous and self-contradictory than they are disingenuous, and they're not really cynical. Indeed, their weaknesses make them rather likable, and it could be argued that they show something of the "spiritedness" one appreciates in domestic animals (tame but not so tame as to be uninteresting), and that like court buffoons they combine a certain cheekiness in the criticism of authority with an accurate sense of the limits on its expression. In this, they are prototypical loiterly narrators. So the contrast with the witch Cañizares is striking, and not solely because of the village violence that swirls around her in the episode of Berganza's meeting with her. Cañizares is an out-and-out cynic—and this at the same time as her information about the dogs' origins strongly suggests that they may themselves be the offspring of another witch (Montiela), babies cursed at birth and magically turned into pups by a third old crone, named Camacha.

By the time of Berganza's encounter with Cañizares at the end of her life, she has become (a little like the dogs themselves) a hospitaler, and she subscribes openly to good Christian doctrine, vehemently denying (in public) that she's a witch; but she freely admits to Berganza (in private) that she still loves to rub on the magic ointment and take off for the pleasures of the sabbath. She both recognizes that this is hypocrisy and is complacently unself-critical about it, affirming self-righteously that "hypocrisy does no harm to others" and asserting self-indulgently that "the habit of vice becomes second nature" while relying for forgiveness on God's goodness (she seems to be planning death-bed repentance). "I cover up my faults with the cloak of hypocrisy," she confides, accepting all the esteem and honor that come her way as a result ("my conduct is a credit to me") while cheerfully revealing the shallowness of her "conversion":

> "Now that I can't go fast because of age, or pray because I go dizzy, or go on pilgrimages because of the weakness of my legs, or give alms because I am poor or think good thoughts because I am addicted to grumbling [soy amiga de murmurar] (and in order to do good one must first think good thoughts), all my thoughts are bound to be evil. Nevertheless . . ." (235, translation modified)

So this is the "nevertheless" of the cynic, Sloterdijk's "yes, but," separated by the crooked smile of its comma.

Contemporary feminists might legitimately see Cañizares's cynicism as a self-defensive, "bottom-up," protective tactic dictated by cruel life circumstances, unlike the manipulative cynicism of the powerful. The dogs don't read it that way, however. Cañizares makes them uncomfortable because her character has bearing on their own situation. If her claim about their parentage is correct, then their ability to speak—although it may mean they're turning human again—is likely to be taken as evidence that, as witch's children, they're creatures of the devil. The theory might be that, in the way that witches are deluded in their cynicism, believing themselves without responsibility ("hypocrisy does no harm to others") when they're actually the devil's instruments, so too the dogs might be being ventriloquized in spite of themselves—ventriloquized by the forces of evil. It's a version of the problem of responsibility that attaches itself to all cultural agency—subjects are always subjected to culture while believing themselves to be autonomous agents—but made terrifying in this case by the ever-present threat of the Inquisition. Furthermore, the dogs' hopes and fears are complicated by the prophecy accompanying Camacha's ensorcellment. It may apply to them and indicate that they're returning to human form (but also, in that case, that they're a witch's brood). Or again, if they're not Montiela's children, it may simply not apply to their case at all, which would be a relief (but wouldn't account for their ability to speak). That there might be further alternative readings of their situation doesn't cross their minds. In particular, as fictional characters, they're unaware of the possibility that occurs to a reasonably alert reader, that they're the mouthpieces, not of the devil, but of an author, and of an author whose hypocrisy—manifested in the literary precautions he takes to disengage his responsibility from the tale he tells—resembles the conscious hypocrisy, the cynicism of Cañizares more than the dogs' own unconscious inconsistencies. Is the author's gesture, self-defensive as it is, merely a form of understandable *discreción* of the kind fervently recommended by Cipión, or does it have an uncomfortable affinity with the more calculating maneuvers of Cañizares? And can anyone tell the difference?

The one thing that's clear in this murky business is that, in this text, the general problem of the kynical (the dogs, Cañizares, Cervantes) lies in the fact that, whereas, on the one hand, they must speak out about human failings because *murmuración* comes naturally to them, they can't, on the other hand, bring themselves, for whatever reason, to speak openly. When Berganza is still an ordinary dog and can only bark, he's all for denouncing evils straightforwardly: he would love, for example, to expose the fraudulence of shepherds (204) and advise a magistrate on the control of prostitution (251). But his experience in unintentionally exposing the hypocrisy of Cañizares has taught him a lesson: no one on this occasion actually changes—for good or ill—their previous estimation of the witch; but the village, with near unanimity, treats Berganza himself as a creature of the devil (237). It's not the evildoer but the critic, the denouncer of evil, who gets into trouble. So when Berganza acquires the ability to communicate with humans, does he go back and try to clarify matters for the benefit of defrauded sheep owners and deluded villagers? Does he return to the magistrate who had him put out of his court for barking? No, he mutters cautiously about all this to Cipión behind a bed, hoping no one will hear him. And in the same way the text itself covers its own tracks and ensures that it can't be charged with responsibility for whatever Berganza might say. The question that's asked isn't whether such behavior is wise or necessary (it seems to be inescapable), but what its moral status is, given in particular the disturbing model of Cañizares.

Berganza's experience, as it happens, offers two models for approaching this question, each with implications for judging the moral value of the text's ventriloquial performance. One model clearly implies cynicism on the part of the text; this is the model of the *perro sabio* or trained dog, the role Berganza plays for a while with a group of soldier-entertainers. The other model is that of the *Canis loquens* as the dubious outcome of witchcraft, and its implications are at best murky and difficult to read: its figuration will be as the proverbial dog at a game of skittles. As *perro sabio* Berganza does a jumping trick: "I learned to jump for the King of France and not to jump for the bad landlady." Not jumping, in other words, is denunciatory and critical while jumping flatters authority. But not only does Berganza jump or not jump on the command of his trainer, both his criticism and his sops to authority are crowd pleasers and correspond to popular prejudice:

"Come on, Gavilán, my boy, jump for that old fellow you know who dyes his beard; and if you don't want to, then jump for the pomp and the show of Doña Pimpinela de Plafigonia, who was a friend of that Galician girl who used to serve at table in Valdeastillas. Don't you like that order, Gavilan my boy? Then jump for Pasillas, the undergraduate who signs himself a licentiate when he has no degree at all. Oh, you are a lazy hound! Why don't you jump? Ah, now I get your games: now jump for the wine of Esquivias, which is as famous as that of Ciudad Real, San Martin and Ribadivia."

He lowered the cane and I jumped, and took note of his malicious tricks. (226–27)

This is inescapably a *mise en abyme* for the novella itself, in which the author, like the trainer, uses his dogs (cynically) as a vehicle of social criticism, but in which his criticism of the hypocrisy of others might also pass (even more cynically) for a crowd-pleasing turn, with no critical "bite" at all and having no object other than receiving applause and making a little money. Such criticism is dubious because in effect it isn't really critical at all, as the joy with which it is received clearly indicates.

But then there's the other model, which is that of witchcraft and the dog at the skittles game, a figure for criticism that—unlike the *perro sabio*'s—is potentially unwelcome. This model is suggested by Camacha's prophecy: according to this bit of doggerel, Berganza and his brother (who may well be Cipión) will return to their true shape ("su forma verdadera") only when the mighty are put down and the humble exalted "por poderosa mano para hacello" ("by that hand which has the power to perform it"). The Biblical overtones of course suggest a reference to the last trump (God's final criticism of humanity), but that can't be, the dogs think, because although they're already half-transformed into humans, nothing around them has changed in the least. Perhaps, then, the prophecy is an allegory, like the wheel of Fortune. Or maybe it's a straight description of some sort of everyday occurrence, such as a game of skittles, "in which those who are standing are knocked down and those who fall down get up again, and this by the hand of him who is able to perform it" (239)? The problem here is that the dogs have been involved in Fortune's ups and downs all their lives and have witnessed plenty of skittles games without achieving human form ("la forma que dices"). So, since the prophecy is inapplicable, Cipión concludes triumphantly, they can't possibly be Montiela's offspring, but "just dogs." He forgets, of course, to ask what it means in the case that they've unexpectedly acquired the faculty of speech. And his conclusion ("nos estamos tan perros que vees") is phrased, if it means "we're dogs as you see," in a way that's odd. The verb *estar* normally refers not to permanent or essential identity (*ser*), but to a temporary condition; so the phrase might translate as something like "we're dogs for as long as we seem to you to be so."

The obvious possibility the two friends don't consider in their exegetical efforts is that the phrase "their true shape" doesn't describe "human" form but that of talking dogs, that is, the shape they've actually achieved and the status, of kynical critics ("perros murmuradores"), that is currently theirs. For if that's the case, their participation in the turns of Fortune's wheel and the many skittles games they've witnessed no longer disconfirm the prophecy but tend to confirm it; and the apparently transitional form they've attained—neither dogs nor humans but something in between—isn't inconsistent with it at all. If the prophecy refers to human form, it may well do so according to a definition of the human as not some superior state but as *Canis loquens* (or maybe *perro sabio*), as if the human was a state of arrested development or a missing link along the way to "true" (*Homo sapiens* or *hombre sabio*) humanity . . . ? By this reckoning, humanity would be a spotty, mongreloid species, whose powers of speech and claims to a higher culture coexist and conflict with a fundamentally animal nature. And Berganza and Cipión, by the same reckoning, qualify therefore, just as they are, as figures for the human—but also, and simultaneously (since Camacha's prophecy applies), as the ensorcelled offspring of a witch. Ergo, to be human is to be, exactly like Berganza and Cipión, a thing of thoroughly dubious ancestry—that uncanny, unaccountable, and perhaps evil, and in any case *mixed* thing, a dog who talks.

If so, the art of *tropelía*—that is, the art by means of which Camacha transformed Montiela's babies into pups—isn't some horrible exception.[6] It names a universal condition, the norm of existence, by virtue of which human children can become dogs but also dogs can acquire the gift of speech. For *tropelía*, as it is explained in the text, "makes one thing appear to be another." It defines existence, according to the principle of Fortune's wheel, in terms of a dynamic of transformability and hence as a state of permanent delusion, since through a kind of principle of endless digression—exploiting the potential for otherness that's inherent in everything—a given thing can always become its other. There's no *ser*, just *estar*, as in Cipión's grammatically odd but thematically apt formulation. Humans have a latent dogginess in them, which *tropelía* can make manifest (thus Camacha turns Montiela's babies into pups); but dogs, in turn, have a potential, realized by Berganza and Cipión, to turn into humans. All they have to do is learn to talk, which our heroes have done through a *tropelía* that matches, and inverts, Camacha's—the art of Miguel de Cervantes. For, if *tropelía* is witch's magic, and one that also defines the world of Berganza, in which there's no permanence and discursive digressivity is the only way to come close to catching the "truth" of things, it's a possible and highly suggestive name for the transformative art of the novelist— not now the novelist as dog trainer manipulating a performance, but the novelist as the author of fictions whose truthfulness lies in their demonstration that things aren't what they seem but always contain an other, potentially realizable, possibility of being into which they can be "turned." Humans, therefore, aren't humans at all because they're potentially describable as talking dogs, and to think otherwise is to fall victim to hypocrisy or false consciousness, that is, the belief or the desire to believe that things can be and are what they seem (a definition of ideology). In this literary sense, *tropelía*, is the instrument of an antihypocritical project or ideology critique. And taking advantage of the etymological relation of *tropelía* to *trope*—a "turn" or figure of speech—we can say that the author's function is, by means of his troping, to disabuse those who suffer from the hypocritical illusion that humans are humans and dogs dogs by demonstrating, in the figure of the talking dog, the permeability of the two categories, their mutual "tropability."

That makes the author, as a master of digression, something other than a merely cynical street entertainer. It makes him a practitioner of loiterature but by the same token a troublemaker, one whose affinity with witches is deeply disturbing. For it may mean that, like them, he's cynically denying responsibility for the harm of which he's a deluded instrument, meddling in critical *tropelía* without concern for its effect on the social order, like Cañizares comfortably practising hypocrisy in the belief that it "does no harm to others." A troublemaker nonetheless, and one whose interventions, whatever their moral status—and taking as they do the form of a demonstration that humans aren't humans but talking dogs—are as likely to be welcome, in a society that rests on firm hierarchies, excluded middles, and impermeable categories, as a dog at a skittles game. For in countries where skittles is played in the open (a street or courtyard, say), it's normal enough for dogs to hang about a game. But their presence is regarded as a potentially disruptive one: they figure an unwanted element of potential disorder—an admixture of nature in the game of culture—that needs to be kept under surveillance and control. Kynics are dogs who talk but who talk (unlike most of the talking dogs who are humans) from the angle of vision of dogs; their view that humans are themselves so many talking dogs is a case in point—it's a canine view of the human, not a human view. Their existence, therefore, is a threat to the cherished illusions of human culture, illusions that would be destroyed if the kynical deviation into a doggish view of things ever took hold. Like dogs at a skittles game, kynics are tolerated, but only so long as they don't disturb the game in progress. They do well, therefore, to keep a low profile and hold their criticism down to the level of muttering, *murmuración*. Discretion has to be their watchword if they don't want to be thrown out of the game of culture. For, grumble as they may against it, there is no other game; and watching it critically from the sidelines, like a street cur at the edge of a group of skittles players, is still a way of being in it.

Between these two models—the dog at the skittles game, the trained hound entertaining the crowd—there's not much point in trying to discriminate, in the end. For each is a condition of the other. Troublemaking criticisms are made palatable by the hypocrisy—indeed the cynicism—of showmanship (their artistic presentation as a piece of entertainment). But the entertainment has a critical content, however watered down it may be by caution and the desire to please. To be a canine philosopher is to navigate between these two options, of criticism and showmanship, which taken together define the spottiness of the kynical trade, a spottiness inherent in the kynic's status as a talking dog of mongrel ancestry. The fact that this mixed status and ancestry is shared with the missing link that is "us," humanity in general, is in the end almost immaterial, since it is the kynic's particular task to draw the conclusions it suggests. Such conclusions, of course, can only be *critical* with respect to humanity's *hypocritical* failure to acknowledge its mixed status and the consequences thereof. But they're necessarily *hypercritical* when it comes to judging the critic's own spottiness, as one who takes on the task of correcting others for faults that one's own criticism exemplifies.

So to be a critic of culture is to end up being more critical of oneself than of the culture one criticizes and more conscious of the conditions of criticism, obscure and embarrassing as they are, than of the vulnerabilities of the critical target. Such, at least, is the lesson I draw from the canine philosophers of the "Coloquio," a text that might fairly be said to have inaugurated the whole tradition to which this chapter is devoted, of kynical talking-dog literature as a criticism of the critic.

A CYNICAL EXPERIMENT

On the face of it, Bulgakov's *Heart of a Dog* is in complete contrast with the "Coloquio," in this as in many other respects. Most centrally, the theme of mongrelization is transferred in this novel from the critic to the object of criticism while, as I've mentioned, its values are reversed (dogginess, as naked and cynical self-interest, not "human" hypocrisy, is what holds the species back). And, by the same token, the criticism itself (*Heart of a Dog* is a witty and savage satirical allegory of the Russian Revolution and the Soviet society it spawned) becomes outspoken rather than muted: no shamefaced muttering in dark corners for Bulgakov, and little in the way of rhetorical precautions in his text (the allegory is patent). The price the author was to pay for so much kynical outspokenness would have been predicted without difficulty by Cervantes (or Cipión): after 1930, all of Bulgakov's books were banned from publication for more than thirty years, and *Heart of a Dog* wasn't available in the Soviet Union until 1987.

I confess I was a bit tempted to ban it from my own corpus, too, not for outspokenness but because, as a result of these thematic inversions of the major kynical tradition, learning from dogs seems scarcely to be the issue here. Sharik is no philosoph(iz)er hound like Berganza; nor is he, like Tulip, a gifted teacher. He's not even a model of negative learning (learning to be a dope), like Millie. But he *is* a salutary example (and so pedagogical, nevertheless, in his own way) of what the world would be like if we talking dogs were, so to speak, all dog, with no leavening of human "weakness" in the form of hypocrisy. That is, he represents a closure of context that's equal but opposite to the closure that is hypocrisy, the closure inherent in materialism, opportunism, and philistinism, in the crudest and most grasping sense of these words. If anything, Bulgakov's point—the question he asks—is about the possibility of our learning *not* to be doglike.

And, as a result, *Heart of a Dog* does still belong to the Cervantine tradition in one important respect. There's an awareness of the transferability of criticism from the object back onto the critical subject, which means that the concept of critical authorship—figured *en abyme* by the experiment in which Sharik the dog becomes the dog-man Sharikov—does come in, at least by implication, for disabused examination. The universal doggishness of Soviet society, for which Sharikov is the central figure, has as its corollary that there's something doglike also—something cynical and self-interested—in Sharikov's creators, a pair of fictional scientists who (like latterday witches) dream up the experiment that gives birth to him. But they, in turn, implicate the real-life author who dreamed up the text and created Sharikov as a creature of writing. And, because the text insists on the disastrous consequences of the experiment, a theme that's barely hinted at in Cervantes comes into clear focus in Bulgakov. This is the theme of the responsibility incurred by the intellectual, as one whose hand washing takes the form of pursuing knowledge (or carrying out a social experiment, or writing satire) without regard to its consequences. Just as Cañizares exempted herself from the consequences of her hypocrisy, blind to the extent to which, in so doing, she made herself an acolyte of the devil, so Bulgakov's cynical characters are oblivious to everything but their own immediate aims: the pursuit of knowledge, to be sure, but also of professional status and social rewards.

The street cur Sharik, then, becomes the despicable dog-man Sharikov, not as a result of a witch's curse but as the outcome of a disastrous "mad scientist" experiment that's thoughtlessly undertaken by a couple of ambitious, and doglike, scientists. The experiment unleashes, as its unexpected result, an allegorical equivalent of the Russian Revolution, here pictured as an unmitigated social catastrophe. As poetic justice requires, it's the authors of the experiment who suffer most cruelly from its effects. They're thus designated as "tragic" victims, hubristic but responsible; and we're reminded that intellectuals aren't only subjects of (subjected to) the culture in which they may occupy a quite marginal position (say, as a researcher or social critic); they're also among the major agents of cultural production. The revolution, in 1917, was notably the doing of a group of critical intellectuals who seem not to have known, any more than Bulgakov's professor and his assistant, what they were doing. To ignore the responsibility that flows from the intellectual's power as an agent of culture is, in other words, the form of cynical hand washing that's characteristic of the intellectual class. However true it may be to say that cultural agency is itself "subjected" and that its outcome, therefore, can never be fully or accurately foreseen, it's nevertheless the duty of intellectuals to "experiment" with care, lest they find themselves playing the role, not of Cervantes's witches, but of apprentice sorcerers. For the cynic who sees only self-interest turns out, as we are coming to see, to be always the instrument of another cynical power, like Barbara Bush and her foundation, or Cañizares and the devil. That, in Bulgakov's rewrite of it, is what the myth of Faust turns out to have always signified.

Experimenting with rejuvenation, Philip Philippovich (the Professor) is led to transplant into the brain of Sharik, a stray dog he has taken off the streets, near death from starvation and abuse, the pituitary gland of a young hoodlum who has died in a brawl. Sharik's name ("little ball") seems to refer, as if by predestination, to this small round gland, whose function baffled medicine for centuries and in which Descartes was led to locate the human soul and hence the link between body and mind. And indeed, to the surprise and embarrassment of the Professor, Sharik now proceeds to grow into the semblance of a slightly shaggy, low-browed, small-statured man—not a human mind in a dog's body (as the dominant kynical tradition might have predicted) but, rather, a dystopian version of Ackerley's fantasy: the mind of a dog in the body of a man. We don't get a canine philosopher, then, but a human who acts like a dog. Sharik rapidly acquires human speech (having learned it passively from years of being cursed on the street and deciphering butcher's and "fish trust" signs). He learns to dress himself and, having acquired from the bureaucracy the documentation that certifies his human identity (with the name Polygraph Polygraphovich Sharikov), he begins to function as a member of society. But tellingly, he remains overpartial to strong drink as well as to food, kitchens, and (female) cooks, while certain refinements of speech and deportment elude him. Notably, he retains from his canine existence a prolific vocabulary of Russian curses, table manners are a problem, and he persists in catching fleas with his teeth instead of his fingers.

And this doglike human, so thoughtlessly created in the interests of scientific research (and the Professor's career), turns out to have exactly the character and social origins, as a "proletarian" (born of a street cur and a criminal), to become a favored member of Soviet society. Sharikov is quickly on friendly terms with the "house management committee" (aka Party Central Committee?), and makes his way in the *nomenklatura*, becoming director of the subsection of the Moscow Communal Property Administration charged with ridding the city of cats (allegorizing perhaps, as Laura Pérez suggests to me, the cynical employment of the lumpenproletariat by the Party higher-ups to do the Revolution's dirty-work in eliminating the class enemy?). When he was still Sharik, he had licked the Professor's boots, fawned on him in return for food, and admired his master's way of "nipping" back, in dog-eat-dog fashion, at the house management committee. But Sharikov now turns out to be a thief, a coward, a would-be blackmailer, and a rapist, who makes Philip Philippovich's life a nightmare.

Forced, then, to cohabit with a vulgarian who prefers the crudities of the circus to the refinements of theater and opera, who boorishly simplifies the arguments of Engels and Krautsky into the crudest of doctrines ("just take everything and divide it up," 89), and who reduces the elegant apartment itself to a material and moral shambles by his pursuit of cats and his sexual attack on the cook, the repentant Professor concludes that, although he has been able to turn a dog into a hoodlum, the next step — turning the hoodlum into a man — is beyond his powers. Only Sharikov's love of food and drink allows him to be controlled in some degree; but in the end, the only solution will be to overpower him and submit him to a reverse transplant operation. So in the final pages of the novel we see a four-legged Sharik again, still able to talk a bit, but already slumped peaceably at the Professor's feet and congratulating himself, as any dog might, on being "set for life" in this comfortable apartment with its warm radiators and plentiful food. Both man and dog—bourgeois intellectual and proletarian—are contented, it seems, when the ratio of power between them is right (and the underdog gets some basic creature comforts—which was not the case before the revolution). Cipión and Berganza, with their abiding interest in finding a "good" master, would understand perfectly.

Although he lives to rue his misconceived experiment, however, the Professor is far from imagining, so clear is his conscience, that he and his surgery might somehow have been responsible for the disasters that beset him: from Philip Philippovich's point of view, the error lay only in using a criminal as donor. But the novel's irony implies more searching questions. What is the responsibility of the scientist himself in Sharikov's origins? And (to translate the allegory) to what extent was the revolution, as an ill-considered social experiment, the result of blindness and lack of foresight on the part of a group of intellectuals, who were pursuing good Enlightenment ideals (social emancipation, the empirical pursuit of truth) without attending to their likely social consequences? Can the errors of the revolution be blamed *solely* on the dubious "social origins" (in serfdom) of the Russian proletariat, its unreadiness for power, as the Professor's entirely self-serving assessment with respect to Sharikov would suggest?

The problem with this latter interpretation is that it doesn't take account of the cozy relation between man and dog (intellectual and proletarian) that the novel dwells on in both its initial and its final episodes. Under normal circumstances, intellectuals and proletarians (men and dogs) are, it seems, such good friends that, in the matter of responsibility, there's nothing to distinguish between them. They're like the mind and the body, yoked together (mongrel fashion) by the pituitary: the man (mind) needs his dog (body), to lick his feet and be controlled, giving Fido-like affection; but the dog (body) concomitantly needs a man (mind) to be its master. Trouble arises only when an in-between figure like Sharikov emerges to disturb the balance, a figure not fully human (*Canis loquens*, not *Homo sapiens*) but endowed with sufficient semblance of humanity, in combination with the doglike motivations he has maintained, to become the master. It's the reversal of the comfortable man-dog tandem, such that the doglike (the body, the proletarian) are suddenly in charge, according to the doctrine of the dictatorship of the proletariat, that results in disorder. But that reversal can only be the result of the Professor's unconsidered intervention, his cynical experimentation, in substituting a human pituitary for a dog's.

At *ultimate* fault, perhaps, is the original chumminess of the animal (dog, body, proletarian) and the human (man, mind, intellectual), so oddly yoked together in conformity with a thematics of mongrelization. But *immediate* responsibility for the social disorder resulting from the upset in the balance of power lies squarely with those who inconsiderately undertake, out of curiosity, to interfere with the status quo. That is, it lies with Sharikov's "authors," scientific and (I'll suggest presently) literary. But how could a man like Philip Philippovich, opera lover and distinguished medical scientist—all mind, so to speak—imagine that there might be some connection between himself and a shaggy, starving street dog like Sharik? and that in operating on the dog he was therefore incurring responsibility for the fate of his own species? (How could contemporary animal experimenters, or the doctors in Nazi death camps who experimented on Jews, imagine that similar responsibility might be at stake? They just want[ed] to "contribute to knowledge.") Cynical hand washing—the denial of responsibility—is always the product of an ideology of distinction.

The novel's figure for the connectedness the Professor ignores is, of course, the pituitary gland, which it intriguingly refers to throughout the text by its scientific name, "hypophysis," meaning a growth (from *phyein*, to cause to grow) below the brain. The term is used, though, I suspect, because it also seems to imply something like "growing from below," as if it referred perhaps to the attachment of the human brain to a lower, animal form of life that the possession of a pituitary enables it, simultaneously, to (seek to) transcend. To possess a pituitary isn't simply to share a defining anatomical feature with (among other animals) dogs, although that is part of the novel's point; it's also to have the potential to grow and simultaneously to be condemned to fall short of that potential, to be unable to achieve the refinement and maturity for which one nevertheless strives. It's in the perspective of the pituitary that upward-tending, Faustian figures like Philip Philippovich are deluded, because they ignore the sense in which they share a plane of existence with animals like Sharik and brutes like Sharikov, who is thus not the only figure of arrested development in the text.

So, just as Sharikov is always "barking" out ejaculations, "yipping" in anger, "yelping" with pain, or "whining" in self-pity, the Professor "barks" too on occasion, and "nips" the house management committee.

Furthermore, Sharik is not the Professor's only pet; he has a very doglike human companion—a sort of "Man Fido" (since Crusoe is in the intertext)—in the person of his faithful assistant, young Dr. Bormenthal, who is, of course, always facing off jealously with Sharik or Sharikov, but who is also regularly detailed to do the Professor's dirty work (supplying cadavers; overpowering unwilling experimental subjects like Sharik and administering the ether; standing up to Shvonder, the head of the management committee; and so on), so that the latter can be "free" to get on with his work and at the same time keep his hands nice and clean. Bormenthal is the puppyish figure of the ever-faithful disciple, eternally beloved (and made use of) by professors. He thus mediates between, and so connects, Sharik and Sharikov on the one hand, and the distinguished Philip Philippovich on the other (as if he were their pituitary), even as the distinction the two scientists claim is figured in part by Bormenthal's German name and in part by their habit of speaking German together when they don't wish to be understood by the "lower orders" (as Ackerley would have said). (This, by the way, is the clue I responded to, as a post-World War II reader, in associating Philip Philippovich's experimental [a]morality with that of the death-camp doctors.)

All this friendship and connectedness between man and dog, professor and disciple—with its kynical reminder that we humans are, by hypophysical determination (and whatever our degree of mental development), dogs at heart—also means, however, that we can't read the novel's satire of boorish Soviet society in which the doglike Sharikovs are the master, or its concomicant satire of the Professor's cynical denial of responsibility, as if the connection between Sharik(ov) and Philip Philippovich didn't imply a further connection, that between the satirist critic himself and his (double) target. After all, the Professor's experiment (designed to find out what happens if a human pituitary is implanted in a dog) has as its counterpart the thought-experiment that is the novel (what would happen if dogs could become human? Answer: Soviet society). Furthermore, the novel grounds its own satirical stance, with respect to the boorishness of the Soviet masters, in bourgeois intellectual values of refinement, sophistication, and wit that correspond precisely to the Professor's own urbane tastes, and so replicate his self-definition as a "distinguished" member of the human race, distinct from the doggish, mongrelized majority.

As a consequence, the novel's critique of Philip Philippovich's cynicism extends, by the logic of *tu quoque* (as irony always does), to the "distinction" implied by its own urbane and witty writing, contrasted as it is with the character, diction, and doings of a vulgarian like Sharikov. For, as I've already pointed out, Bulgakov is as much the author of Sharikov's days as Philip Philippovich and, like Cervantes engaging in literary *tropelía*, he's working in a domain of fictional experimentation no less murky—since it can't know its own consequences or measure its own responsibility—than the domain of scientific experimentation in which the Professor engages with such self-satisfied and self-disculpating detachment. If Sharikov owes his existence to the Professor's cynical experiment, his name (Polygraph Polygraphovich) makes it clear that he has another progenitor, the producer of (multiple) writing(s).

The only difference is that, where the Professor denies—even to himself—his own involvement in dogginess and hence the impossibility of his being able to engage with impunity in "animal experimentation," the novel's author can be thought to be more kynically *acknowledging* his intellectual cynicism and the spottiness of his motivations, his knowledge that satirical criticism rests on the delusion of distinction and the denial of personal responsibility. It's a wry acknowledgment, and it works by implication only. But it doesn't fail to suggest a sort of solidarity in cynicism that connects intellectuals like Bulgakov to intellectuals like Philip Philippovich, even when the first kynically criticizes the cynicism of the second. What they share is disdain for people like Sharikov and hence a willful denial of what, in their own being, connects them to such people. Criticism thus turns back, once again, on a critic, the forthrightness of whose criticism seemed at first to imply no possible connection between the critical object and the subject. And once again a critic is left to hope (to hope against hope) that acknowledgment of the spottiness of his position will be enough to excuse his participation in something (the cynical hand washing of deluded intellectuals) that he himself, when he encounters it in others, rightly finds inexcusable.

SPOT, OR HIS MASTER'S VOICE

It's hard, then, in the long run, to distinguish sharply between the kynical and the cynical, the critic and the criticized. Delusion and lack of self-knowledge are on both sides, and social differences—the kind of differences that make criticism possible at the same time as they justify attempts at social engineering—are interpreted, as much by critics as by engineers, as entailing distinction. Neither can predict with any accuracy the outcomes their social interventions may produce nor identify the deeper motivations that may underlie them. It's just that one—the spotty kynic—acknowledges these conditions as the inevitable conditions of agency and recommends care (care as caution, care as worry over responsibility), whereas the other ignores them and is culpably self-disculpating, unself-critically denying the facts of responsibility. The one—whom I'll now call the "krytic"— is the kynically spotty, self-critical hound, for whom the paradoxical message: "Don't trust us spotty ones!" serves as a motto. The other is simply hypo-critical, that is, insufficiently (self-)critical—a category that includes plenty of practicing critics.

If not all critics are krytical and the krytical are at best spotty, we need to take all the lessons we can get from canine philosophers; and the spottier the philosopher the more salutary the lesson. But sometimes (institutions in particular, being what they are), there may be no mongrel philosophers around. In such circumstances, the kynically deprived can always avail themselves of the lesson encapsulated in "the most valuable trademark in the world." I'm referring to the His Master's Voice/RCA Victor logo, with its appealing black-eared white terrier, for whom my private nickname has always been, because of the ear, Spot. (Warren Motte informs me his real name is Nipper.) It's worth looking up page 224 of Michael Taussig's *Mimesis and Alterity*, though, where there's a reproduction of a stunning and spectacularly spotty version of Spot (taken from a Cuna needlepoint mola).[7] It was from Taussig that I learned also, to my surprise but also my delight, that many people believe Spot not to be listening to the sounds of "his master's voice" (the official interpretation: Spot as Fido), but to be speaking into an ancient piece of recording apparatus (a little as if Millie used a dictaphone to dictate her story to Barbara Bush). Spot as *Canis loquens*, then.

Given this ambiguity, we can say that, like the famous rabbit-ducks that illustrate the trickiness of visual figure and ground, Spot is a figure of reversibility. But he figures the reversibility implicit in the theoretical concept of the subjection of agency.[8] He reminds us that, as *Canis loquens*, we can't dictate doggy messages without being simultaneously dictated to, if only by the human language that we speak (but "language," here, can stand for discursivity, that is, the full range of cultural conditions that mediate, and so produce, human interactions). The condition of our cultural interventions, in other words, is that they be themselves culturally determined. Is Spot delivering some devastatingly kynical piece of cultural critique into his little dictaphone? He might be; but blink, and Spot the krytic becomes Fido, giving fascinated and exclusive attention to what it is that "his master's voice"—the cultural machine—is dictating to (and through) him.

Culture, in short, is a reproducing machine. And we're the dogs through whom it reproduces its messages, whether we hearken to them Fido-fashion, or whether they speak anyway when we dictate "our own" messages into the machine. We're inseparably part of the machine, the part without which it couldn't function (and indeed wouldn't have a function); and yet, oddly—because we're dogs and it's a machine—we're also (partially) separable from it and able to affect (in some degree) its working. In other words, because we talking dogs are its agents as well as its subjects, culture is bound to have a digressive structure; and it reproduces digressively, therefore, through change (but change that's neither fully predictable nor genuinely radical). It's the degree of (partial) separability entailed by culture's digressive, machine-dog structure that makes it possible for us dogs to be critical (including krytical). On the other hand, the degree of inseparability it also entails means that the price of exercising our critical "faculty" has to be the krytical knowledge that criticism inevitably feeds back into the machine it criticizes and contributes to its (digressive) self-reproduction. Blink, I'm a cultural subject; blink, I'm a critic (krytic) of culture; blink, I'm a subject again. Same difference, as people say.

Still, it is a difference, and it means that we have an option: the option to be either digressive or nondigressive subjects. We can be content to be talking machines ourselves, just human phonographs blindly and unself-consciously reproducing the messages of culture— or we can be talking dogs, having the ability to "talk back" into the machine (the machine that's simultaneously talking through us even as we talk into it). To *forget* that, whatever we do or say, the machine is reproducing itself through us—to believe, in other words, in the independence of our own individual agency—is precisely to become a human phonograph identical with the machine itself. That's the paradox of ideology, as Althusser pointed out (I'd want to add that nevertheless the machine continues to function digressively).[9] To remember that condition of agency, making an anamnestic effort, doesn't of course release us from it. But it does remind us of our spottiness, and awareness of spottiness is the condition of our enjoying even the small degree of separability from the machine that the krytical can attain.

Yes, I know I'm presenting the alternative too starkly. And yes, I realize that the privilege of the krytical isn't much of a privilege. But, like most privileges, those associated with the conscious exercise of the ability to digress are privileges indeed when you compare them with the alternative. Dogs would teach us that if they could talk. And whether they talk to us or not, the literature of talking dogs suggests that that's what we should be learning from them.[10]

Three Loiterly Intellectuals

Flâneur Reading (On Being Belated)

On my campus, 747-FAST is the number that connects you electronically to the library database and allows you to charge out a book without setting foot on the premises. (Of course, the book doesn't arrive for twenty-four hours, and meanwhile you've missed the pleasure of browsing the shelves for yourself.) Speed, I know, first began to affect the practice of reading with the emergence of print technology and the invention of the book, so it's a bit late to be complaining about it now. But folks who tell us we shouldn't mourn the probable passing of that self-same book in the information age (because it too was once new technology resisted by belated people) are ignoring a couple of points. For one thing, what's disturbing these days isn't so much the probable disappearance of books, which can be faced with some equanimity, as the possible loss of certain modes of reading—I'll call them "critical" reading—that require time and are incompatible with haste. The speed reader doesn't have time for reflection and is inclined to take things at face value.

For another thing, there is a whole culture of speed, which (taking a hint from Baudelaire) I'll call the culture of impatience, which has its roots less in the age of incunabula than in the industrial revolution and the era of entrepreneurial capitalism. This culture threatens many reflective practices by speeding up communication so that language is necessarily taken to be transparent. Citing Paul Virilio, Rey Chow has drawn attention to modernist writing as a form of resistance to the culture of impatience,[1] and I'll follow suit by attempting to describe a complementary phenomenon, the emergence of "flâneur reading" as a critical practice that takes the culture of speed as its object. Walter Benjamin long ago described the flâneur as the writer betaking himself to the marketplace[2] (inevitably himself, of course); he saw the flâneur figure in terms of an encounter between practices of writing, but also of reading, that had developed as part of an aristocratic and/or monastic culture associated with *otium* (ease or leisure), and the exigencies of capitalist *neg-otium*, the busyness and productivity of a new industrial and bourgeois age. But what this means is that the flâneur was a structurally belated figure from the start, and I want to propose that as a consequence of this belatedness there was in the flâneur a potential for resistance to the pressures of the capitalist marketplace (and in particular its doctrine of progress) that Benjamin doesn't allow for. If anything, such resistance has become even more crucial now, with the proliferation of technologies of near-instantaneity (the telephone, the fax, e-mail), than it ever was in Baudelaire's time, when the railroad and its companion invention, the telegraph, were king.

If, as Schivelbusch argues, the railroad (despite upholstery) gave the bourgeoisie a taste of working-class experience by industrializing travel,[3] the latter-day descendants of the telegraph bombard contemporary white-collar workers, including intellectuals, and give them a taste of blue-collar experience, forcing them to scramble to keep up with what is the postindustrial equivalent of a speeded-up assembly line. If the telegram or most ordinary e-mail messages were a literary genre, they would be at the opposite end of the spectrum of readability from loiterature. In representing the belated value of dilatoriness in the face of cultural acceleration, flâneur writing can be thought, therefore, not solely to have met a market demand as Benjamin saw, but at the same time to have reserved a space, within the culture of progress, for reflective reading. And that space simultaneously provided the precondition for critical attitudes and thought. In short, the *pensiveness* of the flâneur in Baudelaire's poem, "Le Cygne," can be understood as the sign of both a flâneur having become reader of the culture of impatience and of flânerie as an emerging critical practice that might be thought to contain one of the historical germs (like ancient and modern kynicism—see chapters 6 and 7) of contemporary cultural critique.

Betaking himself to the bourgeois marketplace with eyes firmly set on an aristocratic model of leisure, the flâneur, then, was a figure of divided attention and belatedness. As such, he was a likely site for a certain digressiveness to occur, by which he became dissociated from the culture of speed that his observations of modern life were nevertheless subserving. But, in occupying a digressive space within the culture of speed, the flâneur also became a much more *suspect* figure, since his loiterature could be regarded as a form of "loitering with intent," in this case critical intent. As a result, rather than the self-imposed marginalization implied by his nostalgia for the aristocratic value of *otium*, he found himself marginalized in another way, by identification with socially suspect lumpen-proletarian types like the beggar, the ragpicker, or the saltimbank, whom the bourgeois despised, feared, and mistrusted. The story of the emergence, in Baudelaire, of the figure of the flâneur as reader is thus simultaneously the story of his coming to accept and to assume, as an allegorical figuration of the poet, a position that identified the practice of poetry with social misfits, outcasts, and parasites, rather than with the positions of power and prestige to which the dandy in Baudelaire never ceased to give an aristocratic, or would-be aristocratic, inflection. It is the story of his coming to terms with the peripheral social, temporal, and even spatial condition of the loiterly subject (chapter 3).

But rapid change can make a reader of anyone, flâneur or no. It's enough to digress a bit, that is, to become slightly dissociated from the onward rush of progress, in order to discover both the culture's readability and one's own readerly engagement with it as a text. You can experience the effect, for example, by revisiting after a short interval a town you previously lived in or knew well. When I return to Australian cities, Sydney or Brisbane for instance, after having lived elsewhere for about twenty years, I find myself walking around in two cities at once, joined by a common topography. Large patches of the older city have disappeared, but it enjoys surprising reality and substance in my memory (especially the *mémoire du corps*), whereas the new city is incontrovertibly there but lacks all credibility in my eyes. If reading a text is a matter of activating the split between "saying" and "meaning," producing an unverifiable *énonciation* out of an *énoncé* judged inadequate in itself, then one miqht say that the "revisiting" experience makes a once familiar (*heimlich*) urban text into something that has become *unheimlich*, or uncanny: an inadequate city *énoncé* (the city's present configuration) is now sutured to an *énonciation* that "haunts" it, without being fully or securely retrievable (the city of one's memory). This is a strange, two-sided city (a relation of permeable contexts), of which, as the third or mediating figure without whom the two sides would not exist, one has become a sometimes enraptured but often troubled or anxious reader, since one's position is split between two cities, each making claims on the attention but to neither of which one can fully "belong." As in Baudelaire's Paris, what was formerly an everyday environment that could be read off at a glance (like reading the label on a jar of preserves) has become, instead, a "cité pleine de rêves, / Où le spectre en plein jour accroche le passant" (dream-filled city, / where in broad daylight specters catch at passers by; "Les Sept Vieillards").[4] And that can bring out the flâneur in anyone, as you halt at each moment to read, your attention "hooked" (*accroché*) by some new discrepancy between experience and memory.

But Baudelaire didn't need to "revisit" Paris: history took things in hand while he lived there, and made the capital of the nineteenth century, for him, into an uncannily readable text. The short half century of Baudelaire's life span (1821–67) coincides with a period of astoundingly rapid industrial, commercial, and technological "progress" in France, under the burgeoning laissez-faire capitalist economy. A nation that continued to exhaust itself in the postrevolutionary pursuit of political consensus and stability nevertheless became an industrial and colonial power capable of beginning to challenge mighty England itself. Paris—in 1820 still a relatively small, preindustrial city (that of the earliest eighteenth-century flâneurs like Louis-Sébastien Mercier and Restif de la Bretonne, whose writing betrays no special awareness of belatedness)—had become, by the period of the Second Empire, the only European city that could hold a candle to London for size, and it outshone the grimy, dreary English metropolis in glitz and sophistication. The cumulative, complex effects of this sudden cultural transformation were somehow captured and focused, for Parisians, by the urbanism that, especially after 1851, enthusiastically gutted the old, still medieval city and drove new, straight, wide boulevards and avenues connecting with pompous, empty squares through the teeming inner neighborhoods, leading Victor Hugo to quip, in allusion to the authoritarian political regime, that "alignment" was the order of the day.

Small wonder, then, if by reaction resistance became loiterly, readerly, and digressive—a matter of unauthorized but tolerated departures from the norm—given especially the failure of more transgressive modes of oppositionality that had had their day, albeit briefly, in 1848. Flânerie, whatever its political significance before midcentury, became available now for resignification, as a manifestation of resistance to the speed of progress, and hence as a site of reading and (largely implied) critique. Belatedness—no longer merely structural—became a dilatory response to political alignment and the culture of impatience. So, when Baudelaire wrote in "Le Cygne" the famous lines: "Le vieux Paris n'est plus (la forme d'une ville / Change plus vite, hélas! que le cœur d'un mortel)" (Old Paris is no more [a city's form / changes more quickly, alas, than a mortal's heart]), and later in the same poem, "Paris change! mais rien dans ma mélancolie / N'a bougé!" (Paris changes! but nothing in my melancholy / has moved; vol. 1, 85-87), he was arguably recording the introduction of a new, critical dimension into the old flâneur practices of observation and description. These had always been loiterly in style; but the new dimension that becomes apparent in a poem like "Le Cygne" is that of *memory*, which drives a wedge between the changing "city's form" and its belated observer, "a mortal's heart." And with this new distance of the flâneur subject comes *pensiveness*, the stubborn melancholia that is a marker, in this and many other French texts of the period,[5] of historical alienation, and hence of the necessity to *read* the new, changed world—that is, as Baudelaire puts it, to "allegorize" it—rather than merely reproduce its visual aspect as in the descriptive but uncritical prose of flâneur tradition.

Benjamin's flâneur relates mainly to the pre-1848 period: he has affinities with the detective.[6] He's a class spy reporting to the bourgeoisie on the life of the exploited class, at least to the extent that that life was visible on and from the street (for the flâneur rarely ventured into factories or other industrial sites). This flâneur, whose later, "salaried" avatar, Benjamin suggests, will be the sandwich man, is consequently treated, in terms of a thematics of visibility and invisibility, as the agent of panoptic surveillance who simultaneously euphemizes his own bourgeois solitude by imagining his invisibility in the crowd as a *bain de multitude*. His invisibility is that of the inspector, and Foucault might well have seen in his form of (in)activity a precursor of the power-laden practice of examination that was to emerge as characteristic of disciplines like criminology later in the century.[7] The shift that Baudelaire was to introduce into this understanding of the flâneur involved turning him from an inspector (of the working class) into a critical reader (of the class configuration itself), and it required him to overcome his bourgeois sense of solitude and invisibility in order to accept both the reader's connectedness to the city-text and a sense of community with the peripheral figures this new, parasitic, mediatory status associated him with. And that, in turn, I surmise, has much to do with a new understanding of the street, as the flâneur's assigned territory and the site of his operations.

The street was obviously available as an observation post, Benjamin-fashion, where delegates of the middle class could find out something about the existence and political mood of the exploited. But it could also be defined, in doubly negative terms, as a site that was neither the bourgeois "home" (with its famous "douceur du foyer") nor the workplace that was familiar, obviously, to the proletariat as well as to a few representatives of the bourgeoisie. It was an artery of communication used by all, but it was also marked as a quite particular social site by the fact that it had, in addition, more or less permanent, or at least naturalized, denizens of its own: people who didn't have access to official work sites and were also without a "home" in the bourgeois (foyer) sense of the word. These people—the beggars, prostitutes, saltimbanks, *petites vieilles*, ragpickers, and so on who populate much of Baudelaire's city writing—were, like today's homeless and other street people, viewed as "parasitic" figures, taking energy and sustenance from the productive economy while, at best, returning to it only entertainment, like the saltimbanks, or illusion, like the prostitutes.[8] Baudelaire's self-identification with such figures—or more subtly, as Gérard Gasarian argues, his self-allegorization in and through them—is notorious.[9] In Baudelaire the poet-flâneur may be betaking himself to the marketplace, but the symbolic site of his activity is the street as a neutral, marginalized space that doesn't lead anywhere in particular, because it's the place where the productive economy locates a suspect population of loungers, loiterers, and parasites—and so, in my hypothesis, a space of reading split digressively off from a so-called progressive society that was itself deeply divided by class but permeated, nevertheless, across class divisions, by the spirit of the new industrial-capitalist age. The move made by Baudelaire was thus to shift the (street-based) allegiance of the flâneur from the bourgeoisie, the class to which he belonged by birth, to a nonclass: the community of those whose marginalization and parasitism signal them—in the way suggested by Michel Serres—as figures of mediation.

This, however, was no easy shift for Baudelaire to make. He was middle class by origins and education. He was capable of, at least, political identification, on occasion, with the working class and its aspirations. He wasn't capable, though, as in particular Dolf Oehler and Richard Burton have demonstrated, of being, in a sustained way, either the type of intellectual Gramsci calls traditional (working in the interests of ideological hegemony) or the type he calls organic (working for the future ascendancy of the rising, but currently dominated, class).[10] Neither organic nor traditional, he's the prototype of what can be called the critical intellectual, who occupies an unaligned or third position, the digressive position that the dichotomization inherent in nineteenth-century class structure can't quite account for—the position that made the street his natural habitat. This is the position from which a reading becomes possible of the productive, progressive society and its divisions and conflicts, even if that reading amounts—as it frequently does in Baudelaire—to a dismissive "pox on both your houses." The difficulty, though, was that Baudelaire was himself a strongly dualistic thinker, for whom class and other dichotomizations (such as that of day and night) seemed both inevitable and exhaustive, leaving no residue. So it was difficult and even painful for him to conceive of— let alone adopt—a position of oppositionality (there was never much likelihood of his aligning himself with the powerful except in a fit of pique against revolutionaries) that wasn't in alignment with a simple dominant-dominated dichotomy. To conceive of such a fringe position, he needed to be able to come to some sort of understanding of the importance of the phenomenon of mediation, as the third element that opens dichotomous systems to effects of alterity, and whose parasitical function I'm figuring here as the power of reading. And meanwhile, as I'll show at perhaps tedious length, he persisted in interpreting the two-sidedness of the readerly city as a simple dichotomy—expressed particularly as a dichotomy of night and day—denying at the same time the thirdness and mediatory status of the flâneur reader and forced, therefore, to situate him either as a solitary, anonymous, and unaligned figure or (what amounts to the same thing) as a simple instrument of social power.

My guess, then, is that it was the anomalous function of the street— outside of the home and the work place but connecting them, and a site simultaneously frequented by the productive classes and inhabited by the (non)class of society's outcasts and parasites—that gave Baudelaire a way of thinking thirdness, and of making the position of supplementarity palatable to his own (bourgeois) pride and (masculinist) disdain of the function of mediation. The street made it possible for him to connect the flâneur to the "heroism of modern life" that he had identified, as early as 1846, as a key problem for modern art.[11] But the connection must have become easier after 1851, when Haussmann's massive urban transformations began to make the streets themselves into work places, by turning them into the construction sites whose rubble and confusion is recalled, in the same breath as the "bric-à-brac confus" of antique shops, in "Le Cygne"; it must then have become possible for Baudelaire to think of supposedly parasitic, street-bound flânerie as a form of work in its own right, both a substitute for productive employment in its normative sense and a version of the oppositionality suggested by the term *labor* in its political sense, as a metonym for the working-class movement: "le Travail," so capitalized in "Le Cygne." ("La rue," the street, had connoted working-class revolt since at least 1830.) In this hypothesis, poetry as critical flâneur reading, the labor of mediation, thus became for Baudelaire the form of work associated with the street—the work performed by parasites in general and by flâneur reading in particular—in a society whose *dominant* cultural sites are elsewhere, in the home or the factory, for instance.

The emergence in Baudelaire of the figure of the flâneur as reader of the city is tied, then, to an understanding of the city as divided by class struggle but also as split, socially and historically, by a consciousness of the *alterity within* that is critical readability. This is the historical alterity that makes for belatedness in the temporal dimension (as defined by the doctrine of progress), but it's also the social alterity constituted by the existence, within the total community, of a group of out-casts, excluded from *both* major social classes, inner exiles whose hero-ism (by affinity but also by contrast with that of official political exiles like Hugo, to whom "Le Cygne" is dedicated) consists of oc-cupying and assuming—as it were through what might anachronis-tically be called *innere Emigration*—such a position of marginality, along with the parasitic identity it entails. This historically and socially peripheral position makes possible a critical function that society's more respected members (its workers, tradespeople, *commerçants*, man-agers, entrepreneurs, and official intellectuals[12]) are much too *busy*—or insufficiently loiterly—to notice, let alone to fulfil.

I'm arguing, then, that the historical conditions of accelerated cul-tural change that made the city uncannily readable by splitting it, in the eyes of its belated citizens, into an unconvincing presence haunted by an unrecoverable past, were also the conditions that produced the possibility, for the flâneur, of becoming an unaligned but critical reader of the city rather than a class spy delegated by the dominant class to keep tabs on the proletariat. And "Le Cygne," I'll try to show, is the poem of the flâneur as reader in this "exiled" sense. But in order to reach this poem I'll take a slightly dilatory path of my own, making lateralizing moves in the chronology by starting with a famous essay that was perhaps written roughly contemporaneously with "Le Cygne" but was not published until 1863, *Le Peintre de la vie moderne* (*The Painter of Modern Life*) and moving then to an early flâneur poem, "Le Crépuscule du Soir," which dates from 1851, before arriving at "Le Cygne," which is one of a number of breakthrough poems Baudelaire wrote in 1859 and incorporated in the second (1861) edition of *Les Fleurs du Mal*. The full story of Baudelaire as loiterly intellectual would have to encompass also the set of prose poems he wrote in the later years of his life, now grouped under the titles *Petits Poèmes en Prose* or *Le Spleen de Paris*; but "Le Cygne" is the breakthrough text. And that is so, I want to propose, because it is the poem in which the figure of the flâneur as reader emerges, enabling Baudelaire to go beyond the dichotomizations, often organized in terms of day and night, that obscured for him the flâneur's curious, but crucial and critical, position of "inner alterity" within the city. It is the attempted maintenance of such dichotomizations and, simultaneously, an odd promotion of the flâneur figure as disconnected, if not actually extrasocial—isolated, invisible, uninvolved—that can be glimpsed in *The Painter of Modern Life* and "Le Crépuscule du Soir."

DAY, NIGHT, TWILIGHT

The Painter of Modern Life is a justly celebrated essay in which Baudelaire describes art, and more generally the phenomenon of beauty, as the product of mediation. By implication, the readability of modern life, and particularly of the city, is acknowledged—but the flâneur is described as a purely visual consciousness, a walking pair of eyes. This trick, which depends on the common misconception that vision is a direct and unmediated apprehension of the real, is accomplished by means of a strict division of employment—itself enforced by the dichotomization of day and night—between the artist as flâneur, taking in the sights of the diurnal world, and the artist who, no less single-mindedly, produces representations of what the flâneur saw.

This nocturnal figure, the true mediator of modern beauty, has little in common with the "man of the world" who furnishes his raw material. He works feverishly, not in loiterly fashion, and his instrument isn't the eye, the instrument of supposedly unmediated vision, but a hand guided by memory—and this belatedness with respect to the immediate sensations of the flâneur, while it is short term, nevertheless signals the specificity of his task. He doesn't *reproduce* the erstwhile objects of flâneur vision, but *extracts* from them, by a process that Baudelaire calls translation and refers to also as a "mnemotechnics of the beautiful," the beauty that lay concealed beneath their familiar, and thus unprepossessing, everydayness. The present tense of experience becomes beautiful by virtue of a divided attention, on the part of artists, that itself derives from a time lag. The immediacy of the flâneur's experience, by contrast, precludes both dividedness and deferral.

Baudelaire seems unconscious, here, of the potential criticism of the illusion of presentness that's inherent in the phenomenon of memory, although that is exactly the subject of "Le Cygne." Rather, he presents the subject of his case study, Guys, as obliged to work fast, in order not to lose something—he calls it a phantom, in a way that's reminiscent of the haunted city Baudelaire's own poetry describes—something that seems to arise, somehow, in the time gap between the immediacy of flâneur vision and the moment of painterly execution. Thanks to memory, beauty emerges from the clutter and familiarity of experience, but execution must be quick because memory, as a function of time, is inevitably subject to the effects of temporality in the form of forgetting, so that the phantom must be captured and the effect of synthesis that memory makes possible produced before memory fades. It follows, although Baudelaire doesn't make the point, that forgetting is crucial: it is forgetting that produces the painterly city as an effect of *énonciation* arising out of the *énoncé* that is flâneur experience, for this effect exists, it seems, neither in the flâneur's experience nor in the artist's work, but somewhere between them, these being only the joint agency through which it appears, as a third term (what the artist "omitted" from what the flâneur "saw") that's situated in neither. Beauty, in short, is an effect of readability and, consequently, the artist's translation of flâneur experience itself requires translation in turn. The product of his work is described by Baudelaire, in a striking oxymoron, as "a sketch if you will, but a perfected one" (une ébauche si vous voulez, mais parfaite; vol. 2, 700). That is, the artist has done his work in "capturing" the phantom, but the phantom of beauty, as a readable object, does not reside in the still incomplete text that is the work, and so needs to be realized in turn by a further mediating agent, who is of course the spectator of the painting, called by Baudelaire "the translator of a translation" (vol. 2, 698). The process of mediation, once initiated, thus becomes an endless relay, because its product—the effect of beauty—can't be possessed by those who are only the agents of its emergence.

Baudelaire's systematization of this relay effect, which makes beauty a mobile, wandering thing of which art is only the vehicle, lies in his famous distinction between two kinds of beauty. Guys has translated into art the beauty of his own age, with its own particular, relative, and local characteristics; it's for the spectator to perceive, that is, to mediate the emergence of, the other component of beauty, its "eternal" essence. This is a beauty that never exists independently but is *made available* only through the vehicle of each work's transient or "modern" beauty—for every age has its modernity—the transience that makes it only a "sketch" (albeit a perfect one). But now there is no problematics of forgetting, and no need for haste, since the "eternal" phantom is a product of historical memory, and particularly, it seems, of the history of styles. It's the confrontation of artworks from different historical periods that causes the timeless form of beauty to emerge as their common aesthetic component. Eternal beauty is thus a product of reading and something like what we might nowadays call a perception of intertextuality: the simultaneous cognizance of two historically different forms of modernity that are linked by the mediation of spectatorial memory, which is thus another form of belatedness, but long term now, and endlessly expansive, as the concept of "eternal" beauty requires, because it has access to the whole of human history. Baudelaire confronts Guys's contemporary sketches with eighteenth-century fashion plates but also with the hieratic art of ancient Egypt, much as in "Le Cygne" his flâneur figure compares Second Empire Paris with an older city only recently disappeared, or a swan in an urban gutter with the "immense majesty" of the ancient figure of Andromache. The method is the same, and the implications similar with respect to the power of mediatory thought (reading); but the effect of the two texts is different. Whereas in *The Painter of Modern Life* reading is aesthetic—I want to say restrictively so—in "Le Cygne" it is both aesthetic and critical; and that, I suggest, is because in "Le Cygne" the reading subject will have become embodied as a flâneur.

In *The Painter of Modern Life* it is significant, therefore, that the chain of mediations through which the phantom of beauty is produced is presented as, so to speak, no concern of the flâneur's. *His* vision of the world—a world with which he is virtually identified, having no artistic, aesthetic, or critical distance from it—provides the raw material of art; yet he is oddly out of the loop, presented as pure *origin* of a relay that ought by rights to have no origin, because precisely his material is thought of as raw—it passes *through* the flâneur into the chain of production of beauty, transmitted (but without being mediated) by his gaze. Baudelaire, it seems clear, is protecting something here, and what he is protecting, it seems no less clear, is the flâneur's identity, perceived as threatened by the effects of mediation: dividedness, difference, deferral, digressivity. The splitness and loss of presence implied by belatedness and the uncenteredness and loss of control inherent in the agential function of the mediator, through whom things emerge (beauty, signification) that transcend his individuality, threaten the loiterly subject, already socially marginal, with a *ça ne se dessine pas* (chapter 3) to which Baudelaire reacts by reasserting the flâneur's autonomy (and hence his affinity with the so-called bourgeois subject).

The thematics of the *bain de multitude* does not contradict this analysis but confirms it. A consciousness identified with a pure gaze, the flâneur in Baudelaire's understanding is one whose *jouissance* is an orgasm of dispossession, in which personal identity becomes fused with the multiplicity of the crowd:

> It is his passion and his profession to *espouse* the crowd. For the perfect flâneur, the impassioned observer, it is an immense, orgasmic pleasure (*jouissance*) to take up residence in the numerous, the undulant, the moving, the fleeting, and the infinite (vol. 2, 691).

But this is an unthreatening dispossession because, for one thing, the opposed categories (the crowd, the flâneur subject) are in an all-or-nothing relationship of mutual substitutability that denies the messy residues characteristic of mediated differences (which cannot be reduced to identity), and because, for another—but it's ultimately the same thing—the giving up of individual identity to the crowd is interpreted as the mark of a unique privilege, one that quite clearly *distinguishes* the flâneur from the anonymous, undulant mass in which he so readily immerses himself. "To be outside of one's self [*hors de chez soi*] and at the same time to feel everywhere at home in oneself [*chez soi*]" is, we learn, a quite distinctive faculty, the *jouissance* of a prince, and specifically that of "un prince qui jouit de son incognito" (a prince deriving orgasmic pleasure from being incognito). Such an identification suggests a certain residual nostalgia for aristocratic privilege in the flâneur corresponding to what I called the figure's structural belatedness. But it corresponds also to a particular fantasy of power, and one characteristic, if Foucault is correct, of nineteenth-century modernity: the panoptic power of an observer who is invisible to all but has everyone under control, the power of a new, disciplinary society.[13] No wonder Benjamin read this passage and others like it as symptomatic of the flâneur's complicity with the middle class.

I think, however, that in this famous "bain de multitude" passage Baudelaire is mistaking one thing for another: the experience of the "man of the crowd" might equally have been described as an orgy of digressivity, a consequence of the uncenteredness of mediated reality. But the error is significant, in part because it suggests that Baudelaire is compensatorily "correcting" the implications of his own insights into the mediatory function of art by making the flâneur exempt from them, and in part because it can be read as an exemplification of what was at stake in nineteenth-century France, and is, I suppose, always at stake when regimes of disciplinary control are in place: such regimes function to deny the digressiveness inherent in culture as the mediated production of reality. Out of an unwillingness to assume, in the persona of the flâneur, the effects of self-dispossession that are inevitably associated with the function of mediation, Baudelaire finds himself complicitous with a political regime—in this case, that of the Second Empire—whose style (whatever its reality) was authoritarian; and he consequently misses the opportunity to incorporate flânerie, as a practice of reading, into a truly modern theory of art.

Not surprisingly, then, when we turn to a much earlier poem, "Le Crépuscule du Soir," we find a certain hedging of bets going on that has much in common with the equivocations of *The Painter of Modern Life*. But this is a flâneur poem—there's no other figure present who might represent the artistic function—so it's particularly striking that the readability of the city should be enacted here (in the description of twilight) as, so to speak, a *natural* phenomenon of mediation, one for which the flâneur, who remains aloof and disconnected, self-contained except for his gaze, can't be held responsible. On the basis of an absolute distinction between object and subject, twilight as a phenomenon of mediation linking day and night is presented as without implications for its human observer, even though it raises questions both in the context of the day-night dichotomy that enforces the independence of the flâneur in *The Painter of Modern Life* from the artist mediator, and in that of the rather differently signifying but still dichotomous duality of diurnal and nocturnal city experience that structures the whole "Tableaux parisiens" section of *Les Fleurs du Mal* (1861 edition), of which both "Le Crépuscule du Soir" and "Le Cygne" form part.

LE CRÉPUSCULE DU SOIR

Voici le soir charmant, ami du criminel;
Il vient comme un complice, à pas de loup; le ciel
Se ferme lentement comme une grande alcove,
Et l'homme impatient se change en bête fauve.

5 O soir, aimable soir, désiré par celui
Dont les bras, sans mentir, peuvent dire: Aujourd'hui
Nous avons travaillé! — C'est le soir qui soulage
Les esprits que dévore une douleur sauvage,
Le savant obstiné dont le front s'alourdit,
10 Et l'ouvrier courbé qui regagne son lit.
Cependant des démons malsains dans l'atmosphère
S'eveillent lourdement, comme des gens d'affaire,
Et cognent en volant les volets et l'auvent.
A travers les lueurs que tourmente le vent
15 La Prostitution s'allume dans les rues;
Comme une fourmilière elle ouvre ses issues;
Partout elle se fraye un occulte chemin,
Ainsi que l'ennemi qui tente un coup de main
Elle remue au sein de la cité de fange
20 Comme un ver qui dérobe à l'Homme ce qu'il mange.
On entend çà et là les cuisines siffler,
Les théâtres glapir, les orchestres ronfler;
Les tables d'hôte, dont le jeu fait les délices
S'emplissent de catins et d'escrocs, leurs complices
25 Et les voleurs, qui n'ont ni trêve ni merci,
Vont bientôt commencer leur travail, eux aussi,
Et forcer doucement les portes et les caisses
Pour vivre quelques jours et vêtir leurs maîtresses.

Recueille-toi, mon âme, en ce grave moment,
30 Et ferme ton oreille à ce rugissement.
C'est l'heure où les douleurs des malades s'aigrissent!
La sombre Nuit les prend à la gorge; ils finissent
Leur destinée et vont vers le gouffre commun;
L'hôpital se remplit de leurs soupirs. —Plus d'un

35 Ne viendra plus chercher la soupe parfumée,
Au coin du feu, le soir, auprès d'une âme aimée.

Encore la plupart n'ont-ils jamais connu
La douceur du foyer et n'ont jamais vécu!

DUSK

Sweet evening comes, friend of the criminal
Like an accomplice with a light footfall;
The sky shuts on itself as though a tomb,
And man turns beast within his restless room.

O evening, night, so wished for by the one
Whose honest, weary arms can say: We've done
Our work today! —The night will bring relief
To spirits who consume themselves with grief,
The scholar who is bowed with heavy head,
The broken worker falling into bed.
Meanwhile, corrupting demons of the air
Slowly wake up like men of great affairs,
And, flying, bump our shutters and our eaves.
Against the glimmerings teased by the breeze
Old Prostitution blazes in the streets;
She opens out her nest-of-ants retreat;
Everywhere she clears the secret routes,
A stealthy force preparing for a coup;
She moves within this city made of mud,
A worm who steals from man his daily food.
One hears the hissing kitchens close at hand,
The playhouse screech, the blaring of a band.
The tables at the inns where gamesmen sport
Are full of swindlers, sluts, and all their sort.
Robbers who show no pity to their prey
Get ready for their nightly work-a-day
Of cracking safes and deftly forcing doors,
To live a few days more and dress their whores.

Collect yourself, my soul, in this grave time,
And shut out all this clamour from the slime.
This the time of sick men's sharpest pain!
Black night will grab their throats; they cry in vain,

And finish out their fate in common grave;
The hospital is filled with gasps. They have
No further need to think of evenings spent
At fireside—the fragrant soup, the friend.

But most of them have never known the call
Of friendly hearth, have never lived at all![14]

Twilight raises questions in this poem because it *covers* for a thematics
that makes desire a factor of mediation, and more particularly the
motor of a whole culture of impatience described in the first four
verses (Voici le soir . . . Et l'homme impatient se change en bête fauve).
Impatience here is first of all the desire that's frustrated by the slowness
of twilight as mediatory process: it's a desire for nontemporality as
the instantaneity that would give desire immediate gratification. In
this respect impatience is the opposite of the complicitousness—the
complicitousness with time—that's attributed (l. 2) to twilight: it's a
desire for immediacy, for something like an *instantaneous* changing of
shifts between workers of the day and workers of the night, without
intermediary process. At the same time, though, impatience is the
desire for *change*, and as such—and because it cannot bring about
the instantaneity it craves—it becomes instead the very motor of the
mediatory process that is figured here by twilight, the process that
melds every moment into another, so that distinctions that depend
on temporal separation, such as that between workers of the day and
workers of the night, are necessarily blurred, even as the workers change
shifts. Impatience, as the desire for there to be no time, turns out to
be, simultaneously, the very type of desire that mediates time, process,
and change.

This double character of impatience, its own complicity with process
and the intransigence that makes it frustrated by mediation, is captured
within the first two lines of the poem by the presentness, the at-
handness of evening that is first announced (Voici le soir . . .), then
immediately countermanded by indicators of process (Il vient comme
un complice), indicators that are themselves modified in turn by the
abruptness of change that's notified in l. 4: "Et l'homme impatient se
change en bête fauve." Desire is identified in this way as a factor of
readability, in that it brings each moment of city life, as twilight does,
into proximity with predecessor and successor moments through the
effect of impatience, so that a certain two-sidedness of reality (still day,

already night) becomes visible. But impatience being identified also as the desire to escape the effects of desire, by a drastic curtailment of temporality, it thus has an equivocal character—both desire and the desire not to desire—that will show up, in the poem as a whole, as a deep ambivalence and a kind of undecidability.

For, on the one hand, impatience is *condemned* in the poem as the desire of desires: desire is degrading because it is complicitous with evil and criminality, like twilight, and impatience is precisely the desire of humans not to delay in becoming wild beasts (l. 4). This judgment will be the grounds of the observer's disdain for what he calls "tout ce rugissement," and of his unwillingness, therefore, to connect himself with the scene of readability mediated by desire. But on the other hand impatience as the desire to escape from temporality is also exactly what the flâneur himself demonstrates in disconnecting himself from the twilight scene, the scene of readability and mediation, so that his own (unacknowledged) desire—which is nevertheless readable in the way the poem maintains the equivalence and substitutability of categories that twilight simultaneously blurs—is precisely the desire that the poem condemns.

The long central passage (ll. 5–28) thus admits of two interpretations, depending on whether the coming of night is seen as a narrative of substitutability (night replaces day without real change) or as a process determined by the permeability of contexts and marked by the gradual. In this latter understanding, the thematics of complicity, for which Prostitution is the major figure, is pervasive, determining a kind of slide from moment to moment and group to group. It's day workers' desire for rest that links them to the awakening of nocturnal demons, whose agitation is foreshadowed by the onerousness of the diurnal labors that make people long for repose. The bedding down of the ones is thus simultaneous (Cependant, l. 11) with the emergence of the others, whose awakening is further linked, via the wind-tossed gas lamp (l. 14), to the lighting up of Prostitution in the streets. The very image of the complicitous (furtive and occult), Prostitution responds, by its own parasitic animality (Comme un ver qui dérobe à l'Homme ce qu'il mange), to the impatience of mankind to become a wild beast (l. 4), much as the stirring of "démons malsains" corresponded to and was in a sense equivalent with the desire for rest of those who labor by day.

But now, as Prostitution lights up the night, the pleasure industry— with only the slightest moment of transition (On entend *ça et là* les cuisines siffler) swings into action, the whores bring out the conmen with whom they collude (leurs complices), and these in turn introduce the hard-working thieves whose nocturnal work, as the equivalent of daytime labor, announces the end of this period of transition and the onset of Night itself, which will be evoked (l. 32) in the following section. This passage thus reads like a long list, mediated by the complicities of desire and impelled by the urgency of impatience, in which each item—day workers, demons, prostitution, places of pleasure, conmen, thieves—is an unstable entity because it contains an element that produces a shift of identity to or from the next item in line (like a conveyor belt or an escalator in Nicholson Baker, chapter 5). Thus the text mimes a gradual, because mediated, process in time and represents the two-sidedness of readability as an effect of desire.

But this section also reads as a narrative of exchange, in which equivalent categories change places: the day shift heads for bed, the night shift starts work. The emphasis here is on metaphor and sub-stitutability: the demons resemble so many "gens d'affaire" as they wake; the thieves, like so many daytime working stiffs, are slaves (ni trève ni merci) to a perfectly respectable desire for creature comforts (vivre quelques jours, vêtir leurs maîtresses). In conjunction with the awakening of the demons, even the mediatory moment of Prostitution, through its being associated with the lighting of gas lamps, now strengthens this day-for-night thematics whereby twilight produces a reversal without real change, a mere replacement of the personnel that make up the city's permanent work force. Some of the very same elements that functioned in the "process" reading of this passage as mediatory elements, producing a gradual shift, thus now appear, in-stead, as evidence of equivalence accounting for the substitutability of the categories undergoing exchange, and so legitimate a dualistic in-terpretation of the event of twilight as merely the substitution of night for day. In this sense the description corresponds to what impatience desires: the suppression of time through the abolition of mediation.

This result hinges, though, on a notably squeamish treatment of the category of Prostitution, set up by an allegorizing capital letter as the enemy of Mankind and the forerunner of Night (l. 32) so that—since the latter signifies death—it becomes a figure for time, and hence me-diation.[15] Prostitution, which in the "process" reading emblematized complicity, desire, mediation, here stands out as exceptional: the only category that's identified as animal (Comme une fourmilière, Comme un ver), and responding thus to the desire of mankind to change into a wild beast, it is unlike the other daytime and nighttime activities mentioned in the poem in that it is not a form of work, being described, instead, as parasitic (Comme un ver qui dérobe à l'Homme ce qu'il mange). As such, it has characteristics of furtiveness (ll. 17–18) and complicity (l. 24) that link it directly with twilight itself, which comes, as we know from l. 2, "comme un complice." Misogynistically, the work that women do is singled out, then—and I will say scapegoated—as (in thematic terms) not work at all, but a tapeworm of desire that secretly saps the energy and undermines the substance of daytime and nighttime work alike.

I say scapegoated because Prostitution here enacts the curious grammatical anomaly of narrative that can only produce an effect of closure by opening itself up to a digressive mediatory moment (chapter 1). By declaring Prostitution to be not-work (but parasitism) the poem is thematically isolating it, by a kind of quarantining, from the world of labor and safeguarding its narrative of exchange and substitutability from the implications of its own, inevitably mediated, structure, that is, its possible opening onto the kind of shifty, listlike, processual understanding of twilight to which, as we've seen, the poem *also* lends itself. Mediation, which has thus been acknowledged in the poem (by its recognition of twilight as process), but also denied (by the production of mediated categories as equivalent and exchangeable), is thus, finally, vilified (as prostitution, parasitism, complicity) and quite contradictorily, isolated (the principle of connection being treated as an entirely separable category, having nothing in common with those it connects). We might reasonably expect this excluded element of thirdness to "return," therefore, both in the poem and elsewhere in Baudelaire's work; and it will do so, I suggest, in the figure of the flâneur as reader, a figure able to *identify* with the "work" of Prostitution, not hold it at bay.

On the face of it, though, the observer figure in "Le Crépuscule du Soir" (whose description mediates this scene for us and who is thus responsible for the scapegoating of Prostitution) is anything but a mediator. It does no good, for example, to ask whether he has been working from memory (it seems not) or whether he has had to work fast in order to capture the phantom of beauty before it faded. As in *The Painter of Modern Life*, this flâneur has no mediatory function but figures as a pure observer, an unmediated gaze, the two-sided readability of the scene being attributed, not to the presence of a reader, but to the natural process that is twilight, while the function of mediation, as we've seen, is thrown onto Prostitution. Unlike the flâneur of the later essay, though, he is not even interested in the *bain de multitude*, so anxious is he to distinguish himself, not only from the scapegoated figure of Prostitution, but also from the whole population of the poem, day and night workers alike, the impatient and the complicitous. Their desire-driven activities produce only an animal roar (rugissement, l. 30), to which the distant, contemplative speaker's soul is invited to close its ears. This figure—whom we might plausibly assume to be a voyeur, desire-driven in his own way, and whose scapegoating of mediation suggests his own impatience with time—presents himself, then, not simply as invisible and anonymous, like the later "man of the crowd," but as positively disembodied, so intense is his denial of desire.

He is, in short, just a faculty of speech whose location in space can't be determined (is he on the street? standing on a balcony? standing at some other vantage point?), and whose reaction to the scene of desire and the process it mediates—the whole scene of readability—is an affirmation of his own identity as the *opposite* of shifting or digressive, because it's centered on an interiority. These people are headed for the hospice, into the arms of death:

> ils finissent
> Leur destinée et vont vers le gouffre commun;
> L'hôpital se remplit de leurs soupirs.

The speaker, though, distances himself, as if exempt, from the common, time-bound fate, as the possessor of an inner life both spiritual—the "soul" he addresses—and domestic, the "coin du feu," the "douceur du foyer" that he denies to those who are headed for the "gouffre commun" (both pauper's grave and universal abyss), but with which he's evidently familiar himself.

This, then, is a version of the bourgeois subject as "prince incognito": the privileged figure who knows the crowd without being known by the crowd. But it's a version different from what we saw in *The Painter of Modern Life*. Here the flâneur is a prince whose squeamishness about desire and mediation deprives him of all forms of *jouissance*, whether it be the euphoria of digressivity or the diffuseness of power, substituting only a middle-class sense of his own "distinction."

The irony, however, is that his very solitude, almost independently of the dynamics of scapegoating (a scapegoater is always "guilty" of that of which the scapegoat is accused), suggests a kind of affinity, not with the crowd, but between the loathed and isolated category of parasitic Prostitution and this observer who seems, himself, given his abstentionism, to be the only other nonworker on the scene. And there are plenty of passages, of course, especially in the *journaux intimes*, in which Baudelaire will make no bones about—indeed will take provocative pleasure in—proclaiming the affinity of the artist and the prostitute, notably on the score of the "man of the crowd"'s ability to identify with others.

These are, of course, late writings. But in "Le Cygne," also, Andromache—the ostensibly noble figure through whom the flâneur figure of the poem allegorizes himself—is *also* a whorish figure, she (the widow of Hector) who submitted to being married to a slave and whose desire is described, undecidably, as an ecstacy of longing for the dead Hector and an erotic attraction to her living captor:

> sous la main du superbe Pyrrhus,
> Auprès d'un tombeau vide en extase courbée
> Veuve d'Hector, hélas! et femme d'Hélénus![16]

And Andromache, whose son—as a consequence of her dubious survival tactics—became a Greek king, is also the figure in that poem who mediates a fall into history, as power and prestige pass from Troy to Greece. Baudelaire's characteristic misogyny is unabated, here, but it works now, not to scapegoat the other, but as a form of self-recognition.[17] The other is myself; the flâneur, like Andromache, is a mediator. And it is not among the working population that the flâneur discovers his alter ego but in the formerly despised and rejected, marginalized category of the parasitic.

What motivates this recognition might well be the aloneness and disconnectedness of the flâneur, as we've seen it in the two texts just studied. Cut off from the practice of art in *The Painter of Modern Life* by his identification as pure gaze and his association with the crowd but cut off from the crowd, in "Le Crépuscule du Soir," by his unwillingness to acknowledge himself a man of desire, the flâneur is deprived of both forms of belonging (as an artist, as a man of the crowd) by different aspects of his status as "prince incognito." To acknowledge the flâneur as a man of *desire* would be, instead, to acknowledge him as part of—a reader in, as well as of—the world of desire, not a pure observer or disembodied spirit, like the flâneur of "Le Crépuscule du Soir." To acknowledge his mediating status as a *reader* would produce in turn the link that's denied in *The Painter of Modern Life*, between the flâneur as mediator and the mediating artist, "translating" modernity into readable beauty. Both gestures of acknowledgment, taken together, would thus restore the flâneur to forms of connectedness while maintaining his peculiar status and thirdness as the city's "inner other," the observer of those who, by day and by night, make history.

But the price to pay for this maintenance of difference will be abandonment of bourgeois "prince incognito" status in favor of that of the fallen, abandoned, marginalized, nostalgic, and whorish queen. And the community to which it gives access can't be the society whose culture of impatience remains alien to the flâneur and whose alternating shifts—working class and bourgeoisie, day workers and night workers—he reads as participating equally in history's "progress." It has to be the community of those who are in third position and, like Prostitution in "Le Crépuscule du Soir," find themselves marginalized and left out of the narrative of progress as mere parasites and mediators, even though the narrative can't function without them and the part they play is indispensable. These are digressive figures, crepuscular, liminal, often unnoticed, whose place it is, like a swan in a Parisian gutter, to be forever displaced: on the edge, peripheral. They form the community of those who, like Andromache, are history's residue, marooned in a kind of limbo and inevitably belated, therefore, as fast-forwarding history passes them by. They are exiles, then, but (unlike Hugo) "inner" exiles whose privilege, "Le Cygne" will suggest, is to be the critical readers of the culture of impatience as it accelerates away from them, leaving them in its dust.

MYTH AND ALLEGORY

"Le Cygne" is thus a reading of the readerly subject of flânerie—that is, of the readerly subject as a member of a community of marginalized subjects—at the same time as it presents that subject (those subjects) as reader(s) of a city whose history—a history of impatience—has produced them as readers by situating them in the position of belatedness. Myth—"mythe étrange et fatal"—is the name the poem will give to the readability of the flâneur as reader, while allegory—as in "tout pour moi devient allégorie"—is the word by which it will designate the melancholy readability of a history that produces readerly subjects, inexorably, as belated outcasts or "exiles." It's in this relation of myth to allegory, corresponding to the poem's two sections, that it encapsulates a truth about critical reading that we've already seen exemplified in the practice of kynicism (chapters 6 and especially 7): that a reading of the social necessarily implies a reading of the reader, since it is the conditions of the social that have produced the subjectivity capable of reading it (according to the principle of "it takes one to know one"). The flâneur reads the city that, by its heedless flight into the future, produces the flâneur as its reader.

Thus the famous parenthesis:

> (la forme d'une ville
> Change plus vite, hélas! que le cœur d'un mortel)

defines the poem as at once a lament over (readerly) belatedness and a critique of (social) impatience, a culture of speed. But this coincidence of lament and critique is possible only because impatience and belatedness have something in common: each gives temporal expression to desire and, in so doing, historicizes the present, dividing attention between a present moment experienced as inadequate or lacking (an *énoncé*) and a desired other moment (future or past) that, as the present's "other" context, has the status of an *énonciation*, defining the condition of readability not now as a product of duality (night and day) but as an index of historicity. What the parenthesis describes is this discrepant effect of divided attention as a function of desire, and it simultaneously acknowledges what "Le Crépuscule du Soir" denies, that the critic of impatience is himself both a historical subject and a site of desire. It's just that belatedness differs from the anxious anticipation that is impatience in a crucial respect: where impatience seeks to deny time by accelerating it, belatedness makes time its critical resource, and is complicitous with it, distancing itself in this way from a culture fast-forwarding into the future in the very same movement whereby it finds itself outdistanced by the acceleration of history. In other words, it employs a dilatory strategy—the strategy of "Andromaque, je pense à vous"—as the expression of a pointed preference for the past in a present moment devoted to the speed of change.

LE CYGNE

I

Andromaque, je pense à vous! Ce petit fleuve,
Pauvre et triste miroir où jadis resplendit
L'immense majesté de vos douleurs de veuve,
4   Ce Simoïs menteur qui par vos pleurs grandit,

A fécondé soudain ma mémoire fertile,
Comme je traversais le nouveau Carrousel.
Le vieux Paris n'est plus (la forme d'une ville
8   Change plus vite, hélas! que le cœur d'un mortel);

Je ne vois qu'en esprit tout ce camp de baraques,
Ces tas de chapiteaux ébauchés et de fûts,
Les herbes, les gros blocs verdis par l'eau des flaques,
12   Et, brillant aux carreaux, le bric-à-brac confus.

Là s'étalait jadis une ménagerie;
Là je vis, un matin, à l'heure où sous les cieux
Froids et clairs le Travail s'éveille, où la voirie
16   Pousse un sombre ouragan dans l'air silencieux,

Un cygne qui s'était évadé de sa cage,
Et, de ses pieds palmés frottant le pavé sec,
Sur le sol raboteux traînait son blanc plumage.
20   Près d'un ruisseau sans eau la bête ouvrant le bec

Baignait nerveusement ses ailes dans la poudre,
Et disait, le cœur plein de son beau lac natal:
"Eau, quand donc pleuvras-tu? quand tonneras-tu, foudre?"
24   Je vois ce malheureux, mythe étrange et fatal,

Vers le ciel quelquefois, comme l'homme d'Ovide,
Vers le ciel ironique et cruellement bleu,
Sur son cou convulsif tendant sa tête avide,
28   Comme s'il adressait des reproches à Dieu!

II

Paris change! mais rien dans ma mélancolie
N'a bougé! palais neufs, échafaudages, blocs,
Vieux faubourgs, tout pour moi devient allégorie,
32   Et mes chers souvenirs sont plus lourds que des rocs.

Aussi devant ce Louvre une image m'opprime:
Je pense à mon grand cygne, avec ses gestes fous,
Comme les exilés, ridicule et sublime,
36 Et rongé d'un désir sans trêve! et puis à vous,

Andromaque, des bras d'un grand époux tombée,
Vil bétail, sous la main du superbe Pyrrhus,
Auprès d'un tombeau vide en extase courbée;
40 Veuve d'Hector, hélas! et femme d'Hélénus!

Je pense à la négresse, amaigrie et phtisique,
Piétinant dans la boue, et cherchant, l'œil hagard,
Les cocotiers absents de la superbe Afrique
44 Derrière la muraille immense du brouillard;

A quiconque a perdu ce qui ne se retrouve
Jamais, jamais! à ceux qui s'abreuvent de pleurs
Et tètent la Douleur comme une bonne louve!
48 Aux maigres orphelins séchant comme des fleurs!

Ainsi dans la forêt où mon esprit s'exile
Un vieux Souvenir sonne à plein souffle du cor!
Je pense aux matelots oubliés dans une île,
52 Aux captifs, aux vaincus! . . . à bien d'autres encor!

THE SWAN

I

Andromache, I think of you—this meagre stream
This melancholy mirror where had once shone forth
The giant majesty of all your widowhood,
This fraudulent Simoïs, fed by bitter tears,

Has quickened suddenly my fertile memory
As I was walking through the modern Carrousel.
The old Paris is gone (the form a city takes
More quickly shifts, alas, than does the mortal heart);

I picture in my head the busy camp of huts,
And heaps of rough-hewn columns, capitals and shafts,
The grass, the giant blocks made green by puddle-stain,
Reflected in the glaze, the jumbled bric-à-brac.

Once nearby was displayed a great menagerie,

And there I saw one day—the time when under skies
Cold and newly bright, Labour stirs awake
And sweepers push their storms into the silent air—

A swan, who had escaped from his captivity,
And scuffing his splayed feet along the paving stones,
He trailed his white array of feathers in the dirt.
Close by a dried out ditch the bird opened his beak,

Flapping excitedly, bathing his wings in dust,
And said, with heart possessed by lakes he once had loved:
"Water, when will you rain? Thunder, when will you roar?"
I see this hapless creature, sad and fatal myth,

Stretching the hungry head on his convulsive neck,
Sometimes towards the sky, like the man in Ovid's book—
Towards the ironic sky, the sky of cruel blue,
As if he were a soul contesting with his God!

II

Paris may change, but in my melancholy mood
Nothing has budged! New palaces, blocks, scaffoldings,
Old neighborhoods, are allegorical for me,
And my dear memories are heavier than stone.

And so outside the Louvre an image gives me pause:
I think of my great swan, his gestures pained and mad,
Like other exiles, both ridiculous and sublime,
Gnawed by his endless longing! Then I think of you,

Fallen Andromache, torn from a husband's arms,
Vile property beneath the haughty Pyrrhus' hand,
Next to an empty tomb, head bowed in ecstasy,
Widow of Hector! O! and wife of Helenus!

I think of a negress, thin and tubercular,
Treading in the mire, searching with haggard eye
For palm trees she recalls from splendid Africa,
Somewhere behind a giant barrier of fog;

Of all those who have lost something they may not find
Ever, ever again! who steep themselves in tears
And suck a bitter milk from that good she-wolf, grief!
Of orphans, skin and bones, dry and wasted blooms!

And likewise in the forest of my exiled soul
Old Memory sings out a full note of the horn!
I think of sailors left forgotten on an isle,
Of captives, the defeated . . . many others more![18]

Historicizing the present, then, in relation to a desired past, the poem's belated strategy of dilatoriness takes the form of denarrativizing history, substituting for the *telos*-driven narrative of progress, with its concomitant affect of impatience, a certain complicity with temporality. It does so by adopting, in lieu of the perspective of anticipation, that of memory, a perspective that is itself predicated, as we saw in *The Painter of Modern Life*, on forgetting, that is, on loss and dispersal. Productive, in the essay, of an aesthetics of the unfinished (ébauche, si vous voulez, mais une ébauche parfaite), memory corresponds here, however—in the context of the flâneur as reader, as opposed to the artist as producer of suggestive syntheses—to a perspective of residuality. This is the perspective of those whom narrative history bypasses and leaves stranded, on its margins, so that to them the present appears less as a sketch to be completed in the future than as a kind of leftover, fragmented and residual by comparison with an earlier time that's lost but can be remembered (re-membered) and desired, as a now inaccessible prelapsarian era of wholeness and plenitude.

But, in the way that the "ébauche" cannot in fact be completed but opens instead onto a perspective of (re-)mediations, the fragmented present, in "Le Cygne," opens not onto the prelapsarian past, but recalls only a history of other present moments, also and always already marked by residuality and fragmentation. The fall into history, which the poem figures in the fall of Troy and Andromache's consequent exile in Greece, is definitive; that moment of transition, mediated by Andromache, ushers in an experience of historical time as doubly alienated, the impatient drive for progress producing, and leaving in its wake, belated survivors turned nostalgically, like Andromache in Epirus, toward the past. From Troy the torch passes to Greece, and on to Rome, whose heir is the French Empire and its successor, that of Napoléon III; but in the eyes of its belated witnesses, this history is not the progress it claims to be but, if anything, a decline. Thus modern Paris responds to ruined Troy, as a city both unfinished and residual: the rubble of its construction sites coexists with its bric-à-brac, the left-overs of the past that figure the materials of memory, rejected by-products of a history of progress that has no time or place for them. Belated survivors can turn away from the degraded present in which they find themselves, surrounded by the broken fragments of the past, and engage in the nostalgic task of re-collection and re-membering, shuffling the broken pieces and even constructing, like Andromache in exile, not lost Troy, but its simulacrum. And like her, they're broken pieces themselves, history's leftovers, whom in turn a flâneur in modern Paris can belatedly shuffle in his own memory, to make a poem.

Moreover, the flâneur is himself another of history's leftovers. His own belatedness implies the readability *of* the city as a place of memory, but that readability is in turn a function of the marginalized position he occupies *within* the city as man of memory and man of desire—a desire turned, crucially, toward the past instead of being turned, like that of the majority of his contemporaries in the culture of impatience, toward the future. In this way, the flâneur reader now rejoins the desiring crowd of mortals headed for the "gouffre commun," as a desiring subject himself. But the character of his desire positions him as a critical figure within the crowd—critical because marginalized—and by the same token furnishes him with a special community of his own—not the impatient crowd but the community of his fellow exiles from forward-turned, goal-oriented, progressive history, those whose desire points backward, toward the past, and within time produces dilatory, sideward movements, a denarrativization of history that seeks to slow its headlong rush. And it's this occupancy of a digressive reading position and the relationality it produces for the reader that the first part of the poem enacts under the heading of reading as mythification, a concept closely tied to a certain productivity of memory (ma mémoire fertile, l. 5), as the key attribute of the readerly subject.

If reading is a dilatory, denarrativizing practice, however, and consequently critical of the culture of impatience, it has in it also the seeds of melancholy and obsession—the opposite of productivity—which the second section of the poem will proceed to address, and to enact, under the sign, not simply of allegory, but of reading as an obsessive allegorization of the world: "tout pour moi devient allégorie" (l. 31). As a consequence of historical alienation, reading acquires a near-pathological dimension. Thus, in the end, flâneur reading becomes—like postlapsarian exiles in general and like the figure of Andromache in particular—"ridicule et sublime" (l. 31), both noble and pathetic. But that, of course, is because the reader *is*, by definition, an exile: his place in the city is that of marginality and belatedness (the marginality *of* belatedness) and his ability to read is itself the very sign—both a privilege and a curse—of that belatedness and marginality. And consequently the flâneur in this poem, unlike his colleague of "Le Crépuscule du Soir," a mere gaze and a disembodied voice, has a historical identity. We meet him, as a localized, embodied figure, in a carefully specified time and place: "Comme je traversais le nouveau Carrousel" (l. 6). And this time and place, defined as that of the "nouveau Carrousel," is one in which he's conscious of the newness of a city in which he himself walks about thinking of ancient Andromache, and thus conscious also of the shabby figure he cuts by contrast with that newness as an inner exile, one whose desire is turned toward the past.

Corresponding to the flâneur reader's split subjectivity, the city in turn becomes two-sided, readable, or haunted. And that two-sidedness is what reading in the mode of myth and reading in the mode of allegory share as their common quality. For, crossing the "nouveau Carrousel" and recalling Andromache, the flâneur is thinking simultaneously of "le vieux Paris" that has vanished and more particularly of another vanished scene from the same neighborhood that he now sees only in his mind's eye (l. 9), a scene dating from the time when the new city was still under construction. Although we might think it a rather typical episode in the genre of flâneur realism—trivial, accidental, slightly grotesque—this memory of a swan stranded in an urban gutter is what he calls a "mythe étrange et fatal" (l. 24). What makes it a myth is (was) its pregnancy, the call for reading that the swan seems (seemed) to express, stretching its neck and

> tendant sa tête avide
> Comme s'il adressait des reproches à Dieu!

Moreover, it's this interpretability of the swan enigma, as remembered, that has now been confirmed for the flâneur by the thought that came to him of Andromache and her plight—a thought out of place in the "nouveau Carrousel," like a swan in a gutter—as he contemplated the unfamiliar newness of the city. A tantalizingly incomplete *énoncé* has thus now given rise to a meaningful *énonciation*, the thought of Andromache providing the missing clue that makes it possible to say (but the poem doesn't yet say this) that the swan was a myth of exile.

This thought, however, would itself not have arisen had not the flâneur, as mediating third, implicitly compared himself, crossing the new Carrousel, with Andromache weeping for Hector and for lost Troy in Epirus; and equally the link with the swan might not have taken place had there not also been an implicit comparison in the flâneur's mind between his own shabbiness and the swan's grotesque out-of-placeness. He, in other words, as a reader, is intensely *implicated*, by virtue of his own reading situation, in the myth whose interpretation he mediates. And furthermore, as a result of this readerly intervention on his part, a complex lateralization of history has taken place, the outcome of a digressive, dilatory move that has made an ancient widowed queen, a swan seen at some former but recent time (jadis, l. 13), and a flâneur-poet in Haussmann's new Paris, all parts of one another's context, and so, in a sense, contemporaneous.

Memory, in this way—"[l]a mémoire fertile"—fits the pieces together to make a myth that's both the *product* of history's forward march (whose *disjecta membra* it utilizes) and a critical *comment* on the "thought"-lessness inherent in progress's own historicization of the present through eager anticipation of the future. For the pensiveness of the flâneur (imagine him standing stock still, visited by revelation, in the middle of the square) matches the swan's own mutely critical stance (Comme s'il adressait des reproches à Dieu), while Andromache, weeping beside her false Simoïs,

> Pauvre et triste miroir où jadis resplendit
> L'immense majesté de vos douleurs de veuve,

is the very figure of reflection. She combines reflection as pensiveness and reflection as mirroring (the flâneur, the widow, the swan) in a complex image of thought, and so of critical reading, not as something that stands outside of time, like the flâneur in "Le Crépuscule du Soir," but as that product of time which, within time, retards, holds back, and resists the nevertheless irresistible forward march of history.

But time-bound thought is also, by the same token, subject to desire: it's the desire for meaning, a meaning situated in the past, that would take thought itself out of the condition of temporality and historicity. In pensiveness, therefore, lie the roots of melancholy, turning myth into allegory. For the meaningfulness of the present, as reading establishes it, lies only in the awareness of a loss of meaning with respect to a past that, however far back one may go—from modern Paris to ancient Andromache—remains, like Troy, irrecoverable. The present, for a belated reader, is thus not only a site of desire but the site of a desire that by definition can't be assuaged, the meaningfulness that constitutes the object of desire consisting only in knowledge of loss, including the loss of meaning, and hence of desire's endless insatiability. Allegory, then, is the name given by the poem to the structure of readerly desire as it resolves into a problematics of supplementarity, the three-way encounter of flâneur, widow, and swan on the place du Carrousel, with its excited but uncentered mirrorings, becoming now an endless inventory-taking, in the poem's mind, of the figures of lack that confirm his reading of the swan. In this way, where the poem might have derived from the uncenteredness of the three-way encounter a sense of energy deriving from the powers of endless diversion (Friedrich Schlegel's *permanente Parekbasis*), it resolves instead into the expression of an *idée fixe*.

The swan, as myth, posed the question of the meaning of the unknown: meaning resided in no one place but consisted of a complex set of relations, among which it moved. The mythic reading situation is dynamic. In allegory, though, as in the melancholy that's associated with it, nothing moves, so that the power to change becomes invested exclusively in the city, the site of the culture of impatience. Thus,

> Paris change! mais rien dans ma mélancolie
> N'a bougé! palais neufs, échafaudages, blocs,
> Vieux faubourgs, tout pour moi devient allégorie,
> Et mes chers souvenirs sont plus lourds que des rocs.

This, it seems, is because meaning—the meaning of the swan—is now, always already, known and available: it has become conceptualized, and statable, as lack and hence as perpetually unsatisfied desire. Reading as a form of resistance to linear history ceases in this way to be an ironic, dilatory, or delaying tactic, grounded in the practice of inspired digression, and becomes instead something single-minded, stubborn, and in its own way, closed on itself and unresourceful. It's still resistance, doubtless, and still critical; but it has become sullen and brooding, there has been a distinct loss of energy. For any given *enoncé* there is now only one possible *énonciation*, and that *énonciation* can't open in turn onto further possibilities of signification. Allegory, as the poem conceives and enacts it, produces the two-sidedness of readability but without giving access to third, fourth, or fifth sides.

So the poem becomes a list, but a list disinclined to digress; it rehearses the membership of a very tightly controlled paradigm. The text now consists of a chain of metonymic figures of exile and desire, each signifying in relation to the other by virtue of readability, but signifying only the endlessness of the pursuit of meaning and the insatiability of desire, until finally the text ends, without closure, on its etcetera: "à bien d'autres encor!" The familiar figures are now, as it were, *transfixed* in their desire, the swan "rongé d'un désir sans trêve" (l. 36), and Andromache "en extase courbée" (l. 39). The new figure of the "négresse" who joins them is likewise pictured as "piétinant" (trampling, unable to advance) and staring of eye (l'oeil hagard, l. 42). Then the poet's consciousness begins to flood with examples, and these are no longer individual, particularized figures but plurals, like the orphans of l. 48 and later the sailors, captives, and vanquished ones (ll. 51–52), or else abstracted generalizations: "whoever . . . ," "those who . . ." (ll. 45–48). Thus is formed the populous community of exiles of which he is a member; but the population has become increasingly faceless as it grows and as it becomes evident that each figure is a cipher, standing for the same inescapable problematics of loss, exclusion, and desire. And simultaneously the lateralization of time that's produced by flâneur reading has led, it appears, to a complete spatialization of the poet's memory, so that it can now be figured as a forest traversed by the single horn call of *one* "vieux Souvenir" (l. 50).

Allegory, in other words, goes beyond the denarrativization of history and an art of dilatoriness. It dehistoricizes time itself and makes it neither progressive nor digressive, but a *piétinement*, an impeded walking on the spot; and a kind of dreary sameness ensues. Such displacement as occurs (and the poem, it's true, never ceases to shift restlessly, as the pieces continue to be shuffled in the poet's mind) occurs within a larger sense of heaviness and immobility, that of "rien dans ma mélancolie/N'a bougé (ll. 29–30), and of the *one* image (une image m'opprime," l. 33) that oppresses the poet's consciousness. Gone, then, is the sense of exhilaration and even of a sort of freedom that prevailed at the start, as fertile memory made its great, swooping moves between unexpected and remote protagonists: the flâneur in the "nouveau Carrousel," Andromache in her Grecian exile, an escaped swan stranded in a gutter. Gone, that is, the ability to digress, to change the subject.

A FORK IN THE ROAD

Baudelaire's diagnosis of modernity, then, is that it is the present— but the present marked by a sense of incompleteness and therefore traversed simultaneously by a desire for that incompleteness to resolve, not into a problematics of limitless supplementation informed by lack, but into abolition of that lack: the desire, that is, for there to be no more desire. The culture of impatience, with its belief in progress, is one mindless response to modernity's incompleteness. Against the culture of impatience the art of modernity described in *The Painter of Modern Life* grounds itself in the unfinishedness of "une ébauche . . . mais une ébauche parfaite" and produces beauty only as an effect of supplementation in time. In its dependence on mediation, art thus has an affinity with flâneur reading, which, however, proposes its critique of impatience from a perspective of marginalized belatedness, identifying the past as the present's ignored other context, and making reading itself the practice of supplementation—productive of signification as art is productive of beauty—that remains faithful to that past. We might say, then, in light of these characterizations, that a poem such as "Le Cygne" combines the aesthetic effect of beauty in its sketchlike representation of modernity, with the critical impulse inherent in its flâneur reading of a history of impatience.

From Sterne, though (chapter 1), we know that diversion and melancholy are two sides of one coin, the coin of lack, and Baudelaire's poem in turn enacts flâneur reading as similarly two-sided, poised as it is between myth and allegory, memory and melancholy, digressiveness and obsessive single-mindedness. Flâneur reading has a certain grandeur in the exhilaration of pursuing meaningful "reflection," as contexts reveal their other-sidedness and invite a fertile digressiveness. And it has a servitude, the kind of depressed obsessiveness that creeps in as critical reading begins to harp on a single string: "Desire is lack!" "Culture is inauthentic!" "History is alienating!" "The present is inadequate!" (And I have a thousand examples to support my contention . . .). "Le Cygne" 's importance as a poem isn't just that it's the poem of flâneur reading, then, but that it explores the suture—the crucial lack that makes any present context incomplete—that links these two sides of critical reading and makes them conditions each of the other. On the one hand, reading is a practice of diversion that hints at a kind of euphoria made possible by lack. On the other hand, it is threatened by a lapse into what might be called critical melancholia, as an interminable mulling over of the lack, the endless need for supplementation, that makes the criticism of culture possible. These two sides of flâneur reading are joined, in "Le Cygne," in an odd, but extremely significant, embrace; and in the prose poems they were to combine again, in Baudelaire's extended attempt to invent a form of poetic cultural criticism in a volume that would capture, under a melancholic title (*Le Spleen de Paris*), "the somersaults of consciousness" (vol. 1, 276).

One of the conditions of possibility for critical practice, as the exercise of a certain kind of readerly, digressive "freedom" in circumstances of marginalization, is, then, its potential for melancholia. The ability to enact cultural criticism through an art of digression is founded on a certain uncenteredness of things, a lack of fullness in their constitution—the wound to my Uncle Toby's groin—that can, and does, become an object of lamentation, as in the case of "Le Cygne," and even a debilitating, incapacitating fixation. Criticism of culture as inauthentic and/or alienating can thus always founder on the depressing discovery that criticism itself has no grounds on which to operate that aren't themselves those of inauthenticity and/or alienation, the very condition of Baudelairean modernity. But to allow that awareness to limit or cripple the power of criticism itself is to yield to a form of inattentiveness to, or forgetfulness of, the resources for diversion and diversity that result from thirdness and the permeability of contexts. Melancholia is thus always an inability to divide one's attention, as opposed to discovering a place where the road opens into a fork, and as Yogi Berra advises, taking that fork. But criticism takes the forked road: divided attention, distractedness, and digressivity, are its very conditions of possibility.

In exploring the relations between loiterature as it entails a poetics of pleasure, based on the relaxation of disciplinary and/or ideological constraint, and loiterature as it enacts a critique of the alienations of modern culture, I've been taking Yogi Berra's advice in this book. But now we have another two-sidedness to explore, given Baudelaire's demonstration that critical reading itself has a fork, divided as it is between the pleasure and power of digressivity and the premature closure of lamentation, monotony, and melancholy. I'll take that fork in the two remaining chapters, looking first (chapter 9) at a certain Orientalist tendency in the work of an otherwise exemplary flâneur critic, Roland Barthes, as evidence that critical melancholia has everything to do with contextual closure, and then turning to read the work of Meaghan Morris (in chapter 10) as a marginalized intellectual whose practice of "pedestrianism" doesn't lose sight of, but actively exploits the resources of digressivity.

The remarkable thing about Baudelaire, though, as their common ancestor, is the degree to which his work and his career combined a certain cantankerous and choleric, not to say melancholic, rigidity of contextual closure—manifested in his clinging to dualistic analyses and his reluctance to envisage the consequences of thirdness, as in the single-mindedness with which he holds to certain embittered opinions and cultivates a kind of historical despair—with an astonishing talent for laterality, for shifts and moves and digressiveness that open up unexpected lines of flight.[19] That this Baudelairean dividedness is in actuality a predicament—and, as such, less contradictory than it is exemplary of modern critical consciousness—is perhaps the claim of "Le Cygne"; and it has been the task of this chapter to begin to explore some of the complexities such a predicament generates.

Pointless Stories, Storyless Points

Conversely, a book is conceivable: which would report a thousand "incidents" but would refuse ever to draw a line of meaning from them; it would be, quite specifically, a book of *haikus*.—Roland Barthes, *Roland Barthes by Roland Barthes*

Rosencrantz: Incidents! All we get is incidents! Dear God, is it too much to expect a little sustained action?—Tom Stoppard, *Rosencrantz and Guildenstern Are Dead*

When Barthes's *Incidents* was published posthumously, there was a mild outcry in the world of the Paris literati.[1] There are two relatively unremarkable texts in this volume ("La lumière du sud-ouest" and "Au Palace ce soir . . ."); the scandal bore on two others, "Incidents," described by the editor in a cautious preliminary note as "a notation, a collection of things seen and heard in Morocco, essentially in Tangiers and Rabat, and then in the South, in 1968 and 1969," and "Soirées de Paris," a series of diarylike accounts of his evenings' insignificant doings that Barthes kept between 24 August and 19 September 1979, just after writing a critical study of the "journal intime" as a genre for *Tel Quel* and not long before his untimely death. Because these last mentioned texts, especially the latter of the two, are open about the author's homosexuality, it was felt in some quarters that one of the more reticent of France's gay male intellectuals had been "outed," and in a manner thought (not without homophobia) to demean the great man's memory. I'm interested, though, in the nonnarrative or antinarrative formal qualities of the two texts, as examples of loiterature in its "cruising" mode (chapter 3); and I want more particularly to look at what they tell us about the kind of intellectual I call "critical"—the intellectual who doesn't fit easily into either of the Gramscian categories of the "organic" or the "traditional"—when that intellectual, whose position is normally unaligned, is "on vacation" or "taking time out," and isn't, ideologically speaking, *on guard*. More specifically still, I'll ask what these two mildly scandalous texts, written ten years apart and relating to rather different life experiences, have in common. What differences connect them? What incidences — interactions, intersections, intrications, mutual interruptions — join them?

In the heyday of the British Empire, POSH (standing for Port Out Starboard Home) was a notation used by shipping clerks to indicate the most prestigious passengers on the ships that plied the thin red line passing through Suez. Without too much artifice, the acronym might be taken as a way of articulating the intrication of *at home* and *out there*, the permeability of contexts, that defines the various economies — commercial, cultural, and in this case sexual — of the colonial enterprise, an intrication that has, if anything, intensified in the so-called postcolonial era. In that sense, we're all posh; and in choosing to look critically at the forgetfulness of the at home/out there intrication that relates Barthes's two texts (one supposedly Parisian, the other patently Moroccan), I'm not attempting, therefore, to make one of modern culture's poshest (most prestigious) intellectuals into some kind of scapegoat. I'm looking for a way to describe the texts, and to read their sadly missed author, as *paradigmatic*, in the sense of typical as well as listlike. It's not because they're exceptional but because they're *ordinary*[2] that these texts — themselves unsystematic explorations of the everyday (the familiar everyday of Paris and the everyday of the Oriental other) — seem interesting and indeed have a certain poignant quality. Not the trivial Barthes, whose bodily desires some would have liked to hush up, nor yet Barthes the cultural icon, but the ordinary Barthes — "R. B." — is the fellow I want to spend some time with here; and that is because he permits us to grasp something of how the construction of the everyday relates to contextual closure.

The main genres of gay male narrative tend to be autobiographical, but their thematics is no less characteristically one of encounter. For obvious reasons, gay subjectivity can scarcely regard itself as autonomous or fail to take account of itself as a relational phenomenon, traversed by the complex dynamics of alterity. The coming out story (say Paul Monette's *Becoming a Man* or J. R. Ackerley's *My Father and Myself*[3]) has affinities with the Bildungsroman, while the AIDS story, which follows a declining curve uncannily symmetrical to the coming out story's mounting curve (as the poignancy of Eric Michael's punning title, *Unbecoming*, underlines), responds to homophobic mythification of the disease with an equally metaphoric counter-myth: not AIDS but a homophobic society is the killer.[4]

The cruising story, though (John Rechy's *Numbers* or Renaud Camus's *Tricks* can serve as examples[5]), tends not to have a narrative "curve" at all, and closure is as irrelevant to it as it is defining in both the coming out story and the AIDS story. The structure here (if "structure" is the word) is episodic, repetitive (but in a Kierkegaardian sense, in which repetition implies difference) and, in a word, digressive—the "incident" is its narrative material. The goal (encapsulated in the famous seventies T-shirt slogan: "So many men, so little time") isn't the narrative or argumentative one of *comprehension* but the encyclopedic one of *comprehensiveness*, not synthesis but seriality, and the dynamic is therefore that of the etcetera principle. The outcome is a text structured like a list, an enumeration, an inventory or a catalog, a "telling" in the etymological sense of counting out, and corresponding more to a purely descriptive practice of notation than to an art of composition.

This open-endedness of the cruising narrative, of which both "Soirées de Paris" and "Incidents" are paradigmatic examples, has everything to do, I believe, with the ambiguity and uncertainty of the social relations (the circumstances of encounter) in which the gay male cruiser is involved. These social relations aren't governed by the clearly legislated, if practically unnegotiable, double bind of the closet, although their semisurreptitiousness gives them a closety feel. They're not subject either to the overt hostility in response to which AIDS narratives are so angry a genre, although the "adventurous" side of cruising, the slight sense of danger it can generate, accords with the knowledge that gay-affirming behavior (the constitution of a community of desire, for example) is inevitably pursued in a social context that can prove lethal to it. Cruising activates the *range* of phenomena that arise from the fraught relation—not fully separable yet anxiously autonomous—that links male homosociality and male homosexuality.

It is, in short, a subcultural (or "private") phenomenon inhabiting—or, as Michel de Certeau might say, poaching on—a "public" space, that of the subculture's Other. Thus, the desiring community the cruiser "counts out," encounter by encounter, is potentially limitless, by virtue of the continuum linking gay and straight, the homosexual and the homosocial. But by the same token, the gay cruiser's identity is ambiguous in that it coexists with any number of "straight" identities—

respectable middle-class man, college kid or whatever—under cover of which the cruiser's presence on the streets is legitimated. It follows that to believe in a gay male community uniquely constituted by a commonality of desire or in an identity purely defined by erotic object-choice takes quite a bit of forgetting. Yet it's just such forgetting that constitutes the community of desire the cruiser is exploring, and it's as a subject to such forgetting that the figure of the cruiser interests me, therefore, in this essay. For there's something *single-minded* about sexual cruising, a single-mindedness that's reminiscent of the figure of the collector (think, say, of Balzac's Pons). And this same single-mindedness shows up, albeit in displaced fashion, in Barthes (whose sexual hunting is euphemized in "Incidents" as touristic curiosity and pursued in "Soirée de Paris" with a kind of defeated diffidence). It shows up as thematic *redundancy*, a form of insistence that's very unusual in the digressive art of loiterature, which is more apt to change the subject than to harp on one string. But the cruiser, in "Soirées," becomes an obsessive collector of examples of the commoditization of relations, and in "Incidents," of what Barthes elsewhere calls the "romanesque." And it's the forgetting implied by these two forms of single-mindedness that I want to try to identify in what follows.

Not surprisingly, cruising is fast becoming a metaphor for gay research, which picks about in straight culture, in its own single-minded (and so forgetful) way, for often equivocal evidence of gayness, extending the limits of the gay community by collecting the apparently limitless number of "encounters" and *trouvailles* that seem to qualify. Neil Bartlett (chapter 3) figures his activity as a kind of folk historian of the gay male community in London as a matter of cruising the archives. In *Bringing Out Roland Barthes*, D. A. Miller likens his critical work to a kind of cruising of the Barthes text in search of "moments" (or incidents?), "responses to a handful of names, phrases, images, themes" that lead the critic to intuit a "gay writing position" that can be thought to inform the whole.[6] The cruising researcher's haul is predictably incomplete and often a bit dubious, and the writing in turn—an "album," says Miller, a bulletin board or scrapbook in Bartlett's metaphor—takes on the episodic, fragmented, and digressive quality of cruising narratives themselves, condemned to the incidental but celebratory of the incomplete, as the etcetera principle mandates. Like Bartlett's or Miller's, my own writing is bound, in turn, to be discontinuous and episodic—all stops and starts—and (in its own way) simultaneously rambling and single-minded or forgetful. In short, cruisy.

But I'm not so interested in detecting intimations of gayness, which in fact neither text makes any bones about (their closety character comes from the curious circumstance that each was prepared for the printer but never published in Barthes's lifetime). My antenna is tuned rather to try to pick up something else, of which gay male theory and historical research have been, I think symptomatically, relatively oblivious, namely the incidences that might connect the emergence in the West over the last century or so of a gay male sexual identity with the historical apogee of colonial empires, like the British and the French, that conceived of themselves as modern. I mean by this that, as opposed to the straightforward and unembarrassed exploitation of subject peoples characteristic of earlier empires, the modern empires imagined themselves to be *at the service* of colonized countries and populations, whose historical development they were furthering. That this doctrine was ideological mumbo jumbo covering invasion and despoliation is one thing; but that it was widely believed is another, as is the fact that "good relations" and "friendship" between metropolitan powers and former colonies—in the guise of commonwealths and associations and privileged trading partnerships—remain today, after the collapse of historical colonialism, as the alibi of our own postcolonial world.

Is the marginalized male homosexual subject at home particularly apt—as Alan Hollinghurst suggests in his novel *The Swimming-Pool Library*—to put himself at the service of colonial power abroad?[7] Is there a relation between this desire to be of service (to the colonial other? or to the colonial power?) and the ideology of service that legitimated the whole colonial enterprise (the white man's burden and the rest of it)? What of the element of racism so often manifest in gay male desire (I mean the *pertinence* of race in so many gay male desiring relations)? Does it derive from some sort of (perhaps mutual) identification between gay white men and subaltern colonial subjects? Rather than approaching such delicate topics, as Hollinghurst's fiction does, through the personage of the gay male colonial administrator (subject to the "service" ethic), I want to look at the at home/abroad intrication in the phenomenon of gay male sexual tourism, which has the merit of focusing attention on the indubitably exploitative character of (post)colonial relations, disguised as they may be as commercial—or even purely friendly–"human" exchanges. For a Wilde or a Gide, in flight from persecution or repression at home, "French" North Africa provided a refuge so relatively comfortable that they may well not have reflected—as the R. B. of "Incidents" much later seems not to have done—on the degree to which their comfort was that of the colonial master. And in contemporary Thailand—a country that, ironically, maintained a certain political independence during the colonial period "proper"—the economic power of the West has made it impossible now to eliminate a flourishing sex industry fueled by male tourists, gay and straight (who are drawn by the cruel fallacy that the younger the prostitute the less likely he or she is to be infected with the HIV virus).

Cruising is relevant in connection with sexual tourism as a colonial and postcolonial phenomenon because, as I've mentioned, the gay man who cruises, like the sexual tourist, is never a uniquely sexual subject but must acknowledge the possibility of being anamnestically inter-pellated in *other* identities as well—as a man, a consumer, a teenager, a businessman, an intellectual, a Westerner. . . . How, I want to ask, does Barthes, as a (forgetful) gay male cruiser at home and sexual tourist abroad, deal with the problematics of his "other" identity as a colonizing/postcolonial subject, a problematics that becomes in-escapable to the extent that he scarcely bothers to disguise his (never explicitly commented on) sexual preference for "boys" of Maghrebi origin? What incidences link the commoditized erotic relations that are so prominent in the cruisy Parisian text with the striking de-emphasis of commoditization in the touristic Moroccan text? Does commoditization, in other words, function as a displaced figure for the incidence of colonialism in sexual relations? And, if the *stress* on commoditization in "Soirées de Paris" functions as a sign of the sexual cruiser's forgetting of his (nevertheless readable) colonial identity, does the corresponding *de-emphasis* of commoditization in "Incidents" in-dicate (given the functional equivalence of items that can displace one another) *another* way of forgetting "coloniality," one that corresponds structurally to the sexual tourist's desire to naturalize his relation to the (commoditized, colonized) cultural other? Finally, does such a desire for natural(ized) relations on the part of the colonialist/tourist subject tell us something about Orientalism itself, as the deluded belief in an "authenticity" of the other but also as a belief in a possible authenticity of contact with the other within the nevertheless commoditized context of colonialism? These are the hypotheses that underlie the comments that follow.[8]

Intellectuals, one might say, are people who are still at work even when, by conventional measures, they're not working. If that's so, there are many more intellectuals than the class is normally held to contain; but also the figure of the "intellectual at leisure" (as Barthes noticed in *Mythologies*) is a sensitive and perhaps crucial one.[9] Can the off-duty intellectual be permitted a degree of relaxation, or should he or she instead (being never more intellectual than when not working) be held to the highest standards of intellectuality? In the nineteenth century the figure of the flâneur, as a forerunner of the contemporary category of the unaligned or "critical" intellectual (chapter 8), already raised this question of intellectual *informality*, suggesting that loiterly intellectuality has advantages over disciplined forms of knowledge in its greater openness to otherness and its preference for comprehensiveness over system (or comprehension). But the flâneur was a marginal social figure whose critique of closed context was nourished by the peripheral situation of loiterly subjectivity (chapter 3).

Barthes, though—with his series of books in digressive relation to one another and the general "drift" of his career from Marxist-oriented analyst of power to unaligned professor of desire[10]—can stand, given the high cultural and academic status he achieved, for a twentieth-century phenomenon: that of the officialization, and the institutionalization, of the critical intellectual. He thus permits us to ask what happens when a man whose *work* is that of a critical intellectual (modeled on the leisurely practices of flânerie) takes time out and in so doing rediscovers flânerie itself (as in "Soirées") or goes on vacation and becomes (as in "Incidents") a sexual tourist. What happens when the circumstances are ripe for an ordinary man to emerge, not in the figure of the intellectual as man of leisure, but in that of the critical intellectual at leisure? I'll argue that it's the apparent neutrality of the critical intellectual, as neither traditional nor organic, that's questioned by the case of Barthes, in his off-duty mode as the author of "Incidents" and "Soirées de Paris." And I'll suggest that the melancholia that surfaces in this Barthes, especially in "Soirées de Paris," is a sign of his forgetfulness, as an ordinary fellow, of the critical intellectual's function, which is to remember other contexts and to be conscious of contextual alterity: to recall, for example, that "at home" is linked to "out there" and "out there" to "at home."

But in the first instance, what happens in "Soirées de Paris" is that the intellectual at leisure turns his critical powers and the flâneur practice of "notation" onto the very cultural sphere in which, as a working intellectual, he also evolves, a sphere figured by the urban environment of Saint-Germain-des-Prés, which is represented as a place where commoditized values are the norm, so that sexual hustlers and young intellectuals on the up-and-up form a single, only partly differentiated, population. What happens in "Incidents," though, is that the practice of notation is devoted to recording instances of the "romanesque," that is (I quote the editor's comment, 8) to "a putting into writing of encounters—incidents—that might have been woven into a romance (novel), were it not that all and any narrative weaving . . . has been omitted"—in other words, novelistic subject matter without the novel, or pure "tellability" without its attendant narrative. In particular, the editor is at pains to point out, the "romanesque" has nothing to do with "Morocco, its people, culture or social problems," which are excluded, I take it, along with narrative (and argumentative) elaboration. The romanesque, in other words, is a case of pure intellectual unalignment, although it requires an emphatic denegation to make it so.

D. A. Miller seems to go along in general terms with this theory of the romanesque as pure tellability divorced from narrative. He oddly omits "Incidents" from his commentary, but interestingly reads the romanesque as a site of emergence in Barthes's writing of the gayness that has no place in the narratives of heterosexual culture (43–51). The problem, though (aside from the assumption that gayness is independent of heterosexual "narratives"), is a double one. First, whatever the emergences it may favor, a story that goes untold can't for that reason be regarded as inoperative: rather it becomes significant by virtue of its having been omitted, and as an object of forgetting. Second, the narrative most obviously excluded from "Incidents" isn't so much that of heterosexuality in general as it is that of colonialism in particular. There's an omission of the colonial story in "Incidents" that has the same structure of denial, in short, as the editor's overemphatic claim that Morocco and its history ("This is a misunderstanding that must be immediately set aside") are irrelevant to the romanesque.

If it's necessary, as Miller thinks, to forget heterosexual narratives for gayness to emerge, the gay male sexual tourist, as a cruiser, is also the subject of another, perhaps related, forgetting, which is that of the colonial context of his episodic investigations. *That* forgetting is also a condition, or part of the condition, of the emergence of his gayness. But there's a name, of course, for European descriptive practices that take "the East" as their object while forgetting their embeddedness in the history of colonialism. That name is Orientalism—and in (mis)naming his "incidentalist" practice of the romanesque as an art of haiku it's almost as if Barthes had forewarned us to expect it to be, like his naming of it, an Orientalist practice. Orientalism, then, in "Incidents," can be seen as a condition of emergence of the text's gayness. As for "Soirées de Paris," without going so far as to claim it as an Orientalist text, I do want to propose that the link between its stress on commoditization in the Parisian context and the Orientalist cultivation of the romanesque in "Incidents" lies, again, in the incidences of colonialist power in gay desire, coloniality being repressed, *along with* commoditization in "Incidents," but *by means of* a displacement that substitutes the commoditized for the colonial in "Soirées." It's as a subject of the double forgetting of the colonial, which seems to function as a condition of the emergence of gayness in each text, that I see R. B., the ordinary fellow, showing up in the critical intellectual Roland Barthes, in conformity with Michel de Certeau's description of the way the higher flights of knowledge find themselves humiliatingly interrupted by the banality of their everyday involvement in the ordinary histories and mechanisms of power (8).

Let's say, then, that there's a colonialist illusion (or alibi) and a postcolonial illusion (or alibi). The colonialist illusion *naturalizes the commoditized relations* that colonialism puts in place; in this, I'll argue, it's like the illusion sought by every tourist, including the sexual tourist, and "Incidents" is in this sense the text of colonialist illusion. The postcolonial illusion, though, *naturalizes colonial power itself*, and in this respect it's like the illusion of the (homo)sexual cruiser who forgets the identities that make him, say, white, middle class, and wealthy, and is thus able to relate on "equal" terms with, say, working-class or racially "other" men, or street kids and hustlers. As in "Soirées de Paris," it's only the community of desire that seems relevant. In this latter case, furthermore, it's not inconvenient, to either the cruiser or the postcolonial subject, to acknowledge the commoditization of relations—which thus becomes available as a substitute for the repressed consciousness of coloniality—whereas it's precisely these commoditized relations that must be played down in the colonial situation "proper," so that, like tourists, colonizing subjects can believe themselves to be linked in some more "natural" or "human" (unmediated) way to the colonized people with whom they have dealings. "Soirées de Paris," as a postcolonial text, thus foregrounds the commoditized relations that "Incidents" is led to de-emphasize, but in each case with a comparable result: the denegation of coloniality at the level of intersubjective relations, a crucial forgetting.

In "Soirées" (to look first at the chronologically later text), there are a number of *tapeurs* (people who want something out of you) and other nuisances. Barthes unfailingly treats them with long-suffering tolerance — except on one occasion, when he permits himself the luxury of rudeness. He has been talking a bit wearily with Jean G. about this young man's run-of-the-mill novel ("neither the text nor the boy pushes my buttons"), but now suddenly, when they're interrupted by a "Moroccan ex-hustler" with a hard-luck story and a request for a loan, Barthes reacts ("his rudeness gives me the energy to refuse") with unexpected intensity: "I refuse . . . ; he makes an angry gesture and knocks over chairs in his abrupt departure" (65). What should we make of this sudden flurry of violence? Why does a "Moroccan ex-hustler" provoke such a response? Barthes appears to have the (racist) habit of referring to all culturally Islamic Maghrebis as "Arabes" (66–67); but he also seems regularly to specify Moroccans within that group, as though they held a particular interest for him, a fact that recalls the Moroccan setting of "Incidents." Moreover, Barthes mentions having known this particular Moroccan ten years before (i.e., in the period of "Incidents").

While recalling the Morocco of "Incidents," this fellow—a former hustler who is now a *tapeur*—encapsulates also the main characteristic of the male population of "Soirées," which is that there's no clear distinction between "densely packed hustlers" on the street (55) and, say, the importunate Argentinian on the terrace of the Flore (54) or the young men (Eric, Jean, Olivier) to whom Barthes may dedicate an essay or in whose first novel he takes a benevolent interest. The interest all these men show in him is self-interested, and R. B.'s own erotic interest in most of them (the Argentinian is an exception) is itself a commoditized one (indeed, in the case of the hustlers, at least, it seems to be the commoditization of relations that he finds erotic). There are, in short, only different ways to *faire du gringue*, of being on the make. The rush of psychic energy provoked by the Moroccan recognized from the past has to do, then, with something unwelcome about his integration into the present Parisian scene, as if this were a betrayal of something remembered from another time and place and as if it were important for Barthes to maintain a separation between the "at home" scene of Saint-Germain and the "out there" of his Moroccan excursions of ten years earlier. The ex-hustler whom R. B. so energetically rejects stands, in other words, partly as evidence of an occluded link between the Moroccan text and the Parisian one and of an incidence of the former in the latter and partly also as an emblem of the repressed colonial subtext underlying the cruisy erotics of the commoditized Parisian scene.

For although R. B. is usually unspecific about the "racial" character-istics of the "boys" he notices (and Eric, Jean, Olivier, etc., are clearly European), the one moment when he comments: "a very handsome *white* hustler stops me" (72, my emphasis), taken together with the references to "Arabes" (66–67) and the habit of specifying "Moroccan" identity on occasion, adds up to an acknowledgment of the sociological fact that a preponderance of the street boys in Saint-Germain are immigrants or the children of immigrants from the Maghreb, and of the psychological reality that it's to these that R. B. is predominantly drawn. Although the world of Saint-Germain is presented to us as gen-erally cruisy and more specifically a commoditized world of universal hustling (both sexual and intellectual), it turns out, on closer reading, to be also a colonialist world—one in which the fact of colonialism (the historical reason why there are so many Maghrebis in Saint-Germain) is so taken for granted by the narrative subject that its omnipresence can be deduced only from scattered clues.

This (the repression of colonialism itself) is what I call the postcolo-nial illusion. So it's faintly ironic that the middle-aged R. B. among the young so often seems to strike dated Gidean poses, stubbornly reading his *Monde* ("very difficult to read one's paper in peace," 66) or "a little of Pascal's *Pensées*" (61) while the terrace jumps all around him, or going home to read Chateaubriand in bed ("I go back with relief to the *Mémoires d'outre-tombe*, the real book," 55) as Gide read Bossuet in the Congo jungle. R. B.'s postcolonial Africa, in short, is the rue de Rennes with its "densité des gigolos," or the rue Saint-André-des-Arts where one night the natives seemed restless, "there were so many young people out it was actually hostile" (70). It's as if the initially blotted out colonial context *returns*, in transformed guise, in the person of all these "jeunes." And the need to repress it becomes so intense that it finally leads R. B. into forms of insensitivity considerably more egregious than Gide's (who, as an earlier Barthes noticed, blithely obliged his poor bearers to struggle daily with heavy packing cases containing bound volumes of Shakespeare and Goethe). "I do not like," he writes like a true curmudgeon of a heavy-handed documentary on the problems of youth, "that very contemporary sort of message in which you have to sympathize with down-and-outers (limited horizon of the young, etc.)" (72).

Such irritation with the young, I'm arguing, indicates that the occluded horizons may be those of the writer, and that they include a wider range of "paumés" (down-and-outers) than he thinks: in particular, the context that is blocked out is in large measure colonial. (Not coincidentally, straight after the reference to the handsome white boy on this same page, two "Laotian creatures" (72) are mentioned— Barthes is attracted to one of them.) But the alibi for this is of course that R. B. has woes of his own to concentrate on. The genre of his writing isn't travel writing (like Gide's *Voyage au Congo*) or even the memoir (like Chateaubriand's *Mémoires d'outre-tombe*): it's the "journal intime," and accordingly it focuses on its narrator's own depressed mood, "exhausted and enervated" (61), "in despair too at not feeling at home [anywhere]; without real refuge" (60), unable to work in the afternoon (59, 63) but going out only to face a wasted evening, a "vaine soirée." D. A. Miller is perceptive in saying that the death of "his" mother has made "the" mother (writing, for instance) unavailable to him; but R. B.'s sense of being at a loose end, of existing desultorily and randomly, has to do also with what he calls his hesitation with respect to "the management of desire" (69). With hustlers he's forever paying in advance and not being surprised when they fail to show (59) or making a "vague rendez-vous" that neither will keep. His more intellectual young friends he "convinces" to leave town—and then feels abandoned ("and yet that is what I would like, anxious to clear my life of all these messes," 62). A whole afternoon goes by in fruitless cruising: "first of all at the Bain V, nothing . . . it occurred to me to go looking for a hustler in Montmartre, which is perhaps why, in bad faith, I found nothing. . . . At La Nuit, absolutely nothing. . . . I hang around the house . . . leave the house again and go see the new porn film at Le Dragon: as always . . . dreadful" (66–68). And the upshot of this dreary day is as follows: "I dare not cruise my neighbor. . . . Downstairs into the black room; I always regret this sordid episode afterward, each time suffering the ordeal of my abandonment" (68).

This vocabulary of ordeal and the euphemistic "descente à la chambre noire" show us that R. B.'s solitude in the crowded orgy room is paradigmatic of the "Soirées" as a whole, which are tinged with the experience of the infernal (Barthes is thinking of Dante) because the middle-aged narrative subject (he's thinking of Proust) is caught in the mechanism whereby to desire is to become undesirable, so that in the end it's easier—less painful—to disengage from a connection than to undergo the hurt of rejection. Thus with Olivier: "I sent him away, saying I had work to do, knowing it was over, and that more than Olivier was over: the love of *one* boy" (73). And it's in this self-inflicted *délaissement* that he thinks of Chateaubriand, the true model of melancholy (le vrai livre), but adding quickly the self-denigrating rider so typical of the loiterly tradition: "But suppose the Moderns were wrong? What if they had no talent?" (55).

There's a homology, then, I'm proposing, between this depressive self-enclosure among the young and the foreclusion of the colonial from the Parisian everyday. But if this self-pitying, self-enclosed personage is "R. B.," it's not just because Barthes is playing ordinary man to Chateaubriand's "Enchanteur" in a manner characteristic of loiterly writing. Rather it's because, in so doing, he's yielding to the banality of allowing personal misery to displace the consciousness one might expect of a critical intellectual and committing the everyday lapse of failing to see that the commoditized intersubjective relations that make the management of Desire so painful for him are part and parcel of relations of global power that makes things painful for those he calls "paumés." Forgetfulness that there's "a context" (that is, an unrecognized "other" context) is the most ordinary lapse of all— but it's just such a decontextualization, in turn, that makes things seem pointless. For the genre of these "vaines soirées," finally, isn't only the diary or "journal intime" (with its focus on the individual subject). They're also, as foreshadowed in the dinner table conversation of the first evening (53), a series of "histoires plates," or stories that fall flat—the point of which quite obviously lies in their absolute pointlessness. But pointlessness arises precisely when a story is divorced from the context that holds the key to its significance. The "histoire plate" lacks narrative energy (the romanesque: the element of tellability) just as its listless narrator lacks psychic energy. But it does so, indeed, *because* of this self-involvement on the narrator's part, and as a function of the "limited horizon" that prevents this forgetful, cruisy subject from grasping the missing dimension of his experience.

To restore this missing point(edness) ought to mean restoring the repressed element, then: the missing context of the colonial. And indeed, what "Incidents" suggests when read in relation to "Soirées" is precisely that for R. B. the possibility of (an illusion of) reciprocated desire and of an erotics of (apparent) simplicity, naturalness, and directness, in which "the management of Desire" would become innocent and easy because removed from the complexities of commoditization, is bound up with a restoration of the romanesque. That is, it's dependent on restoring a form of tellability that's lacking in the "histoires plates" of the Parisian "vaines soirées" but is generated *away* from the familiar and dreary everyday of home, as a function of the touristic gaze on the everyday of the (colonial) other. But here too there will be foreclosure, for although the romanesque is restored in this colonial text, it's restored as pure *punctum*, as a point(edness) without a story that actually repeats the forgetfulness of the "histoire plate" as a genre, a story that's pointless because of its repressed context. So the missing point, it seems, can only be restored at the price of forgetting the story in which it's embedded. Which can only mean that the "point" missing from one narrative (the "histoire plate") is the *same* as the "story" that's suppressed in the other (productive of the romanesque), its name being, in each case, colonialism.

What's called the context of a given story is always another story. Thus it is that colonialism, as the context that's missing from the aimless stories of "Soirées de Paris," is also the colonialism as (hi)story that's missing from "Incidents," whose pure tellability, as a collection of points without a story, is as *inane* as the collection of stories without point that constitute Barthes's "vaines soirées." It's the same omission, in other words, that makes home so *dreary* and abroad so piquant, so *exotic*.

The tourist's dilemma derives from being *sold* access to another culture that's (presented as) desirable only to the extent that it's authentic and natural, that is, directly accessible. If one is to be content with packaged "Englishness," say, there's absolutely no need to go to England (as Des Esseintes in Huysmans's *À Rebours* demonstrated): one can stay home and read the brochures. The reason tourists actually travel to other countries can only be that they have a desire—contradicted, of course, by the touristic circumstances—for unmediated contact, a noncommoditized experience of the other. Thus, their main business seems often to be to forget their status as tourists: they avoid "touristy" places and things, they love carnivals (Munich, New Orleans, Rio, Sydney), when it's easier for tourists to "mingle" because the locals are themselves behaving like tourists; they put their faith in "seeing" the sights, mistaking vision for a direct, unmediated mode of contact; and, finally, they seek sex with the natives, confident that it provides "natural" access to the other in her or his "naked" reality. . . .

However, it's the very desire for authenticity that marks the tourist as a tourist, since such authenticity is not a concern of anyone else: locals (who may be intent on turning a buck or having a good time) are the last people to ask, or to care, whether what they're doing is genuine or not. And the same desire for authenticity is what links tourism, as the denegation of commoditization, to Orientalism and related isms, in which denial of the alienated relation of colonizer to colonized and the affirmation of the possibility of unmediated and authentic knowledge of the other depend on forgetting the status of the colonizing subject (who becomes "simply," say, a sexual subject). "Incidents," as an album of touristy verbal snapshots divorced from any narrativization that might situate them in a history of global power, and as a series of brief objectivized perceptions whose subject is only rarely represented, falls squarely into this pattern of denegation and forgetting that makes touristic and colonial "self"-forgetting homologous practices.

When the observer does come into focus in "Incidents," it's in the role of off-duty intellectual, reading Lacan a little self-consciously in the Moroccan South (39) or, a bit more frequently, functioning as a linguist who notes features of the French spoken by carpet salesmen and street boys and on one occasion achieves a kind of community-in-philology with a group of kids through a common interest in the fact that, in French, "the genitalia form a paradigm of occlusive consonants: *cul/con/queue*" (57). Mainly, though, the apparent neutrality of the observer is produced by a kind of absence of the writing subject from the scene that's being described, so that the focus of interest falls on the population that is the object of his observation. This population, in turn, falls into three main groups: European hippies (portrayed satirically, 16, 18, 34), *colons* and *pieds noirs* (observed unsympathetically, 24, 26, 31, 32), and finally Muslims (usually drawn sympathetically if amusedly and—haiku oblige—in somewhat aestheticized fashion).

But whereas the coolness of the portrayal of the Europeans signals that the observing subject is functioning here as a critical intellectual, aligned neither with the dominant colonial class nor with the Islamic other (and practicing with respect to each a kind of policy of critical neutrality), the fact that his description of Islamic culture lapses so often into a kind of Orientalist shorthand—a naturalized language of the authentic—nevertheless shows us that, within the carefully critical Roland Barthes, there resides a less self-conscious, more banal, touristic and colonialist R. B.

Barthes's Orientalist predecessors—Chateaubriand (again), Nerval, Gautier, or Flaubert—all had stories to tell, and, often enough, stories of sexual initiation: Loti is their natural successor, and the Gide of *The Immoralist*, inventing the coming out genre in a context of Orientalist travel, provides the link with R. B. as a gay male sexual tourist. But these stories (Nerval being a partial exception) are rarely the colonialist story, and it's through his own suppression of this story, replaced by eroticized "haikus," that Barthes continues this tradition, while suppressing narrative altogether, in the storyless "points"—the *punctum* without the plot—that constitute for him the romanesque. Oddly enough (since the concept of the *punctum* arose in connection with photography[11]), Barthes's "haikus" reproduce the *scènes et types* postcard genre of the colonial era[12] whenever they focus on an anonymous Moroccan: thus we get "a young Moor," "a young Black," "my shoeshine boy," "and old peasant in a brown djellaba," "four men from the country," various students and so forth. Stereotypically, Oriental brutality (21, 23, 37–38) and inefficiency (43) are noted alongside *pied noir* insensitivity and bêtise; practices of Ramadan are noted, but for their incoherence (29) and picturesqueness (29–30). Mainly, though, what we're given is a collection of Orientalist genre scenes, whose unspoken point is that *this* is typical of the other's everyday, something one wouldn't see "at home":

The child I find in the corridor was sleeping in an old cardboard box, his head sticking out as though cut off. (15)

Sitting on the balcony, they wait for the tiny red lamp to be lit on the tip of the minaret, marking the end of the fast. (29)

Medina: at six in the evening, in the street studded with peddlers, one sad fellow offers a single chopping board on the edge of the sidewalk. (32)

M., sick, huddled in a corner on a mat, concealed his bare, burning feet under his brown djellaba. (39)

Two naked boys have slowly crossed the wadi, their clothes in bundles on their heads. (41)

The supposed romanesque, here, is a version of the picturesque, then, and a product of the tourist's desire for instant (immediate) authenticity; like the man with the single chopping board, these little pictures propose one endless item, the "eternal" Orient, chopped up into a series of telling details.

Concomitantly with this fantasy of immediate access to the life of the other, R. B. seems as happy in his sexuality here as he is miserable in "Soirées de Paris." The excruciatingly alienated negotiations of Parisian Desire have become idyllic encounters, candid and engaging, rather touching and even natural: "Visit from an unknown boy, sent by his friend! 'What do you want? Why are you here?'—'It's nature!' (Another boy, on another occasion: 'It's love!')" (23). I'm not suggesting, of course, that R. B. doesn't know that these kids are hustling in their fashion: what makes them attractive to him is the blandness of their denial of commoditization, a denial that makes it feasible for him to deny it in turn. "C'est la nature!" "C'est la tendresse!"—whether he believes them or not—are the words he wants to hear, words that by Orientalist definition, since they're quoted here as instances of the Moroccan romanesque, he couldn't expect to hear in Paris. By the same token, the (one-way) gift economy that governs sexual relations between the Parisian visitor and the Moroccan kids functions as a (barely credible) denial of the commodity economy that makes Desire such a hellish torment. Mustafa keeps the sandals he was asked to hold (24); Farid, having warned R. B. against beggars, proceeds to beg a pack of cigarettes and then five thousand francs (22–23). One imagines the outburst such mendacity might provoke in Paris (deadbeats are arrogant in our day and age; 72); here, it's as engaging as the gesture of the child who brings R. B. a bouquet as thanks for having typed his name (40). Indeed, it signifies that, even in their impudence, all these Moroccans are engagingly transparent, readable, and *childlike*. The Orientalist illusion of innocence is complete.

So when R. B. is *tapé* in Morocco, it doesn't have the same meaning as on the terrace of the Dome. All the panhandling that goes on can be treated—naturalized and indeed sentimentalized—as evidence of the other's desire for the European subject, and so of the reciprocity of desire that was so absent in Paris. Even the most banally commercial approach can be (mis)taken, thanks to the polysemy of the verb *taper* itself, which means "to put the bite on, to fuck," for a sexual invitation, as in the case of the carpet seller whose approximate French is the occasion for some erotic titillation, thinly disguised as linguistic analysis: "A demonstration of phonological pertinence: a young man in the bazaar (with an appealing glance: *tu/ti* (non pertinent) *veux tapis/taper* (pertinent)?" (Want a/wanna carpet/fuck?; 19). Barthes the intellectual is very visibly inhabited here by a touristic and colonialist R. B. anxious to misread blatantly commoditized relations as a natural expression of desire. But in this respect the two most typical boys in the text are the half-French Gérard (38), so anxious to offer his Oriental charms (for only in Islam does it count as a "final, irresistible, argument" that he is "uncut"), and young Mustapha, described with breathtaking *candeur* (or colonial self-deceit?) as "un être blanc de toute hostilité" (devoid of all hostility, the choice of the word *blanc* [white] being startlingly overdetermined; 32). If Europe's Orientalist dream is of a colonized other offering itself willingly, openly, and above all *spontaneously* (naturally) to be fucked (or, in Barthes's more euphemistic vocabulary, *niqué* or *tapé*), in a desiring relation assumed to be unmarked by asymmetries of wealth and power, then that's the dream we find personified in R. B. as a sexual tourist in Morocco, transforming the other's everyday into a magically idyllic site where something freely given (called the romanesque) becomes available, something on which the painful narratives of history have no bearing.

But it was, of course, Roland Barthes himself, in *Mythologies*, who taught us, long before he was to write either "Incidents" or "Soirées de Paris," that the denial of history is the beginning of ideology and the myths of ideology serve only the distribution of power that's in place. That there's an R. B. forgetful of Barthes's lesson doesn't mean, though, that critical intellectuals are any more hypocritical or lacking in self-knowledge than other mortals. What it does mean is that spottiness comes naturally to them (as we saw in chapter 7), and that therefore vigilance has to be their stock-in-trade; moreover, such vigilance never needs to be exercised more carefully than when they are on vacation or taking time off. For, as I've said, being at leisure for them is indistinguishable from being at work.

The theoretical upshot of the preceding comments might be an understanding of the everyday, not as something that is "just there" but as the ideological product of decontextualization, in the sense of a failure to recognize that there is a context other than the "present" context. Such decontextualization splits the everyday into two apparently opposed versions: the *familiar* everyday (Barthes's Saint-Germain), figured in "Soirées de Paris" as a pointless story or "histoire plate," and the other's everyday (Barthes's Morocco) that furnishes in "Incidents" a storyless point(edness), as a site of the *exotic*. If the everyday is that which we decontextualize by dehistoricizing it, then to restore the missing, or forgotten, "other" context is, in each case, to reinsert what's seen as purely local (or present) into a global (or historical) framework—in the present case, the framework of (post)colonialism—and this recontextualization gives point to the pointlessness of the familiar while it simultaneously furnishes the (hi)story missing from the decontextualized poignancies of the Barthesian romanesque, the Orientalist, the exotic. And, furthermore, if identity (that of gay man, for instance) is the product of forgetting (the forgetting of other possible identities), this forgetting can be connected, in turn, to the decontextualization that produces the everyday. One's everyday, in other words, is selected by the identity (or the set of identities) one *assumes*, in both senses of the word ("accedes to" and "takes for granted"), and such identities are the product of a limitation that excludes our potential to be other. Barthesian melancholy might be described as an effect of such foreclosure.

To approach the same issue from another angle, one might also say that in the everyday, whether familiar or exotic—and concomitantly in the construction of identity—a certain connectedness is lost; and, as the case of R. B. demonstrates, this connectedness can be that of the subject and the object when either one of these comes to embody an "other" context, such as the (post)colonial context, that gets ideologically forgotten. Thus we've seen that, in the case of the exotic, it's the object that becomes disconnected and is emphasized, therefore, over the (touristic, colonialist) subject, whose presence on the scene is "omitted" (and with it the question of how this European subject came to be the witness of the other's Moroccan everyday). Correlatively, in the familiar world of "Soirées de Paris," it's the (commoditized, colonial) object that becomes an amorphous, poorly differentiated mass of "tapeurs" and "jeunes," lacking in *relief* (the romanesque) because nothing and no one stands out, while the narrative focus falls heavily on the subject and his subjective problems. The concluding sentence, in which Barthes observes morosely that "the love of *one* boy" is henceforth over for him, captures perfectly this interdependence of an object become anonymous and a subject consumed with self-pity. It follows from this analysis that the restoration of context, the opening of the present and the local onto otherness, at the same time that it links in a historical and global framework the domains of the everyday that are illusorily perceived as distinct (on the one hand Paris, on the other Morocco), also reconnects the subject (say, R. B.) and the object (say, the "boys" of Paris and Morocco), establishing the "how come" of their being brought together in one place and demonstrating that the one can't rightly be thought to the exclusion of the other. Not only are we all "posh," as I said at the outset, but we're also, in the same sense, all "paumés" as well, since "at home" and "out there" are inextricably linked.

Where Baudelaire (chapter 8) had to learn with difficulty to acknowledge his affinity, as a loiterly intellectual, with the marginalized figures of the nineteenth-century street (the "paumés" of his era), the most obvious sign of Barthes's forgetfulness of the lessons of loiterliness, in "Incidents" and "Soirées de Paris," is his anxiety to distinguish himself from the losers, deadbeats, and down-and-outers (whether these be the hustlers and *tapeurs* of Saint-Germain, or the cute kids of Morocco) who populate his now (post)colonial world. "L'arrogance du paumé," he writes in curmudgeonly mode, "voilà l'époque," (deadbeats are arrogant in this day and age). But it is precisely the arrogance he attributes to them that signals something about our own day and age: that it is no longer easy to forget other contexts and that the history that brings together a "posh" if melancholy intellectual and the "paumés" of a Parisian *quartier de nuit* will return and insist—even, and perhaps especially, when it is ignored.

Reading and Being Read (On Being Pedestrian)

Disciplinary discourses characteristically devote considerable attention to establishing their object as valuable and worthy of study. The discipline of economics depends crucially on the importance attached to the economy, that of literature on the value it discovers in verbal artifacts that are produced as inexhaustible reservoirs of meaning. Not coincidentally, the value assigned to the object of disciplinary attention justifies the methods current in the discipline: if literature is a mine of potential significations, then the close reading method that is still central to literary criticism is the appropriate and desirable one. Literary criticism conceived as a critique of the literary in the sense of, say, the laying bare of its ideological investments and complicities, its dependence on *doxa*, is a relatively recent development—and it is one of the developments in literary studies that has fostered the even more recent emergence in the academy of what is commonly called cultural studies, to which the practice of critical rather than appreciative reading is central. What I want to address is the kind of problem of legitimation that arises when a discipline relies on a method of reading that is a hermeneutics of suspicion and consequently is critical of the discipline's object.

Cultural studies (CS) is scarcely a discipline; it is more a loose set of critical practices. But it is very much concerned, as if it were a discipline, with the two legitimating questions of the value of its object and the validity of its method, the problem being that if it is a critique of culture, then culture can scarcely be declared to be precious or valuable, although it is undeniably important, while the validity of the method is undermined by its belongingness to the culture it criticizes. In the sense of what Raymond Williams liked to call a "whole way of life," the concept of culture as it is understood in CS is historically tied to the moment of radical transformation brought about in Western Europe by various revolutions, industrial and political. The rapid spread of industrialization and of capitalism, the growth of large cities and the increasing dominance of the middle class in all the spheres of political and everyday life, the advent (in short) of "modernity," inescapably produced the sense that the conditions of existence had changed irreversibly and were now incommensurable with what they had once been (and at first could still be remembered to have been, only a short span of years earlier).

Social formations and the conditions of life they determine could no longer be conceived, in any sense, as natural: their susceptibility to change implied that social reality was a mediated phenomenon and required a concept such as that of culture to account for it. But, by contrast with the authenticity that came to be attributed to earlier ways, the culture of modernity was necessarily experienced, at the same time, as false and alienating—a culture of inauthenticity. As Raymond Williams's classic book, *Culture and Society, 1780–1950*, demonstrated, modern culture consequently became an object of criticism from the start, whether from the right or the left of the political spectrum (Edmund Burke and William Cobbett are Williams's paradigmatic figures).[1] Furthermore, with the advent of marxism, powerful concepts such as those of commodity fetishism and of ideology began to emerge as analyses of the mystifying forces that were now perceived to dominate social existence.

Authenticity belonged only in the past or in the future—or else it was attributed to groups held to be magically impervious to modernity's corrupting influences: a cultivated elite, perhaps, or in later versions the working class or marginalized groups and subcultures whose remoteness from the exercise of power seemed to guarantee them a certain cultural autonomy as well. With its siting in the institutions of power on the one hand, and, on the other, its focus on popular culture and its concern for dispossessed populations, cs has inherited, in a rather contradictory way, both of these tendencies. It has turned its face, though, from a third tendency. Art was regularly cited as a refuge of genuineness and hence as the site of an implicit or explicit critique of the debased culture of modernity; but, as James Clifford has shown, it was with the emergence of cultural anthropology that an ethnographic version of authenticity came to be attributed to groups conceived as living outside of history because remote from the European (or American) "center," and "primitive" or "exotic" culture, the culture of groups held to be untouched by modernity, came to share some of the qualities that Western modernism attributed to the productions of high art.[2] The museum, with its ethnographic and artistic wings, came in this way to be something of a sacred site, in which the values of integrity and genuineness had taken refuge.

For CS, though, not the museum but profane, fallen, and commercial sites are the locus of its work—the street and the freeway, arcades, department stores, and shopping malls, the media and industrial or popular culture—and this work is, generally speaking, not so much the work of appreciation as a work of suspicion. Knowledge for CS takes the form of accumulating demonstrations of the alienations of which capitalist and industrial (now postindustrial) culture is guilty, or else of identifying sites and forms of resistance to these alienating forces, a resistance most often taken to indicate residual or marginal possibilities of a surviving "genuine" culture, thus functioning as a critique of the general culture's falsity. As itself a manifestation, or a would-be manifestation, of such resistance CS tends to define its own value as a form of knowledge not by reference to its debased object (the general culture) but by virtue of its own critical practices, the method that is thought to align it with the other oppositional forces, increasingly sited in the domain of the popular and the marginalized, that are thought to be at work within modern culture. It thus implicitly grounds these critical practices, which are the source of its own validity as a (pseudo- or proto-) discipline, in solidarity with groups and practices thought to enjoy an authenticity that CS denies its object: culture as our shared "whole way of life."

There is understandable reluctance, therefore, to inquire too industriously either into the relation of institutionalized CS with popular and marginalized cultural sectors or into the theoretical possibility of validity and trustworthiness within a general culture defined by its inauthenticity. In short, a largely unexamined dualism seems to prevail by which it is assumed that the distance that permits criticism of a debased object guarantees the criticism immunity from the effects of its involvement with the object. But the very motivation of CS, which lies in its suspicion of modernity, necessarily feeds back into its practice, which is itself one of the manifestations of modernity, and thus forms an implied critique of its own position. And poststructuralist thought, with its slogan: "There is no outside" (of text, of power, of ideology, of culture . . .), confirms that what we need is a critical perspective that does not rely on opposing a positive term, such as authenticity, to a negative term, such as alienation or inauthenticity. Instead, such a perspective would take into account what it means for a cultural subject to occupy a dissociated position with respect to the cultural mediations that produce *all* subjective positions, including the position of dissociation. We need, in other words, to be able to understand and accept critical knowledge as a function of the culture that is its object, not as something grounded in an assumed externality with respect to that culture.

I take this to mean that, instead of relying on the authenticity-inauthenticity pair, cs as a set of critical practices might be more appropriately grounded in a theory of split subjectivity. Such a theory would account for critical positioning within culture in terms that are consonant with the mystification the critique attributes to cultural subjects, in such a way that the word *alienation* might name not only the split that defines mystified subjects as sites of *misrecognition*— what Althusser called an imaginary relation to the real conditions of production[3]—but also the distancing from self that makes possible criticism as a mode of *recognition* (the recognition of misrecognition) that is simultaneously a self-recognition (a recognition that one is oneself a site of misrecognition). The word *split*, in poststructuralist theory, designates a relation of difference such that the two "sides" of the relation can neither be absolutely separate one from the other nor completely and seamlessly joined; and it would follow from this definition that if the critical relation is a relation of split with respect to its object, then the recognition of the object (as "inauthentic") that constitutes the critical subject (as other than the "inauthentic" object, other—that is—than its own Other) simultaneously implicates the subject in the inauthenticity of the object. To recognize modern culture as alienating, in short, is to acknowledge the dependence of critical recognition itself on a phenomenon of cultural alienation; and to understand criticism as one form of the alienation it criticizes is to recognize that critical practices exist not externally to their object but within a structure of constructed differences in which there are only relations without a positive term.

Reading is often cited as a model of cs as a critical activity, and it is the theory of reading, I think, and more particularly of ironic reading, that can account for critical practices in a way that bypasses the authenticity-inauthenticity dualism and validates the critical relation as the other of mystified misrecognition without denying its implication in the alienating culture it criticizes. The reading relation is regularly cited as one that questions rigid distinctions of subject and object, self and other, and substitutes for them a relation of split. The text-reader relation is one of mutual dependence: discourse becomes text, that is, meaningful, only by virtue of its being read, but the reading subject is the site of a self-recognition that is mediated by the otherness of a text. To "read" culture as a critical subject is simultaneously, therefore, to produce it as *textual* (subject, that is, to the condition of interpretability that is the precondition of any hermeneutics of suspicion), and to recognize oneself as a cultural *subject*, that is, a product of otherness (the otherness of the cultural text), and subject(ed) therefore to the conditions of readability in turn (for to be a cultural subject is to be a site of misrecognition). Reading, in other words, is a matter of being read, of being read by the culture that is simultaneously the object of one's reading. It denies the possibility of strictly "individual" agency and enacts instead a theory of the subjection of agency; and therein lies the relevance of an understanding of the mechanisms of irony to a theory of critical reading, that is, a critical recognition of misrecognition that is itself necessarily mystified.

For irony is the phenomenon that most clearly manifests the inseparability of reading and being read, the fact that, if the readability of the object is the condition of all critical practices, then readability is in turn a feature of the critical subject, who can be critical only by virtue of a law that decrees *all* cultural agency, including critical agency, to be textual in nature, that is, subject to readability. This means, quite simply, that criticism has mystification as its precondition, not only in the sense that criticism takes as its object the mystification of cultural subjects, but also because criticism shares with mystification the structure of alienation and must acknowledge, therefore, the likelihood of its being mystified in turn. In order to treat its object as mystified, the critical subject must be prepared, in other words, to recognize *itself* as a likely candidate to become the mystified object of another critical reading, which in turn has mystification as its own precondition, and so on. For the critical reader, the only alternative to being read in this way is to perform one's own self-reading, and then a self-reading of that self-reading, and so on—there is no escape, for a reader, from the condition of readability because readability is itself the condition of the reader's critical practice. The only question, then, is whether and to what extent *being read* is something that one can do for oneself; and if grammar suggests not (one cannot be the active subject of a passive verb), the theory of split subjectivity—which goes beyond grammar by understanding discourse as a matter of enunciation, the conditions of which are not merely grammatical—implies the answer "both yes and no." It does so because it makes mystification a condition of criticism, but criticism the recognition of mystification, which puts the critic in exactly the position of being the active subject of a passive verb. These issues—of the involvement of the critic in the critical object and of the dose of self-mystification implied by critical frailties—are those that the tradition of loiterature (especially of kynical spottiness [chapter 7] and flâneur reading [chapter 8]) has permitted us to visit before.

Enoncé and *énonciation* are poorly translated into English by terms like *statement* and *utterance*. In an énoncé, meaning is exhausted in the predications of the sentence, and the subject is a grammatical instance, equivalent to the predicated meaning(s). Thus, "I hope it won't rain," as énoncé, means what it says (or if you will, it says no more than it means), and "I" is simply the site of a hope that there will be no rainfall. As an enunciation or utterance, however, the statement demonstrates readability—it requires interpretation, and the mediation of what is called context intervenes, so that "I hope it won't rain" is taken to mean both *more* and *other* than it says: for example, that the speaker is planning a picnic or a military campaign, or that, deeply depressed, she or he is hoping desperately for a sunny day to cheer her- or himself up. A subject of enunciation is produced *only* as a difference with respect to the subject of the énoncé and cannot exist as a positive term in its own right; but the same is true also, in the final analysis, of the subject of the énoncé, the supposed literalness of which is in fact context-dependent, as cases of ambiguity demonstrate. The two, in short, always co-occur, and they do so in a split relation of difference, the existence of each being dependent on the other without its being possible to separate them absolutely; so that reading can be described as the production of just such a split between an énoncé and an enunciation, and the measurement of their distance. If the word *text* designates discourse-as-read, then text is the site of a discursive split: what it "says," as énoncé, is *not* what it means, in context, as enunciation, and vice versa, each of these terms (*énoncé* and *enunciation*) being only the negative of the other: it is that which is *not* its other.

It is possible to read nonverbal discourse in this way as well as verbal texts. Traffic lights, for instance, *say* "stop" or "go," but they simultaneously *signify* something else: perhaps the impersonal reign of law in a disciplined society whose technological development has reached dangerous proportions. And the theory of the commodity as an object that says much less than it means and requires to be read so as to restore its occulted context (which, in this case, is the context of its production) can be thought of as a central model for the work of CS as a set of suspicious critical practices for which it is axiomatic that the discourse of culture in our everyday lives is a text that signifies other than what it says. Roland Barthes's *Mythologies*, for instance— rightly regarded as a founding text of CS—was an early demonstration of this axiom. It is, in short, a constant assumption of CS that culture is a set of discursive énoncés, verbal and nonverbal, whose function as enunciations is concealed from cultural subjects by a naturalizing effect attributable to the workings of power but can be restored to these mystified subjects, in some degree, by an act of critical reading that makes culture into a text.

As a practice of suspicious reading, CS therefore has an important structural feature in common with irony, which is also a textualization of énoncé. Irony points to an occulted context that changes the significance of an énoncé, demonstrating a critical difference between what it might be innocently taken to say and what it means; irony, too, is the critique of a mystification. To quote to a speaker his or her statement of a few hours earlier, "I hope it won't rain," at the point when the picnic has been swamped or the invasion has been disrupted by bad weather—or worse, because of factors even more unforeseen than meteorological uncertainty—is to produce an ironic enunciation that functions as a demystifying reminder that our statements and other acts occur within contexts that are in an important sense wholly or partially unknown to us and that we cannot "hope" to control. The ironic utterance, however, has the intriguing feature that, as an enunciation, it does not have an énoncé of its own, but only, so to speak, a borrowed one; nor does the critical énoncé the ironic enunciation implies need to be formulated for the demystifying effect of irony to be realized (it is "supplied" by the ironist's audience). The subject of an ironic enunciation is the subject of a discursive act of mentioning,[4] or of citing (in the strong sense of that verb, as when one cites someone before a tribunal); its "content" as an énoncé is furnished, therefore, by the mystified utterance of *another* subject (or, in self-irony, of the speaking subject as other-than-itself). The effect, at least superficially, is to separate the discursive *critical* act of demystification from another discursive act that is marked as mystified, as if the two had nothing in common. It is an act of dissociation, an attempt to distinguish the subject of ironic enunciation from the subject of the énoncé.

I say "superficially," though, because this operation of irony, as a form of critical reading, has much in common with the phenomenon that is called scapegoating. Scapegoating disculpates a scapegoater (or a whole scapegoating community) by throwing the "sin" onto a scapegoat; but the whole point of the operation depends on there being a commonality between scapegoat and scapegoater(s) such that the sin is in fact shared. Irony, as a citation of mystification, often functions as a critique of ideology, where ideology is understood in Althusserian fashion as a case of misrecognition in which a subject assumes the power, as an individual, to control meanings that are in fact contextually produced, ignoring the implications of the énoncé/enunciation split and enacting, therefore, an imaginary relation toward the real conditions of cultural production. The famous *bêtise* of, say, M. Homais (in Flaubert's *Madame Bovary*) lies in his being spoken by a discourse—the jargon of scientificity and progress—of which he *believes* himself to be an active subject. As the supposedly active subject of an actually passive verb, he is a mystified figure who is incapable of reading his own cultural positioning and can only *be read*.

Faithful to the logic of scapegoating, Althusser thought that the ability to read ideology implied a "scientific" position of reading, exempt from the effects of ideology. There is, however, no outside of ideology from which to criticize the ideological, and it was Barthes who pointed out that the ironist as demystifying reader is always subject to being read as a mystified subject in turn, just as the scapegoater always and by definition proves guilty of that of which the scapegoat stands accused.[5] Irony as ideological critique has no grounding except in ideology—an "other" ideology from the ideology that is the butt of irony. How, Barthes asks, can one take *bêtise* as one's butt without thereby laying claim to intelligence, that is, committing an act of *bêtise* in turn (for what is *bêtise* if not the act of attributing intelligence to oneself when one is in fact mouthing banalities)? The act of ironic enunciation thus turns out to have an implicit—that is, readable—énoncé that is not entirely separable, therefore, from the mystified énoncé it cites; and the relation of that énoncé (say, "I am intelligent") to the énoncé that is castigated as *bête* is, once again, one of split. There *is* a difference between two ideologies (say, M. Homais's ideology of progress and the Flaubertian ideology of artistic autonomy and distinction), but both the subject of the cited énoncé and the subject of the ironic act of enunciation are *within ideology*. Like Emma escaping banality in a way that is itself banal, the ironist, therefore, as a critical subject, is readable as mystified; and the ironist's act of reading the other (as mystified) cannot be separated from a concomitant vulnerability to *being read* (as mystified) in turn.

More particularly, there is inevitably a high degree of resemblance between the ideology that is the ironist's butt and that which grounds the ironic enunciation. Intelligence, as Barthes saw, is just another form of the *bêtise* it likes to castigate, the other of that *bêtise*, and both Homais's ideology of progress and Flaubert's ideology of distinction are versions of a nineteenth-century bourgeois worldview. As a matter of empirical observation, it seems probable, indeed, that we do not ironize just any statements, but precisely those from which we seek to distance ourselves because we feel that they may implicate us. There is an element of there-but-for-the-grace-of-God in irony, and like those who laugh at human folly for fear of weeping, we ironize precisely the kind of ideological discourse that we can imagine ourselves falling into. We would not criticize sexism, racism, or homophobia so energetically, for example, if we did not, at least obscurely, recognize elements of sexist, racist, or homophobic irrationality in ourselves; and if reading, as a general phenomenon, is describable as a phenomenon of self-recognition in and through the other, that characterization is particularly evident in the case of irony as a mode of ideological critique; indeed, it constitutes the so-called irony of irony. But there is a difference between the self-recognition of irony and of critical reading, and that of appreciative reading: irony enacts self-recognition, precisely, as a *critical* moment, the self one recognizes in the other being a mystified subject, the subject of a misrecognition of self.

The important implications of this analysis seem to me to be threefold. First, the fact that there is no position from outside of ideology from which to criticize the ideological (no "authentic" site from which to castigate "inauthentic" modernity) does not incapacitate the critical impulse, but instead imposes on it the conditions of ironic discourse. These conditions, second, can be encapsulated in the maxim that mystification is the condition of criticism and that one cannot read critically, therefore, without finding oneself open, in turn, to the possibility of being critically read. "It takes one to know one" is the maxim that governs all forms of critical reading. Third, however, the critical subject, as a site of self-recognition in and through the mystified other and hence of a recognition of self-misrecognition, cannot be expected to escape mystification but *may* be expected to inscribe in critical discourse some representation of this recognition of misrecognition.

What I want to pursue in the remainder of this chapter is a brief examination of how these three implications are played out in a specimen of the critical writing of one particularly subtle and especially nimble practitioner of cs, the Australian writer Meaghan Morris. For this purpose, they can be encapsulated, perhaps, as a rule of *negativity* and an imperative of instability or of *mobility*. The critical position is a "negative" one to the extent that it cannot be grounded in a position outside the system it criticizes: it occupies a position of difference in a system that admits no positive terms. Critical discourse as it is practiced by Morris enacts this situation, like an ironic enunciation, by seeking to signify without incorporating an énoncé of its own, that is, by exhausting its enunciative capacity in the act of distancing itself from the other. But to the extent that, again as in irony, the critical position inevitably proves to be contaminated by the ideological or mystified positions of which it is critical, the acknowledgment of self-mystification takes the form of constant critical repositioning, as if, conscious of the inescapability of *being read*, the critical subject were resolved at least to duck and weave, to present a moving target, demystifying each successive position she is led to occupy by immediately moving to another. "Feminism" is the name Morris seems often to give to the negative positioning of her critical practice; and taking a hint from her essay on shopping centers (malls), which she would have liked to sub-title "Pedestrian Notes on Modernity,"[6] I would like to call pedestrianism her tactic of instability and the moving target, which adds an ironic and self-ironic sting to the loiterly practice of digressiveness.

Tactics like these doubtless have something in common also with the practices of cultural critics like Gayatri Spivak and Trinh T. Minh-ha, in whom they have been perhaps better recognized and more favorably assessed. It is certainly not coincidental that such moves have been developed by writers whose own historical identity is subject to multiple forms of marginalization: as women and as women "of color," as postcolonial and "third world" subjects, as cosmopolitan or "homeless" intellectuals whose situation is exotic wherever they find themselves. Marginality, of course (see chapter 8), names the critical position par excellence, but it also defines the reasons for that position's instability. And as a woman (albeit not "of color"), as an "independent scholar" working largely outside of the academy, and as herself a colonized subject (from a so-called white-settler colony, it is true, but one that is now in postcolonial economic thrall to the United States and the Pacific Rim), Morris also writes in significant ways from the margins. But oddly enough, white middle-class feminist intellectuals are vulnerable to forms of hostility that women of color such as Spivak and Trinh are in part protected from, thanks to the (somewhat racist?) immunity from criticism that "spokespeople for the oppressed" can enjoy among guilty white liberals and lefties. Morris's writing has been roundly attacked in her own country and declared, for example (although in this case by a relatively sympathetic reader), to be as "tangled as a plate of spaghetti".[7] There are good reasons for my not wanting to disentangle the spaghetti in what follows: I want rather to look at one essay, entitled "Banality in Cultural Studies" with a view to trying to suggest how and why its spaghettiness might have the power to frustrate the expectations of certain readers but to delight and stimulate others.[8] It does these two things, I think, by simultaneously enacting, and theorizing its enactment of, a certain ironic negativity and an associated imperative of critical mobility that can leave even well-intentioned souls, if they are not alert, wondering what is "the point." But isn't a certain *pointed* "pointlessness" exactly what one might expect of a discourse from the margins?

"Things To Do With Shopping Centres," in which Morris initially advocated and exemplified a pedestrian critical practice, is simultaneously an exploration of critical marginality and a kind of dry run for this pointed circling around a certain failure, or unwillingness, to make a point that reappears in "Banality in Cultural Studies." It is less an essay about shopping malls (more commonly called "centres" in Australia) than it is a meditation—illustrated by the example of the "Green Hills" neighborhood shopping center in Maitland (New South Wales)—on how the practice of shopping might be approached as an exemplification of women's involvement in modernity, itself understood as a history of change. And it specifically identifies itself as an attempt to describe that involvement in terms *other* than the standard story of "commodity semiosis" (218) as the production of a paradise of the Imaginary that converts shoppers—always feminized in this story and embodied as women—into so many unreflective, reflex-driven consumers. Thus, Janet Wolff's understanding of the female shopper as inheritor of the flâneur tradition[9] is both taken up and significantly modified in the figure of the pedestrian user of the mall who functions for Morris as an emblem both of women's "ambivalent" participation in modernity and, simultaneously and interchangeably, of her own complex critical self-positioning as a writer about "things to do with shopping centres." Where a Barthes yields, in his more curmudgeonly moments of melancholia (chapter 9), to a certain contempt for the *paumés*, who, although he fails to acknowledge it, signify his own participation, as an intellectual, in historical processes, Morris identifies as a model for her own critical procedure (and so identifies *with*), the ordinary ("pedestrian") woman shopper whose enjoyment of time spent at the mall does not preclude hard-headedness and skepticism. "Like effective shopping, feminist criticism includes moments of sharpened focus, narrowed gaze—of sceptical, if not paranoid, assessment" (197).

Pedestrian mall users—those, that is, who arrive by means other than the private car—tend to stay there longer and thus, like loiterly subjects, have time to develop their "slow, evaluative, appreciatively critical relationship" (203) to the shopping center (whether they actually shop or not). This ambivalence (critical/appreciative) corresponds to Morris's own project, as a critic of popular culture, to find "a place to speak other than that of the fascinated describer" (196), whether this describer stands *outside* the spectacle (like the detached flâneur of Baudelaire's "Le Crépuscule du Soir," chapter 8) or alternatively—and as recommended in particular by Iain Chambers—celebrates popular culture by fascinated immersion *within* it, "a 'wide-eyed' pose of critical amazement at the performance of the everyday" (196–97). Morris's pedestrian critic is thus *not uninvolved* in what she describes (Morris refuses, for that reason, to discuss malls she has not herself visited and used), and yet she is no easy dupe of "commodity semiosis." And concomitantly she seeks a mode of writing that lies somewhere between the genres of (distanced, objective) formal description and (purely subjective) personal reminiscence, capable of combining critical and analytic distance with acknowledgement of the fact that the critic too is part of the scene, and in no way dissociated from it.

This critic is the inheritor, then, of the Baudelairean flâneur figure of "Le Cygne" (chapter 8), conscious of participation in the history of modernity (whether it be "Paris change" or Maitland evolving through the acquisition of a mall) while no less self-consciously withholding assent (whether it be to Baudelaire's culture of impatience or the "male paranoia" of small-town boosterism that Morris identifies as having provided the alibi for the commercial creation of "Green Hills"). And, a bit like the Baudelairean figure again, Morris's pedestrian critic knows that the best way to bring off her balancing act between involvement and critical distance is to keep moving so as to avoid succumbing, on the one hand, to the blandishments of the object itself (the glittering new Paris or the somewhat tawdry charms of a country-town supermarket-cum-discount-outlet), but also, and on the other hand— this being where she parts company with the Baudelairean example— to a certain proclivity to become stuck, like Baudelaire's flâneur, in a single critical position: the temptation to lapse into melancholy. The practice of pedestrianism as a continual movement of the attention doesn't preclude stopping and staring, like the flâneur, as a perennial enjoyer of the sights and scenes of nineteenth-century urban streets or late twentieth-century suburban malls. But it enjoins less a *pensiveness* dangerously oriented toward melancholic self-pity than a consistently *ironic* practice not unrelated to that of the ancient Cynics but which in this case necessarily implies self-irony as well and, with it, a practice of mobility, a permanent digressiveness that differs somewhat from the Greek model. Like Diogenes deflating Plato with a plucked chicken from the marketplace, Morris demolishes the standard theories of commodity fetishism and the "Garden of Eden" analysis of consumerism by pointing to a dreary rack of raincoats or a pile of mass-produced thong-sandals in a discount store (222). Her pedestrianism thus has in common with cynical philosophy (chapter 6) a strategic attention to the unattended to, the "trivial" detail capable of deflating a whole theory; but the mobility she practices is less a matter of changing critical *objects* (moving, like *pícaro* dogs, from master to master, chapter 7) than of disconnecting the critical subject position itself from any fixed orientation, given that there is no position from which to read that isn't subject, in turn, to the condition of readability. And if she identifies Maitland's mall as a way of traveling without leaving home for a small-town community anxious to keep up with modernity but not to abandon its local ways, the critical practice she describes as pedestrianism could therefore be characterized, inversely, as a way of leaving home—learning to do without a permanent intellectual home base—without having to travel any real distance, since modernity—to the marginalized but participant, "ambivalent" critical subject—is no further away than the short stroll or quick bus trip that takes you to the local mall.

As I mentioned earlier, there has always been a certain defining tension in CS around the notion of the popular, and by extension, of the ordinary, the everyday. Is popular culture an exploitative and trivial manipulation of the "masses," as a lengthy tradition maintained and continues to maintain? Or are the people, as in particular "British" (Anglo-Australian and to an extent American) CS has argued for a generation now, resourcefully oppositional in their modes of consuming debased, mass-produced material? Inspired by Baudrillard's use of the concept of banality and aided and abetted in particular by Michel de Certeau, Morris's move in "Banality in Cultural Studies" is to reconfigure the debate by recording her "irritation" with its terms. The banality attributed to the popular by its detractors is matched only by the banality with which its defendants turn out stereotyped arguments in its favor; and what is actually at stake in *both* cases, she shows, is the legitimation of the position of the cultural critic. To declare popular culture banal is to situate oneself as discriminating; to insist on its oppositionality is to project onto the popular a position which is that of the critic; and in each case the people are being *used*—treated as "dopes"—a situation that is ironic in view of the fact that modern (post-"Frankfurt School") CS began as a refutation of the "dope" theory of the popular. In some such way as this, one might summarize the conceptual content of "Banality in Cultural Studies" as an énoncé.

As an enunciative performance, though, the text is *doing* something even more interesting, and in this too it is aided and abetted by Certeau's *The Practice of Everyday Life*, an extremely careful reading of which anchors Morris's essay.[10] Certeau's key move lies in his affirmation of the *ubiquity* of ordinariness, and this idea does not only subtend Morris's identification of "banality" in British CS's compulsively repetitive celebrations of popular cultural consumption. It implies also that there is an irony in *any* attempt, including Morris's own, to produce a discourse of knowledge as something distinct from the ordinariness of "common opinion," or *doxa*. The irony is that the would-be subjects of knowledge will find themselves mouthing banalities in turn, as the production of knowledge turns out to be, not separate from, but deeply involved in the everyday stories of economic, political, and cultural conflict, the "polemological space" that for Certeau is the space of culture itself. To point repeatedly, as Morris does, to the ironic return of the banal, in this sense, in the work of a number of male cultural critics—Baudrillard, Fiske, (Iain) Chambers, and Certeau himself—who are insufficiently attentive to the refraction in their own discourse of their institutional situation as university intellectuals, may seem a pointlessly negative ironizing, to the extent that, as Certeau suggests, such ironies can be thought to be inescapable and no more positive alternative seems available. But that there *is* an alternative is indicated elsewhere and otherwise than in the essay's conceptual content. This alternative is enacted in its enunciative practice, which shows by counterexample that a practice of pedestrianism might substitute for critical practices that aren't careful of their own enunciative positions and fall, therefore, into the banality of making use of the popular for purposes of self-legitimation.

Pedestrianism, as the word implies, does not turn its back on banality or on the ironic implications of Certeau's analysis; it is, on the contrary, a response to those implications, one however that is *careful*— in the strong sense of "full of care"—in a way that the discourses Morris distances herself from are not. There is in fact nothing pointless about the essay's restless negativity; but as is pointed out from the start its point can be reached only by "a rather circuitous route" and does not have to do with achieving some sort of *resolution* of the tensions that arise in connection with the ostensible topic of banality ("I'm not sure that banality can have a point"). Instead it "takes the form of pursuing an aim rather than reaching a conclusion" (14). The point enacted by the essay's pedestrianism is one that relates to the possibility—the "aim"—of a feminist practice of criticism, which I can begin describing by saying that it is somewhat reminiscent of Julia Kristeva's statement in an essay entitled "Woman Can Never Be Defined" that:

> In "woman," I see something that cannot be represented, something that is not said, something above and beyond nomenclatures and ideologies. . . . It follows that a feminist practice can only be negative, at odds with what already exists so that we may say "that's not it" and "that's still not it."[11]

If a *careful* reading of Certeau occupies a central position in Morris's essay, it does so for a number of reasons. He offers the grounds of her ironic critique of banality in cs. He also, as I am about to indicate, offers a certain theorization of her own critical practice. Finally, she will be led, as I have mentioned, to use Certeau ironically against Certeau himself, but also therefore against the position that she herself just occupied, a position that turns out, in this way, to have been temporary and tactical—one from which she is ready to "part company" (35) as it reveals its own involvement in banality. If she thus distances herself from the theory that underwrites her own tactics of distancing and then self-distancing, it is the better to exemplify the point that becomes briefly explicit for the first time, precisely in her discussion of Certeau: that we need to be "very careful of our enunciative and 'anecdotal' strategies—more careful than much cultural studies has been in its mimesis of a popular voice—and their relation to the institutional places we may occupy as we speak" (27). Notice that although the essay's point *is* in fact made in the énoncé, it gains its power from an *enunciative enactment of what enunciative care entails*, which is a willingness not only to distance oneself from the positions of others but also to abandon one's own position. That *enunciative* point, in other words, is more crucial than any more specific point one might find oneself making in an énoncé.

Morris's appropriation of Certeau's vocabulary of "strategy" and the occupation of "places" in the very formulation of the kind of care that will lead her to part company from Certeau consequently has something emblematic about it. For it is clear that two ideas of his, in particular, are crucial as theoretical underpinnings of the practice of pedestrian criticism as an enactment of enunciative carefulness. One is the concept of culture as polemological space, which substitutes for concepts like a "whole way of life" a conflictual model of social relations, defined by the interaction and interdependence of—that is, by a relation of split between—powerful "strategies" and oppositional "tactics" that are something like what Lyotard calls "the strength of the weak."[12] It is true that Certeau himself tends to describe this model in rather dualistic terms rather than as a relation of split. For him *space* can be occupied and panoptically surveyed by the powerful as the "place" that is proper to them and is their property, while *time* is the friend of opportunistic oppositionality, whose tactics depend on good timing and, as Morris writes (in a phrase that is quite suggestive of her own enunciative practice), "use 'the place of the other,' in a mode of insinuation" (29). Certeau also tends to describe his model, dualistically and I think mistakenly, as a relation between language as an imposed or given "grammar"—a set of rules—and individual acts of enunciation that appropriate the language and make use of it for individual or local operations of resignification. This Saussurean *langue* vs. *parole* duality is inappropriate because it is not language as such that one resignifies but other enunciations (discursive acts that constitute interpretable, and therefore reinterpretable, texts).

Certeau is therefore closer to the potential his model of tactics and strategies has as a relational dynamics of difference when he cites acts of reading and of quoting as examples of the oppositional appropriation of discursive positions constructed by the manipulations of power. In this rewrite of the model, the "proper" is no longer a positive term or a natural given but simply a discursive construct, and language is not the site of the proper but the mediator between conflictual positions that construct or deconstruct significations. By extrapolation, therefore, culture becomes not so much the site (a "space") as the *condition of possibility* of political struggle, viewed as the differential construction of meaning, now manipulative or strategic, now opportunistic and tactical. And in this understanding, the negativity of critical repositionings or resignifications of powerful discourses displays its affinity with irony as a citational act having the power to demonstrate the ideological character of a given discourse (its complicity with a dominant power) by recontextualizing it, so that its constructedness is shown up as a form of readability (its vulnerability to *being read*). It is ideology, in other words, that mediates ironic and/or critical relations, in the way that language or culture, in my corrective rewrite of Certeau's model, mediates the conflict of strategies and tactics—and indeed, as I once tried to show without quite formulating it in this way, irony might well be described, like Morris's critical practice, as a tactical discursive intervention that displays the strategies of dominant ideologies.[13]

But as we know, irony has its own irony, which is that the ironic critique of ideology necessarily turns out to be conducted from an ideological position of its own—and banality, like Flaubert's *bêtise*, is one of the possible synonyms of the ideological. The banal as Baudrillard understands it is an exact echo of Althusser on the ideological—it is the assumption that, as Morris puts it, "the subject is more powerful than the object" (20), where "object" refers to the butt of the subject's irony or critique, the small-*o* other, but also to the big-*O* Other of which the small-*o* is a metonym and which speaks through us when we believe we are speaking, as individual subjects, on our own behalf.

Banality is the way the object will keep turning up in the subject, and the second key idea of Certeau's is therefore that, just as there is no outside of ideology, there is no escape from the banality of the everyday which is everywhere and so shows up deflatingly, like ideology in irony, precisely in those positions that attempt to distinguish themselves from it—as the intellectual does in attempting to produce "knowledge" as something distinct from "common sense." Such distinctions are always only differences and the relation is one of split, so that, as in irony, the more one constructs knowledge as the other of the everyday, the more it will turn out to be inhabited by the banality of common sense.

The ordinary, then, as Certeau puts it (Morris 27), has the ironic power to "reorganize the place from which discourse is produced" and notably the place from which scholarly and/or critical discourse is produced. If Certeau's definition of the social as a polemological space authorizes critical discourse as an oppositional, ironic, appropriative or tactical negativity with respect to dominant discourses (whether in society at large or in cs itself), the law of banality as Certeau formulates it implies that the criticized banality (as ideologicity) will ironically show up in turn in the criticizing discourse. That is why a truly careful critical practice will seek to *keep moving*, shifting from one negative position to another, not in an attempt to "out-run" banality, of course, but with a view to demonstrating the extremes of carefulness its ubiquity requires of us. The practice of pedestrianism does not seek to deny or even to distance itself from banality; rather, as an art of being constantly on the move, it has self-conscious awareness of banality as its motor.

Morris begins her essay, then, with a series of ironic demonstrations of the ironies that befall the practitioners of cs in their representations of the popular, ironies that arise whether the discourse seeks to discriminate between the popular as banal and itself as not banal, or whether in assigning active agency to the popular it ends up attributing to it forms of *bêtise* and/or demonstrating banality on its own behalf. Baudrillard distinguishes, in spite of himself, between an "aesthetic order (fatality)" and "mass cultural anarchy (banality)" as the literal and the figural—but falls into figuration and, like his platitudinous seducer, who "assumes . . . that the subject is more powerful than the object," winds up ironically reoccupying "the place of control of meaning" himself (20). Celebratory accounts of popular culture as active forms of consumption, such as those of John Fiske and Iain Chambers, turn out under examination to be "narcissistic in structure" because the popular serves as a mask for the intellectual's own voice or, alternatively, self-defeating because the supposed celebration is a version of the thesis of "cultural dopes" in the critique of which "the project of cultural studies effectively and rightly began" (24). Furthermore (I am summarizing quite brutally some extremely subtle analyses), in all these accounts there is a perceptible feminization of the popular; they are antifeminist representations of "mass culture as woman" (23).

In the essay's central section these discriminatory accounts are then relativized by recourse to the "more positive" approach of Certeau, whose definition of popular culture as a "way of operating" and whose perception of the ubiquity of the ordinary mean that "the practice of everyday life has no place, no borders, no hierarchy of materials forbidden or privileged for use" (30–31). Understanding the popular, the ordinary, the everyday, the banal to inhabit the intellectual's discourse as part and parcel of its constitution, Certeau bypasses the problems that haunt the mimesis of the popular in sites of knowledge; and his own practice of quoting the popular from an institutionally secure place in the scholarly institution does continue, Morris thinks, to "allow ways for the other to speak" (34) by virtue of his recognition of the critic's own historicity and involvement in the cultural system. Nevertheless she is led finally to "part company" once more, making yet another ironizing move with respect to Certeau that repeats the structure of the ironic reversibilities she discovered in Baudrillard and the British writers. For Certeau's muse—the Ordinary Man—is very decidedly gendered; and similarly the position of enunciation from which he constructs the notion of banality that allows for the other to speak is itself a "tenured (masculine) 'we'" (31) that blurs all the manifestations of its popular other—"Black, Primitive, Woman, Child, People, 'Voice,' 'Banality'"—into an undifferentiated "myth of *common* otherness" against whose polemological challenge the "same singular writing subject of historical production" survives (36). Thus— because he fails to pluralize and particularize popular otherness into its component othernesses, of which his own discourse would become one—the dualism of subject and object that Certeau's construction of banality had "reorganized" returns in his own enunciative practice as the banality of "an old pathos of separation," polarized between categories like elite vs. popular, special vs. general, singular vs. "banal" or ordinary. Certeau is *careful* but *not careful enough* of his own position of enunciation.

Where to go after this ironization of the position that subtended the earlier ironizations? It was the "tenured" quality of Certeau's discourse—its stability and sameness as the product of a "singular" and, parenthetically, masculine writing subject to whom the phenomenon of internal splitting is unknown—that led Morris to distance herself from the position represented by his work. In the final pages of her essay, the externalized irony by which she distanced herself successively from Baudrillard, Fiske, and Chambers, and then from Certeau, turns to an internalized, self-splitting irony—a self-detenuring irony—as she describes a close shave in which she was rescued at the last minute from her own desire to "allegorize" the popular and its Certeau-esque ability to make trouble by doing a reading of the Hitchcock film *The Trouble with Harry*. But, she says:

> I did not long enjoy the contemplation of my intention. "Did you notice," asked Bill Collins [host of the TV movie show] in his med-itative moment, "how everyone in this film seems to *want* to feel guilty?" "That's not the point!" I told the television, ready with my counterthesis. "Well," declared that irritating voice, "there's a Ph.D. in that!" (39–40)

This anecdote (as we're warned to expect at the start) is itself allegorical (15). It teaches us that to say "That's *not* the point!" or "That's *not* it!" is nevertheless always to come perilously close to making a point, promoting a counterthesis, making use of the popular for the purposes of self-legitimation, falling into the banality of occupying an unself-critical position with respect to banality, through failure, in particular, to take account of one's placement with respect to Ph.D. granting institutions. It reproduces "an old pathos of separation." "[T]o retrieve a given theory of popular culture from a text framed as an *exemplum* of both [i.e. of theory and of popular cultures] would be to produce, at the end of my trajectory, precisely the kind of 'banality' I was setting out to question," says Morris, making both the self-irony and the point of her anecdote quite explicit.

For with all this irony and self-irony, she does have a point—but it's not Certeau's (or Hitchcock's) point about the troublesome ubiquity of the banal, and it's more like a question, or an "aim" to pursue, than a point to be *made*. If it is true that every attempt to speak of the banality of our shared culture from a position that implies some epistemological ambition—the construction of "valid" knowledge as nonbanal—necessarily participates in the "old pathos of separation" and so, ironically, winds up revealing itself to be banal in turn, is there a tactic that might, in Certeau-esque fashion, make "trouble" with the rule not as a denial or an evasion of the conditions it defines but as a way of "making do," that is, of resignifying them? More particularly, might it be the privilege of a voice that does not speak from the position of a "tenured (masculine) 'we'" to disrupt the discriminatory gestures and attendant ironies of banality to which academic and intellectual positions of enunciation are demonstrably subject? That would be Morris's hope for "the cultural practice of a feminism (for example) already situated *both* by knowledge and social experience of insecurity and dispossession *and* by a politics of exercising established institutional powers" (39)—a feminism, in other words, that could speak from both sides of the fence, the side of tenure and the side of dispossession. Might there, in other words, be a way of institutionalizing insecurity? of dispossessing the institutional? of politicizing knowledge from the perspective of a social experience of disempowerment, which is that of feminists "for example," but also of other groups with particular historical experiences of their own?

To put this another way, the "interesting possibility" left open by Certeau (but not realized by him) would be, according to Morris, that "the voice of that which academic discourses—including cultural studies—constitute as popular [might begin] to theorize its speech" (41). That is, not (banally) just to speak but *both* to speak from the untenured position *and* to produce (untenured) knowledge of what it means to speak without tenure. The prime condition for realizing this possibility would be that feminists (for example)—enabled as they are by the experience of dispossession in combination with the practice of institutional politics—exercise care "*not* to become subjects of banality in [the] old double sense: not to formulate edicts and proclamations, yet to keep theorizing" (41). If theorizing here means attending in particular to the "complexity of social experience investing our 'place' as intellectuals today" rather than relegating it to a merely adjunct or instrumental position—attending, that is, to what was earlier called "enunciative and 'anecdotal' strategies . . . and their relation to the institutional *places* we may occupy as we speak" (26)—it also clearly means keeping moving, that is, problematizing positions and then problematizing the position from which the problematizing was carried out, and so on, following a "that's not it" by a self-addressed "that's still not it!" It means, in short, something like following the enunciative procedure—the critical practice I have called pedestrianism—of which Morris's essay is itself an exemplary demonstration.

I hope, then (by now the reasons must be evident), that no one wants me to round off this chapter neatly, and to part company with my book, by making a point of my own. I want rather to allow the resonances between Morris's critical practice and the writing I've baptized loiterature—the way each comments on the other—to hang in the air, doubtless to decay as time and further reflection erode them. Does loiterature qualify as a historical model of the position of negativity Morris names feminism? Is it—whether or not it models a way of doing cultural studies—a way of making intellectual trouble through a tactical alliance with the ordinary (the trivial, the banal, the natural) that inhabits all our cultural contexts as their inescapable "other context"—the ordinary that makes trouble for tenured positions but can equally disrupt trouble-making gestures themselves when and if they forget themselves to the extent, rather than enacting a *visée*, of making a (critical) point?

Can we, in short, regard loiterature as a "pedestrian" way of inhabiting modernity, one that has nothing in particular to *say* (although much to record) but communicates a great deal by the kind of oblique device that's called in French *suivez mon regard* (follow the direction I'm looking in), about the kinds of reticence modernity inspires in some (many? maybe all?) of its subjects? Does loiterature just loiter? Or does it loiter with intent? And if the latter, is *that* the intent—to register a certain withholding of assent not by saying so but through dilatory discursive gesturing: beating about the bush, digressing, failing to come to the point? Or can it be that "the" intent, if such there be and whatever it may be, crumbles as soon as I formulate it, as a result of its having become, willy-nilly, a point?

There's a kind of plausible deniability in loiterature that gives it a more than passing resemblance, I think, to the "ambivalence"—not to say the inscrutability—Meaghan Morris attributes to the pedestrian shopper in a mall. Is she there just because she's there? Does she intend to shop? Is her "appreciation"—a word that implies enjoyment but also something like assessment—somehow and in some sense *critical?* That plausible deniability (which affiliates loiterature with the shopper in a way different from Morris's modeling of her own overtly acknowledged critical intent on her) makes me wonder, sometimes, whether I haven't been (agreeably) wasting my time—since, in the end, I can come to no conclusion—in writing about loiterature. But it may also be true that I've stumbled onto one of the modern ages's best kept secrets: that one can make trouble, precisely, not only by blocking the ability to conclude in general but also, and in particular, by blocking the ability to conclude about what it means to block the ability to conclude. If so, that's a not insignificant discovery.

So, reader, let's not try to decide. (Let's try not to decide.) Let's betake ourselves, instead, like Campuzano and Peralta in Cervantes (chapter 7), to the Espolón. Let's repair, like Benjamin's flâneur, to the marketplace. Let's go hang out in the mall.

Notes

1. DIVIDED ATTENTIONS

1. Frank O'Hara, "Ann Arbor Variations," *The Collected Poems of Frank O'Hara*, ed. Donald Allen (New York: Knopf, 1971), 64–66.
2. My biographical information about Frank O'Hara is from Brad Gooch, *City Poet: The Life and Times of Frank O'Hara* (New York: Knopf, 1993).
3. Charles Baudelaire, "Le Cygne," *Œuvres complètes*, vol. 1, ed. C. Pichois (Paris: Bibl. de la Pléiade, 1975), 85–87.
4. In *Popular Culture: The Metropolitan Experience* (New York: Routledge, 1986), Iain Chambers argues, on the basis of a quotation from Walter Benjamin, that it is inappropriate to subject popular culture, as an object of "distracted attention," to "the apparatus of contemplation" associated with intellectual modes of analysis. The Benjamin passage (Chambers, 12) is from "The Work of Art in the Era of Mechanical Reproduction": "[The] public is an examiner, but an absent-minded one" (see Walter Benjamin, *Illuminations*, ed. Hannah Arendt [New York: Schocken Books, 1969, 241]). Benjamin has already noted that architecture is the prototype of works of art subject to distracted reception, and he writes that "[r]eception in a state of distraction . . . finds in the film its true means of exercise" (239–40).

   In *Charles Baudelaire: A Lyric Poet in the Era of High Capitalism* (London: NLB [Versus], 1973, 131–32), Benjamin associates Baudelaire's comment on the sensation of being in a crowd—one is a "kaleidoscope endowed with consciousness"—with the spectator's experience of film and the worker's experience of the assembly line without, however, using the word *distracted*. Finally, in *Dialectic of the Enlightenment* (New York: Continuum, 1993, 127), Max Horkheimer and Theodor Adorno describe cinema as a "relentless rush of facts" that makes the consumer "distraught" and consequently vulnerable to "ideological enforcement." It seems possible to extrapolate that, struck by the isomorphism of the assembly line as a mode of production and the cinema as a mode of reception, these Frankfurt School thinkers regarded distraction as a mode of alienation characteristic of modern times. *My* point would be that it functions as a *pharmakon*, remedy as well as poison.

5. O'Hara, "The Day Lady Died," *Collected Poems*, 325.

6. Peter Stallybrass and Allon White, *The Politics and Poetics of Transgression* (Ithaca NY: Cornell University Press, 1986), 94–100.

7. Denis Diderot, *Rameau's Nephew: D'Alembert's Dream* (London: Penguin, 1966), 33. (Denis Diderot, *Le Neveu de Rameau et autres dialogues philosophiques* [Paris: Gallimard (Coll. "Folio"), 1972], 31.)

8. O'Hara, "Ann Arbor Variations," *Collected Poems*, 66.

9. See Charles Baudelaire, "Le Vin des Chiffonniers," *Œuvres complètes*, vol. 1, 106–7, and Stéphane Mallarmé, "Le Tombeau de Charles Baudelaire," *Œuvres complètes*, ed. H. Mondor and G. Jean-Aubry (Paris: Bibl. de la Pléiade, 1945), 70.

10. It is.

11. Sophocles, *The Oedipus Cycle*, trans. Dudley Fitts and Robert Fitzgerald (San Diego: Harcourt Brace Jovanovich, 1977), 37.

12. Karl Marx and Friedrich Engels, *Manifest der kommunistischen Partei* (München: Fink, 1969): "Alles Ständige und Stehende verdampft, alles Heilige wird verweiht, und die Menschen sind endlich gezwungen, ihre Lebensstellung, ihre gegenseitigen Beziehungen mit nüchternen Augen anzuschauen." [All that is respectable and permanent melts into fog, all that is holy is desanctified, and humans are finally forced to look soberly on their life situation and mutual dealings.] Translation by Ross Chambers.

13. Friedrich Schlegel, Fragment 688, *Kritische Ausgabe*, vol. 18, *Philosophische Lehrjahre (1796–1806)*, ed. E. Behler (Paderborn: Schöningh, 1962), 85.

14. Michel Tournier, *Les Météores* (Paris: Gallimard [Coll. "Folio"], 1975), 222–26. My thanks to Mireille Rosello for drawing this passage to my attention.

15. Roland Barthes, *Le Plaisir du texte* (Paris: Seuil [Coll. "Points"], 1973).

16. See in particular, Maurice Blanchot, "L'expérience de Mallarmé," *L'Espace littéraire* (Paris: Gallimard, 1955), 30–41. For an exegesis of Blanchot's thought, see John Gregg, *Maurice Blanchot and the Literature of Transgression* (Princeton: Princeton University Press, 1994).

17. Translated by Ross Chambers from Jacques Réda, "Un voyage aux sources de la Seine," *Recommandations aux promeneurs* (Paris: Gallimard, 1988): 95–145; quotation 100–102. My thanks to Warren Motte Jr. for alerting me to this text.

18. See Ross Chambers, "Reading and Being Read: Irony and Critical Practice in Cultural Studies," *the minnesota review*, 43–44 (1995), 113–30; and see chapter 11.

19. Bambu Productions (Fox Lorber Video).

20. I am extrapolating in this argument from Gerald Prince, *A Grammar of Stories* (The Hague: Mouton, 1973).

21. Peter Brooks, *Reading for the Plot: Design and Intention in Narrative* (New York: Knopf, 1984), 107–8. For a substitutive/dispossessive model of narrative "exchange" that problematizes the concept of textual unity by emphasizing the potential in narrative discourse for digression and dilatoriness, see Ian Reid, *Narrative Exchanges* (London: Routledge, 1992).

22. See Ross Chambers, *Story and Situation: Narrative Seduction and the Power of Fiction* (Minneapolis: University of Minnesota Press, 1984).

23. Nicholson Baker, *U and I: A True Story* (New York: Vintage, 1991), 121.

24. Laurence Sterne, *The Life and Opinions of Tristram Shandy, Gentleman*, ed. James A Work (Indianapolis: Odyssey, 1940), 1.22.27–28. All references are to book, chapter, and page in this edition.

25. Just for the pleasure, I quote Sterne's account of Montaigne's thoughts on sleep: "The world enjoys other pleasures, says he, as they do that of sleep, without tasting it or feeling it as it slips and passes by—We should study and ruminate upon it, in order to render proper thanks to him who grants it for us—for this end I cause myself to be disturbed in my sleep, that I may the better and the more sensibly relish it—And yet I see few, says he again, who live with less sleep when need requires; my body is capable of a firm, but not of a violent and sudden agitation—I evade of late all violent exercises—I am never weary with walking—but from my youth, I never liked to ride upon pavements. I love to lie hard and alone, and even without my wife—This last word may stagger the faith of the world—but remember, 'La Vraisemblance (as *Baylet* says in the affair of *Liceti*) n'est pas toujours du Côté de la Vérité.' And so much for sleep." (4.16.291)

26. On the alternative relation of lamentation and digression, see Andy Elbon, "Lapsus/Gradus" (Ph.D. dissertation, University of Michigan, 1993). I thank Andy for the many insights his work has contributed to mine.

2. ON STEPPING OUT OF LINE

1. Jules Verne, *Around the World in Eighty Days*, trans. William Butcher (Oxford: Oxford University Press, 1995). All other quotations are from this edition, to which page numbers in parenthesis refer. (Jules Verne, *Le Tour du monde en quatre-vingts jours* [Paris: Livre de Poche, 1966].)

2. François Maspero, *Roissy Express*, trans. Paul Jones, photographs by Anaïk Frantz (London and New York: Verso, 1994). Page numbers in parenthesis refer to this edition. (François Maspero, *Les passagers du Roissy-Express* [Paris: Seuil (coll. "Points"), 1990].)

3. Thomas Kuhn, *The Structure of Scientific Revolutions* (Chicago: University of Chicago Press, 1962).

4. Raymond Williams, *Culture and Society, 1780–1950* (New York: Columbia University Press, 1983).

5. On "like"-sentences and "not"-sentences, see Anne Freadman, "Untitled (On Genre)," *Cultural Studies*, 2, 1 (January 1988), 74–80.

6. See Jean-François Lyotard, *The Inhuman: Reflections on Time*, trans. Geoffrey Bennington and Rachel Bowlby (Stanford: Stanford University Press, 1991) esp. 119–28. (Jean-François Lyotard, *L'Inhumain: Causeries sur le temps* [Paris: Galilée, 1988].)

7. Diderot, *Rameau's Nephew*, 52.

8. Roland Barthes, *The Pleasure of the Text*, trans. Richard Miller (New York: Hill and Wang, 1975). (Roland Barthes, *Le Plaisir du Texte* [Paris: Seuil, 1973].)

9. See Maurice Blanchot, *The Space of Literature*, trans. Ann Smock (Lincoln: University of Nebraska Press, 1982), esp. 38–48, "Mallarmé's Experience." (Maurice Blanchot, *L'Espace littéraire* [Paris: Gallimard, 1955].)

10. See Jean-François Lyotard, *The Differend: Phrases in Dispute*, trans. Georges van den Abbeele (Minneapolis: University of Minnesota Press, 1988). (Jean-François Lyotard, *Le Différend* [Paris: Minuit, 1983].)

11. Jean-François Lyotard, "On the Strength of the Weak," *Sémiotexte*, vol. 3, 2 (1978), 204–12. ("Sur la force des faibles," *L'Arc*, 64 [1976], 4–12.)

12. See Michel Serres, *The Parasite*, trans. Lawrence R. Schehr (Baltimore: Johns Hopkins University Press, 1982). (Michel Serres, *Le Parasite* [Paris: Grasset, 1980].)

13. Pacific Arts Video. Translations from the soundtrack by Ross Chambers.

14. On the subjection of agency, see John Mowitt, *Text: The Genealogy of an Antidisciplinary Object* (Durham NC: Duke University Press, 1992), from whom I take this phrase.

15. Karl Marx and Friedrich Engels, *Basic Writings on Politics and Philosophy*, ed. Lewis S. Feuer (New York: Doubleday, 1959), 339.

16. Peter Sloterdijk, *Critique of Cynical Reason*, trans. Michael Eldred (Minneapolis: University of Minnesota Press, 1987), 88. (Peter Sloterdijk, *Kritik der zynischen Vernunft*, 2 vols. [Frankfurt: Suhrkamp, 1983].)

3. LOITERLY SUBJECTS

1. Gérard de Nerval, "Les Nuits d'Octobre," *Œuvres*, vol. 1, ed. Albert Béguin and Jean Richer (Paris: Bibliothèque de la Pléiade, 1966), 77–118; translations of quotations by Ross Chambers. Colette, *The Vagabond*, translated by Enid McLeod (New York: Ballantine, 1955). (Colette, *La Vagabonde*

[Paris: Livre de Poche-Albin Michel, 1980].) Neil Bartlett, *Who Was That Man? A Present for Mr Oscar Wilde* (London: Serpent's Tail, 1988).

2. See Michel Foucault, *Discipline and Punish*, trans. Alan Sheridan (New York: Random House, 1978). (Michel Foucault: *Surveiller et punir* [Paris: Gallimard, 1975].)

3. The general paucity of loiterature written by women is explained in part by the same reasons that account for the invisibility of the female *flâneuse*. Women who could not linger in the street under pain of being suspected of adultery or prostitution or both could become observers of life outside the home only from the vantage point of a window or balcony, or (for working-class women) of a street-stall or barrow. Shopping later provided respectable women with an alibi for flânerie. See Janet Wolff, "The Invisible *Flâneuse*: Women and the Literature of Modernity," *Feminine Sentences: Essays on Women and Culture* (Berkeley: University of California Press, 1990), 34–50.

4. Walter Benjamin, "The Storyteller," *Illuminations*, 83–109.

5. On the complexity of Nerval's attitude to both speed and delay, see Ross Chambers, *Gérard de Nerval et la poétique du voyage* (Paris: Corti, 1969).

6. See Nancy Miller, "Woman of Letters: The Return to Writing in Colette's *La Vagabonde*," chap. 9, *Subject to Change* (New York: Columbia Univerisity Press, 1988), 229–64.

7. I am working here with a conception of community that owes much to Jean-Luc Nancy, *La Communauté désœuvrée* (Paris: Christian Bourgois, 1986) translated by Peter Connor as *The Inoperative Community* (Minneapolis: University of Minnesota Press, 1991). I don't understand community either as a matter of conformity (the totalitarian model) or as a contractual phenomenon (between "individuals" and "society") but as a function of the recognition of self in alterity and of alterity in self, and hence of a mediated play of differences.

4. CHANGING THE SUBJECT

1. Friedrich Schlegel, Fragment 668, *Kritische Ausgabe*, vol. 18, 85. On Schlegelian *parekbasis* in relation to irony see Paul de Man, "The Rhetoric of Temporality," *Blindness and Insight*, 2d. ed. (Minneapolis: University of Minnesota Press, 1983), esp. 218–23.

2. See Sneja Gunew and Ian Reid, eds., *Not the Whole Story* (Sydney: Local Consumption, 1984).

3. The prefix di-/dis- of "digression" and "discourse" appears to imply dispersal and, if not exactly directionlessness, at least some uncertainty of direction.

4. Randa Sabry, "La digression dans la rhétorique antique," *Poétique*, 79 (1989), 259–76.

5. Sabry, "La digression," 263–66.

6. See especially Philippe Hamon, *Introduction à l'analyse du descriptif* (Paris: Hachette, 1981); and see *La Description littéraire: Anthologie de textes théoriques et critiques*, ed. Philippe Hamon (Paris: Macula, 1991), 12: "Le 'ETC.' dont Claude Simon clôt le 'Générique' de *Lecon de Choses* . . . pourrait être l'emblème de toute description."

7. Xavier de Maistre, *Voyage autour de ma chambre* (Paris: Corti, 1984), 50. All further references are to this edition. Translations by Ross Chambers.

8. The method is strikingly similar to that of Walter Benjamin in his famous essay "Unpacking My Library," *Illuminations*, 59–67. It is also comparable to Michel de Certeau's description of the "rhetoric" of walking in the city as governed by a combination of asyndeton (interruption) and synecdoche (pars pro toto). See Michel de Certeau, "Marches dans la ville," *L'Invention du quotidien, I: Arts de faire* (Paris: Gallimard [Coll. "Folio"], 1990), 139–64; trans. by Steven Rendall as "Walking in the City," *The Practice of Everyday Life* (Berkeley: University of California Press, 1984), 91–110.

9. Samuel Beckett, *More Pricks than Kicks* (New York Press, 1972). All further references are to this edition.

10. See Dante Alighieri, *Purgatorio*, canto 4.

11. In letters to Constantine Curran (early July 1904) and Grant Richards (5 May 1906), Joyce famously referred to moral paralysis and cultural hemiplegia—half-life or half-death—as a central concern of *Dubliners*. See Richard Ellmann, ed., *Selected Letters of James Joyce* (New York: Viking, 1975), 22 and 81–84.

12. (This is one of those digressive/concessive footnotes that dehierarchize "main" arguments.) I am giving "language" and "desire" somewhat idealized definitions here. A less simplistic theory (such as I sketched in *Room for Maneuver* [Chicago: University of Chicago Press, 1991]), rather than distinguishing desire from language and equating the first exclusively with disorder and the second exclusively with order, would recognize both their mutual entailments (no desire without language, no language without desire) and the fact that *both* desire and language are sites of split, reproducing within themselves the conditions of cleavage or *brisure* implied by the nature/culture nexus, which puts the ordering principle of culture and the disordering force of nature in a relation of mutual dependence. Language is simultaneously a site of cultural order and of natural disorder; desire seeks order and produces disorder; digression is a product of the split in

language and of the split in desire, as well as of the mutual embrace of desire and language.

13. Paul Auster, *City of Glass* (New York: Penguin Books, 1987), 156. All further references are to this edition. *City of Glass, Ghosts,* and *The Locked Room* together form *The New York Trilogy* (New York: Penguin Books, 1990).

14. See Mallarmé, "Crise de vers," *Œuvres complètes*, 360–68: "[le vers], philo-sophiquement, rémunère le défaut des langues, complément supérieur," 364.

15. But it may disguise a reference to Louis Wolfson, the author of *Le schizo-phrène et les langues*, on which Auster has written an essay under the title "New York Babel," *Ground Work: Selected Poems and Essays 1970–1979* (London and Boston: Faber and Faber, 1991), 119–26. Wolfson's name itself gestures toward Freud's "Wolf-Man" and resonates with Poe's William Wilson (see note 16).

16. The Poe intertext of *City of Glass* is a rich one. In addition to "William Wilson" (a tale about alter egos that begins: "Let me call myself, for the moment, William Wilson"), it includes the Dupin stories and, especially, "The Man of the Crowd," in which a narrator follows a mysterious old man through the city.

17. See Walter Benjamin, "Der Flâneur," *Charles Baudelaire: Ein Lyriker im Zeitalter des Hochkapitalismus* (Frankfurt: Suhrkamp, 1969); translated by Harry Zohn as "The Flâneur" in *Charles Baudelaire: A Lyric Poet in the Era of High Capitalism* (London: Verso, 1985). Jeffrey T. Nealon, "Work of the Detective, Work of the Writer: Paul Auster's *City of Glass*," *Modern Fiction Studies*, 12, 1 (Spring 1996), 91–110, reads the detective-writer relation in light of Blanchot and Heidegger; my chapter was written before this article appeared.

5. TIME OUT

1. Nicholson Baker, *The Mezzanine* (New York: Vintage, 1990).

2. Nicholson Baker, *U and I: A True Story* (New York: Vintage, 1991), 73.

3. Barthes, *The Pleasure of the Text*.

4. Certeau, *The Practice of Everyday Life*, 121.

5. See Ross Chambers, "The Etcetera Principle: Narrative and the Paradig-matic," *French Literature Series*, 21 (1994), 1–24.

6. René Descartes, *A Discourse on Method: Meditations and Principles* (London: Everyman's, 1987), 88.

7. Amélie Oksenberg Rorty, "The Structure of Descartes' Meditations," *Essays on Descartes' Meditations*, ed. Amélie O. Rorty (Berkeley: University of California Press, 1986), 1–20.

8. See L. Aryeh Kosman, "The Naïve Narrator: Meditation in Descartes' *Meditations*," *Essays on Descartes' Meditations*, 21–43.

9. Nicholson Baker, *Room Temperature* (New York: Vintage, 1990), 41.

10. Marcus Aurelius, *Meditations* (London: Penguin, 1964), 168.

11. Walter Benjamin, *The Origin of the German Tragic Drama* (London: NLB, 1977), 182. (*Ursprung des deutschen Trauerspiels* [Frankfurt: Suhrkamp, 1963].)

12. Jacques Rancière, *The Ignorant Schoolmaster* (Stanford: Stanford University Press, 1991). (*Le Maître ignorant* [Paris: Fayard, 1987].)

13. The etymology of *to list* (of a boat) is obscure. It seems unrelated either to the noun *list* or to the archaic verb *to list*, meaning to desire (as in "The wind bloweth where it listeth").

14. Serres, *The Parasite*.

6. LEARNING FROM DOGS, I

1. Sloterdijk, *Critique of Cynical Reason*.

2. *Millie's Book, as Dictated to Barbara Bush* (New York: William Morrow, 1990); J. R. Ackerley, *My Father and Myself* (New York: Poseidon, 1968), *We Think the World of You* (New York: Poseidon, 1960), and *My Dog Tulip* (New York: Poseidon, 1965). These are the editions to which page references in parentheses refer (I abbreviate the three Ackerley titles as MF&M, WTTWOY and MDT respectively).

3. Quoted without reference to source in Peter Parker, *Ackerley* (New York: Farrar, Straus, Giroux, 1989), 269. On the implications of bestiality in humans' relations with their pets, see Midas Dekkers, *Dearest Pet: On Bestiality* (London and New York: Verso, 1994).

4. The pun is Nelson Moe's, and I thank him for it.

7. LEARNING FROM DOGS, II

1. Miguel de Cervantes, "The Dogs' Colloquy" in *Exemplary Stories* (London: Penguin, 1972), 195–252 ("Novela y coloquio que pasó entre 'Cipión' y 'Berganza', " *Novelas ejemplares* [Barcelona: Juventud, 1958], 443–502); and Mikhail Bulgakov, *Heart of a Dog* (New York: Grove Weidenfeld, 1982). These are the editions to which page references in parentheses refer.

2. E. T. A. Hoffmann, "Nachrichten von den neuesten Schicksalen des Hundes Berganza," *Fantasiestücke in Callots Manier*, Sämtliche Werke, vol. 2, 1 (München: Deutscher Klassiker Verlag, 1993), 101–77. I've not been able to find a translation of this story in print.

3. There was, however, one female Cynic in a position to enlighten them as to their gender-privilege. Asked why she, a woman, took up philosophy,

Hipparchia responded that if she were going to waste her time she would rather do so as a philosopher than as a housewife. On Hipparchia, see Michèle Le Dœuff, *Hipparchia's Choice: An Essay Concerning Women, Philosophy, Etc.* (Oxford: Blackwell, 1991). (*L'Etude et le rouet, I: Des Femmes, de la philosophie, etc.* [Paris: Seuil, 1989]).

4. Certeau, *The Practice of Everyday Life*.

5. Michael Nerlich, "On the Philosophical Dimension of *El casamiento engañoso* and *El coloquio de los perros*," *Cervantes's "Exemplary Novels" and the Adventure of Writing*, ed. Michael Nerlich and Nicholas Spadaccini (Minneapolis: Prisma, 1989), 247–329.

6. On *tropelía*, see L. J. Woodward, "El casamiento engañoso y El coloquio de los perros," *Bulletin of Hispanic Studies*, 36 (1959), 80–87.

7. Michael Taussig, *Mimesis as Alterity: A Particular History of the Senses* (New York and London: Routledge, 1993).

8. I borrow this phrase from John Mowitt, *Text: The Genealogy of an Interdisciplinary Object* (Durham NC: Duke University Press, 1992).

9. Louis Althusser, "Ideology and State Ideological Apparatuses (Notes towards an Investigation)," *Lenin and Philosophy and Other Essays* (New York: Monthly Review Press, n.d. [copyright 1971 by NLB]), 127–86; and Chambers, *Room for Maneuver*.

10. More friends than usual have contributed to these two linked chapters (6 and 7), and especially to chapter 7, by encouragement, criticism, and suggestions. I acknowledge in particular the help of Laura Pérez, Mireille Rosello, and James Porter; for her frank criticism of an early draft I'm deeply grateful to the late Marie Maclean.

8. FLÂNEUR READING

1. Rey Chow, *Writing Diaspora: Tactics of Intervention in Contemporary Cultural Studies* (Bloomington: Indiana University Press, 1993), 165–74.

2. Benjamin, *Charles Baudelaire*, 34: "Baudelaire knew what the true situation of the man of letters was: he goes to the marketplace as a *flâneur*."

3. Wolfgang Schivelbusch, *The Railway Journey: The Industrialization of Time and Space in the Nineteenth Century* (Berkeley: University of California Press, 1986) [*Geschichte der Eisenbahnreise* (München: Carl Hauser Verlag, 1978)].

4. Baudelaire, *Œuvres complètes*, vol. 1, 87–88. All quotations from Baudelaire are taken from this edition and are cited in parentheses by volume and page number. Translations by Ross Chambers unless otherwise indicated.

5. See Ross Chambers, *The Writing of Melancholy: Modes of Opposition in Early French Modernism* (Chicago: University of Chicago Press, 1993).

(*Mélancolie et opposition: Les débuts du modernisme en France* [Paris: Corti, 1987].) On the "mnemonics of dispossession," see Richard Terdiman's acute conjunctural reading of "Le Cygne" in *Present Past: Modernity and the Memory Crisis (Ithaca: Cornell University Press,* 1993), 106-47.

6. Benjamin, "The Flâneur," 35-66. ("Der Flâneur," 35-71).

7. See Foucault, *Discipline and Punish.*

8. On parasites and the significance of parasitism, see Serres, *The Parasite.*

9. Gérard Gasarian, "La figure du poète hystérique, ou l'allégorie chez Baudelaire," *Poétique,* 86 (avril 1991), 177-91.

10. See Dolf Oehler, *Pariser Bilder, I (1830-1848): Antibourgeoise Aesthetik bei Baudelaire, Daumier und Heine* (Frankfurt: Suhrkamp, 1979); and Richard Burton, *Baudelaire and the Second Republic: Writing and Revolution* (Oxford: Clarendon Press, 1991)

11. See *Le Salon de 1846,* vol. 2, 415-96, esp. 493-96. See also Ross Chambers, "The Flâneur as Hero (on Baudelaire)," *Australian Journal of French Studies,* 28, 2 (November 1992), 142-53. This chapter undertakes a reconceptualization of that article.

12. This list is inspired by the mounting levels of the "Parisian inferno" in Balzac's account of modern life as frenetic activity under the impulsion of "gold and pleasure" in "La fille aux yeux d'or" ("The Girl with the Golden Eyes"), part of his *Histoire des Treize.* Baudelaire's view of modern city life was certainly indebted to Balzac's vision.

13. Foucault, *Discipline and Punish.*

14. Translation from Charles Baudelaire, *The Flowers of Evil,* trans. James McGowan (Oxford: Oxford University Press ["World's Classics"], 1993), 193-95.

15. On time as a parasite, see "L'Ennemi" (1. 16): " . . . Le Temps mange la vie, / Et l'obscur Ennemi qui nous ronge le cœur / Du sang que nous perdons croît et se fortifie" (Time devours life, and the occult Enemy who gnaws at our life increases and gains strength from the blood that we lose).

16. I owe this reading to Wolfgang Fietkau, *Schwanengesang auf 1848: Ein Rendezvous am Louvre: Baudelaire, Marx, Proudhon und Victor Hugo* (Reinbek: Rowohlt, 1978).

17. Ross Chambers, "Perpetual Abjuration: Baudelaire and the Pain of Modernity," *French Forum,* 15, 2 (May 1990), 169-88.

18. Translation from Charles Baudelaire, *The Flowers of Evil,* 173-76.

19. For an important schizoanalytic reading of Baudelaire, see Eugene Holland, *Baudelaire and Schizoanalysis: The Sociopoetics of Modernism* (Cambridge: Cambridge University Press, 1994).

9. POINTLESS STORIES, STORYLESS POINTS

1. Roland Barthes, *Incidents*, trans. Richard Howard (Berkeley: University of California Press, 1992) (*Incidents* [Paris: Seuil, 1987]). I silently modify Richard Howard's translation on occasion. On the outcry over *Incidents* see Svetlana Boym, "The Obscenity of Theory: Roland Barthes's 'Soirées de Paris,' and Walter Benjamin's 'Moscow Diary,'" *Yale Journal of Criticism*, 4, 2 (1991). On "Incidents" and its place in Barthes's personal and intellectual evolution, see Lawrence R. Schehr, "Roland Barthes' Semierotics," *Canadian Review of Comparative Literature/Revue Canadienne de Littérature Comparée*, March–June 1994, 65–79.

2. On the ubiquity of the banal, especially in intellectual discourse, see Certeau, *The Practice of Everyday Life*, esp. 8 [22–23].

3. Paul Monette, *Becoming a Man* (New York: Harcourt Brace Jovanovich, 1992); Ackerley, *My Father and Myself*; and see chapter 6.

4. Eric Michaels, *Unbecoming* (Sydney: EMPress, 1990); see also, for example, Hervé Guibert, *To the Friend Who Did Not Save My Life* (New York: Serpent's Tail, 1994) (*A l'ami qui ne m'a pas sauvé la vie* [Paris: Gailimard, 1990]), and David Wojnarowicz, *Close to the Knives* (New York: Vintage, 1991).

5. John Rechy, *Numbers* (New York: Grove Weidenfeld, 1976); Renaud Camus, *Tricks* (New York: Serpent's Tail, 1996) (*Tricks* [Paris: Mazarine, 1979]).

6. D. A. Miller, *Bringing Out Roland Barthes* (Berkeley: University of California Press, 1992), 7.

7. Alan Hollinghurst, *The Swimming-Pool Library* (New York: Vintage, 1989).

8. These reflections arise in part from Jonathan Dollimore's point, in *Sexual Dissidence* (Oxford: Clarendon Press, 1991), that "over and again in the culture of homosexuality differences of race and class are intensely cathected" and the "crossing" of gayness with race and class has "a complex, difficult history, from which we can learn" (250). This chapter was written before the appearance of Christopher Lane's *The Ruling Passion: British Colonial Allegory and the Paradox of Homosexual Desire* (Durham NC: Duke University Press, 1995), which examines the "crossings" of masculinity, homosexual desire, and empire in British colonialist and imperialist writing.

9. See "The Writer on Holiday," Roland Barthes, *Mythologies* (New York: Noonday, 1991), 29–31. ("L'Écrivain en vacances," *Mythologies* [Paris: Seuil, 1957], 30–33).

10. I borrow the phrase from Steven Ungar's title, *Roland Barthes: The Professor of Desire* (Lincoln: University of Nebraska Press, 1983).

11. See Roland Barthes, *Camera Lucida* (New York: Hill and Wang, 1981). (*La Chambre claire* [Paris: Gallimard/Seuil, 1980]).

12. See Malek Alloula, *The Colonial Harem* (Minneapolis: University of Minnesota Press, 1986). (*Le Harem colonial* [Genève: Slatkine, 1981]).

10. READING AND BEING READ

1. Raymond Williams, *Culture and Society, 1780–1950* (New York: Columbia University Press, 1983).

2. James Clifford, *The Predicament of Culture* (Cambridge MA: Harvard University Press, 1988).

3. Althusser, "Ideology and State Ideological Practices."

4. See Dan Sperber and Deirdre Wilson, "Les ironies comme mentions," *Poétique* 38 (1978), 399–412.

5. *S/Z* (New York: Hill and Wang, 1974), 205–6. (*S/Z* [Paris: Seuil, 1970], 212).

6. Meaghan Morris, "Things to Do with Shopping Centres," *Grafts: Feminist Cultural Criticism*, ed. Susan Sheridan, (London: Verso, 1988), 193–225: "[I]f this project on 'Things to Do With Shopping Centres' could have a subtitle, it would be 'Pedestrian Notes on Modernity'" (201).

7. See Meaghan Morris, "A Small Serve of Spaghetti," *Meanjin* 3 (1990), 470–80.

8. Meaghan Morris, "Banality in Cultural Studies," *Logics of Television*, ed. Patricia Mellencamp (Bloomington: Indiana University Press, 1990), 14–43.

9. Wolff, "The Invisible Flâneuse," 34–50.

10. Certeau, *The Practice of Everyday Life*.

11. See Elaine Marks and Isabelle de Courtivron, eds., *New French Feminisms: An Anthology*. (Amherst: University of Massachusetts Press, 1980), 137.

12. Jean-François Lyotard. "La force de faibles." *L'Arc*, 64 (1976), 4–12.

13. See Chambers, *Room for Maneuver*.

Index

In the STAGES series